GOD'S PEOPLES

GOD'S PEOPLES

COVENANT AND LAND IN SOUTH AFRICA, ISRAEL, AND ULSTER

Donald Harman Akenson

CORNELL UNIVERSITY PRESS

ITHACA AND LONDON

First published 1992 by Cornell University Press

Printed in the United States of America

Art on part opening pages: Voortrekker Monument, Pretoria, Republic of South Africa.

⊗The paper in this book meets the minimum requirements of the American National Standard for Information Sciences—Permanence of Paper for Printed Library Materials, ANSI Z39.48-1984.

Library of Congress Cataloging-in-Publication Data

Akenson, Donald H.
    God's peoples : covenant and land in South Africa, Israel, and Ulster / Donald Harman Akenson.
        p. cm.
    Includes bibliographical references and index.
    ISBN 0-8014-2755-X (alk. paper)
    1. Covenants (Religion) 2. South Africa—Civilization.
3. Afrikaners. 4. Israel—Civilization. 5. Ulster (Northern Ireland and Ireland)—Civilization. I. Title.
BL617.A44 1992
231.7'6——dc20   92-8758

In memory of my father
Donald Nels Akenson
1910–1990

Contents

MAPS AND FIGURES *ix*

ACKNOWLEDGMENTS *xi*

Part I THE ADAMANTINE WORD

1. The Oldest Code *3*
2. A Very Big Deal *13*

Part II COVENANTAL CULTURES IN THE MAKING

3. The Afrikaners: A Culture in Exile, 1806–1948 *45*
4. The Covenantal Culture of the Ulster-Scots to 1920 *97*
5. Zionism and the Land of Israel to 1948 *151*

Part III THE COVENANT AND THE STATE

6. Northern Ireland: A Protestant State for a Protestant People, 1920–1969 *183*
7. The High Noon of Apartheid, 1948–1969 *203*
8. Israel: A Singular State, 1948–1967 *227*

vii

Part IV THE COVENANT IN RECENT TIMES

9. A Covenant Comes Apart: Ulster, 1969 to the Present   *263*
10. A World Unhinged: Afrikaners and Apartheid, 1969 to the Present   *295*
11. Israel, 1967 to the Present: Completing the Circle   *311*

Part V ENVOI

12. Conclusion: Living with God's Peoples   *349*

NOTES   *359*
INDEX   *395*

Maps and Figures

MAPS

1. Africa, 1914 *48*
2. Irish counties *104*
3. The Ulster plantation *107*
4. Irish religious proportions, 1834 *110*
5. The British mandate *174*
6. South Africa, 1985 *298*
7. Israel, 1947, 1949, and 1967 *312*

FIGURES

1. The Afrikaner Covenantal Oath *47*
2. The Balfour Declaration *163*
3. The Ulster Covenant *187*

Acknowledgments

For direct support in writing and publishing this book, I am grateful to the Social Sciences and Humanities Research Council of Canada; the School of Graduate Studies and Research, Queens University, Kingston, Ontario; the Stout Research Centre of Victoria University, Wellington, New Zealand; the Institute of Social and Economic Research, Rhodes University, Grahamstown, South Africa; and the Jackman Foundation.

Scores of scholars in South Africa, Israel, and Ireland, as well as in Canada, Great Britain, and the United States have been generous with their time and knowledge. Because this is a controversial volume, I shall not name them individually; I am grateful nonetheless.

D. H. A.

Part I

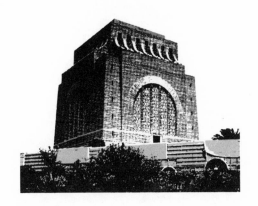

THE
ADAMANTINE WORD

1

The Oldest Code

(1)

Any careful reader of the Bible realizes that, often, stones speak louder than words. I had read a good deal about Ulster, and about South Africa, and about Israel, and I had faith in the fundamental accuracy, if read judiciously, of the historical record of each country. At a distant intellectual level I realized that these three cultures—the Afrikaner, the Ulster-Scot, and the Israeli—had many things in common. But it was a flat, two-dimensional recognition.

Then I visited the Voortrekker monument in Pretoria, South Africa. It is an extraordinary structure, not only a monument to a culture's past but also a map of a collective mind. The monument is a national museum for the Afrikaners, but it could just as well serve as a defensive outpost. Its walls are as thick as were some parts of the Maginot Line, and it has sally ports and ambushments that would do credit to a medieval fortress. Each salient protects another.

What struck me was that I had encountered the mind that built this structure before, and in far distant countries. Although built in different eras and using sharply different technologies, the bawns of the Ulster-Scots, fortified farmhouses designed to protect against the indigenous Catholics, and the military-agricultural encampments of Israeli "pioneers" on the West Bank of the Jordan, hunkered down amid the Palestinian Arab population, came from the same cast of mind: the creation of an interlocking defensive structure that asserted at once its own existence and the ability of those inside the structure to defend themselves against the alien and hostile outside world.

Later I realized that many of my friends and acquaintances in these three societies often spoke the same way, even though they used different languages—not everyone, not all the time, but frequently enough to make me recognize that Northern Ireland's Presbyterians, the Afrikaners, and most Israelis have held in common several fundamental concepts. This kind of observation intrigues a historian, and immediately I began to look backward. It soon became clear that the Afrikaners of the seventeenth through early twentieth centuries (usually called "Boers" in contemporary usage) and the Ulster Presbyterians of the same era had been even more alike ideologically in those years than they are today. What they had in common was their understanding of how the world worked. And that understanding stemmed directly from the Hebrew scriptures.

Dan Jacobson, the son of Jewish immigrants to South Africa and himself the author of a lucid literary commentary on the scriptures, recalled of his own childhood:

> I had as one group among my neighbors yet another chosen people: the Boers, or Afrikaners. Their national or collective myth about themselves owed almost everything to the Bible. Like the Israelites, and their fellow Calvinists in New England, they believed that they had been called by their God to wander through the wilderness, to meet and defeat the heathen, and to occupy a promised land on his behalf. How literally they took this parallel may be gauged from the fact that the holiest day of their national calendar bore the name "Day of the Covenant." A sense of their having been summoned by divine decree to perform an ineluctable historical duty has never left the Boers, and has contributed to both their strength and their weakness.[1]

Anyone acquainted with the Irish Troubles of the twentieth century will quickly note the word "covenant," for it is to one such covenant that the government of Northern Ireland owes its existence. On 23 September 1912, more than 218,000 men—virtually the entire adult male Protestant population of Ulster—signed "Ulster's Solemn League and Covenant." This Ulster covenant was modeled on a Scottish Presbyterian original of the late sixteenth century which, in its turn, took its doctrine of the reciprocal responsibilities of God and a righteous civil polity directly from the Hebrew scriptures.

No one is greatly surprised that, although Israel is a secular state, much of that polity's behavior is conditioned by sacred texts. "It is in the very nature of the Jewish state," Dan Jacobson notes, "that the Hebrew scriptures will always be a source of pride and reassurance to its inhabitants, whether they are believers or not. To no other people does the Bible speak so intimately, or in such a directly inspiriting fashion."[2]

That the societies and governments of Afrikaners, Israelis, and Ulster-Scots have differed from one another in a myriad of ways is an observation so obvious as to be otiose, and the last thing anyone with sense would do is present them as simulacra, varying in latitude but not in attitude. The three societies are different indeed, but bear in mind the shrewd comments of a master historian: "We can always pinpoint differences, it is the easiest of all scholarly tasks, since everything is always different in some ways from everything else across time and space. What is harder and takes priority is to discover similarities."[3]

What events in Ulster and in South Africa since the seventeenth century, and in the state of Israel in the twentieth century, have in common is that they can be understood only by direct reference to the very oldest strands of the cultural fabric that is shared by western societies: the memory of events that occurred as much as four millennia ago and are recorded, sometimes in blurred form and other times with eerie sharpness, in the scriptures.

(2)

The three modern cultures with which I here deal are thoroughly politically incorrect in the opinion of the haute bourgeoisie who determine today's political and moral chic. So I must confess a certain incorrectness in my own attitude. I like my friends among the Afrikaners, the Ulster-Scots, and the Israelis. They share something—concreteness of outlook and directness of expression—that makes me trust them: not agree with them but trust them to let me know where I stand (mostly in the wrong in their view, but they let me know with clarity and admirable honesty).

Every European nation at one time or another has had leaders or prophets who say that their country is chosen of God and is, in effect, the successor of the children of Israel, and that its citizens are living in a promised land. They and their followers may even believe those things for a little while, but the concepts are very pale and they fade quickly. This book is about something very different: three cultures that are the real thing.

As even a glance at the table of contents makes clear, this book is a study in analogical history. Either the reader will be convinced that the ancient Hebrews had a distinct and robust way of constructing their world and that this conceptual apparatus significantly influenced at least three distinct modern cultures, or the book fails. My own view is that unless one uses the lens of the ancient Hebrew covenant as a primary mode (not sole but primary) of viewing the Ulster-Scots, the Afrikaners, and the Israelis, then the optics are all askew and neither their history nor their future will make much sense.

None of the three modern cultures I deal with likes to be compared with the others. These apprehensions are understandable. When such comparisons are made, usually it is for the purposes of slagging one, or all, of them. That sort of thing is well illustrated in an article concerning Israel written by Edward Pearce in the *Sunday Times* of London: "What we are perilously close to getting in that country is a sort of Hasidic Rhodesia, narrow, blind to its own interests and dwindling. . . . Any group of people, the Rhodesians, the Afrikaners and for that matter the Ulster Protestants, are damaged and diminished by the need to keep somebody else in his place and to justify themselves as decent fellows."[4] That is grossly unfair. The article from which these sentences are drawn uses analogy without employing evidence: one of the tricks of propaganda. There are indeed very significant parallels among the three societies, but these must be delineated clearly and with evidentiary backing. Any other use of analogies is mere billingsgate.[5]

There are many ways of understanding the development of these three societies, and more than one of them is right. Systems of historical explanation are like that: given a common definition of historical accuracy (by which one means the evidentiary canons of the historical profession) and accepting the rules of logic and the laws of probability, one can construct several valid historical explanatory systems. Some will be better than others by virtue of being more elegant or more efficient, but everything else being equal, the system one prefers is frequently a matter of taste. And taste in the historical profession is largely determined by the kind of problem to which the historian is drawn. So, here I am reflecting my own interest in certain kinds of historical problems—those which are cross-cultural, international, comparative, and which involve behavioral and ideational patterns of very long duration.

Because I have spent the last three decades studying and writing about places where one usually is not granted a hearing (or a reading) unless one's own ethnic or religious background is first openly declared, let me add that I have no ethnic or religious investment (either pro or con) in these three cultures. My own ancestors, dour and depressed Swedes, converted themselves into "Bible Readers" about the end of the Napoleonic Wars. They took the Bible very seriously and consequently were a thorn in the flesh of the Lutheran establishment. Eventually, in the middle of the last century, they were in effect run out of Sweden and settled in Minnesota. (Their story, in fictionalized form, can be found in Vilhelm Moberg's brilliant quartet, published in English as *The Emigrants*.) In the New World, they called themselves "Baptists," but the name was a flag of convenience, for they refused to have anything to do with other Baptists, suspecting the others were having too much fun. For well over a century, they kept alive many of their mid-nineteenth-century Swedish cultural patterns and, most important, the practice of reading, rereading, discussing, and memorizing the scriptures.

Despite this heritage, were it not for the precepts of Rabbi Judah Goldin, I would not dare to confront here the daunting body of writings that we Christians arrogantly call the "Old Testament." There is nothing old about it. If ever any book was alive and disturbingly fresh, this is it. Yet the mountain of scholarly literature associated with the Hebrew scriptures—from commentaries to form criticism to historical treatises—is a barrier that can put anyone off. Year after year, Judah Goldin patiently taught Yale undergraduates that the only way to encounter the scriptures was to read them directly. Slowly. Rabbi Goldin had a characteristic exercise: he required the regular memorization of sizable chunks of scripture. He did not mind what version one used, but his weekly examination required the writing out of the week's passage by memory perfectly, word by word, comma by period by semicolon. This was a useful moral as well as intellectual discipline for precious Yale undergraduates, who as a rule did not think it hubristic to explain to the world how it should arrange itself: to learn firsthand what a jot and a tittle are is salutory.

This bit of personal history is germane, because Judah Goldin was right. One has to treat serious writings seriously, and there is no more serious text than the scriptures. Although himself an immensely learned man and an adept at highly recherché forms of biblical criticism, Judah Goldin believed that such methods inevitably were secondary. What counted first, and what had to be directly experienced, was the scriptural text. Many scholarly methods were potentially helpful, but all were secondary to the text.[6]

Fortunately, this emphasis upon encountering the scriptures meshes perfectly with the way that the two Christian peoples with whom I am here concerned approached the scriptures. Ulstermen and Afrikaners both read the scriptures as manuals of instruction, and, much more than most Christian denominations, they paid attention to the "Old Testament." Within the Jewish tradition, there of course has been a long skein of learned commentaries on the scriptures, but until recently (when a significant body of Jewish scholars overcame the earlier Jewish rejection of biblical criticism) the commentaries have been extremely respectful of the text in its present form.

In the discussion that follows, references are to the Protestant "Old Testament." The Christian societies with which we are concerned learned their religion from the Protestant Bible, so this makes sense. In fact, for our present purposes, all the central versions of the scriptures—Jewish, Protestant, and Roman Catholic—are fundamentally the same. The Roman Catholic scriptures include a few tertiary items not included in the Protestant canon, but nothing crucial. In their most common form, the Hebrew scriptures contain the same material as does the Protestant canon, although arranged in a slightly different order and with some books that are separate in the Protestant version, amalgamated and given slightly different titles. This makes no substantive difference. The first five books of the scriptures—the "Torah," the "Pentateuch," or "the books of Moses"—are virtually identical in both, although the books take different names.

Although there are several good "modern" translations of the scriptures—particularly the Revised Standard Version (1952), the New Jewish Version (1962 ff.), and the Jerusalem Bible (1966)—I refer to the Authorized Version of 1611, often called the King James Version. This version is used for three reasons. First, it was the specific vehicle through which the Presbyterians of Ulster acquired their belief in Yahweh, so in this one instance we can use the same English Bible as did our historical subjects. Second, the King James Version, more than any other, has a historical resonance in the culture of the English-speaking world. As the novelist and critic Robert Stone has noted, "The greatest vehicle of mass literacy in the English-speaking world has been the King James Bible. It has been the great primer."[7] For historians it is only natural that whenever possible, we go back to our cultural roots. And, third and most important, the Authorized Version of the scriptures is as fine a body of writing as exists in our language. Surely one can tolerate an archaism now and then in return for hearing English as celestial music.

The scriptures are a collective document, which means that some pieces were composed earlier than were others and that some portions have been redacted by later editors. To a modern historian, the ways in which biblical scholars have tried to sort out the various canons, have assayed the levels of historical accuracy in the text, have interpreted mythic referents, and have traced the evolution of biblical genres are at once fascinating and impressive. But in the present context, these achievements are largely irrelevant, because, in the cultures that we are here trying to understand, the scriptures were accepted as a reality in themselves. Usually the scriptures were taken literally, but always and in all their parts, seriously. Thus, from this viewpoint, the scriptures are historical phenomena because they have been believed and their concepts have become parts of human systems of belief. Indeed, in the three cases we are here dealing with, the scriptures have been the single most compelling determinant of the way people have thought about their world.

Northrop Frye presented his lapidary discussion of the Bible as literature under the title *The Great Code*.[8] Transformed from a literary metaphor to a historical one, the concept of the scriptures as a code is perfect. They are a code not in the sense of something to be deciphered, to be broken, but in the sense that one speaks of organisms as having a genetic code. For certain societies, in certain eras of their development, the scriptures have acted culturally and socially in the same way the human genetic code operates physiologically. That is, this great code has, in some degree, directly determined what people would believe and what they would think and what they would do. Equally important, the code has provided the fundamental working of these societies' cosmologies. In this second aspect, the great code determined the ground rules under which new information entered the particular culture, how this information was evaluated, and what were the alternative courses of behavior in any particular situation. Societies that took the Hebrew scriptures as their basic cultural code were formatted just as firmly as a present-day computer disk. Although one acknowledges the complex evolution of the scriptures, the historical fact is that the average believer, in the societies here under study, experienced the scriptures as a single item, a single embodiment of divine wisdom. Thus, Frye is right: the scriptures are not a string of fascicules but a single great code.

I think that the most productive way of approaching this great code is to adopt a posture of feigned innocence. By this I do not mean anything mendacious: rather, that we should try to encounter the scriptures with everything we have learned about them from modern criticism, and with as many of our own cultural predispositions as we can identify and control, forced temporarily out of mind. This is particularly essential for Christians and for anyone who, though no longer a believer, comes from a Christian background, because the Christian reading of the Hebrew scriptures can be a massive and distorting lens placed between us and the text. In some ways, this remark may seem a solecism, for were not the Ulster Presbyterians and the Afrikaner Protestants Christians? Certainly, but as I argue in detail later, in contrast to most Christian denominations, they mediated their reading of the Hebrew scriptures much less through the "New Testament" mindset than did virtually all other Christian groups. They assimilated the Hebrew scriptures directly and did not read them as a mere prologue to the Christian era.

Neither should we read the scriptures through the lenses of nineteenth- and twentieth-century liberal Jewish theologians and commentators. They have tended either to theologize away the grittier aspects of the Word, or to engage in apologetics, in the sense of showing how certain harsh laws and obsessive taboos made, they claim, great sense. Liberal Jewish commentators have joined the mainline Christian interpreters in our own day in a misleadingly nice, almost smarmy, interpretation of the scriptures. The Bible is sulphurous in spots, not nice. Sanitizing the scriptures may make the modern reader more comfortable with them, but most believers through the ages have not wanted to be comfortable: they have wanted to be right. And the great code is about right, and its inevitable biblical concomitant, might.

One aspect of our modern knowledge of the scriptures can be kept to the fore without tainting our innocent reading. Simply, the great code is the single most venerable cultural artifact in our western world. It has had a longer continuous run than any other set of culture constructs. It is far and away the oldest element among the components that comprise the culture of the western world in the late twentieth century.

Exactly when the fundamental strata of oral history upon which the scriptures are based were laid down is something of which scholars will never be certain, but most seem to agree that it was sometime in the middle Bronze Age. The Stone Age came to an end in the Near East somewhere around 3000 B.C. The patriarchal era, the crucial time for the forming of the Hebrew collectivity, began about a thousand years later. William Foxwell Albright spent his lifetime worrying about the dating of the patriarchs, shaking his dating one way and another, like a dog worrying a bone. The dating of the patriarch Abraham is the crux. By present-day scholarly consensus (general if not quite universal), the bracketing timeframe for the patriarchal narratives is 2100–1550 B.C. Albright eventually concluded that the nineteenth or twentieth century B.C. was the best fit, and his conclusion has stood up well.[9]

Reporting this dating is easily done, but the skein of cultural continuity that it indicates is humbling. We are scarcely surprised that our contact with Bronze Age cultures is broken: the Sumerians and Babylonians are names that most people know chiefly from two-line references in world history texts, and, in the New World, though the Mayan chronology stretched back to the equivalent of 3372 B.C., virtually nothing of that culture has come forward to us as a living tradition. Yet the story of Abraham still directly affects the world in which we live.

The Mosaic law probably dates from the mid-thirteenth century B.C. (the late Bronze Age), but it assimilated Near Eastern law codes going back to the middle Bronze Age. Some of these codes may have originated as early as 1920 B.C., which is virtually coterminous with the age of the patriarchs.[10] Everyone who has been sent to Sabbath or Sunday school knows of the Mosaic code, in the form of the Ten Commandments, and even most nonreligious of adults in our society know something about it. Undoubtedly, more persons worldwide could give a brief account of the Ten Commandments than could identify the president of the United States. But who has any idea what the laws and beliefs were of the Bronze Age people who inhabited, say, the British Isles, cradle of what we think of as a venerable civilization? The people who built Stonehenge are parodied by the modern "druids," but their real culture is resistant to all but the most specialized scholarly investigation; the builders of those inexplicable Hibernian religious structures, Dowth, Knowth, and New Grange, have left traces that are crudely iconographic but convey no message to us; the pre-Celtic inhabitants of Scotland, the Picts, remain a virtually complete mystery. And yet we all know that Thou Shalt Not.

The Iron Age in Palestine can be taken as roughly the twelfth to the sixth century B.C., the period in which most of the material in the Hebrew scriptures settled into a near-permanent form. In that era, dynastic Egypt was in decline, Phoenicia was becoming the first international trading power, and classical Greece was pulling together the disparate threads that would make a major civilization. Yet, with none of those three extraordinary cultures do we have continuity, although we have enough knowledge of them, unlike the uncharitable Bronze Age cultures of the British Isles, to view them with admiration. But our sense of empathy with them is synthetic, in the sense that the corpus of classical learning we so admire was long lost to the west and only discovered after a long break; and both Egyptian and Phoenician cultures are known to us not through a continuous line from the past to the present, but as a result of modern archaeology and epigraphy.

With the Iron Age culture of Israel, the west has never lost touch.

2

A Very Big Deal

(1)

At the heart of the scriptures is a deal, hard and clear. This is the covenant between Yahweh and his people. The term "covenant" has such an extensive literature that one can easily miss the fact that at heart it is simply a bargain. The details of this agreement shift over time, but the kernel does not. If Israel will be his people, Yahweh will be their God. This, though easily stated, is as profound a commitment as any set of human beings can make. This is the opposite of the Faustian deal, but it has one element in common with it. Whereas the covenant is a collective, not an individual bargain, and it is with the Almighty rather than the devil, it is identical in this regard: once you sign on, you belong to him. The contract is Israel's perpetual enlistment in the divine army; it binds the entire nation and does so generation after generation from time unto eternity. This is a very big deal indeed.

In its fully evolved form, the covenant is conditional. Thus, the statement of domestic blessings in Leviticus begins with an "if:"

If ye walk in my statutes and keep my commandments, and do them;
    Then I will give you rain in due season, and the land shall yield her increase, and the trees of the field shall yield their fruit.
    And your threshing shall reach unto the vintage, and the vintage shall reach unto the sowing time: and ye shall eat your bread to the full, and dwell in your land safely. (Lev. 26:3–5)

13

The earliest forms of the covenant are not explicitly conditional. After the flood, God tells Noah that he is creating the rainbow: "I do set my bow in the cloud, and it shall be for a token of a covenant between me and the earth" (Gen. 9:13). Nor is the early covenant limited to any distinct group of persons or, indeed, to the human race. It is, God says, a covenant "between me and you and every living creature of all flesh; and the waters shall no more become a flood to destroy all flesh" (Gen. 9:15).

That inclusive, unconditional covenant soon is displaced. God focuses his attention on Abram, a man living in Canaan with his wife, Sarai, amid his father's houses and lands. Why the Almighty chooses Abram is the sort of question that rarely arises in the scriptures, and that is a signal point: God chooses whom he will and when people, individually or as a group, are chosen, they have only two alternatives: to accept God's choice or not. Abram, chosen by God, is told to get out of his father's house, to leave his relatives behind, and to go into a land that God would show him:

> And I will make of thee a great nation, and I will bless thee, and make thy name great; and thou shalt be a blessing:
> And I will bless them that bless thee, and curse him that curseth thee: and in thee shall all the families of the earth be blessed. (Gen. 12:2–3)

In accepting this divine commission, Abram becomes a different person. He is reborn. The Almighty symbolizes this newness by changing Abram's name to Abraham, meaning the father of many nations:

> And I will make thee exceeding fruitful, and I will make nations of thee, and kings shall come out of thee.
> And I will establish my covenant between me and thee and thy seed after thee in their generations for an everlasting covenant, to be a God unto thee, and to thy seed after thee.
> And I will give unto thee, and to thy seed after thee, the land wherein thou art a stranger, all the land of Canaan, for an everlasting possession; and I will be their God. (Gen. 17:6–8)

Notice that the covenant has been restricted, from all living creatures to one man and his descendants. Although the covenant is not yet expressed as being fully conditional, the Almighty has something that he requires Abraham and his descendants to do as a consequence of being chosen: "Ye shall circumcise the flesh of your foreskin; and it shall be a token of the covenant betwixt me and you" (Gen. 17:11).

The next stage of the covenant's evolution occurs when God chooses (for reasons that characteristically are never explained) another particular man: He appears to Moses in a burning bush. An adiabatic fire appears and is followed by God's voice: "I am the God of thy father, the God of Abraham, the God of Isaac, and the God of Jacob" (Exod. 3:6). God proposes to send Moses to the Egyptian pharaoh who is keeping the descendants of Abraham in bondage. Moses is to lead them out of Egypt, "unto a land flowing with milk and honey" (Exod. 3:8). As a token of his confidence in Moses, God answers Moses' question, "Who shall I say sent me?" The first answer is an enigmatic, oracular, "I am that I am" (Exod. 3:14), which, in a later dialogue with Moses is expanded: "I appeared unto Abraham, unto Isaac, and unto Jacob, by the name of God Almighty, but by my name Jehovah was I not known to them" (Exod. 6:3).

This introduction of a new name for the deity has attracted impressively recondite commentary, indicating as it does the inclusion of a new substratum of oral tradition behind the written scriptures. But such scholarship can too easily obscure the precise literary purpose for placing the tale where it is. The scriptures, it is frequently noted, usually work in parallels within verses and within stories.

Now, "parallel" when used in biblical studies is a very protean concept. It encompasses the way that "parallelism" is frequently used in literary studies (to mean metric and structural similarities, analogies, congruencies, and tropes), but it means something more. Parallelism is also a moral concept. In the biblical moral universe, man does something and God reacts, or, alternatively God acts and mankind reacts. But this is not cause and effect in the simple Newtonian moral universe of, say, David Hume, who essentially viewed cause and effect as one billiard ball hitting another and sending it on to the next and so on infinitely. In the Bible, the moral universe is three-, not two-, dimensional, and often God reacts to mankind's folly (or, sometimes, virtue) by producing consequences in a totally unexpected manner, indeed, on a totally new plane.

There is a parallel, undoubtedly consciously drawn, between the story of the Abrahamic covenant and that of Moses. In the story of Abraham, God changed the name of humankind's representative as a part of the completion of the relationship. And here the name of the Almighty is changed. The compilers of the Pentateuch clearly expect the reader to absorb the stories of Abraham and of Moses in tandem.

Parallels in the scriptures do not lie still. They are not immobile symmetrical comparisons, but take on the nature of a dialectic that moves the story forward. Thus, whereas the arrangement between Abraham and the Almighty has led to the introduction of one condition—circumcision—Moses now goes up to Yahweh's mountain and returns not only with the Ten Commandments but with a complex set of rules that the children of Israel must follow (see Exod. 20–24; cf. Deut. 5–25). Now, crucially, Yahweh is iffy about things: ". . . *If* ye will obey my voice indeed, and keep my covenant, *then* ye shall be a peculiar treasure unto me above all people" (Exod. 19:5, italics mine).

The if-then mode (another form of parallelism) characterizes the covenant in its full form. It is this if-then nature of the covenant that means it is not flippant to think of the covenant as a deal between God and the Hebrews. Indeed, so clear are the details of this deal that a modern-day lawyer could write out a contract embodying precise standards of performance on each side. An idiomatic Hebrew phrase of the biblical era was "to cut a covenant"[1] and, in truth, God and man had cut a deal.

If-then. It is a more complex relationship psychologically than it is legally. On the surface, the causality flows only one way: if the Chosen People follow Yahweh's rules, he will give them virtues, peace, and prosperity. If they are his holy servants, the scriptures say, he will bless them. But psychologically the causality is easily reversed. That is, a person, or an entire nation, may observe that things are going well, that people are becoming rich and fecund, and thus will conclude: I (or we) must be righteous, for we are being blessed. Undoubtedly the reader will notice that this mechanism is part of the morphology of what Max Weber called the "Protestant ethic," a belief that success in the visible world signified righteousness in the invisible. So, one might suggest that I am being grossly anachronistic in noting a similar mechanism as existing in biblical terms. But here is a psalm ascribed to King David:

> I was also upright before him, and I kept myself from mine iniquity.
> Therefore hath the Lord recompensed me according to my righteousness, according to the cleanness of my hands in his eyesight. (Ps. 18:23–24)

In fact, that kind of causal reversal is integral to if-then thinking on moral matters. It is a small and natural step in covenantal thinking to affirm that the possession of might (whether in the form of economic prosperity or military power) is evidence that one is morally right.

The if-then contract with Yahweh is a very risky arrangement, because the penalty clauses invoked for lapses by the Chosen People are extremely severe:

> If thou wilt not observe to do all the words of this law that are written in this book, that thou mayest fear this glorious and fearful name, THE LORD THY GOD;
> Then the Lord will make thy plagues wonderful, and the plagues of thy seed, *even* great plagues, and of long continuance, and sore sicknesses, and of long continuance.
> Moreover he will bring upon thee all the diseases of Egypt, which thou wast afraid of; and they shall cleave unto thee.
> Also every sickness, and every plague, which *is* not written in the book of this law, them will the Lord bring upon thee, until thou be destroyed.
> And ye shall be left few in number, whereas ye were as the stars of heaven for multitude; because thou wouldest not obey the voice of the Lord thy God. (Deut. 28:58–62)

Both directly in Yahweh's voice and indirectly through the prophets, the Chosen People are warned that Yahweh is a "jealous God" (Exod. 20:5, 34:14; Deut. 4:24, 5:9, 6:15; Josh. 24:19). A jealous God, like a jealous lover, is capable of violence; this is no metaphor. In the scriptures, God is very clearly credited with physically punishing those who wander from the paths defined by the covenant. Because Yahweh controls all the earth, he is able to vent his wrath in a variety of ways. For instance, in Moses' time, a man named Korah, a protocongregationalist, argued that every one of the Israelites was chosen by God and therefore that all persons were the equivalent of priests and were able to worship Yahweh directly. Korah and 250 of the leading men of the children of Israel rebelled against the rule of Moses and against the way that the Levite priests monopolized the positions of religious prominence. Moses wanted these religious democrats (to use an anachronistic but not inaccurate phrase) killed, and in an especially memorable way as they were breaking the terms of the covenant. Moses asks Yahweh to have the earth swallow up these dissenters and that is what happens. Korah, 250 princes of the people, their houses and goods all drop into a pit and the earth closes around them (Num. 16:1–34; also 26:10).

Equally spectacular is Yahweh's displeasure when expressed in the form of fire. In a situation in some ways similar to the Korah episode, two sons of Aaron (Moses' brother and the head of the Levite priests) usurped the priestly pecking order by taking "strange fire" in their censers as an offering to Yahweh. Immediately he sent down fire, "and devoured them, and they died before the Lord" (Lev. 10:2). On another occasion, during the forty years of wandering in the wilderness, "the people complained, it displeased the Lord: and the Lord heard it and his anger was kindled; and the fire of the Lord burnt among them, and consumed them that were in the uttermost parts of the camp" (Num. 11:1).

A little later, Miriam (Moses' sister) and Aaron questioned the religious leadership that Yahweh had bestowed on Moses. "Hath the Lord indeed spoken only by Moses?" they ask. "Hath he not spoken also by us?" (Num. 12:2). The Lord hears this and responds by inflicting leprosy upon Miriam, a case so severe that she becomes white as snow. Only after special intercession by Moses does Yahweh decide to heal her (Num. 12:10–16).

The if-then contract, therefore, implies a set of lessons that is anything but valetudinarian. There is no hedging, no casuistry here, just the unmistakable message that if you do not keep the deal with Yahweh, then he, the Lord of all the earth, is capable of turning the very earth, and all of its processes, into your scourge.

The same diamond-clear, diamond-hard morality is taught through Yahweh's sanctioning of purges and pogroms. At one point, when Moses was away conversing with Yahweh, a spontaneous apostasy spread among the people. They broke the fundamental commandment "Thou shalt have no other gods before me" and made a golden calf and danced around it naked. Moses, as Yahweh's spokesman, called together the Levites, each to bring his sword. "Thus saith the Lord God of Israel. . . . Go in and out from gate to gate throughout the camp, and slay every man his brother, and every man his companion, and every man his neighbour" (Exod. 32:27). They did so. About 3,000 men died in this purge. Much later, during the period of the divided kingship, members of the royal family of Ahab took to worshiping Baal. Jehu, king of Israel, learned of this and wreaked havoc. He captured the seventy sons of King Ahab and, after killing them, put their heads in a basket and sent the basket to their home city. Then, Jehu killed all the remaining members of the house of Ahab that he could find, their retainers, and their priests (2 Kings 10:1–11). Obviously, such tales are not intended to pink the conscience delicately. They say: keep the deal or else.

In enforcing the bargain, Yahweh frequently uses heathen peoples to punish Israel. For example, during the era of the judges, the children of Israel again fell into apostasy:

And the anger of the Lord was hot against Israel, and he sold them into the hands of the Philistines, and into the hands of the children of Ammon.

And that year they vexed and oppressed the children of Israel eighteen years. (Judg. 10:7–8)

Roughly four centuries after that event, King Manasseh, the king of Judah, began to worship idols and lead the people astray. Yahweh, through one of his prophets, sent this terrifying judgment: "Behold I am bringing such evil upon Jerusalem and Judah that whoever heareth of it, both his ears shall tingle" (2 Kings 21:12). In a remarkable image, this judgment continues: "And I will wipe Jerusalem as a man wipeth a dish, wiping it, and turning it upside down" (2 Kings 21:13). Most graphically instructive of all the scriptural warnings was the purge directed by Yahweh against Ahaz, the king of Judah who led his people in the worship of molten images and had sacrificed by fire to these false gods some of his children:

> Wherefore the Lord his God delivered him into the hand of the King of Syria; and they smote him and carried away a great multitude of them captives, and brought them to Damascus. And he was also delivered into the hand of the king of Israel, who smote him with a great slaughter.
>
> For Pekah the son of Remaliah slew in Judah an hundred and twenty thousand in one day, which were all valiant men; because they had forsaken the Lord God of their fathers.
>
> .   .   .   .
>
> And the children of Israel carried away captive of their brethren two hundred thousand, women, sons, and daughters, and took also away much spoil from them, and brought the spoil to Samaria. (2 Chron. 28:5, 6, and 8)

Thus Yahweh sanctioned a pogrom that cost the house of Judah in one day 120,000 men and then combined this with a purge whereby the warriors of the Israelite half of the Hebrew nation took 200,000 women and children of Judah as spoils.

Note here the moral economy that the if-then contract between God and his Chosen People implies. In it there is no suggestion that one should do right for the sake of doing right. Virtue is not its own reward, nor is vice its own punishment. The if-then deal is unambiguous: both individuals and the nation are to do good because that is how one does well, and they are to eschew evil because doing bad results in one's doing badly. This naked moral empiricism is apt to offend or embarrass many modern sensibilities. Granted, as an act of personal religious devotion, it is perfectly reasonable to try to theologize this hard empiricism, to gentle it, to smooth away the hard edges, but that sort of votive exercise should not intrude upon our reading of what the text actually says. And what the scriptures say, read seriously and often literally, formed the fundamental pattern of mind of the three societies that are the focus of our attention.

(2)

If God is one of the names that people give to whatever they believe is the ultimate reality, then Yahweh is a remarkably understandable ultimate, and that is one of his wondrous features. Despite vast later efforts to etherealize him, the God of the Hebrew scriptures is solidly anthropomorphic. Had Yahweh been some Pythagorean abstraction, we would today not know his name—or, probably, that of Israel. But, as William Foxwell Albright argued, "It cannot be emphasized too strongly that the anthropomorphic conception of Yahweh was absolutely necessary if the God of Israel was to remain a God of the individual Israelite as well as of the people as a whole. . . . It was precisely the anthropomorphism of Yahweh which was essential to the initial success of Israel's religion."[2]

The Hebrew God is aniconic and perfect. The first characteristic is a matter of inconvenience (one longs to see his face) and the second a matter of definition. Despite a great deal of ritual incantation about the mysteriousness of Yahweh, he is quite comprehensible. (Indeed, in biblical contexts and in later commentaries, when believers refer to Yahweh as being mysterious and beyond comprehension, they usually mean that he is disagreeable or rather frightening, but since he is by definition inerrant, his atrabilious nature must be some part of a divine perfection that we cannot understand.) Emotionally and psychologically, Yahweh works just like a human being. Not just any human, to be sure, but he has mood swings, is frustrated, becomes angry, is generous, only on a cosmic scale. His dialogue with Job is one of the best conversations ever recorded. His words as given through the prophets are emotionally shrill, but they certainly are emotionally clear. But Yahweh is most forthright and most graphic in the Pentateuch wherein the ground rules of the covenant are worked out. Anybody who spent time on a playground as a child and survived can understand Yahweh, for his stock in trade is making deals and enforcing them.

I would suggest that the covenant between Yahweh and Israel is the only image of Yahweh that exists. It is not a direct picture, and certainly not a graven image. Rather, the covenant is like a palimpsest which shows us in shadow what he really is.

One might say that God created the covenant in his own image, and for devotional purposes that is a useful observation. But as modern historians, looking for human explanations for human history, we could easily suggest the opposite: that whoever created the depiction of the covenant (a collective development effected over several centuries) created Yahweh in their image. That is, the priestly caste that articulated the rules of behavior and of priestly precedence found in the scriptures (the covenant's rules) made sure that the rules not only had a divine origin, but also a divine enforcer. The character of the Almighty enforcer, therefore, had to be tailored to fit the character of the covenant.

Hence, in the Hebrew scriptures, the covenant itself is the transcendent reality. Once the covenant is extant, it is impossible to speak of God without automatically referring to the covenant. Or, to put it another way: God cannot exist outside the covenant. Hence, the ultimate ground of human experience in the scriptures is this deal, the covenant, hard, inflexible, comprehensible.

(3)

The covenant as the ultimate ground of experience in the scriptures encompasses not only Yahweh, but his parallel construct, the Chosen People. In 1935, in a classic essay, Henry Wheeler Robinson suggested the usefulness of the concept of "corporate personality" in interpreting the Hebrew scriptures.[3] By this phrase Robinson meant two things. First, like a corporation in the modern legal sense, the Hebrew people were a single personality. They conceived of themselves as a single entity. And this corporate identity extended over time and included all members of the Chosen People, past, present, and future. Second, the corporate entity could be represented at special moments in its history by a single individual who could embody in his own singular personality the corporate personality of the entire nation.

The late Elizabethan phrase that is used in the Authorized Version, by which Yahweh tells Moses that the people "shall be a peculiar treasure unto me" (Exod. 19:5), captures the essential nature of this corporate identity. The children of Israel are peculiar in the now-archaic sense of their being special, and also in the modern sense of being singular—different from every other people. What makes them both different and special is that they have been given a treasure, the covenant, for which they are now responsible. Indeed, for a long period in their early history, the children of Israel maintained a reliquary of the holiest order, the ark of the covenant, which accompanied them on their wanderings and ultimately was housed in the holy-of-holies in the temple of Jerusalem. The ark was the physical manifestation of the possession of a spiritual treasure by the Chosen People—and was as close as the children of Israel ever came to carving an image of Yahweh.

The singularity and specialness of the Chosen People are bound up with the concept of "seed." God says to Abraham:

> For all the land which thou seest, to thee will I give it and to thy seed for ever.
> And I will make thy seed as the dust of the earth; so that if a man can number the dust of the earth, *then* shall thy seed also be numbered. (Gen. 13:15–16)

And again:

> And I will establish my covenant between me and thee and thy seed after thee in their generations for an everlasting covenant, to be a God unto thee, and to thy seed after thee. (Gen. 17:7)

The matter of seed runs through the scriptures in a very literal and explicit fashion. It should not be turned into a pale metaphor. The references are directly biological and have to do with human reproduction. This is most clear in the story of Onan, one of the sons of Judah (Gen. 38:1–10). One of Judah's other sons, his firstborn, "was wicked in the sight of the Lord; and the Lord slew him." Judah, wishing to continue his family line, urged Onan to have sexual congress with the widow of Onan's brother and then to marry her and raise the child that would result from their physical union. Onan agreed to have sexual intercourse, but, "lest he should give seed to his brother," practiced coitus interruptus: he ejaculated on the ground. Now to a modern reader this decision seems reasonable, but Yahweh saw the sperm being spilled and it "displeased" him. "Wherefore he slew him [Onan] also." Manifestly, seed refers to biological reproduction and it is through the seed in the biological sense that the corporate existence of the Chosen People is achieved generation after generation. Biology is central to the definition of the Chosen People. That is why those long genealogies are found in the scriptures. Whether or not the genealogies are historically accurate or whether they are schematized lines of descent is of no moment. What is salient is that they purport to chronicle the way the seed of Abraham, through the mechanism of human reproduction, was carried through time, increasing in each generation the corporate host that is the Chosen People. The mentality here is significant. One is not being arch when one notes that segments of the scriptures (for example, 1 Chron. 1–9) read very much like one-half of a purebred stud book, the half that contains the sire's line. People keep track of blood lines only if they think such things are important, and judging by the amount of attention given to genealogies in the Hebrew scriptures, such things are very important indeed.

In this context, the practice of circumcision makes great sense. Yahweh's instructions to Abraham are within the context of maintaining the covenant: "And the uncircumcised man child whose flesh of his foreskin is not circumcised, that soul shall be cut off from his people; he hath broken my covenant" (Gen. 17:14). Circumcision is a real physical act, an intentional offering to God of a piece of flesh, similar in that regard to the several other forms of flesh sacrifice practiced by the Hebrews of the time. By offering up part of the male reproductive organ of each of their offspring, the Chosen People reaffirmed in each generation that physical reproduction was part of the covenant with the Almighty.

Biology, therefore, becomes as vital as belief in determining the corporate entity, the Chosen People, so there is a strong emphasis upon keeping pure the lines of reproduction: that is, of not marrying outside the Hebrew nation or race (neither term quite fits the unique polity that evolved under the covenant). Moses, as an old man, rehearsed for the people the covenantal ordinances that bound together, and bound to Yahweh, the Chosen People. One of these is as follows:

> When the Lord thy God shall bring thee unto the land wither thou goest to possess it, and hath cast out many nations before thee, the Hittites, and the Girgashites, and the Amorites, and the Canaanites, and the Perizzites, and the Hivites, and the Jebusites, seven nations greater and mightier than thou.
>
> . . . . .
>
> Neither shalt thou make marriages with them; thy daughter thou shalt not give unto his son, nor his daughter shalt thou take unto thy son. (Deut. 7:1 and 3)

Joshua, in his last counsel to the people, gave similar advice, that they must not intermarry with the people of the nations that they conquered (Josh. 23:12).

One graphic story illustrates with particular clarity the horror with which the scriptures view intermarriage. At one time the men of Israel "began to commit whoredom with the daughters of Moab" (Num. 25:1). Since in the scriptural ideology, blood impurity always leads to sacral impurity, one is not surprised to learn that as a result of their mixed marriages, the Chosen People made sacrifices and bowed down to the gods of Moab. The Lord, angered by this development, brings a fierce plague upon Israel. While many of the people are weeping in repentance before the holy tabernacle, a manifestly unrepentant Hebrew man brings a non-Israelite woman to his tent. Phinehas, the grandson of Aaron, takes a javelin and follows the couple to their tent. There, as the couple have sexual congress, he thrusts the javelin through the man's back and all the way through the woman's belly. This priestly murder satisfied Yahweh: "So the plague was stayed from the children of Israel." Even so, the Chosen People already had lost to the plague 24,000 individuals, all as a direct result of not keeping their seed pure (Num. 25:1–9).

Now, to equate this emphasis upon group purity with modern racism would be a mistake, for righteousness rather than race is involved. The reason that intermarriage with outsiders is denounced is that it leads to infidelity to the covenant in general and to the worship of false gods in particular. Yet the conceptual grid for the Chosen People's protection of their righteousness is not much different from modern racist thinking.

Racist	Chosen People
Our group is superior.	Our people are convenanted to purity.
Other races are inferior.	Other peoples are not; they are less pure.
Therefore, intermarriage will introduce inferiority into our race.	Therefore, intermarriage will introduce impurity into our people.

The way in which the covenant implies both belief and blood purity (that is, adherence to Yahweh as the one god and the maintenance of the purity of the Abrahamic seed) puts one in mind of a certain toy popular in the nineteenth century. The "thingamatrope" consisted of a disk painted on opposite sides with two quite different images. The toy was fitted with a device that allowed the disk to be spun very quickly on its vertical axis.

When it spun, the two separate images merged to form a single picture. That is what happens with belief and blood in the Pentateuch: the whirl of Israel's history makes them one.

If defense of the purity of the seed is in part a social act (such as is effected by inhibiting mixed marriages), at other times it is necessarily military. Yahweh told Abraham, "I will bless them that bless thee, and curse him that curseth thee" (Gen. 12:3). Moses, in giving his great charge to the Chosen People, indicated what this would entail:

> And ye shall chase your enemies, and they shall fall before you by the sword.
> And five of you shall chase an hundred, and an hundred of you shall put ten thousand to flight: and your enemies shall fall before you by the sword.
> For I will have respect unto you, and make you fruitful, and multiply you, and establish my covenant with you. (Lev. 26:7–9)

When the Chosen People win a military victory, Yahweh of course is given the credit (see Josh. 23:9; Num. 21:3). At other times he is credited with having taken it upon himself to destroy directly those who have cursed Israel. For example, at one point Yahweh sends an angel to kill all the leading Assyrian warriors (2 Chron. 32:21; 2 Kings 19:35). When the angel is done with his job, 185,000 Assyrian warriors are scattered on the ground, dead.

Those who cursed Abraham's seed were not always punished in such large numbers, but often just as effectively. Take the case of Eglon, a king of Moab who enslaved the Chosen People for eighteen years (Jud. 3:12–30). The people were delivered from his heavy hand by one of history's first recorded professional assassins. This was Ehud, a left-handed man who had a special two-edged dagger made, eighteen inches long, which could be hidden under his clothes. This he strapped along his right thigh. The assassin went to King Eglon, an immensely fat man, and presented him with a gift from the children of Israel, and, having given him the gift, added that he had a secret message to give him in private. Alone with the Moabite king, Ehud said, "I have a message from God unto thee." He rose, swept the dagger out from under his clothes, and thrust it into the king. Because of the obesity of the Moabite, Ehud could not pull the dagger out. This assassination was the signal for an Israelite rebellion and the killing of 10,000 Moabites. Thus was Moab subdued and Israel made triumphant.

(4)

From the if-then character of the covenant follow three interrelated habits of mind. Each of these is made possible because the covenant is essentially empirical in nature. In fact, the covenant could be converted into a hypothesis easily tested by a twentieth-century observer: if condition A occurs, then response B ensues. There is nothing mystical about it. It is a matter of cause and effect, stimulus and response, action and reaction.

The first mental habit that derives from the nature of the covenant is the tendency to make sharp distinctions between the sacred and the profane. Virtually all cultures make this distinction in one way or another, but in the scriptural code the line is drawn especially clearly. This clarity is perhaps best captured in the book of Leviticus, for example:

> But I have said unto you, Ye shall inherit their land, and I will give it unto you to possess it, a land that floweth with milk and honey: I *am* the Lord your God, which have separated you from *other* people.
> Ye shall therefore put difference between clean beasts and unclean, and between unclean fowls and clean: and ye shall not make your souls abominable by beast, or by fowl, or by any manner of living thing that creepeth on the ground, which I have separated from you as unclean.
> And ye shall be holy unto me: for I the Lord *am* holy, and have severed you from *other* people, that ye should be mine. (Lev. 20:24–26)

There it all is: the reference to the covenant, to the benefits derived from it (a land of milk and honey), if the Chosen People keep separate (sacred) from other peoples (the profane). Notice that all the natural world is divided just as is human society, into clean beasts and unclean (sacred and profane). Such a division of the world into easily understandable black and white categories is emotionally comforting, because it erases those ambiguous gray areas of human experience that cause so much anxiety. Thus, the Hebrew conceptual grid is very attractive. It has a major disadvantage, however: people who exist within such an ideology—whether as individuals or as a corporate group—do not have much room to maneuver.

Individuals can engage in new experiences and can encounter new persons only with great care. They must decide whether the stranger at their door is one of themselves, and act accordingly. And, as a nation, the children of Israel are given little opportunity to compromise with their enemies. Undeniably, human beings, being endlessly ingenious, can argue long about the details of the divine distinction between sacred and profane, but there is no avoiding the fact that ultimately all decisions are supposed to be made within the stark rubrics of the sacred-profane dichotomy.

The second habit of mind that follows from the covenant is functionally related to the sacred-profane distinction, namely the legal mode of thinking. It is entirely appropriate that the book of Psalms begins with a hymn to the law and to those who follow its precepts:

> Blessed *is* the man that walketh not in the counsel of the ungodly, nor standeth in the way of sinners, nor sitteth in the seat of the scornful.
> But his delight *is* in the law of the Lord; and in his law doth he meditate day and night.
> And he shall be like a tree planted by the rivers of water, that bringeth forth his fruit in his season; his leaf also shall not wither; and whatsoever he doeth shall prosper. (Ps. 1:1–3)

The law in the scriptures is of three sorts: apodictic, false-apodictic, and casuistic. Apodictic commandments consist of absolute laws in their pure form. Such laws state a rule of behavior but give no indication of the consequences if the command is not obeyed. The so-called great commandment is the purest example:

> Hear, O Israel: The Lord our God, *is* one Lord:
> And thou shalt love the Lord thy God with all thine heart, and with all thy soul, and with all they might. (Deut. 6:4–5)

The Decalogue ("Thou shalt not kill," etc.) is perhaps the best-known apodictic framing of behavioral imperatives (see Exod. 20 and Deut. 5). What I term "false-apodictic" (the term is mine, although I cannot imagine that in the vast libraries of commentary someone has not used it before) refers to laws such as "And he that smiteth his father, or his mother, shall be surely put to death" (Exod. 21:15). This is not true apodictic law, because there is an unstated if-then clause. The statute really says *if* a person strikes his father or his mother, *then* he or she shall be executed. The same holds for the famous formula "Eye for eye, tooth for tooth, hand for hand, foot for foot" (Exod. 21:24). *If* a person maims another, *then* an equivalent revenge-maiming shall be visited upon him. The third, and most common form of law in the Hebrew scriptures is casuistic. This is if-then thinking at its most explicit and precise: "If a man shall steal an ox, or a sheep, and kill it, or sell it; he shall restore five oxen for an ox, and four sheep for a sheep" (Exod. 22:1). This kind of statute gives rise very quickly to case law and to the search for precedents in the common event of cases arising that are not exactly covered by biblical statutes. What, for example, should be the punishment for a man who steals an ox but is apprehended before he either can kill it or sell it? Does he merely return the animal or must he pay the five-oxen compensation, or something in between?

The omnipresence of the Hebrew legal code is one of its crucial characteristics. It translates the sacred-profane distinctions that stem from the covenant into practical rules for everyday life. Granted, some of the requirements, particularly the food taboos, are complicated and involve some inconvenience, but the rules are specific and can be met with a reasonable amount of effort. This legalistic approach to behavior yields a mentality that is both very exacting in its grasp of details and highly pragmatic. Yahweh's law is a practical discipline, and because the laws are so precise and so practical, it is easy for members of the group to monitor accurately who is and who is not conforming fully to Yahweh's covenant. And, simultaneously, the laws are a continuing and visible reminder to Israel that they, the Chosen People, are not the same as everyone else, the profane.

The third habit of mind engendered by the if-then character of the covenant is that the Chosen People think historically. To what extent the material in the scriptures represents accurately written history is one of those questions about which holy and unholy wars have been fought, but for our purposes that question is not germane. Whether or not they got the details right, the Israelite scribes (and before them the keepers of the oral version of the tales and genealogies) *tried* to do so. The intellectual grid that is formed by the scriptures is nothing if not historical. And how could it be otherwise? The covenant is presented in terms that imply sequence (if-then); the emphasis upon the Abrahamic seed results in a desire to plot the descent of the seed over time (as is evidenced in the long sequential genealogies); the legalistic cast of mind implies not only a concern with the sequence of events in individual cases, but with the aggregation of wisdom (case law) over time. History in the scriptures therefore is central. That the past can be known and recorded is an assumption that makes the existence of scriptures possible.

Within this historical mindset are four secondary characteristics. First, the scriptures teach the Chosen People to think in terms of cause and effect. That is no small thing. Also, the scriptures implicitly teach that if one is to think well in cause-effect terms, what is happening on both sides of the equation must be specified very precisely. (Modern social scientists call this "operational specificity.") So, for example, when someone sins, his transgression is specified and his punishment is precisely defined: cause-effect. A second aspect of the scriptural-taught ability to think historically is something so obvious that it is easily overlooked: the scriptures teach those who read and hear their contents to think in terms of time in general and in terms of chronology in particular. Just how seminal an intellectual influence this is becomes obvious when one contrasts the Hebrew scriptures to, for example, the holy texts of most Far Eastern religions. There all events at more than one lifespan's remove from the scribe are reported as if time occurred on some great white wall, and as if every event in the past were shown on that wall, equidistant from the present. In contrast, the Hebrews meter time, and they use the same measuring system consistently, all the way back to creation. Modern scholars sometimes point amusedly to earlier attempts to date happenings in the scriptures by calculating the passage of time as shown in the Hebrew genealogies (Archbishop Ussher's classic seventeenth-century chronology that dates the creation of the world at 4004 B.C. comes to mind). But one should not patronize the scribes. That they used lifespans instead of years as a way of measuring time is hardly primitive: until well into the present century, the standard agricultural lease in England, the first country to undergo the radical transformation that we call the Industrial Revolution, was in terms of "lives," not years. A third aspect of the historical mindset is that the Hebrews' discourse became numerate: accurate numerical description, or attempts at it, are part of clearly defining cause and effect. Thus, large portions of the Pentateuch are given over to early enumerations (the book of *Numbers* contains some of the best examples). These population censuses were an attempt to gain a definition of the Chosen People and to chart their growth. And fourth, the historical sense also produced a very precise sense of geography in the holy texts. The point I want to stress here is the prodigious topographical detail in the scriptures. Spatial description is as essential an axis of historical description as is chronology: the Chosen People move not only through time, but through specific, tightly boundaried space.

All this sounds very modern, and it is. Yet to note this fact is to fly in the face of what is virtually a small industry, the line of scholarship that emphasizes how different the biblical sense of history is from that of our own time. Of course it is different: the historical sense of each generation and each culture is different from that of every other, and the Hebrew nation had some singular mental habits of its own. But its historical sense was not all that much different from our own. Granted, the scriptures start with the Almighty as the ultimate cause of everything. Yahweh, in fact, becomes a very specific actor and, once his bargain with Abraham is sealed, he is known only through the covenant. He therefore operates in very specific ways, not unlike any great historical figure. It is easy to be misled by the later theologizations of Yahweh. As Harold Bloom has argued, "Modern scholars, Jewish and Gentile alike, cannot seem to accept the fact that there was no Jewish theology before Philo. 'Jewish theology,' despite its long history from Philo to Franz Rosenzweig, is therefore an oxymoron, particularly when applied to biblical texts. . . . Yahweh is an uncanny personality, and not at all a concept."⁴

It is sometimes argued that the scriptures are radically different from modern historical discourse in that they inevitably imply a lesson. History, in the scriptures, teaches, but so too does modern history. It is true that modern historians like to dissemble concerning the lessons that they draw and to disguise them behind certain tricks of professional distancing. Yet, actually, we are forever drawing lessons. Has anyone read any volume about, say, the history of the Vietnam War that did not contain an implied lesson? Even the most anodyne of modern histories—for example, the studies of the *longue durée* by the Annales school—are undertaken in order to teach the reader something about the nature of human existence and hence they contain an implicit lesson, however subdued. It is sometimes suggested that the Hebrew scriptures, replete as they are with poetic expressions, are thereby rendered incompatible with our own way of thinking. "It is a language in which every other word is a concealed metaphor" was Henry Wheeler Robinson's view of the sacred tongue, expressed half a century ago.⁵ Today his observation would alienate few historians, for, if there is one thing that the application of critical theory has forced professional historians to realize it is that *all* words enhull concealed metaphors, those of the allegedly antiseptic historians of our own time as much as the Yahwist scribes of three millennia ago.

That the historical sense of the Hebrew scriptures should be so similar to our own should surprise no one, for it is from those scriptures that western society learned how to think historically. What should surprise us, however, is the constant denial of this fact by people in my own trade: professional historians. Indeed, professional historians love to point to Hecataeus, to Herodotus, to Thucydides as our founding fathers. This putative descent was even more a matter of pride in an earlier generation when the classical languages and literature were dominant studies in the humanities. The classics were, well, so much classier as intellectual antecedents than were the texts that had their origin in the oral tradition of a group of Semitic nomads from the back of beyond.

Nevertheless, the Hebrew scriptures, not the classics, were the medium in which, from the time of Constantine onward, most literate westerners first encountered the study of the past. These scriptures—which, unlike the classics, were not lost to western society during the alleged Dark Ages—are markedly older than those of classical antiquity. Older roots, unbroken continuity, and a vastly wider audience: that is why the scriptures, not the Greek classics, are the hammer and anvil by which our western sense of history first took shape. In our understanding of history as narrative and as process we in present-day western society are the descendants of the children of Israel, and that is no mean heritage.

(5)

Before drawing together my argument about the covenant and the scriptures as a conceptual grid, let me note three motives that serve as reflex points in the framework. These are land, the Exodus, and blood sacrifice. These are points of great sensitivity within the grid and anything that touches one of them energizes the entire grid and calls forth an immediate, focused, sometimes violent response.

As mentioned earlier, the scriptures are full of topographical details. The scriptures are never garrulous, so these items, though they are obscure to most modern readers, must nonetheless be important. In part, the significance of the topographical details is cognitive, allowing the Chosen People to move not just down the path of time, but through physical human space as well. Time and space both act as coordinates. The Chosen People, in agreeing to the covenant, receive not only the blessing of the law but the land. In the covenant, possession of the land is tied to the perpetuation of Abraham's seed: "For all the land which thou seest, to thee will I give it and to thy seed for ever" (Gen. 13:15). Later, after the Exodus from Egypt, Moses is reminded by Yahweh:

And I am come down to deliver them out of the hand of the Egyptians, and to bring them up out of that land unto a good land and a large, unto a land flowing with milk and honey. (Exod. 3:8)

The scriptures' emphasis upon the Promised Land is not allegorical. There are literally hundreds of detailed references to specific places, and although the land on occasion may be described poetically, the children of Israel know that it is real. The land is part of their deal with Yahweh, as he explicitly recognized: "And I have also established my covenant with them, to give them the land of Canaan, the land of their pilgrimage, wherein they were strangers" (Exod. 6:4).

In the scriptures, almost as much time is spent chronicling the activities of the Israelites when they are not in the land (during their journeys toward it or when they are absent from it during the Babylonian captivity) as when they are there. The land becomes, therefore, something like the monarch in the Jacobite toast, "To the once and future king." It is past glory and future hope. In the periods when the children of Israel are not in residence, the land is the terminus that they know they eventually will attain if they behave righteously. That is Yahweh's promise. And when they are lodged in their homeland, they know that they reside there by virtue of the divine will and cannot be dislodged by force of enemies, unless they themselves fall from righteousness.

The Israelites' first entry into the Promised Land was presaged by the great Exodus from Egypt. This is one of three stories that form the narrative tripod upon which the Hebrew scriptures rest. (The other two are Abraham's direct encounter with God and the giving of the Law to Moses.) The Exodus is so central that it serves as one of the definitions of Yahweh: "I am the Lord thy God, which have brought thee out of the land of Egypt, out of the house of bondage" (Exod. 20:2). The deliverance from Egypt is one of the greatest acts of God on behalf of his people. The narrative itself is absolutely riveting, its first section being nothing less than a contest between the most powerful person on earth, the Egyptian pharaoh, and the God of the Israelites. This segment has the episodic and repetitive structure and the highly vivid detail that characterizes texts which are close to their roots in oral tradition (Exod., chaps. 7–12). Moses, eighty years of age, and his eighty-three-year-old brother Aaron ask for the Israelites' release. At first they display minor miracles to Pharaoh as a testimony to the strength of their god: Aaron's staff turns temporarily into a snake and the same rod is later used, at the Lord's command, to turn the waters of Egypt into blood. That not sufficing, a series of plagues is called down upon the Egyptians: frogs, lice, flies, a disease of cattle, boils, hail, locusts, three days of darkness, and finally that awful and climactic event, the death of Egypt's firstborn, both of humans and domestic animals. At last, the Israelites are allowed to depart. But even then, Pharaoh "hardened his heart" and sent 600 elite charioteers after them, just as they were approaching the Red (or Reed) Sea. (Exod., chap. 14) In what must stand as not only one of the first, but probably the greatest of *deus ex machina* conclusions, Yahweh, through Moses and the winds, parts the waters so that the children of Israel can pass on dry land. The Egyptian charioteers who follow them are drowned, for when Moses stretches out his hand, the sea returns to its normal character. According to linguistic scholars, the victory song that follows, "The Song at the Sea" (Exod. 15:1–21), is one of the oldest parts of the scriptures, probably dating from the eleventh or twelfth century B.C.[6]

> The Lord *is* my strength and song, and he is become my salvation: he *is* my God, and I will prepare him an habitation; my father's God, and I will exalt him.
> The Lord *is* a man of war: the Lord *is* his name. (Exod. 15:2–3)

The song continues in the unembarrassed strains of an era when triumphalism had yet to obtain a bad name and is followed by a description of Miriam, sister of Moses and Aaron, leading the women of Israel in a victory dance.

The centrality of the Exodus cannot be overstated. "One thing . . . is unmistakable," observes Judah Goldin,

> the exodus from Egypt is not simply referred to occasionally but recalled countless times and in a variety of connections. . . . In the seventh century B.C. there was a current popular exclamation, "As the Lord liveth who brought up the Israelites out of the land of Egypt." In the second century A.D. you might frequently run into sundry people who, to overcome demons or evil powers, would recite the formula: "The God who drowned the king of Egypt and the Egyptians in the Red Sea." Rabbis of the same century said that "In every single generation a person must look upon himself as though *he* had gone forth from Egypt," and to this day the Jews recite this statement as they celebrate Passover.[7]

Mention of the passing over of the angel of death brings us to the third reflex point in the scriptures' conceptual grid, the matter of blood sacrifice. A lot of mammals and fowl are ritually slaughtered in the scriptures to gain Yahweh's indulgence. In a historiographic survey of the scholarly literature on the Hebrew scriptures, Horace D. Hummel noted in 1966 that "it is particularly striking that so little further exploration has been made into the nature and meaning of sacrifice. The relative neglect of this area is all the more surprising because of the intense interest in other areas of Israel's cult."[8] The literature remains thin, but the avoidance of the topic should not surprise anyone. The killing of living things to propitiate a deity offends modern sensibilities, and we would like to ignore the details, if possible, or at least allegorize them. The scriptures, though, will not let us blur the focus. They provide very precise instructions, filling several biblical chapters, on how to dispatch ritually and to dismember liturgically various living things. The opening of the book of Leviticus serves as a fair example.

Five species from the animal kingdom are defined as acceptable for ritual slaughter: castrated bovines (I suspect that bullocks and oxen were employed by the Israelites because bulls were votive objects in ancient Egypt), sheep, goats, turtledoves, and pigeons. This is the instruction for killing a sheep or goat:

> And if his offering *be* of the flocks, *namely,* of the sheep, or of the goats, for a burnt-sacrifice; he shall bring it a male without blemish.
> And he shall kill it on the side of the altar northward before the Lord: and the priests, Aaron's sons, shall sprinkle his blood round about upon the altar.
> And he shall cut it into his pieces, with his head and his fat: and the priest shall lay them in order on the wood that *is* on the fire which *is* upon the altar:
> But he shall wash the inwards and the legs with water: and the priest shall bring *it* all, and burn *it* upon the altar; it *is* a burnt-sacrifice, an offering made by fire, of a sweet savour unto the Lord. (Lev. 1:10–13)

One could multiply such details, but the point is clear: the children of Israel were quite serious about ritual killing of at least five species.

A natural question arises—was there a sixth sacrificial species—humankind? The scriptures show that the Hebrews were very frightened of the idea of child sacrifice and there are repeated prohibitions against it. This abhorred practice was associated with the gods of other nations. The king of Moab, for example, when the Israelites pressed him hard in battle, offered up his eldest son as a burnt sacrifice (2 Kings 3:27). When the Bible refers to human sacrifice, it usually mentions a child as the burnt offering; these sacrifices probably involved ritual killing and burning in a manner similar to the Israelites' procedures for their five sacrificial species. The biblical descriptions of child sacrifice sometimes mention a specific alien deity to whom the offering is made: Molech (Lev. 18:21; 20:2–4) and Baal (Jer. 19:5), although the actual deity is sometimes unnamed (Deut. 12:31; Mic. 6:7; Isa. 57:5). The fascinating characteristic of these denunciations of child sacrifice is that the practice is not denounced because it is intrinsically evil. There is no talk of the sanctity of human life, nor in these instances is it even implied. Child sacrifice is wrong because it is associated with the worship of false gods. Not incidentally, this particular form of idolatry wastes Abraham's seed by cutting the lines of genealogical descent. Therefore it wounds and diminishes the corporate body that is the Chosen People.

Was such a concern, bordering on hysteria, justified? Surely the Israelites cannot have been inclined to the ritual murder of children. But note that Ahaz, an apostate king of Judah who reigned in Jerusalem for sixteen years, burned his own children in ritual sacrifice (2 Chron. 28:3). One of the psalms refers to an apostasy during Moses' time, when some Israelites fell from the faith, served idols, and sacrificed their sons and daughters (Ps. 106:37–38). Ezekiel, in one of his warnings to the people, refers to two whorish women of Israel who resided in Egypt; among their sins was the slaying of their children as an offering to idols (Ezek. 23:39). Ezekiel's story was told in the form of a parable, but it probably referred to some historical memory. Undeniably, this matter of child sacrifice hit a nerve. In part, this anxiety stemmed from the fact that the ritual slaughter of large mammals (cattle and sheep), as employed in the worship of Yahweh, was fundamentally the same process that the neighboring religions followed in their ritual slaughter of the highest mammals, humans. The technique was the same and, moreover, the idea of child sacrifice had something enticingly logical about it: the offering of the treasure of highest value, Israel's seed, its children. So, against the very logic of their own ritual tradition, the Israelites had to be turned away from the ritual killing of humans.

That child sacrifice potentially could fit easily into the Yahwist religion is indicated by the heart-rending story of Jephthah, one of the "judges" of Israel, and his daughter. Jephthah was at war with the Ammonites:

And Jephthah vowed a vow unto the Lord, and said, If thou shalt without fail deliver the children of Ammon into mine hands,

Then it shall be, that whatsoever cometh forth of the doors of my house to meet me, when I return in peace from the children of Ammon, shall surely be the Lord's, and I will offer it up for a burnt-offering. (Judg. 11:30–31)

As events worked out, Yahweh delivered the Ammonites into Jephthah's hand. He enjoyed "a very great slaughter," and returned home triumphant:

> And he smote from Aroer, even till thou come to Minnith, *even* twenty cities, and unto the plain of the vineyards, with a very great slaughter. Thus the children of Ammon were subdued before the children of Israel.
>
> And Jephthah came to Mizpeh unto his house, and, behold, his daughter came out to meet him with timbrels and with dances: and she was *his* only child; beside her he had neither son nor daughter. (Judg. 11:34–36)

His daughter's response is to accept her fate. She goes into the mountains for two months of solitude and then returns home where her father carries out his vow: he kills her and offers her up for a burnt offering.

This is a truly extraordinary tale. It is noteworthy that the bargain Jephthah made with Yahweh (a small covenant, really) is never questioned. Jephthah made the deal and he had to fulfill his half of the bargain: that is how covenants work. The Israelites do not condemn Jephthah for his awesome deed, although the daughters of Israel are said to have lamented annually his daughter's terrible death. So, in this one case, ritual sacrifice of a child is accepted as part of a covenant with Yahweh.

The aspect of the story that redeems it from being simply a tale of the trading of an only child for a military victory is the selflessness of the young girl. She encourages her father to keep his vow. Rather than break the covenant, she gives up her life, and thus the story becomes not one of superstitious mayhem, but of the ultimate self-sacrifice.

Indeed, the same mechanism holds in one of the Bible's centerpiece stories, Abraham's offering up of his son Isaac. Abraham is told by Yahweh:

> And he said, Take now thy son, thine only son Isaac, whom thou lovest, and get thee into the land of Moriah; and offer him there for a burnt-offering upon one of the mountains which I will tell thee of. (Gen. 22:2)

He obeys:

> And Abraham rose up early in the morning, and saddled his ass, and took two of his young men with him, and Isaac his son, and clave the

wood for the burnt-offering, and rose up, and went unto the place of which God had told him. (Gen. 22:3)

Isaac, realizing that there is no lamb, asks his father about it. He is told that God will provide the lamb for the burnt offering. When they come to the holy place:

Abraham built an altar there, and laid the wood in order, and bound Isaac his son, and laid him on the altar upon the wood.
And Abraham stretched forth his hand, and took the knife to slay his son. (Gen. 22:9–10)

Only at the last moment, when Abraham is about to kill his son, does an angel of God call out and stop the proceedings. The Lord is pleased, "For now I know that thou fearest God seeing thou hast not withheld thy son, thine only son from me" (Gen. 22:12). Yahweh provides a ram for the slaughter, caught by its horns in a nearby thicket.

The usual reading of this text—and the one that is favored consciously by the scriptural scribes—is that the hero of the piece is Abraham. He was willing to do the extraordinary, was he not? But I think that anyone who heard this story in the long-gone age when ritual sacrifice was a normal part of the religious life must have experienced a moment of identification with Abraham's obscene task and then a surge of revulsion. Recall that the scriptures work very hard at repressing the temptation to child sacrifice and that they label persons who follow this practice as heathens. Thus, we have an overt text and a latent subtext that run in opposite directions. Abraham on the surface is depicted as a hero, devoted to his God, but the subtext is that here is a fanatic, devoid of even the most elementary brakes on his careering zealotry.

The real hero of the story, as in the Jephthah tale, is the sacrificial victim. Isaac voluntarily allowed himself to be trussed up. Of his own choice, he was willing to become a sacrificial animal. Isaac, like Jephthah's daughter (oh, why can we not know her name?), takes the Israelites' deeply felt, deeply feared, deeply repressed attraction to child sacrifice and transforms it into a moment of self-sacrifice. The willingness of Isaac and Jephthah's daughter to die for the covenant and, indirectly, for the Chosen People, becomes one of the noteworthy themes in the histories of all peoples of the covenant: for thus the concept of ritual sacrifice is transformed into self-sacrifice for the common good, something very different and, I think, finer.

(6)

If we ask why this ancient conceptual grid has lasted so long and has had (and still has) such an extraordinary influence on the way people think and act, we can only give ourselves half-answers. I speculate later about why the scriptural code has been so perdurable and so strong, but readers should be aware that in a sense I am only fooling them, because actually we are all wrapped within a tautology. The tautology is this: the only reason we can seriously posit for the scriptures' longevity and influence is that they contain the characteristics that resulted in their longevity and influence; and since the scriptures' conceptual grid has survived so long and been so influential, whatever characteristics we adduce that the grid possesses are the sort that produce the grid's survival and cultural importance. This is a big circle and is not very satisfying. Nevertheless, with the sinking heart of a modern person trying to explain something that is beyond the frontier of modern methods, let me make some observations.

It is possible to argue that the reason the Hebrew scriptures have had such a long run is that they became encapsulated in an obscure sect, Christianity, that by an extremely unlikely set of occurrences became the dominant religion of the western world. But that really is no help. To say that historical accidents account for things is merely to admit that we do not know why things happened. Accident is not a historical explanation. As for the encapsulation of the Hebrew scriptures in Christian traditions being the cause of their survival, it would be more accurate to suggest that one of the reasons that the Christian religion did so well is that its rhetoric was based directly upon the highly persuasive rhetoric of its Hebrew antecedents. Without the Hebrew scriptures, there are no Christian Gospels.

In any case, to overemphasize the influence of Christianity is to neglect the heirs of the children of Israel, the people called the Jews. To them the scriptures, especially the five books ascribed to Moses, have been *alive*. For the Jews, the scriptures have never been a cultural ossuary, holding the bones of a long dead civilization; they are the living, unbroken continuity of modern Judaism with the religion of the ancient Hebrews. But to ascribe the permanence and the cultural hegemony of the scriptures to their having been kept and treasured by the Jews is to make deceptively linear a complex causal circle. In fact, the causality can be reversed. The Jews existed because the scriptures called them into being: no scriptures, no Jews. And one can accurately say that it was the scriptures that preserved the Jews, as much as the other way around.

So, instead of concentrating on the custodians of the ancient writ, one can more profitably reflect on the nature of the text itself, for, ultimately, the scriptures preserved themselves.

The character of the scriptures can be contrasted with twentieth-century poetry. I read present-day poets with pleasure and enthusiasm, but this is a studied activity, like chess. Unlike the scriptures, modern poetry operates according to some very strict and artificial assumptions. It takes forms that are learned and frequently learnéd. In that way, modern poetry is very different from the scriptures. Frank O'Connor, in his wonderfully wise survey of Irish literature, *The Backward Look,* distinguishes between what he calls "primary literatures" and the rest.[9] Primary literatures—the Hebrew scriptures, early Greek writings, pre-Christian Celtic cycles—are far from being simple or unsophisticated, but they share a characteristic that is totally missing in modern poetry: they speak to a general audience and in a manner that is virtually oracular. In their sources they are very close to the oral literatures that were their original form. Primary literatures are the means of confronting the full complexities and terrors of human life. They are literature, but they are not merely literary. They permit us to understand things otherwise unfathomable and to survive what otherwise would be unendurable. For the people who create them, hear them, read them, and believe in them, primary literatures are a means of controlling a world that is otherwise uncontrollable.

Without being reductionist, one may fairly note that the Hebrew scriptures are much more forceful than are other western primary literatures, chiefly because they fit together so well despite the myriad sources and hands involved in their creation. They work. They provide a readily comprehensible explanation of most things that a preindustrial people could care about, and they give directions for living the totality of life. The covenant, the fundamental deal that underlies the entire Hebrew Bible, is perfectly understandable to anyone who has bought and sold sheep or cattle or has made virtually any kind of small business bargain. The covenant is not ethereal, and it is not intellectually demanding. Anyone can comprehend it, if not in full (for no holy mystery can be understood in full), then certainly in its fundamentals. Within the covenant framework, God is a concept easy to grasp. He is the being that makes the deal and once the Abrahamic covenant is put in place, God does not appear except in relation to the covenant, the bargain that everyone understands. That there is only one God for Israel (and, as the theory of godship develops, that there finally is only one God in the universe) makes the Hebrew scriptures much more consistent than those of the other primary western literatures, all of which have multiple gods. That Yahweh is frequently unpleasant is beside the point. At least he works consistently through the covenant, and he keeps his word.

The pervasiveness of Yahweh and his covenant is beautifully congruent to the concept of the Chosen People. The Israelites in the scriptures assume a single corporate personality. That personality itself becomes a ground of reality, for it runs back in time to Abraham and forward in time to the very end of the future. Similarly, in its pervasiveness, the Mosaic law and its legal derivatives are congruent. Law, like the concepts of Yahweh, of the covenant, and of the Chosen People, surrounds everyday life, in this instance with a set of rules that (when they are exegetically expounded) cover every possible human situation.

If we think of the covenant, of Yahweh, of the Chosen People, and of the law as forming a well-integrated conceptual grid, then we should also realize that it is not a passive grid. In fact, it is a decision-making matrix. It seems that the grid was designed to make decisions about the real world. One can feed into it virtually any problem and get an answer. This is possible because the scriptural grid combines a perpetual alertness to sacred-profane distinction (in modern language, "digital"—yes-no—decisions, as in a computer) with an empirical mindset. Real information is collected about the cause and effect of a whole array of human actions. Historical thinking characterizes the network, so that a library of relevant precedents is available, a reference set that stretches over a very long skein of time.

Therefore, not only does the scriptural grid *work,* in the sense that its components fit together smoothly and with a good deal of grace; the grid actually performs work. One feeds a question into it, and, integrating the given data and its accumulated library of experience, and calling into account the nature of law and of the covenant, the scriptural grid can make a decision. Whether or not one accepts that decision is a different matter, but one must accept the basic principle of utility: something that works, survives.

That something so useful, so efficient, so all-encompassing would be preserved and maintained by its adherents seems obvious. Equally, one can see how easily its characteristics would be useful to non-Jews. Cultures that in any way define themselves as being a Chosen People (such as the Afrikaners and the Ulster Presbyterians) could appropriate and preserve the essence, if not all the details, of the ancient Israelite system.

What is less obvious is that this conceptual grid could have its greatest impact upon individuals and societies that no longer conceive of themselves as being in the thrall of the Hebrew scriptures.

Just how difficult it is to escape the influence of the ancient scriptural grid is best illustrated by the development of early Christianity. Although we know much less than we would like to know about the historical Jesus, it is generally (if not quite universally) agreed among biblical critics that the most radical parts of the New Testament, the Beatitudes (Matt. 5:3–12; Luke 6:20–46) are for the most part authentically representative of Jesus' views, if not his exact words. It is impossible to read the Beatitudes without recognizing that Jesus was rejecting the covenant. He was truly revolutionary. He replaced the if-then empiricism of the Hebrew scriptures with something so alien that it could have come from another universe: he called for the practice of virtue for its own sake and not because, as in the covenantal system, right produced might. We do not know much more about Jesus' views directly, but the interesting thing is how the early church dealt with him. The church was unable to follow his example in breaking free of the covenantal grid. So, although on the surface they appeared to reject Judaism, Jesus' successors interpreted the life and teachings of Jesus *within* the context of that grid. His successors transformed him into a covenantal figure. (Indeed, the scriptures that discussed his life and work are sometimes called the "New Covenant.") He is given a virgin birth: thus the concept of seed is not elided, only now Jesus comes not from Abraham's seed but directly from God himself. Myriad details of his life are claimed by biblical writers to be fulfillments of prophecies found in the Hebrew scriptures. His crucifixion is interpreted as a blood sacrifice. And, early Christian dogmatists claim that belief in his message ("if") results in eternal salvation ("then"). Hence, though claiming to have broken free of the Hebrew covenant, the Christian Church did not. Why? Because the Hebrew conceptual grid was not simply a conviction or a belief, but rather something lying so deep within the mind that it ultimately determined the possibilities of conviction and belief.[10]

(7)

Now to turn to the modern world: the Protestant Reformation and thereafter. It seems obvious that those societies that pay most attention to the Hebrew scriptures are those societies most apt to react like the ancient Israelites on certain pivotal matters.

What should we watch for? First, a mindset that places a good deal of emphasis upon social law. Whenever possible in such societies, social law will be enforced through religious congregations, rather than by civil jurisdictions. Second, such polities are apt to draw particularly sharp definitions of who their enemies are and to be thoroughly unforgiving to them. In an oft-reprinted lecture given in 1904 at the Jewish Theological Seminary of America, Talmudic scholar Louis Ginzberg noted that " 'Love your enemies' is not a Jewish precept, and one may doubt whether there are any examples of compliance with it."[11] Third, when covenantal societies think about the Almighty, the deity is apt to be heavily anthropomorphized and thoroughly warlike. One of Yahweh's most compelling guises is as a war god. He leads his people to victory over Egypt under Moses, to the conquest of the land of Canaan, to the repulse of the Midianites under the "judges," and to the defeat of the Philistines by David. Henry Wheeler Robinson pointed out that "careful study of the narratives will show how closely Yahweh is identified with the victory in each case."[12] Fourth, societies strongly influenced by the Hebrew grid will be profoundly attached to specific pieces of land. This will not be mere land hunger, but land will be seen as sacralized, as holy, and as a Promised Land. Fifth, the motif of the Exodus, the escape from Egyptian bondage preparatory to the journey to the Promised Land, will have special emotional appeal. Sixth, such societies are likely to set great store by the concept of group purity, either religious or racial or both. They will be given to quotations of the scriptural prohibitions on the mixing of their pure seed with the impure seed of lesser peoples.

These societies will not be given to easy compromises, committed to religious or racial pluralism, or overly concerned about keeping the good opinion of the outside, profane world. To keep the deal that is the covenant, a society must be uncompromising, adamantine, self-contained.

Part II

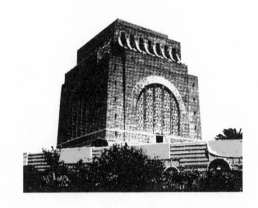

COVENANTAL CULTURES IN THE MAKING

3

The Afrikaners:
A Culture in Exile, 1806–1948

(1)

On 8 August 1938 a strange sequence of events began.* In Cape Town, a crowd gathered. Aside from a few puzzled English-speaking spectators, the group was Afrikaans-speaking. Many of the Afrikaners in the crowd were dressed in the costume of a century earlier; they watched two dozen ox-drawn wagons and their drivers and

*Since 1960 the vocabulary describing South Africa's various constituent groups has changed a lot, and it still is in flux. Hence I want to make clear what terms I use here. "White" has generally taken the place of "European" in official and scholarly usage. The implication of the older terminology, however, that the white groups share a common origin in European culture remains. "Nonwhite" is the umbrella term for everyone else. I wish there were some other term, since it is potentially derogatory to define any group negatively. But because segments of the nonwhite groups dislike being called "black," there is no alternative. Actually, in its negative semantics, "nonwhite" has a certain doleful accuracy: it refers to everyone against whom systematic racial discrimination has been practiced: everyone but the whites. "Afrikaners" refers to those previously known as "Boers." Occasionally (as in "Second Anglo-Boer War"), I employ the older term because it is conventional histor-ical usage. For the sake of consistency, however, I generally use "Afrikaner" in this book, frequently as an intentional anachronism. The peoples stemming from the British Isles, often misdesignated as "English" or "British," I refer to by inclusive terminology: "British-Isles origin" or, "Anglo-Celts." I also use the rough synonyms "English-speakers" or "Anglo-phones." "Blacks" refers to those people once denominated "Kaffirs," then "natives," then "Bantu." In this book, "black" includes neither the "coloured" (brown or "mixed race") people nor the Asians. "Khoikhoi" designates the people who were called "Hottentots" in the nineteenth and earlier twentieth centuries. "San" here refers to those who were once known as "bushmen." (Some scholars use both "Khoikhoi" and "San" as equivalent to Hottentot.) I use "native" sparingly, and without its nineteenth-century connotations.

passengers, all in the costume worn by the original Voortrekkers, who had left the Cape of Good Hope rather than accept British domination and the inhibitions on their way of life that the empire implied. The organizers of the parade exhorted the crowd to take the Voortrekkers as models and to affirm the vows said to have been taken nearly a century ago by their forefathers on the eve of an impending battle with the Zulu. After the crowd recited the oath, the wagons and passengers began their own long trek northward.[1]

From other spots in South Africa, eight other ox-wagons and costumed crews set out soon thereafter. They were headed for two festivals planned for 16 December 1938. One celebration would be in Pretoria where the cornerstone of a massive monument to the Voortrekkers was to be dedicated, and the other was to be at Blood River, where on 16 December 1838, the battle with the Zulu had turned into an epochal and sanguine victory. These commemorative activities were not very well planned and at first attracted only mild interest. But as the several ox-wagons wound their way through the small towns and the countryside, members of the Afrikaner population came to realize that it was not their past that was passing slowly by, but their future that was moving ineluctably forward: the procession was a collective affirmation that they, the Afrikaners, would eventually control South Africa and thus their own destiny. The intensity and the sponteneity of Afrikaners excitement about the trek centenary was a surprise to everyone, including the celebration's organizers. Across the country, Afrikaner men took to affirming their ethnic identity by growing beards. Women made Voortrekker costumes and, as the procession approached, turned out their families in period dress. In hamlet and town, as the ox-wagons passed, there were proud ceremonies. Streets were renamed in honor of the Voortrekker heroes. Long speeches were made and, frequently, the covenantal oath was repeated. It became the custom that, as the wagons approached a town, the locals would unhitch the oxen and pulled the wagons into the center of town themselves. As the wagons drew closer to Blood River and to the site of the planned Voortrekker monument, a torchlight marathon began in Cape

---

Rather, I intend the connotations that are becoming general among indigenous peoples of North America and the South Pacific: inhabitants of the country who were displaced by the European invasions, military, economic, and cultural. People whose ancestral origin is the Indian subcontinent (present-day India and Pakistan) are called "Asiatics" or "Asians" in official usage. "Indian" refers to people of the *entire* Indian subcontinent, not just the present-day state of India.

"My brethren and fellow countrymen, at this moment we stand before the holy God of heaven and earth, to make a promise, if He will be with us and protect us and deliver the enemy into our hands so that we may triumph over him, that we shall observe the day and the date as an anniversary in each year and a day of thanksgiving like the Sabbath, in His honour; and that we shall enjoin our children that they must take part with us in this, for a remembrance even for our posterity; and if anyone sees a difficulty in this, let him return from this place. For the honour of His name shall be joyfully exalted, and to Him the fame and the honour of the victory must be given."

Figure 1. The Afrikaner Convenantal Oath

Town, timed so that the torch, a symbol of freedom and of white civilization, would arrive at journey's end just as the wagon trains pulled in.

The final ceremony at Pretoria took three full days (that at Blood River was somewhat less ornate) and concluded with the laying of the cornerstone of the monument. Approximately 100,000 people attended the Pretoria ceremony alone, slightly less than one-tenth of all Afrikaner men, women, and children in the Union of South Africa.[2] It is clear that the overwhelming majority of the Afrikaner population (and a small sliver of the British Isles-derived populace) participated in some aspects of the centenary celebrations. Whatever the celebrations were—religious events, ethnic affirmations, cultural assertions—they were not epiphenomenal. They meant something very important. For Afrikaners involved in the celebrations, the events of 1938 were at once a public affirmation of their ethnic and national identity and a deeply moving personal experience.[3] One thus can easily understand the fear, awe, and exhaltation experienced by fifteen-year-old Johannes Meintjes (later to become the pioneering

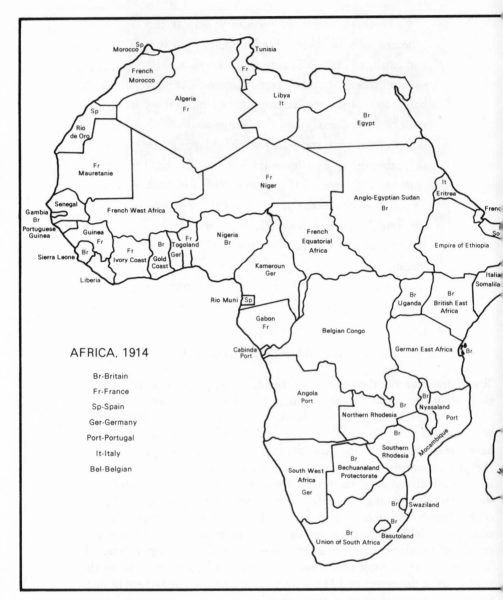

AFRICA, 1914

Br-Britain
Fr-France
Sp-Spain
Ger-Germany
Port-Portugal
It-Italy
Bel-Belgian

Map 1. Africa, 1914

Afrikaner historian of the Great Trek) when, before 4,000 people in the glare of torchlight, he recited a nine-stanza poem that concluded with the exhortation: "Trek! God will show the way!"[4] If the Great Trek had been the Afrikaners' march into exile, then Covenant Day, 16 December 1938, was their assurance that they were nearly home.

To white South Africans whose origins were in the British Isles, the 1938 centenary celebrations were matters of easy ridicule, but anyone with any prescience had to be frightened, for the Afrikaners were serving notice that they were nearly ready to seize control of what they believed was their rightful homeland. Alan Paton was among the most perceptive of the contemporary observers. He was a strong anti-imperialist, so he was sympathetic to the Afrikaner views. Paton, who was bilingual, had himself grown a commemorative beard for the celebrations and had journeyed from Johannesburg to Pretoria by wagon to be at the site of the promised Voortrekker monument. He was washing off the road dust in one of the communal showers that had been set up for the travelers when a bearded Afrikaner next to him, unaware that Paton was not an Afrikaner, offered his own view of what the centenary celebration meant. "Now we're going to tip those English on their arse" is a colloquial English version of his words, and that was a fair summary of what the Afrikaner resurgence meant for the rest of the white community in South Africa.[5]

(2)

Coming to grips with the way in which covenantal constructs were wired into Afrikaner culture gives one an opportunity to encounter one of the most interesting, stimulating, and frustrating of historical literatures. South African history, because of the country's existence as an international moral dilemma, has attracted more than its fair share of first-rate historians. It has also attracted zealots, ideologues, reactionaries, racists, and just plain fruitcakes. The fringe writers aside, a bewilderingly wide range of opinion on most issues exists among responsible and serious historians of South Africa. Because the influence of academic historians as keepers of the various forms of the public memory has been so strong in South Africa, their work requires comment.

Considered as a result of a collective (if far from cooperative) enterprise, the structure of South African historiography is strangely twisted and bent.[6] The historiography reminds me of the appearance of a modern steel-and-glass office block after a high-intensity fire, which has stripped the building of its outer veneer, leaving only the structural armature, angular and warped. So too, the various approaches that dominate modern South African historical writing appear strange to readers accustomed to reading the history of nations that today operate in a much less morally intense environment. The *gravitas* that characterizes most professionally written European and North American history is missing in most South African writing, for all save the coolest of analyses are responses to a hidden agenda, one anchored in the problems of today and, more so, of tomorrow. Hence, very little has been written in terms of trying to understand South Africa's long-range history solely for the sake of comprehending how it works, the way, for example, the Annales school has attempted to provide for France. And one cannot imagine a morally neutral *folkliv* movement such as is pursued in the Scandinavian countries in order to preserve the past of the everyday citizen, for the demotic past is too volatile a topic and too much involved in the political mythology of the Afrikaner people.

That is not bad historical practice; it just is different from the way things are done elsewhere.

The problem of race relations of course is the matter that sets the agenda for the South African historical profession—and race is paramount even when it is unspoken and even when its reality is denied. Although it would be inaccurate to speak of formal "schools" of South African history, it seems to me that there are four distinct strands. One of these is historical writing, mostly in Afrikaans, produced as part of the historical justification of the actions of the Afrikaner people. The implicit logic in this literature is "if you understand us, you will understand that we are right." Second, South African historical studies is one of the few arenas where one still can encounter genuine paleo-Marxists—adherents of the extreme doctrine of structural Marxism that leaves no room for anything save economic structure and its contradictions as the determinants of human behavior. This line of Marxist analysis has virtually disappeared from modern western historical writing but survives, as do many vestigial cultural practices, on the margins of dying empires. When such writers trace the way in which the Afrikaner culture and its resultant apartheid were entirely products of capital accumulation and its contradictions, it is impossible not to hear the voices of their predecessors among Western European historians who spent the 1950s and 1960s simultaneously defending Stalin and delineating western economic contradictions.

A third strand of historical writing, the neo-Marxist, has been immensely productive. These individual scholars, while accepting the importance of economic substructure in societal relations, have understood the importance of culture in modulating the way those basic substructures work. If South African historiography has not yet produced its own E. P. Thompson, the day is probably not far off. And fourth, there is an omnibus strand, composed of scholars often mislabeled "liberals." This is a code word: usually said with a slight curl of the lip, "liberal historian" usually means a non-Marxist, and it covers a broad range, from economic liberals to social "pluralists." They deserve better. Anthropologists and sociologists with historical interests, historians well informed by theoretical work in various social sciences, and other writers who embrace a pluralism of theoretical outlook are producing valuable studies of individual industries and of specific locales, employing both neo-Marxist and non-Marxist social theory. Whatever else it is, the historical writing of these scholars is not "liberal" in the derogatory sense of being flaccid and mindlessly empirical.

Historians, no less than other people, have "primordial beliefs"—beliefs so deeply embedded in their own personalities as to preclude their being examined rationally or tinctured by true empathy. One emotion runs so deep in the English-language literature on South African history that it can justly be labeled a primordial belief and in essence racist; namely, that the Afrikaners are an irredeemably bad lot. No one seems to like them very much and a lot of historians dislike them a great deal. Stated so baldly, this would seem to describe an unlikely situation, yet with certain unusual exceptions, the historical literature by English-language historians of South Africa has either denigrated the Afrikaners' culture, or, more grandly, simply refused to admit that it exists save as an accouterment to economic substructures or as an excuse for self-aggrandizing political nationalism. As I indicate later, there is a fear, expressed quite overtly by some South African historians, that if one tries as a historian to get inside the Afrikaner mindset, one will unintentionally advance the case of Afrikaner racist mythology. This I do not accept.

There is a long and clear tradition of English-language writers bad-mouthing the Afrikaners. The Afrikaner historian Michael Streak published a monograph, *The Afrikaner as Viewed by the English, 1795–1854*, which included long excerpts from the English-language publishers of his period.[7] Most of those excerpts would today be actionable in any country that has a reasonable Incitement-to-Hatred Act. The tradition began with the travel narrative of John Barrow, published in two volumes in London in 1801 and 1804, and continued in unbroken skein through the nineteenth century. Two examples from the second half of the century, not extreme ones, indicate the way observers from the English-language world thought about the Afrikaners. The first, by Anthony Trollope, was published in 1878 and the second, by Dorothea Phillips, in 1899. Despite obvious differences, the products of these two writers were cut from the same cloth. Each author was bent on being fair and understanding to the "Boers" but the manner of each was unconsciously patronizing. "The Dutch Boer is what he is not because he is Dutch or because he is a Boer, but because circumstances have isolated him," Trollope explained.[8] Later he added: "We can hardly be entitled to expect more refinement today among the Boers of South Africa than among the English of the time of Queen Elizabeth."[9] Phillips was understanding in her way as well. She inveighed against English people who came to South Africa "and instead of studying the idiosyncrasies of the Africander, they assume a condescending and arrogant attitude toward the people of the land, and expect them to behave as if they were English."[10] That seems to be a plea for cultural pluralism, except that she quickly added, "But as they are not English, they naturally do not come up to the stranger's expectations, and are consequently relegated to outer darkness."[11] Both travelers repeated a constant theme in the nineteenth-century anti-Afrikaner literature: Afrikaners are lazy. "The people whom I have in mind," reported Mrs. Phillips, "told me that they had come to the Transvaal in the great 'trek' forty years before. . . . Needless to say, having once planted the garden, made the wall of the Kraal (also of stones), there was nothing more to be done for the rest of their lives except to sit smoking the pipe of peace and drinking bad coffee. Their fathers had done the same: why should they try to improve on their methods?"[12] Trollope had reported that "things in the Boer's house no doubt are generally dirty. An earthen floor will make everything dirty—whether in Ireland or in the Transvaal. The Boer's dress is dirty—and also, which is more important, that of the Boeress. The little Boerlings are all dirty;—so that, even when they are pretty, one does not wish to kiss them."[13] The two writers also embroidered upon a third theme common in the English-language literature. "I have heard the Boers spoken of as a dishonest people," Trollope reported, and then he quoted two sources. One claimed that "no Boer would make a considerable purchase without relieving the grief which was natural to him at parting with his money by pocketing some little article gratis—a knife, or a tobacco pipe, or perhaps a few buttons." The second report said that all shopkeepers were forced to include the cost of Boer thieving in setting their retail prices.[14] Mrs. Phillips developed the same motif. "I remember a store-keeper telling me that at Nachtmaal he always had a large extra staff simply to watch what the customers pocketed, the items being added to the account, without remarks being made on either side. He also told me that a store-keeper of his acquaintance had lost his whole Boer connection for ever because he was not so wise in his generation, but prosecuted one of these pilferers."[15]

Neither Trollope nor Phillips was writing jingoistic propaganda. Each was trying to understand the Afrikaners, but their unconscious, high-Victorian prejudices were inescapable. One could multiply such examples.[16] The salient point is that attempts to understand Afrikaner society in the twentieth century—including those efforts conducted by historians—frequently have fallen into updated versions of those nineteenth-century prejudices. Dan O'Meara, in his provocative *Volkskapitalisme,* cites examples of scholars who refer to the Afrikaners as "paranoid," as "out of touch with reality," and as "the gullible tool of manipulating leaders." One study, by a social scientist, concludes that Afrikaners are "immature psychopaths" in a sociopathic culture.[17] Such remarks are the late twentieth century's equivalent of calling the Boers lazy and dishonest in the Victorian era. O'Meara shrewdly notes that an inherited "pro-British" spirit exists. This, I think, by now is largely unconscious, but it explains, in O'Meara's words, why "a number of non-Afrikaner authors have failed to read, or at least take seriously, what Afrikaners write about themselves, giving nationalist historians legitimate cause for complaint." O'Meara adds, however, that "not all histories of Afrikaner nationalism suffer from such obvious ideological limitations."[18]

Actually, recent historical literature simply implies (without ever quite saying so) that for the purposes of historical explication Afrikaner culture does not exist, or that it is merely a political nationalism comparable to fascism. For the structural Marxists this is easily done, as they have an a priori explanatory structure that does not recognize culture as an independent actor in the determination of human history: at best, culture is like a panel of repoussé metalwork, a set of images hammered into relief by the constant behind-the-scenes pressures of economic forces. Within this framework, Afrikaner cultural awareness is seen as a result of the process of class formation and, ultimately, Afrikaner racism is presented as one peculiar form of capitalism's later stages.

Neo-Marxists are much more sophisticated, and they recognize that the Afrikaner culture mediated the formation of capitalist society in South Africa, even though in their view the culture was ultimately the product of

South Africa's peculiar economic structure. The trouble with the neo-Marxist viewpoint is that it does for Afrikaner culture what pre-1950s American historiography did for the American black: it denies that the culture had any independent power. Thus, while honestly attempting to analyze Afrikaner culture (just as, in a similar way, many of the earlier historians of the American south tried sincerely to deal with black culture), they assume the culture either to be powerless, or, at best, to be a passive and tertiary determinant of events. It is unfortunately true that what one despises (either consciously or unconsciously) one denigrates: in this case by depicting Afrikaner culture as weak, passive, and lacking the dignity of self-volition. This is a particularly ironic academic development, because popular consciousness (especially among English-speakers) attributes enormous power to Afrikaner culture and ethnic identity.

What happens when South African historians tackle Afrikaner culture as a subject head on? In recent years the results have been curious. Among those labeled "liberal" (meaning non-Marxist and non-Afrikaner) historians, there have been various efforts at "disproving" the historical beliefs of the Afrikaner community. A highly skilled and rhetorically successful essay in this vein was published in 1983 by Marianne Cornevin, titled *Apartheid: Power and Historical Falsification.*[19] Cornevin focuses on a decalogue of historical assertions common in South African historical literature, especially that published in the Afrikaans language. These assertions include the following: whites and blacks arrived in South Africa at the same time; blacks were nomadic until they encountered the whites; the Voortrekkers forayed into an empty land that belonged to no one. And so on: ten historical beliefs commonly held in Afrikaner society are efficiently shown to be wrong, a task Cornevin accomplishes with a minimum of posturing and without triumphalism. The process is an example of how disinterested professional historical skills can be put in the service of both the present and the past.

Cornevin's effort contrasts sharply with *The Political Mythology of Apartheid* published two years later by Leonard Thompson. As the doyen of South African historians in North America, and as the most academically powerful of the non-Marxist historians of South Africa, Thompson carries immense weight. To anyone acquainted with the way historians outside South Africa have dealt with the nationalist and ethnic mythologies of the nineteenth and twentieth centuries, however, Thompson's effort is depressingly reductionistic and presentist. It is reductionist in its fundamental conception of myth as something that is either accurate or inaccurate and thus can be either proved or disproved. "In assessing political myths," he posits, "we may apply three criteria. One is the special province of the historian, who is a technician in the handling of historical evidence. If a myth is compatible with the evidence, it passes a crucial test. If it distorts the evidence, it fails the test and is bad history—*and to that extent an implausible myth*" (emphasis mine). Thompson adopts a second criterion: "One may also assess a political myth in terms of its scientific probability." And, he adds, "The third criterion for assessing political myths is utiliarian . . . *whether its effects are good or bad*" (emphasis mine.)[20]

Thompson's viewpoint is quite extraordinary. It harks back to an almost-forgotten era, when militant atheists went about "disproving" biblical myths and thus, they thought, reducing peoples' belief in them. The entire enterprise is misdirected. Myths are complex interworkings of attitudes, faiths, and accurate and inaccurate empirical observations, which—if they are viable—have not so much a defensible logic as, to their adherents, a satisfying *psycho*logic. And viable myths permit their adherents to hold, without disquiet, beliefs that are rationally incompatible with each other, and to hold views about empirical reality that are not verifiable by any rational process. When one studies systems of myth (or, if one prefers, belief systems), the most important task of the scholar is to see how the systems work, and this has to be done on the terms of the myths themselves: do the pieces, however bizarrely shaped, fit together? Does the belief system speak to the emotional as well as to the intellectual needs of its adherents? Does the myth system explain to its believers how the world works?[21]

Getting the low-level historical facts right is certainly one of the basic tasks of the professional historian, and it can be done without rancor. In the context of South African life, it sometimes takes courage for historians to challenge Afrikaner mythology, especially if they are Afrikaners themselves. In March 1979, the distinguished professor F. A. van Jaarsveld took part in a symposium at the University of Pretoria, giving an address on the meaning of the Day of the Covenant and on the need to make it a more inclusive national festival. Part way through his speech a band of protestors entered the lecture hall, hauled him from the podium, and smeared him with tar and feathers.[22]

Van Jaarsveld's historical revisionism was evidence of considerable moral courage, but for English-language historians to approach the cultural constructs of the Afrikaner population with a reductionist, debunking attitude neither requires courage nor offers evidence of good historical technique. Instead, it shows the continued existence of what O'Meara has called the inherited pro-British spirit. Look at those Afrikaners, the argument implies; they cannot even get their own history right.

That the constructs of Afrikaner culture often have not been treated with the empathy and seriousness that one expects of good professional practitioners is in part attributable to the fact that much of the cultural analysis of the Afrikaners in the English-language literature has been simplistic and intellectually flabby. In many such histories, the concept of Calvinism has been made to carry much more weight than it can bear. (This is in sharp contrast to the case of Ulster, where Calvinism has been unduly ignored by mainline historians.) The concept of "Calvinism" has been used both to refer to the specific doctrinal formulations that stem from Jean Calvin and as a portmanteau label for the Dutch-derived culture in South Africa. Hermann Giliomee and Richard Elphick argue that historians of the seventeenth and eighteenth centuries, such as the noted maritime historian Charles Boxer, and some modern writers have used Calvinism to explain the Afrikaners' view of themselves and to explain their racism, without employing anything approaching an adequate evidentiary base.[23] Heribert Adam has demonstrated how little the widespread emphasis upon "primitive Calvinism" explains about South African history, especially about apartheid.[24]

"Calvinism" has been useful both to those who dislike the Afrikaners—the words "primitive," "fanatic," and "fundamentalist" have been attached to it—and to those who have wished to provide an apologetic for Afrikaner culture.[25] Thus, W. A. de Klerk in *The Puritans in Africa: A Story of Afrikanerdom* (1975) uses eighteenth- and nineteenth-century "Calvinism" to associate the Afrikaner culture with "roots in the Protestant ethic of a particular order," one that involves "a rational plan from the radical Right."[26] Both the adverse and positive mentions of Calvinism directly state or strongly imply (1) an assumption that Calvinism in the theological sense of the word permeated early Cape society, (2) that a clear and linear connection links the "Calvinism" of, say, 1815, and the Afrikaner sense of ethnic identity that emerges much later in the nineteenth century, and (3) that in some mysterious way the Afrikaners skipped the Enlightenment: not that they rejected it, but that they somehow never learned of it.

These ideas arise from scholarship that is far from being state-of-the-art, but they open the way for some spurious, but extremely clever, historical swordplay from the intellectual right, most intriguingly on the part of the political philosopher André du Toit. The "right" to which du Toit belongs is not the far right of the South African political spectrum (in fact, in conventional political terms, du Toit is considered to be "left"), but the international intellectual right of Allan Bloom: the tradition that great ideas issue from great minds and that real intellectual history should pay little attention to the demotic mind, focusing instead on the writings of the articulate and gifted. In two important and closely related essays, published in 1975 and in 1983, du Toit has argued that there exists a "Calvinist paradigm" in South African history and that it is bogus.[27] Du Toit candidly admits that his critique is part of his own present-day political agenda. "As long as this nineteenth-century myth [of Afrikaner Calvinism] serves to give spurious historical weight to twentieth-century social ideology, both the practice of history and the practice of politics will suffer."[28] Those are the closing words of his 1983 essay in the *American Historical Review* and presumably they are the ones he wishes his reader to remember.

Du Toit's essays have two trains of argument which at first seem puzzlingly unrelated; they are not. The first consists of a demonstration that before roughly 1850 there is little evidence of widespread beliefs of a Calvinist sort. This means that there cannot be a direct and linear connection between the belief system of the seventeenth- and eighteenth- and early-nineteenth century Afrikaners and the beliefs of their descendants of the late nineteenth and twentieth centuries.

This argument on du Toit's part is convincing, but far from being a major revision, it is merely a repetition of what at the time of du Toit's writing was already well proved. A series of publications about Afrikaner culture had already established the fact that the belief system that has dominated modern Afrikaner society was a product of the 1870s and thereafter. What one may call the modern Afrikaner belief system was recognized as being a synthetic construct, one that was catalyzed into being by rapid economic change and by the wars with the United Kingdom in the last three decades of the nineteenth century. Floris Albertus van Jaarsveld had demonstrated in 1961 in *The Awakening of Afrikaner Nationalism* that "it was only during the years 1868–1881 that many Afrikaners developed a national consciousness and became a 'people' or a 'nation.' "[29] Irving Hexham, whose work du Toit well knew, had published in 1981 a volume entitled *The Irony of Apartheid* in which it was very clearly argued that the mythology that du Toit insists on calling the "Calvinist paradigm" was not fully developed until the end of the Second Anglo-Boer War.[30] And, most important of all, in 1975, T. Dunbar Moodie in an internationally acclaimed tour de force had detailed the

way in which the Afrikaners' "civil religion"—a close synonym for du
Toit's "Calvinistic paradigm"—had been synthesized between the Second
Anglo-Boer War and the creation of the apartheid state.[31]

What was du Toit playing at, in telling historians what they already
knew? Here the second train of his argument comes into play. In his 1975
essay, du Toit had made it clear that only "ideology" could underlie the
actions of a state, and that an ideology was a coherent set of action-related
ideas. These ideas could not be mere political sentiments based on a
national identity. They had to be the kind of tightly reasoned, highly
articulate statement made and read by political philosophers.[32] Thus,
there could be no common ideological core in Afrikaner society, for the
demos cannot have an ideology. By adopting such an exclusive definition
of ideology, du Toit was able to argue that only in quite modern times—
since 1948—had an ideology of Afrikaner nationalism arisen; and this
ideology was apartheid.[33]

Thus, du Toit's definition of "ideology" was an attempt to force the
analysis of Afrikaner behavior out of the historical mode. And his attack
on the putative "Calvinist paradigm" was less an attack on a specific set
of historical beliefs (although he was indeed extremely good at tidying up
some minor datings and attributions), than an attack on the historical
mode of analysis in general—at least if that analysis involved Afrikaner
demotic culture.[34]

Two important matters come to a head here. The first issue is whether
or not it is self-corrupting to study the evolution of the Afrikaner worldview. Dan O'Meara has said that "I would argue that despite many
differences at the level of conclusions, both the Afrikaner nationalist and
[the] liberal literature share uncritically the same principles of investigation and explanation—they operate within a similar epistomological
framework. As a result, the liberal analysis of Afrikaner nationalism remains at the level of counter-ideological history. It presents but a pale,
negative mirror-image of the assumptions of Afrikaner nationalist analysis."[35] André du Toit, in a free-swinging 1984 attack on F. A. van Jaarsveld, the first serious analyst of Afrikaner myths, concluded: "I have
argued that as an effort towards the 'historical' understanding of modern
Afrikaner nationalism and of the ideology of apartheid this literature
amounts to the reinforcement of the myth."[36] Both O'Meara's and du
Toit's statements are inaccurate: anyone who could read either the work
of van Jaarsveld or of Moodie and find it to be even an unintentional
endorsement of Afrikaner nationalist theories, or even a negative mirror-
image of those myths, has a will strong enough to move mountains.

But worse, O'Meara's and du Toit's viewpoints imply a set of coercive normative views that would kill serious scholarship. I can imagine no other western society for which historians of repute would contemplate such an argument. In a devastating single-page reply to du Toit, F. A. van Jaarsveld concluded by quoting a report in the Johannesburg *Sunday Times* which had done a feature on du Toit (18 July 1982). "Dr. du Toit, a political philosophy lecturer . . . admits his attack amounts to an academic tarring and feathering of Professor van Jaarsveld."[37]

A second question: in dealing with the historical development of Afrikaner culture, should one be dealing only with ideologies as articulated by an elite, or with both high culture and low? Focusing on high culture might simplify things, as it would make most of the history of the Afrikaner disappear, but that is unhelpful if one is looking toward history for enlightenment. Any sensible discussion involves both high culture (in the few areas wherein it was present, particularly theology) and a recognition that there was a popular culture, a rich one, within Afrikaner society. Emphatically, one should not fall into the old-fashioned concept of sketching a "national mind," nor should one endorse the idea that there was something called "Afrikanerdom" in the nationalistic sense of there having been an Afrikaner people, moving surely forward, mystically aware of their collective identity from earliest times. Nor should one equate Afrikaner social values and popular customs with "Afrikaner nationalism." Instead, we should accept the idea that there are well-developed ways in which the social sciences model the attitudes and beliefs of large groups of people. For our purposes, the Afrikaners are merely a statistical population. In the case of the great mass of people who leave behind no precise statements of their beliefs, one makes inferences about their attitudes and beliefs the way social scientists always have: by observing their behavior. Of course considerable variation has always existed within Afrikaner society, but that is true of most statistical populations. Hence, one can reject the idea that any sort of automatic unity of the Afrikaner population existed, while at the same time noting certain general tendencies that were, first, emergent, and ultimately, ascendant.

(3)

The pre-1948 years of Afrikaner history are best divided into four periods: the Dutch colonial era before 1806, including the first British occupation of 1795–1802 (which will receive no attention here); the period between the long-term occupation of the Cape by the United Kingdom in 1806 and 1870, when the Afrikaner identity began to crystallize; 1870–1910, a period of rapid cultural development; and 1910–48, when the Afrikaner identity began to assume the character of an endoskeleton strong enough to determine and to control the apparatus of a modern state.[38]

In a manner of speaking, entering the era of 1806–70 in Afrikaner cultural history is like walking into a huge and nearly empty factory. A few tools lie around—we can call them concepts, ideas, or constructs— and some other items, things that the tools, when placed in the right hands could make something out of, are there; these miscellaneous items we can call historical events and folk memories of those events. But it is the vast emptiness that is most striking. Almost as noticeable as the things that are lying around are the things that we might expect to be there but are not.

That is: the Afrikaner population in this era has left behind little evidence of anything that resembles a high culture and not very much concerning their popular culture. Few contemporary books exist from the period 1806–70, and certainly none articulate a reflective communal ideology. Archival material in the form of diaries and manuscripts that give a direct insight into how the Afrikaner population, largely rural and highly dispersed, thought, are very limited. Even newspapers are rare, since printing facilities were almost nonexistent. Most of the available information on this era is either secondhand or written retrospectively, late in life, by aged participants, so that we have serious problems interpreting what material there is.

What we do *not* find is a people with an agreed sense of mission. We do not find a social group that believes it is a Chosen People. We do not find "Calvinism" in the sloppy, generalized sense of the word. And crucially, we do not even find Calvinism in the technical, theological sense. After an intensive study of eighteenth- and nineteenth-century Afrikaner theological development, J. Alton Templin concluded that "in the absence of trained theologians among the Boers on the frontier and in the republics, a lay piety developed among respected and pious leaders. Consequently, South African theology was not explicit, seldom systematic, seldom orthodox, and not based on educated theological leadership. Most religious leaders knew little more about Calvinism than the name."[39]

Yet, certain cultural tools were lying around, simple ones that could fit the hands of almost anyone who picked them up. If there is one single thing about Afrikaner history in the first two-thirds of the nineteenth century about which one can be sure, it is this: the ideological-cultural tool kit that everyone shared was the Bible, and most especially the "Old Testament." Even that extreme skeptic André du Toit notes that Voortrekker rhetoric shows the direct influence of the Old Testament and that this "can hardly be disputed." He agrees that on the frontier "the use of biblical terminology, allusions to and analogies with events and figures in the Old Testament, and an easy recourse to providential language" was ubiquitous.[40] What the familiarity with the Bible and adoption of its metaphors and rhetorical modes actually meant—did the Trekboers and Voortrekkers really believe the Bible?—can be debated. But the ubiquity of these cultural tools in their hands cannot be doubted. If the prevalence of biblical metaphors and biblical rhetoric did not influence the way that early Afrikaners thought and acted, then their society comprised the only one yet discovered which does not conform to the contention of linguistic science, that language influences thought.

What must be heavily underscored is that the demotic cultural tool kit was the Hebrew scriptures. The reading of the Bible and the folk theology that emerged among the Afrikaner clergy and laity, although in theory Christian, was not Christianized. "Afrikaners used the Old Testament almost exclusively; Christology was almost nonexistent," is the conclusion of the most intensive investigation of the subject yet conducted. "In South Africa," says J. Alton Templin, "this assumption that Christ is prefigured in all Old Testament narratives disappeared."[41] This means that the distorting lens that Christianity places in front of the Hebrew texts was removed, and that the Afrikaner people of the first two-thirds of the nineteenth century encountered unmediated the covenantal grid of the ancient Hebrews.[42]

Those were the most important of the tools. Also scattered around the great barracks of a factory were historical events and memories of those events. The memories perhaps were inaccurate, but not less real for that. There is no advantage here in serving up a potted history of Afrikaner society from 1806 to 1870, but let us note the existence of certain items that might later be of value in shaping the collective outlook of the Afrikaner population. In noting these items we need not become entangled in nuances of interpretation, for the "right" interpretation of events as defined by present-day professional historians is totally irrelevant to how the Afrikaner of the late nineteenth and early twentieth centuries interpreted these same events.

Consider the following:

ITEM. The Afrikaner people brought with them into the nineteenth century a pattern of conflict in relations with nonwhite races. The pattern went back virtually to the days of Jan van Rieback, founder of the first settlement. Small-scale race wars and the practice of slavery were deeply woven into the fabric of Afrikaner society. The origin of the pattern may be argued, but not the reality.[43]

ITEM. From 1806 onward, the Afrikaners were under alien rule. This was the suzerainity of the United Kingdom, an Anglo-Celtic culture that was radically different in almost every way from that of the largely Dutch-derived Afrikaners.[44] Afrikaner roots went back to 1652 and, because between 1706 and 1795 there had been scarcely any immigration into the Cape,[45] a singular and distinct society had emerged. When the imperial forces occupied the Cape, first in 1795–1803 and then again in 1806, the Afrikaners' experience was not unlike that of some previously independent Germanic tribe being conquered by Imperial Rome.

ITEM. Not only did the Afrikaner society come under the hegemony of a distant imperialist power, but, from 1820 onward, immigrants from that alien society began arriving in southern African in significant numbers. In absolute terms the numbers were not great—roughly 4,000 settlers from the British Isles arrived in the first half of the 1820s.[46] In 1820 the Afrikaner population was approximately 43,000.[47] The settlers from the British Isles were thoroughly disquieting, however, because, first, they were a potential vanguard of a much greater influx of non-Afrikaner whites, and, second, because they were certain to be favored by the policies of the imperial government and by the functionaries in the colony.

ITEM. The Afrikaners' fears were not imaginary. The imperial administration invoked a thoroughgoing anglicization policy. Nearly all government positions were reserved for English-speakers and, after 1825, all official documents were required to be in English.[48] The combination of this systematic governmental discrimination with the pervasive social condescension toward the Afrikaners on the part of those whose roots were in the British Isles meant that increasingly the Afrikaners at the Cape were made to feel strangers in their own land.

ITEM. When, in the 1830s, the imperial government abolished slavery, it confirmed the Afrikaners' belief that the imperial authorities and their English-speaking allies in the Cape colony intended to destroy the economic and sociolegal base of Afrikaner society.

ITEM. One of the bloodier of a long series of so-called Kaffir Wars occurred in 1834. Although it had nothing directly to do with the emancipation of the slaves, it was easily perceived as connected, especially because in the settlements that followed this war, the imperial authorities protected the interests of the non-whites against the Afrikaners'.

ITEM. In 1836 began the Great Trek from the Cape. The historical writing on this set of events is rich and frequently contradictory. What is known is that a considerable group of Afrikaners sought to escape imperial rule and the increasingly anglicized society of the Cape. The Voortrekkers sought land in the interior of southern Africa, some of it in Zulu territory, and prepared to protect their culture and to preserve what they viewed as proper race relations.[49]

ITEM. In February 1838, nearly 300 Afrikaners, mostly women and children, were ambushed and killed by Zulu.

ITEM. In mid-December 1838, a few hundred Voortrekkers engaged more than 10,000 Zulu warriors under King Dingane. More than 3,000 Zulu were killed at this, the Battle of Blood River. No Afrikaners were killed.

ITEM. Both before and after this battle, some Afrikaners took religious oaths. Although the affirmation of the covenantal oath taken at Blood River did not at that time become an annual tradition, the oath taking became part of the folk memory of the battle.

ITEM. In 1843 Natal, on the east coast, was proclaimed a colony of the United Kingdom and within a year the majority of Afrikaners in the jurisdiction had left.

ITEM. In 1852, the imperial government recognized the independence of the Transvaal, the first of the two significant Afrikaner states. In 1853, the independence of the second, the Orange Free State, was confirmed.

This catalogue need not be continued, for it is long enough to permit us to ask, What, after two-thirds of the nineteenth century, was the Afrikaner worldview? The answer is that instead of a single view, there existed the components of what eventually would become one of the most self-reinforcing, consistent, and all-embracing of modern national conceptual structures. These components were, first, a strong sense of attachment to hard-won land. This feeling of identification with the land, of having spilled blood to redeem it, was strongest in the two Afrikaner republics, but was also characteristic of the inland farmers of the Cape. Second, the Afrikaners possessed a folklore, for the most part of historical memories handed down within families. The Afrikaners thought historically, not in the same way that historians might, but they used history as the ancient Hebrews did, to explain the past in moral terms and to guide their planning for the future. In the absence of newspapers, the historical memory was an oral one, transmitted at the hearth. James Anthony Froude caught a sense of this when he visited southern Africa in 1876. In his report to the secretary of state for the colonies, he provided a capsule history of southern Africa from the Afrikaners' viewpoint: "I tell this story as they tell it themselves, and as it has been told at every Dutch fireside in South Africa."[50]

(4)

The possession of the land and the collective memory of historical events were the raw material of a potential communal worldview. Ultimately, the tool kit that fashioned these raw materials into a seamless web was the one piece of reading material with which every Afrikaner was conversant: the Hebrew scriptures.

That the inchoate became organized, the various shards formed into a communal cultural network, was not an inevitable process. There is no necessary evolutionary connection between the *disjecta membra* of early nineteenth-century Afrikaner culture and the coherent belief system that emerged so strongly in the last third of the nineteenth century: such a development did not *have* to happen. So, why was the vast and nearly empty Afrikaner cultural warehouse, with all those materials and tools scattered around, transformed into a highly efficient cultural factory?

In the first place, because it became less empty. Although precise demographic material is not available, we know that the Afrikaners had an extremely high rate of marital fertility. Once the inland trek had been completed and whatever Malthusian limits had appertained were loosened, their population increased quickly. Once land became easily obtainable, the chief inhibition on family formation by the young was removed. A reasonable estimate is that in the various parts of southern Africa in 1850, there were at least 140,000 Afrikaners, and the numbers were growing rapidly.[51] The main point about the population increase is that it allowed the creation of what today is called "cultural infrastructure." Newspapers became viable. In nucleated areas, schools became general and, most important, the simple day-to-day interchange of news, ideas, and gossip with people outside of one's own family became more frequent. Although it is impossible to obtain accurate literacy statistics, it is clear that year by year more and more of the population became literate.[52] Equally important, the Reformed churches became, community by community, a full religious polity. Churches were built, *dominees* or pastors called, and local theological education began (the first seminary was founded in 1859). The communication of religious ideas became one of the formal concerns of the culture.[53]

Still, those are only preconditions. A set of cultural catalysts was needed and here three related events came into play: the economic future of South Africa was reorientated, an influx of culturally indigestible foreigners took place and, the imperial government intervened aggressively in southern Africa. The discovery of diamonds in 1867 and of gold in the Witswatersrand in 1886, each in quantities worthy of exploitation, did not change overnight the various economies of southern Africa. Granted, some of the changes were swift, but the outstanding result of these discoveries was that the future of the South African economies was transformed: economic power clearly was destined to shift inland to the areas where the newly discovered resources were located. The pastoral inland regions of southern Africa sooner or later would be subsumed in an alien market economy. Thus, the discoveries of diamonds and of gold had the paradoxical effect of making the Afrikaner states potentially economically more powerful, while at the same time threatening the character of their culture, which was based on dispersed agricultural holdings, on common folk memories of historic events, and on similar, but loosely defined, attitudes toward the land and to religion. Within this context, the hordes of miners were as much a cultural threat as an economic one. Not only did they reject Afrikaner political hegemony, but they did not accept the cultural values upon which the Afrikaner states were based.

Simultaneously, the imperial government moved, decisively, clumsily, ruthlessly. Basutoland was annexed by the imperial government in 1868. The diamond fields in Griqualand West were taken in 1871 and the Transvaal Republic was proclaimed imperial territory in 1877. Like any governmental action, these moves by the United Kingdom had a myriad of motivations, but acquisition of pelf has to be adjudged near the top. As the result of the First Anglo-Boer War of 1880–81 (frequently called the First War of Independence by Afrikaner historians), the Transvaal Republic was restored, albeit under unclearly defined crown "suzerainty." Any chance that the two main Afrikaner states, the Transvaal and the Orange Free State, would be left to govern themselves was scotched by the opening of the Witwatersrand gold field in 1886. From then onward, the Afrikaner states were just too rich to be left alone. The long-term result was the Second Anglo-Boer War of 1899–1902 in which the Afrikaners were crushed.

Crucially, the last one-third of the nineteenth century, which could have been the breaking of Afrikaner culture, was its making.[54] In the place of a scattered set of topographical coordinates and historical folk memories and scriptural readings, by the end of the Second Anglo-Boer War, the Afrikaners had constructed a cultural system so strong that it could withstand not only defeat by forces of the world's largest empire, but, ultimately, could outlast that empire.

Clearly, what we encounter here is the emergence of a very unusual cultural system which should not be treated casually. One cannot deal with it in the same way one deals with the political culture of other westernized nations, or one misses its extraordinary power. At the heart of this power lies an ability to effect what one of its most trenchant critics has labeled "self-reification."[55] By that he means that the Afrikaners largely created their culture themselves, by believing that they indeed had a single common culture and that they thereby willed their collective identity into existence.

One can gain an indication of how this self-reification occurred by observing the way the celebration of the sixteenth of December developed.[56] (In the nineteenth century, the name for the commemoration was "Dingaan's Day," which was something less than a tribute to the defeated Zulu king; the name was changed to the Day of the Covenant in 1938, although until 1952 the older name was sometimes employed, even officially; in 1980 it became the Day of the Vow.) It was believed (probably correctly) that oaths had been taken by at least some of the participants in the original battle, and after the victory some of them wanted these covenantal oaths to be reaffirmed annually. In fact, the annual vows had slipped into disuse. It was only in October 1864, at the Natal synod of the Dutch Reformed Church, that a Reverend Mr. Huet proposed that the sixteenth of December should be observed as a day of prayer and thanksgiving for the deliverance of the Cape emigrants. This the synod approved. The interesting point is that the Reverend Mr. Huet was consciously trying to keep alive oral and scattered family traditions that were dying out in Natal, as the jurisdiction became dominated by people of British Isles origin who had no connection with the Voortrekkers. The cleric who seconded Huet's motion in synod was Reverend Frans Lion Cachet, and it was he who organized, in the same year, an annual commemorative service at the actual site of the Battle of Blood River. Cachet was an unusual man amid the pastoral Afrikaners. He had been brought up in the Netherlands and educated at the Scottish Seminary in Amsterdam. But what was most unusual about him was that he had been raised as a Jew and had only become Christian under the influence of a religious revival movement. He had been ordained in South Africa in 1860 and in 1862 became the pastor of Pietermaritzburg.[57] In his oration at the first commemoration ceremony at Blood River, the Reverend Mr. Cachet made some mention of Christian scriptures, but his fundamental text was from Exodus.[58] It read as follows:

> And Moses built an altar, and called the name of it Jehovah-nissi. (Exod. 17:15)

What an obscure text! Had this Jewish convert totally missed the mark? Quite the opposite. The resonance among his auditors was astonishing. The text to them was anything but obscure. It comes from the chronicle of the children of Israel's conquest of the land of Canaan. In this particular tale, Moses, old but still the leader of the people, tells Joshua to attack the Amalekites. During the attack, Moses stands on a hilltop with the "rod of God" in his hands. As long as Moses can keep his arms up, Israel prevails, but when in weariness he lets them drop, the Amalekites start to win. Finally, two men must stand beside Moses, each one upholding one of his arms, and thus the children of Israel easily put the Amalekites to the sword. And Moses built an altar called Jehovah-nissi— the Lord is my banner. Upon hearing Reverend Mr. Cachet speak on this text, the Afrikaner audience spontaneously responded by collecting stones and piling them up, in a simulacrum of the Hebrews' victory altar.[59] They understood.

They also understood that the text did not stop at verse fifteen. It actually concluded with this chilling prediction:

> For he said, Because the Lord hath sworn *that* the Lord will *have* war with Amalek from generation to generation. (Exod. 17:16)

Who Amalek might be (the non-whites, the imperial government) would vary, but an enemy there always would be, from generation to generation. Thus, from its very beginning the celebration of the sixteenth of December was simultaneously a creation of a historical past, a sanctification of that past by its association with sacred history as found in the Hebrew scriptures, a prediction of continued and wearying strife, and a prescription for how to deal with the ever-present enemies: with the fortitude, if perhaps not the exact techniques, of the Voortrekkers at Blood River.

This annual commemorative ceremony caught on more quickly in Natal than elsewhere, because there the Afrikaner population was thin on the ground and was being leeched culturally by anglicization. There was a pressing need for the invention of rituals that affirmed the Afrikaner identity, even if the continuity with Blood River was artificial: historical links do not have to be accurate in order for them to be real.

Because the Afrikaners in the Transvaal and the Orange Free State were under less pressure, their adoption of the sixteenth of December holiday was less viscerally affirmative. In the Transvaal Republic, although the day was declared a public holiday in 1865, the annual celebrations that developed were only minor affairs. In the Orange Free State, although the eldest son of the famed Voortrekker Sarel Cilliers, who had invoked the original vow in 1838, proposed to the Dutch Reformed Church that the battle and the oath should be commemorated each year, it was ignored.[60] The "tradition" came alive in the Transvaal only after the British annexation of April 1877. Celebrations were carried out in 1877, 1878, and 1879; in 1880 between 5,000 and 9,000 armed Afrikaner men (estimates vary) met at Paardekraal (near what is now Krugersdorp), and on the sixteenth of December swore a covenant with each other and with the Almighty. One of the men present later reported that "each of us, without instructions from the leaders, picked up a stone and threw it upon [the altar of stones] . . . as a memorial between ourselves and the Lord. Thus was the vow of Blood River renewed."[61]

It is in the nature of really effective myths that they are self-referential. In this case, the actions at the altar in 1880 created a continuity backward in the time between the men of 1880 and of 1838. Then, after the Transvaal forces did so well in the First Anglo-Boer War, the action of 1880— the Afrikaner men of battle instinctively building a stone altar as a sign of their covenant with each other and with Yahweh—itself became a myth. When, in the 1890s relations with the United Kingdom again soured and another war loomed, the sixteenth of December of 1880 was held up as being in itself a historical event of importance. This self-referential aspect of the evolving Afrikaner culture must be recognized, for it explains why the mythology is immune to the kind of "disproving" that some historians have engaged in. If (as is here the case) the actual act of fabricating historical continuity with the past (which was done by the men of 1880, asserting their continuity with 1838), is *itself* looked at as a sacred event, then there is no way for a skeptic to get inside this intellectual laager.

The celebration of the sixteenth of December is a useful window into the emerging belief system of the Afrikaners because (like the entire system of which it is just a part) it is half empirical, half metaphor. The empirical aspect is by its very nature always proved to be true by actual events. The imperial government from without and enemies from within are always attacking and this confirms the empirically held belief that the Afrikaners always will be under siege. If, as in 1881 at Majuba Hill, the Afrikaners win against these great odds, then it is because of their covenant; and if they lose, it is because they have not sufficiently honored the covenant. Either result confirms the belief.

The deep historical metaphor that emerges with such power is that of the children of Israel. Each year the parallels between the Afrikaners and the ancient Hebrews were drawn more closely at the sixteenth of December celebrations. Paul Kruger, president of the Transvaal Republic, drew these parallels with particular clarity in 1891. At Paardekraal on 16 December that year, he affirmed that

> it is for God that we have prepared the feast in His honor. . . . In the Old Testament, God said to Abraham: "The covenant which I made with you and your descendants, excluding none, shall remain before you and your seed from now to eternity."[62]

Then Kruger traced Yahweh's hand in Afrikaner history beginning with the Great Trek.

The clergyman who delivered the main address at the 1895 sixteenth of December commemoration used this text:

> But my servant Caleb, because he had another spirit with him, and hath followed me fully, him I will bring into the land whereinto he went; and his seed shall possess it. (Num. 14:24)

He expounded: "When we think of the former emigrants, the Voortrekkers of yore, it is then revealed unto us how God, in his divine providence, dealt with them, even as He dealt with the Israelite Nation of old." This parallel implied a divinely commissioned task, to cleanse the land. "He summoned them to the same task: Canaan was inhabited by heathen alienated from God. . . . Israel was bidden make it the Lord's dwelling place."[63]

The almost genealogical belief in continuity with the heroes of Blood River was not severed by the Afrikaners' crushing defeat in the Second Anglo-Boer War. Indeed, it was in 1903, in the then-subjugated Orange Free State, that the sixteenth of December commemoration was *begun* as an annual event. In 1910, when the four previously separate territories formed the Union of South Africa, the day became a public holiday for the whole Union.[64] Undeniably, the sixteenth of December commemorations were emotionally charged and, equally, they were occasions of high rhetoric. But they were not merely rhetorical. The Afrikaner religious and civil leaders were engaged in an exercise in metaphor that required the participation of their audience. If the audience did not recognize the metaphors as pertaining to their own understanding of the world, then there could be no resonance between orator and listener, between leader and follower. Manifestly, however, there was a deep bond of understanding.[65]

Now, the key thing about the metaphors that the Afrikaners were employing as bonding discourse among themselves was that these metaphors were among the most potent in western history, and the most enduring. Ultimately, to liken themselves to the ancient children of Israel was for the Afrikaners to employ a text that was too powerful for them to control. It is a very short step from saying that "we are like the children of Israel" to believing that "we are a Chosen People." In the first instance the speaker is in control; in the second, the text has become the master.

The cultural programming in Hebrew covenantal thinking that emerged in the sixteenth of December commemorations was hastened by the efforts of a band of cultural impressarios whose explicit purpose was to speed the creation of a unified Afrikaner demotic culture. These cultural promoters worked in a variety of fields: historical writing, journalism, religion, and politics. To a remarkable degree, they succeeded in creating a popular mass culture that was South Africa-wide and which provided a set of "vertical" unities that cut across what otherwise seemed to be emergent class lines. For example, in the 1870s, a group of Afrikaner cultural enthusiasts coalesced around the new newspaper *Die Patriot*. The group's name, sometimes translated as the Society of Right-Minded Afrikaners (*Die Genootskap van Regte Afrikaners*), is revealing; they believed that if they could set right the mind of the Afrikaner populace, everything else would follow. Their newspaper denounced the injustice to Afrikaners inflicted by the imperial administration, argued for spiritual continuity with "the heritage of our devout fathers," published regular historical features, demanded the preservation of the Afrikaans language, and pressed for the maintenance of the folk customs of the Afrikaner people. In 1877, the first history of South Africa to be written in Afrikaans was published.[66] Within the succeeding quarter-century a spate of historical works, some in Dutch, some in Afrikaans, gave to the Afrikaner people an articulate version of a common history. Such middle-class expressions as are found in written history might have taken decades to filter down to the popular level, had not the message of history coincided both with what the mass of people were ready to believe and with what the leading Afrikaner politicians wanted them to believe. No one was more important in the creation of a basic mindset throughout Afrikaner society than the president of the Transvaal Republic, Paul Kruger, who was simultaneously an evangelist of the Afrikaner identity and himself a folk icon. It is easy to laugh at some of his views. Kruger literally believed that the world was flat,[67] but in its bullheaded biblical literalness, that belief is highly revealing. It makes one understand that his identification of the Afrikaners with the children of Israel could be so complete that it was not metaphorical but literal.

Paradoxically, although Kruger came from the most conservative of the mainline Dutch Reformed churches, the group known as "Doppers," he was (as were many Doppers) in the vanguard of one European Calvinist tradition. Recall that the South African churches had been almost innocent of theology and of Calvinism in the technical sense during the first half of the nineteenth century. As the Afrikaner population grew and as it became better off economically, their religious network became stronger and the training of the clergy improved considerably. As the clergy became more sophisticated, they inclined toward what is best called neo-Calvinism. This is associated with (but not limited to) the work of Abraham Kuyper (1837–1920), a Dutch theologian and politician of worldwide reputation. He vociferously opposed liberalism in all its forms and regarded Calvinism as a way of life, rather than just a theological system. Both these attitudes sat well with Afrikaner clergy and lay leaders. Most important, from the Afrikaner perspective, Kuyper extricated Calvinism from a puzzle that Calvin had tried to solve but never satisfactorily: how to reconcile predestination with social responsibility. Kuyper argued that there was a difference between individual salvation and national salvation (which is the same distinction that, instinctively, Paul Kruger made in his speeches).[68] Specifically, in Kuyper's neo-Calvinism, there were two sorts of divine grace: the kind of "particular grace" that God gives to individuals through predestination, and the "common grace" that inheres to the whole of God's creations. Kuyper argues that when one is called (elected, or predestined) through particular grace, one gains the ability to see the true order and purpose of God's entire creation. Thus, the social and the individual are melded: for it is first an ability, and, now a responsibility, of those who are elected through particular grace to lead the church, the nation, the world in the discovery of the order and law that God has preordained for all creation. The church, both its clergy and laity, acquires the task of leading the nation. Therefore,

Afrikaner national consciousness and its theology are joined. The nation becomes a sacred tribe.[69]

The durability of this emergent Afrikaner cultural system and, particularly, the importance of the religious templates within that system, were well illustrated during the Second Anglo-Boer War. The sixteenth of December was celebrated not only by Afrikaners in combat brigades, but by women and children in concentration camps as well. As it became clear that the war was being lost, and that the distant empire would again triumph, the Afrikaners did not turn away from their beliefs, but, quite the opposite, they deepened their affirmation. In prisoner-of-war and concentration camps, and among the scattered and clearly losing Afrikaner commandos, religious revivals took place. The feeling among Afrikaners was that Yahweh was punishing his people because they had neglected their task; out of defeat in the Second Anglo-Boer War arose the missionary movement in the Dutch Reformed churches.[70]

These powerful developments were beyond the rational, professional, and emotionally controlled boundaries of United Kingdom imperial procedures. In the midst of the war, Lord Milner ordered an attack on the pile of stones that remained at Paardekraal in 1900, where so many Afrikaners had earlier affirmed their covenant. Milner had the stones loaded onto a train and transported to Durban and then thrown into the sea.[71] Present-day academics who refuse to recognize that historically the Afrikaner culture has been an active, not merely a passive or derivative force in South African history, are engaged in an act as silly, as reality-denying, and as irrelevant as was Lord Milner's.

(5)

The manner in which I have just discussed the way the Afrikaner demotic worldview came together is for the most part in the terms of conventional historical discourse. Words such as "preconditions," "catalysts," and "factors" are used. Yet something is missing. What is lacking is a sense of how the Afrikaners could construct in such a short period of time a worldview that was so awesomely internally consistent and so resistant to all the forces of the outside world.

The answer of course is that they did not create a system of their own, but adopted, with scarcely any modification, the covenantal cultural grid of the ancient children of Israel. One should not hide from this. This was no accidental overlap of two separate cultural systems; these were not simply vague similarities or semicongruities. This was the same system that had been evolved by the ancient Israelites, and one can accurately predict most Afrikaner legal, political, and cultural developments in the first two-thirds of the twentieth century by reading carefully the books of the Pentateuch.

Remember the point from chapter 2, that the covenantal conceptual grid was analogous to computer software: it largely determined how the empirical data of everyday life are processed. And remember too that this covenantal cultural wiring was shown to be effective in a society where the level of religious commitment varied greatly. Of course the Afrikaners had to develop their own *halachah,* their own way of codifying their cultural principles into a set of rules. This they did to some degree after 1910, and fully after 1948.

If we look at the Afrikaner cultural grid in, say 1902–10, it is in full form, although as yet far from being in control of a state. The Afrikaners evinced a belief in their own corporate personality every bit as vivid as that shown by the ancient Hebrews. Virtually every historian who writes in the English language about twentieth-century Afrikaner society includes a footnote or an explanatory paragraph on the word *volk.* Inevitably, each historian points out that the term has no real English-language equivalent. Usually, the author settles on "people" or "nation" as a translation, but these words lack a sense of corporate personality. The Afrikaners came to believe that they constituted one *volk,* as the concept of One People was articulated in the Hebrew scriptures. This concept transcended geopolitical borders: the various jurisdictions and widely scattered Afrikaner settlements merged into a single entity.[72] More important, this identity transcended the boundaries of time. The Afrikaner mythology bonded together in a sacred chain the people of any given present moment with the heroes of the Afrikaner past and, by implication, with the continuing Afrikaner nation of the future. Thus, "Afrikanerdom"—the Afrikaner *volk*—was a transcendant concept. As Dan Jacobson has pointed out, most Christian cultures reformulated and transposed the privileges once enjoyed by the Israelites to a "new Israel," the Christians.[73] But that idea does not have much to do with the Afrikaner sense of corporate personality: the Christian idea of a "new Israel" was too broad and vague to be of use to the Afrikaners. Instead, they embraced the much narrower Old Testament conceptual structure and defined the "new Israel" as specific tracts of land and narrowly defined genetic groups in South Africa.

The importance of topography—of "the Land"—is so central to the

Afrikaner cultural grid that it frequently is taken for granted. The very spine of Afrikaner history (no less than the historical sense of the Hebrew scriptures upon which it is based) involves the winning of "the Land" from alien, and, indeed evil forces. That is why the major Afrikaner historical myths are anchored with specificity not just in chronology but also in topography. The mythic events could not have happened just any place, but only at specific geographic coordinates in "the Land." Always this Afrikaner land, like the land of Canaan, has to be "redeemed." This theme was voiced in crystalline terms by the great Afrikaner poet "Totius" (the Reverend J. D. du Toit). Here is a passage from his 1909 epic *Potgieter's Trek:*

> But see! the world becomes wilder;
>   the fierce vermin worsen,
> stark naked black hordes,
>   following tyrants.
> How the handful of trekkers suffer,
>   the freedom seekers, creators of a People.
> Just like another Israel.
>   by enemies surrounded, lost in the veld,
> but for another Canaan elected,
>   led forward by God's plan.[74]

Not surprisingly, the Exodus theme was among the first aspects of Afrikaner culture to be clearly articulated, and it became a central and enduring feature. The Exodus motif provided a fruitful source of resonant figures of speech. For example, the president of the Transvaal Republic in 1871 likened the original Voortrekkers to "the chosen of the Lord, who, even as the Israelites had trekked from Egypt to escape Pharaoh's yoke, had themselves withdrawn from the yoke of the detestable English government to found their own Government and administration."[75] The biblical idea of the Exodus became more than a figure of speech. The concept was reified. Thus, in a book of 1918 that can be taken as a summation of the Afrikaner understanding of the Great Trek, the Reverend Willem Postma not only presented the Trek as a second Exodus, in which Yahweh led the Afrikaners out of bondage enforced by the imperial government, into a new freedom in their own new Canaan, but he posited that the Afrikaners (and especially his own Dopper Church) were a Chosen People.[76] This confirms that an important shift in meaning had occurred. In their formative cultural state (in the late 1860s and into the 1880s), the Afrikaners had seen themselves as similar to the Chosen

People. Eventually, this likeness was transformed into a belief that they were indeed Chosen People.[77]

Being a Chosen People implied responsibilities and the most important biological and a cultural imperative was purity. In the scriptures the land is given in covenant to a Chosen People and to that people's seed. The primary identification of seed in the Hebrew scriptures is biological and so too was the Afrikaners. Witness van Jaarsveld's comment on the Afrikaner mentality in the Orange Free State in the late 1870s and early 1880s, when the belief system was being formed:

> If one inquires into the basis of this stream of collective nationalism that led to mass solidarity in the Free State, one finds in it the idea of *blood relationship*. This comes out clearly in a memorandum signed by 106 burghers: "We sympathize with our beloved brothers across the Vaal, with whom we are so deeply, so closely related through blood relationship, religion, and language." Similar verdicts were contained in every memorandum introduced at the extraordinary session of the Volksraad in February, 1881.[78]

The idea that blood relationships were central to the corporate identity of the group had both inclusive and limiting aspects. That is, the affirmation that "we are all the same blood" is an inclusive statement, but it also implies that there are limits. Under the Hebrew covenantal grid, the Chosen People were not to have sexual relations with other peoples as this would lead to impurity, moral and physical. Perforce this implies that other groups were in some way inferior. Within the context of Afrikaner life, the Hebrew template fit perfectly. The indigenous inhabitants of "the Land" were viewed as being inferior and, as Afrikaner culture became stronger, sanctions against "miscegenation" increased, particularly as the Afrikaner churches became more and more efficient in controlling the social practices of their members.[79]

Obviously the Afrikaners were not unique in their racial views and practices: the history of western European encounters with indigenous peoples all over the world is an open book on this point. Equally obviously, one cannot point to the Hebrew scriptures as the sole source of the Afrikaners' views on racial purity, because, clearly, the Afrikaners would have had harsh encounters with the indigene no matter what their own ideological framework was. But it was the Hebrew scriptures that legitimated the notion that outside peoples are inherently inferior: the scripture references extend from the story of Ham to the repeated, almost incantatory scriptural denunciations of local native tribes. These racial aspects of the scriptural code were intertwined with all the other aspects of the covenental system—the Land, the Law, and so on—so the need for racial purity was given moral justification and the obtainment of that purity was sacralized.[80]

Notably, Afrikaner views on purity involved separation not just from other racial groups, but from other, less-pure white groups. When dealing with the Anglo-Celts, for example, this emphasis upon purity was at one moment expressed in biological terms, the next in cultural. Thus, in an encomium on the Afrikaner woman, Reverend Willem Postma praised her as the source of the nation's virtue. The Afrikaners' existence, he argued, had been preserved through the steadfastness of its women, who refused to allow their race to be destroyed through intermarriage with other peoples—black or white.[81] In reality, of course, intermarriage between Afrikaners and English-speakers was not rare, but Postma's theme is essential here: mixture leads to impurity and intermixture is denounced on cultural as well as biological grounds. Thus, on the 16 December 1903, one finds J. D. du Toit imploring his people to reaffirm the lines that "fix the boundary between us and all *uitlanders.*" He added that the power of the Afrikaner people lay in "the isolation of our principle."[82]

Given that "seed" and "blood" are closely related to the Hebrew covenantal grid that the Afrikaners adopted, it is no surprise to find the Afrikaners embroidering upon the Hebrew motif of blood sacrifice. The shedding of blood as a means of redemption for the ancient Israelites was accomplished either through animal sacrifice or through individuals selflessly laying down their own lives for their people. Thus, the emergent Afrikaner belief system gave great emphasis to the pain, hardship, and loss of life endured by selfless individuals. The entire alleged fight against imperial authorities, from Slagters Nek in 1815 to the Afrikaner republics' battles against inclusion in the United Kingdom's imperial system, to the horrors of the Second Anglo-Boer War, all became proof texts. Given the scale of human atrocities in our own lifetime, it is easy to overlook those inflicted upon the Afrikaners by the United Kingdom military. In particular, the imperial creation of concentration camps for civilians during the Second Anglo-Boer War became a vivid part of the Afrikaners' collective memory. The number of women and children who died of starvation and disease in the camps—over 26,000—was horrifically high in relation to the population.[83] Given that the Afrikaner population was roughly 700,000 at the time, this meant that 1 in every 17 Afrikaners had died as a noncombatant, through mistreatment.[84] At almost every family gathering after the war, and in every church congregation, at least one woman or child was missing.

Clearly, the fundamental mode through which the Afrikaner cultural grid operated was the same as that of the Hebrew original: its basic mode of thought was historical. In van Jaarsveld's words, the Afrikaners "are a people who lean heavily on their past," and even live in it.[85] Certainly, the Afrikaner historical mode was not the same thing as the antiseptic (if far from value-free) idiom of the professional historian. Instead it was usable history, history that taught a lesson and indicated the horizon of the demotic culture. Hence the Afrikaners' view of the unfolding of history and of the lessons that it taught became one and the same thing as their popular ideology.

In suggesting that by roughly 1910 the main features of Afrikaner culture had been firmly set, I am not suggesting that it was a completed code. For example, although Afrikaner society made very sharp sacred-profane distinctions, and although (as its canons of church discipline reveal) it was given to complex modes of legalistic thinking, the Afrikaners had yet to develop ways of fully implementing their ideology in statute law. The years 1910–48 saw major steps in that direction, but always these moves were limited, first by the imperial authorities and later, by domestic political configurations involving the political roadblock posed by the Anglo-Celtic minority.[86] Only after 1948, when the entire state came under the control of the Afrikaner cultural system, could the implications of the Afrikaner version of the ancient Hebrew's covenant with Yahweh be worked out in detail.

(6)

When a twentieth-century ethnic group adopts a cultural system that is three or four thousand years old, it poses some problems for historians. Mostly it is unnerving and, worse yet, a bit embarrassing. To adapt a comparison that Conor Cruise O'Brien employed to deal with an eighteenth-century group, the Afrikaners of the early twentieth century seem to most historians to be a pretty weird lot, anomalous and eminently unfashionable, creatures of one millennium astray in another, animated fossils. "And to go around complaining that you have been bitten by a coelacanth is likely to excite curiosity rather than sympathy."[87]

Faced with the embarrassment of having been bitten by a coelacanth, professional historians of South Africa in our own time have adopted palliative measures. Some try to wrestle Afrikaner covenantal thinking into a modern form that can be analyzed by contemporary methods. Thus, they present Afrikaner cosmology not as an entire view of the world, and not as an all-encompassing system of ideology and belief, but rather as "Afrikaner nationalism." This makes it comprehensible, but at the cost of trivializing the phenomenon. Like the Hebrew original, the Afrikaner's covenantal grid does imply nationalism, but much more besides. On the other hand, some simplify the situation by focusing only on the racist implications of the Afrikaner cosmology. Undeniably, racism exists in full rebarbative force. Yet to focus too much on racism per se virtually precludes an understanding of such racism. To ignore the whole conceptual structure and focus excessively on any single aspect is like an architectural historian picking out any single pane in a geodesic dome and reporting that the dome is nothing more than a tetrahedron.

So, let us accept the Afrikaners' covenantal grid as being an integral system, a way of processing information concerning all aspects of life and of making decisions on what is proper social behavior; and let us ask what happens when this three- to four-thousand-year-old cultural grid hits something that is undeniably modern: the resource and industrial revolution of the nineteenth and twentieth centuries and, most particularly, the development of industrial capitalism in South Africa. This question leads us to encounter what in my judgment is the most interesting and technically accomplished of South Africa's historical literature, that on the emergence of industrial capitalism. Excellent studies abound, and I hope that my respect for this work is clear, even if I follow quite a different expository path.[88] The best of this historical literature on the emergence of industrial capitalism in South Africa is complex and nuanced and necessarily must be, for the phenomenon of South African capitalism is itself an immensely complicated one. Yet we should not fall into the vice of the historical profession, of forever havering, qualifying, backing-and-filling, and continually pointing out how complicated things are. Things are always complicated, but the essential historical questions frequently are quite simple.

For instance, in assessing the nature of the intersection of the Hebrew covenantal cosmology, as assimilated by the Afrikaners, with the entirely new phenomenon of industrial capitalism, one initially should ask the obvious: which existed first? This is not a silly question, for asking it helps us to avoid our falling into a way of thinking that is surprisingly common, namely, *pro hoc, propter hoc.* The cultural grid that came to be the essence of Afrikaner demotic culture came into being millennia before industrialization in South Africa. Stated so baldly, it seems obvious that to see this cultural grid as being created by industrialization and modernization is risible; yet there are a number of studies that do just that.

A second, equally simple question is this: is it possible for a cosmology, a cultural grid, a belief system, to have any real impact upon a society? There are only two conceivable answers: no, it is not possible, and yes, it is possible. Making the latter choice does not prejudge whether or not such influence occurred in any given instance. Another way of stating this question is to ask, Can culture be an independent variable in any valid historical explanation? The classic structural Marxist answer to the question, whichever way it is framed, is a solid "no." Cultural phenomena (in this case ethnic culture) are explained as being a priori the result of the arrangement of the material world, and ideas (or constructs, conceptual structures, or belief systems) are seen as imperfect representations of the way the world actually is, and consequently, both as derivative and as inevitably illusory and deceptive. In any case, this argument goes, ideas and beliefs cannot be used as independent variables, because they are themselves formed by material circumstances and not truly independent.[89] There is no way to disprove this viewpoint, any more than one can disprove any tautological system. Either one adopts it on faith, or one is an agnostic. Since it seems odd to use one self-enclosed belief system to reject the historical independence of another more enduring one, let us accept the possibility that the emergent Afrikaner conceptual grid, based on the ancient Hebrew model, actually shaped certain aspects of industrial capitalism—perhaps only in a minor way.

A third question: what are we to make of the fact that the conceptual grid the Afrikaners eventually adopted (not created: adopted) was designed for a rural world, not an industrial, or even an industrializing one? The Hebrew covenantal grid was developed by a nomadic people who became agriculturalists and traders and that pretty well fits the Afrikaners before industrialization. In an uncharacteristically lyrical passage, van Jaarsveld noted that

When one pauses to wonder why the parallel with Israel was carried to such lengths, one recollects that, quite apart from the political circumstances, the way of life of the Boers was similar to that of Israel of old. The stories of the Old Testament could never have made such a deep impression on urban communities. One has to appreciate the loneliness, the vast expanses of the veld, the trek into the unknown with all

their possessions and livestock, the patriarchal nature of family relationships and of forms of government, the starry firmament by night
and the scorching sun by day and the dangers of wild beasts and
barbarians that threatened their existence from day to day.[90]

Perhaps. But it was not the Voortrekkers who adopted the full covenantal
cosmology, but their children and their grandchildren. The cosmology
that was assimilated in roughly the period 1870–1910, therefore, was
archaic even before it was fully fleshed out. Yet unless one assumes that
Afrikaner cultural development was frivolous—and I can think of no
group on the face of the earth less frivolous—then their appropriation of
an archaic, rural cosmology must have had a purpose. I would suggest
that this purpose was nothing less than a volitional attempt to control a
world that was getting out of hand. Leroy Vail has written perceptively
concerning rural transformation and industrial modernization in South
Africa:

> What was common for all the region's peoples—the blacks and whites
> alike—was that many of them were gradually losing control over their
> lives as control over that most basic factor of production, the land,
> slipped from their grasp. No longer were rural communities—whether
> black or white—able to exist autonomously, beyond the reach of cap-
> italism and colonial administration. . . . For white Afrikaners, land
> ownership was also important, kept alive as the ideal Afrikaner way of
> life even among the poor whites of the cities and towns.[91]

Within Afrikaner society, what was developing was a contest between a
rural, precapitalist covenantal cultural grid, and the material reality of
modern industrial capitalism, and all this was taking place within the
context of the decline of the second British empire.

Not that this contest was always so obvious in everyday life: several
studies of emergent class consciousness indicate that Afrikaner cultural
structures (particularly the churches) at times hindered class formation,
and then, at other times, they served as the social networks upon which
class activities were based. Still, it is hard to find any specific belief in the
volk culture that is directly and unambiguously ascribable to industrial
capitalism.

If we think of the basis of the Afrikaner covenantal grid as having been
set down by approximately 1910, this does not mean that every filigree,
every detail, was worked out by that time. And certainly, there were
strong rifts within the Afrikaner ethnic group. These battles, however, like

the sparring of two boxers within a ring, were within agreed rubrics. What had yet to be worked out was the institutional implications of Afrikaner demotic culture, especially the degree of required conformity to institutional (as distinct from ideational) norms. There was also the difficult matter of how the Afrikaners were to deal institutionally with, on the one hand, nonwhite groups, and, on the other, with the Anglo-Celts. What occurred in the years 1910–48 was a reticulation of covenantal beliefs. In reflecting on the way that the Afrikaner covenental grid was knitted ever closer together in these years, we must realize that some of the most powerful forces in the shaping and transmitting of the Afrikaner ethnic cosmology have gone largely unrecorded. In common with most civilizations, the historical records of South Africa have mostly been produced by men and they memorialize men; but the real history of the Afrikaner was shaped as much at the hearth as in the kraal or the urban workplace. Granted, it is well known that women play a large part in Afrikaner mythology, especially in their heroic activities during the Great Trek and in their heavy suffering in the concentration camps in the Second Anglo-Boer War. Afrikaner culture is replete with tales of women and girls sacrificing their lives for their men and boys. Their influence is greater, however, than simply that of historical myth. In 1989, Jeffrey Butler analyzed the role of women in small-town South Africa and their contribution to the creation of the Afrikaner sense of identity. Butler suggests that Afrikaner women frequently were more sensitized to issues of cultural identity than were men. "Many Afrikaner women came out of [the Second Anglo-Boer War] with a consuming bitterness and a suspicion that their men were possibly unreliable on ethnic issues."[92] In partial explanation, Butler notes that "married women in ethnically divided capitalist societies were far more confined within their ethnic segment than were the men, especially in South Africa where domestic service was almost entirely an occupation for Africans and coloured."[93]

In everyday small-town life, the Afrikaner women had to deal with shopkeepers, almost all of whom were English-speaking and whose use of English was an implicit form of ascendancy. Thus, rural and village women's groups were in the forefront of the drive for bilingualism which meant, effectively, the right to be served when in public and in commercial situations in the Afrikaans language. Women were also extremely influencial in forming support groups for the Dutch Reformed churches. The largest of these was the ACCV (Afrikaanse Christelike Vroue Vereeniging), a national body that not only supported strong "family" values, but pressed the cause of the Afrikaans language and sought improvements in the school systems. Significantly, the ACCV tried hard to ameliorate (by charitable means) the poverty that threatened to split off proletarian Afrikaners from the rest of the ethnic group.[94] Still, these activities represent only the public aspect of what inevitably was an unrecorded, if ubiquitous, female influence. That women must have been central to the transmission of Afrikaner ethnic values is indicated by the continual references to family values in both political and religious statements by Afrikaner leaders and by the seemingly obsessive emphasis upon female purity.[95]

Even though women's informal, home-based affirmations of Afrikaner ethnicity must have been significant, the limited evidence means that we must deal mostly with formally organized and male-dominated institutions. This is the case with the amorphous "Second Language Movement." The "first" language movement had begun in the 1870s and is associated with the du Toit family and with the formation of the first Afrikaans newspaper in 1876. The Second Language Movement usually is dated from 1905. The importance of language in the reticulation of the Afrikaner belief system in the first half of the twentieth century is easy to miss, especially by English-speakers (not only Anglophones in South Africa, but worldwide). The fact is, language is magic, and that is not a dismissive term. It is magic that works. The concept of the Word is at the heart of many western cultures and language is cherished for its spiritual, as well as practical, benefits. Thus, Reverend S. J. du Toit could say that God had placed the Afrikaners in Africa and had given them the Afrikaans language.[96] Throughout Europe, in the late nineteenth and early twentieth centuries, language movements were used by ethnic and national minorities as a means of preserving or reviving cultural identities. Almost always these language movements made two assertions: first, the ethnic language in question was "ours"—that is, it was in some way indigenous—and second, the languages somehow "fit" the given culture.

The Afrikaans "revival" movement had a problem, however, in that it was not a revival movement. Historically, the ethnic language of the Afrikaner people was Dutch. However, so long had the Afrikaners been away from their linguistic homeland and so tenuous had been the cultural ties to the Low Countries, that in everyday speech, Dutch had been replaced by a rural creole. Although there was virtually nothing written in Afrikaans until the 1870s, the high culture of the Afrikaner community was being expressed in Dutch. For the vernacular culture, Dutch became a foreign tongue. Manifestly, this was an unsatisfactory situation, and it helps to explain why anglicization was such a danger: not only was English associated with the world's then-dominant imperial power, but if one had to learn to write a second tongue, it might as well be English as Dutch. Therefore, the Second Language Movement's goals were, first, to standardize the spoken vernacular of the Afrikaner people; second, to produce a literature sufficient to make Afrikaans into a written as well as a spoken language; third, to gain the adhesion of the elite to Afrikaans rather than Dutch as the language of high culture; and fourth, to use the schools to spread the new ethnic tongue.[97]

This task was seen as a spiritual quest, but there was some shrewd game playing involved as well. If the unique and obscure language of the nineteenth-century rural Afrikaner could be developed as a spoken and written language, it would do two things with marvelous efficiency. One of these would be to provide a cultural bond among Afrikaners across divides of social class, occupation, and geography; moreover, it would exclude outsiders. That most of the "coloured" or "brown" population spoke the creole on which Afrikaans was based was a potential source of embarrassment, so the language enthusiasts responded by ridding Afrikaans of its Khoisan and Malayo-Portuguese elements. Although Afrikaans has one of the simplest grammatical and phonetical structures of any Indo-European language, the attitude of Anglo-Celts toward "foreign" tongues of any sort guaranteed that most Anglophones would not pick up Afrikaans. Thus, to some degree Afrikaner cultural purity would be protected. Of course, using language as a means of sorting out friend from foe is a well-worn template, and a Bible-reading people knew well the story of how 42,000 Ephraimites were put to death by the Chosen People because of a seemingly minor dialectical variation (Judg. 12:6).

By 1925, Afrikaans had triumphed over Dutch. It replaced the older tongue as the second official language of South Africa, equal in theory (if not yet in practice) with English. Of greater emotional moment was the completion of the translation of the Bible into Afrikaans. On Sunday, 17 August 1933, when the Afrikaans Bible was first used in church services, it was at once a religious, linguistic, and political triumph. A nationalist feast was held in celebration in Bloemfontein in which 5,000 persons partook. Putting the Afrikaans Bible in print completed a cultural task first defined by the Society of Right-Minded Afrikaners in 1875.[98]

(7)

The next stage was to use Afrikaans as a barrier to protect Afrikaans youth from modes of thought that would undercut the covenantal grid of the increasingly unified Afrikaner culture. Here the schools were crucial and the battle long. The treaty of Vereeniging, which had concluded the Second Anglo-Boer War in 1902, had provided under section 5 that the Dutch language was to be allowed in the schools. This concession was more apparent than real, however, for the high commissioner for South Africa, Sir Alfred Milner, and his officials intended to break the Afrikaner culture by making difficult its transmission to the young. Hence, in the governmental schools in the Cape, Milner permitted Dutch only as a means of acquiring English and English was used to teach every other subject. The Transvaal and the former Orange Free State had their own separate education laws, but even there Milner used the apparatus of the state to attack Afrikaner culture. In the Transvaal, for example, he had virtually the entire educational bureaucracy removed and a new one appointed in which not a single Afrikaner served.[99] In 1903, regulations were introduced into the Transvaal and into the former Orange Free State to allow, at parental request, the Dutch tongue to be taught in the primary schools for three hours a week, out of a twenty-five-hour school week. Given that the overwhelming majority of the Afrikaner children came from Afrikaans-speaking homes (there were some mixed-marriages wherein English was spoken at home), all save three hours of the children's school week was to be in a foreign tongue. With a certain cunning maliciousness a feature was included in these regulations that put the Afrikaner parents in a cleft stick: they could select for their children either five hours of Bible instruction a week, or three hours of Dutch and two hours of Bible study.[100]

That a genuine cultural war was intended by Milner is made clear in his personal and official correspondence. In one letter he wrote, "The fact is, we are . . . engaged in a fight with a very astute adversary [the Dutch Reformed Church] and there is no harm, in my opinion, in using the wisdom of the serpent against it."[101] In November 1903, Milner had his lieutenant governor respond to a petition by parents who, at the instigation of the Dutch Reformed Church, asked for more local influence in the appointment of schoolteachers and for at least five hours a week of Dutch-language instruction. The reply stated: "The Government knows better than the locality which teachers to appoint," and as for the petition for more instruction in Dutch, Lord Milner "points to 'the general advantage which will accrue from the English language being the medium of instruction for the children of white parents, now that this state has become part of the British Empire.' "[102] Such condescension is not something that its victims forget quickly. Milner, more than anyone else, taught the Afrikaner civic and religious leaders that the schools were a pivotal battleground in a cultural war. After Milner was replaced in 1905 by Lord Selborne, the aggressively anti-Afrikaner tone in educational administration were modified somewhat. When the Transvaal (in 1906) and the Orange River colony (in 1907) were granted responsible government, the two jurisdictions quickly passed education laws, the Hertzog Act in the Orange River Colony and the Smuts Act in the Transvaal. These acts were not identical, but they had in common the precept that the "mother tongue" of each child should be the primary language of education through the fourth standard. (Notice the terminology, for it is not accidental; the language of the hearth, the language learned from one's mother, was to be the educational foundation; and in later agitation for the increased use of Afrikaans, the pure female figure, the mother, and the language of the home were strongly fused.) Further, each child was to be taught a second language, English or Afrikaans as the case might be. Third, it was intended that English-speaking and Afrikaans-speaking children were to be educated together by bilingual teachers.[103] On the surface, these acts, which remained the basis of educational practice for decades, were fair. (Similar arrangements were introduced in the Cape in 1912.) In practice, however, there was a bias against Afrikaans because if the students went beyond standard 4, English became the dominant tongue, and in secondary schools English was nearly universal. The memory of J. D. ("Koot") Vorster, brother of the South African prime minister in 1966–78, illustrates this point. He went to a secondary school in the eastern Cape in 1924 and had only one English-speaking classmate. Nevertheless, "We had to take our classes, except for Afrikaans, in English, because she could not follow Afrikaans. But they never asked whether we could follow English, they just took it for granted."[104]

Even if the bilingual mode of education had not been tilted against Afrikaans, it still would have been objectionable to many Afrikaners, because it caused an inevitable erosion of the Afrikaner culture. During the 1930s and 1940s many (but not all) leaders of the Dutch Reformed churches came to oppose bilingualism, and they were joined by members of the Afrikaner Broederbond, a band of politico cultural zealots (discussed in more detail later). These leaders found the actual integration of Afrikaans-speaking children with children whose home language was English objectionable, because this resulted in "mixing." Under the covenantal way of thinking, mixing is a form of impurity. The head of the Broederbond declared in a pamphlet on education, "We shall have nothing to do with a mixture of languages, of culture, of religion, or of race."[105]

As the opposite of "mixing," "mother tongue education" was idealized. One engagé study of the upbringing of children declared that "if we Afrikaners are insistent upon being acknowledged as a nation, it is necessary to stress that the school must carry over the culture of the nation *pure* from one generation to the next."[106] Therefore, purity precluded bilingualism. As another chairman of the Broederbond stated, "When the school subjects are taken over from the education system of another people, it means that mother-tongue education becomes an introduction to a foreign culture and that through the medium of the mother tongue. The inevitable result is that the indigenous world philosophy is ousted by that of a foreign nation."[107] The Dutch Reformed Church agreed. A spokesman wrote in 1941 that "it is the firm policy of our church, reiterated with emphasis at our last synod, that our children must be educated in schools with Afrikaans as the medium. . . . Not only the salvation of our 'volk' but the preservation of our church depends in large measure on separate schools."[108]

This emerging idea of single-language schools wherein Afrikaner children did not mix with children of British Isles backgrounds, became a source of political controversy in the early 1940s and it was debated in the provincial elections of 1943 and in the general election of 1944. Although it is highly probable that most Afrikaner voters favored this form of educational segregation, support was by no means universal, as the United party supported bilingualism. The debate on the issue had the signal effect of making the demand for culturally segregated schools a major item on the agenda of the Afrikaner republicans. This is important, for it meant that when an Afrikaner republican party came to political power, one of its acts would be to use the schools to protect Afrikaner culture. This would mean segregating white children according to home language and excluding, if possible, foreign ideas and cultures. Here then is a clear indication of the way that the Afrikaners' thinking was developing on the eve of their accession to power. It reveals that an evolving component of what was to become apartheid was the physical and linguistic segregation of children on the basis of culture alone, not race. Afrikaner children were not to be educated with white Anglophone children.

The schools controversy points to the existence of two institutional actors, each of which increased in power year by year. One group was the three Dutch Reformed churches. The main branch, the Nederduitse Gereformeerde Kerk, had become independent from European control in 1824. This body—the NGK—is what is meant by the words "Dutch

Reformed Church." Various geographical and doctrinal splits occurred during the nineteenth century, but in the twentieth century there were only three major bodies. Besides the NGK, there were the Nederduitsch Hervormde Kerk (NHK), in the Transvaal in 1843, and the Gereformeerde Kerk (GK) or, more colloquially, the Dopper Church. After 1902, none of these churches was an established church in the sense of a state church. Yet, unofficially, the NGK was the church of the Afrikaner establishment.[109] In 1926, to take a representative year, it had the allegiance of nine out of every ten Reformed Church adherents (which is nearly nine-tenths of the Afrikaner population). The other two churches had roughly one-twentieth each.[110] It has been argued that the Dopper Church had an influence on Afrikaner culture far out of proportion to its numbers and that may be true.[111] For our purposes, however, the central point is that these three main churches acted very differently than did mainline Protestant churches in North America and Great Britain in the twentieth century. Their ministers and lay leaders were constantly (not just occasionally) active in secular South African politics. Frequently, church leaders defined politics as being one portion of their church's sphere of moral responsibility.

As one example of the way the church influenced the cultural grid, take the matter of "Christian National education." After the Second Anglo-Boer War, a group of schoolteachers, clerics, and laymen—mostly Doppers—founded the Christian National Education Commission whose goal was to create an independent mass school system in which Afrikaner children would not be contaminated by integration with Anglophone children. At its height, in 1905, the commission operated 300 schools, enrolling 9,000 children, almost all of them in the Transvaal. This attempt at cultural purity was too expensive for the Afrikaner community to maintain and, after the educational reforms of 1907 and 1908, the Christian National schools were assimilated into the provincial systems.[112] But that was not the end of the story. The concept of "Christian National education" was generalized and all three Dutch Reformed churches took up the broad ideal that Afrikaner children should have a separate school system. Increasingly, education was spoken of as a sacred trust.[113]

(8)

The same words, "Christian" and "National," were sounded over and over again by activists, especially by members of the Broederbond who favored "Christian Nationalism." This shadowy pressure group, the Afrikaner Broederbond, was formed in 1918, and it went underground in 1922, operating thereafter as a secret organization, based on a cell system. In 1944, there were roughly 2,500 Broederbond members, carefully selected for their doctrinal purity and for the depth of their conviction. Roughly one-third of these members were schoolteachers (a critical tactical asset, given the goal of gaining control over education), and approximately one-tenth were civil servants. Significant numbers of clergy (especially Doppers) and academics from Afrikaans-speaking universities also joined. Large-scale farmers made up most of the remainder. In a small town or in a governmental office, a handful of individuals working together could have a considerable impact. The Broederbond could, for example, push a local school management committee in the desired direction, or manipulate backroom politics to ensure that "real" Afrikaners came forward as political candidates.

Before being proposed for this secret society, an individual was investigated on the basis of several considerations, especially the following: "Does he strive for the ideal of the eternal existence of a separate Afrikaner nation with its own language and culture?" and "Does he give preference to Afrikaners and other well-disposed persons and firms in economic, public, and professional life?"[114] The Broederbond was very strongly behind the centenary celebration of the sixteenth of December in 1938. Not surprisingly, they were also very strong among the Purified National party, founded in 1934–35 with the goal of making South Africa a republic, free of all the old entanglements of empire and, not incidentally, under Afrikaner control. These Purified Nationalists in turn became the central cadre of the Herenigde Nasionale party—the united national party, formed in 1939. Eventually, in 1948, the HNP (usually called either the Nationalists or the National party) won control of the government. From 1948 on, members of the Broederbond were able to exercise considerable influence over the state.[115]

These and similar efforts to turn Afrikaner cultural values into institutions and into political parties and, eventually, into laws, would have failed, if fractures of class or of economic interest with the Afrikaner ethnic group had become unbridgeable. As Dan O'Meara has observed, Christian Nationalism or Afrikaner nationalism "was much more than a complex intellectual-ideological framework representing certain views of the world. The terms also encompassed the mass social and political movement which emerged, comprised of widely disparate groups, mobilised through this ideology."[116]

One of the potentially deepest fissures within the Afrikaner social (and, therefore, cultural) universe was represented by the "poor white problem." In its fundamental lineaments there was nothing unique about this issue. Beginning in roughly the 1870s, Afrikaner agriculture underwent a revolution, a radical transformation from pastoral, subsistence farming to capitalist agriculture, some of it based on arable farming, some of it on highly capitalized stock farming. The destruction of the near-subsistence farm sector by market agriculture occurred somewhat late by European and North American standards, and was for a time inhibited by the Afrikaners' preference for partible inheritance, which kept farm size smaller than it otherwise would have been. Virtually everywhere else that this agricultural revolution has occurred, two problems have characterized the transitional state: rural poverty among those who are being squeezed out by market forces and migration to urban areas by former rural laborers and failed small farmers. These problems in South Africa became especially noticeable among Afrikaners in the decade immediately after the Second Anglo-Boer War. The destruction of homes and outbuildings and the loss of stock caused by the war seriously set back the farming community, and these losses, when combined with increasingly capitalist agriculture, produced an Afrikaner proletariat. Whether they remained in the countryside or settled in urban slums, the poor whites were a great threat to Afrikaner unity, because their class interests might well coincide with an ideological rift. It has been estimated that by the end of the Second Anglo-Boer War, as many as one-fifth of the Afrikaner males involved in the fighting were serving on the imperial side; and it has further been shown that those Afrikaners who entered the imperial service were the white poor.[117] The danger was obvious: an Afrikaner population of poor rural whites and disorientated urban whites was in the making, a group that well might reject the entire cultural grid of assertive Afrikanerdom.

In response, there were the inevitable governmental studies—the Transvaal Indigency Commission of 1908–9 was an early analysis of the problem.[118] The Carnegie Commission undertook a major internationally funded study in 1929–32: their report suggested that one-fifth of the Afrikaans-speaking population lived in abject poverty.[119] The most revealing response, however, was from the voluntary sector. The Broederbond utilized an agency called Helpmekaar (originally set up to help Afrikaners who had been involved in a minor rebellion in 1914 to pay their fines) to distribute donations to aid poor whites to buy houses or to set up small businesses.[120] Similarly, the Afrikaanse Christelike Vroue

Vereeniging, the Christian women's group that was so concerned with ethnic unity, defined the problem of the poor whites as Afrikaner society's major social issue. Members pressed for ameliorative legislation, organized private donations for poor relief, and, most tellingly, argued that improvement in education would allow the children of poor whites to make a decent living in the new urban and industrializing world.[121] Education, of course, is more than simply skills-upgrading and the church women were thinking culturally as well as economically. They realized that unless the children of the poor whites were captured for Afrikanerdom by educational institutions, the potential class rift would become a chasm.

Much the same realization lay behind the extensive charitable activities of the Dutch Reformed Church. As Dunbar Moodie has explained, concerning the late 1920s and 1930s, "The intimate involvement of the [Dutch Reformed Church] clergy in local education was to continue and, in fact, gather momentum. Now the problems of anglicization and poverty were seen as two sides of the same coin, and education as a major solution to both. Christian charity became Christian Nationalist charity."[122] Hermann Giliomee has shrewdly noted, concerning the clash between the Afrikaner cultural grid and the material forces of fast-developing industrial capitalism, that "before the day was won, class interests had to be redefined as ethnic interests."[123]

That is what began to happen in the trade union movement. In theory, workers with the same objective conditions should have roughly equivalent interests. Yet, if that were to come about, the Afrikaners' covenantal grid would be irreparably damaged, for the covenant as a conceptual structure precluded the existence of class. There could be only One People, one *volk*. Within the *volk,* unity and amity, not fracture and friction, must be the divinely ordered nature of things. Thus, O'Meara notes, One-People thinking "involved an active combating of any notion of class struggle," which was replaced "with the principle of mutual cooperation and interest between workers and employers."[124] It was not until the 1930s that Afrikaner cultural leaders took serious note of the potentially divisive nature of trade unions. They noticed two things: Afrikaners were shut out of positions of power in most trade unions and the unions themselves were sources of the cultural heresy of class division among the *volk.* Of 118 unions registered in South Africa in 1937, more than 100 had non-Afrikaner general secretaries.[125] A subsidiary result was that Afrikaners were discriminated against in the more remunerative skilled trades in favor of English-speakers. More important was the danger that Afrikaners in unions would pick up some of the ideologies held by

English-speaking trade unionists. These tenets, whether socialism, communism, or old-fashioned confrontational trade unionism, were inimical to the seamless unity that was desired for the Afrikaner *volk*. Instead of acquiring the class attitudes that poisoned the life of the United Kingdom, the Afrikaner worker "must be made to see himself as an Afrikaner first and last, with more in common with an Afrikaner lawyer or schoolmaster than with an English speaker who worked on the same shop floor."[126]

During the 1930s and 1940s, Albert Hertzog, the son of General J. B. M. Hertzog (prime minister, 1924–39), worked on this problem. He and his associates first tried to acquire their own mine workers union by working from within. From 1934 to 1944 Hertzog was general secretary of the mine workers, the nation's most important white union. Afrikaner "Christian Nationalists" also controlled the railway union. Elsewhere, by 1948, Nationalists were on the march and had split several major unions, but were a long way from being in power.[127] Thus, once a self-consciously Afrikaner party came into power, as it did in 1948, one of the items on its agenda would be to purify the trade union movement, expelling shop floor leaders who espoused the ideology of class conflict and putting trustworthy Afrikaners in charge.

To the same timeframe belongs another movement that, although not complete by 1948, was one of the predictors of the Afrikaner future: the ethnic mobilization of capital. If consciousness of a common ethnicity was to overcome divisive class consciousness, it was not enough to suborn the trade unions. Business ventures must be taken over by Afrikaners. In the 1930s, Afrikaners had control over very few heavily capitalized enterprises, especially outside of the Cape. This mobilization of Afrikaner capital had to be done without becoming self-defeating—it had to avoid raising class consciousness among Afrikaner workers. Thus, the movement for Afrikaner control of capital emphasized that Afrikanerdom was "a single united social group, all in identical straits," and thus, everyone "shared identical interests."[128] How could this identity be claimed? First, the leaders adopted a vocabulary that was "anticapitalist" and "anti-imperialist." Being anticapitalist seems a paradoxical position for such a movement, but what the ideological leaders of Afrikaner Christian Nationalism meant was that they opposed the economic monopolies held by firms from the United Kingdom and by persons of British Isles background. So, actually, they were not anticapitalist at heart, but against the *existing* distribution of the rewards of capital.

Second, the ideologues harnessed their economic movement to the symbolism of the covenantal society. In November 1938, not long before the monumental centenary celebrations of 16 December, Dr. D. F. Malan, head of the Purified Nationalists (and destined, in 1948, to become prime minister) proposed at the unity congress of the two main nationalist parties that they engage in a collective "salvation deed" (*reddingsdaad*). This biblical language referred directly to the blood sacrifices frequently performed by the Hebrew people to gain the blessing of Yahweh. What Malan had in mind was the collection of as much money as possible to help the slum-dwelling Afrikaners of the major cities. Malan took his symbolism one step further. He had chests loaded on the several ox-wagons as they trekked toward their goals during the great centenary celebrations, and they were filled with donations. Thus were melded together the improvement of the conditions of the poor whites, the covenantal concept of collective redemptive acts, and the extended civic liturgy of the Exodus, as embodied in the centennial of the Great Trek. How much money actually was gathered is unknown, but out of the collection came a Broederbond-controlled economic institute, and an Afrikaner clearinghouse for Afrikaners who wished to invest in Afrikaner businesses.

This entire process is sometimes called *Volkskapitalisme* (People's Capitalism), a term coined in 1934 by L. J. du Plessis. At the everyday level, Afrikaners were encouraged to give their custom whenever possible to Afrikaners, rather than to English-speaking business owners.[129] Given the high degree of secrecy of South African business (as compared to firms in North America and the British Isles) it is impossible to know how far this ethnic mobilization of capital had progressed by 1948. What is certain is that during the late 1930s and the 1940s, the Afrikaners as an ethnic group were accumulating capital in significant amounts and that the ideology behind these activities emphasized that the entire *volk* would benefit by the process. Thus, poverty would be overcome not by attacking capitalism, but by overcoming the existing control of the capitalist system by non-Afrikaners; thus would the Chosen master Mammon.

(9)

Finally: the matter of race.[130] The racist beliefs are the most difficult component of the Afrikaners' covenantal mindset to address. This is in part because, for most observers, it is the nastiest aspect of the Afrikaner cultural system. Certainly, in our own time, it is the element that has held the attention of the outside world. Nevertheless, when thinking historically, one must strive to remember that racial beliefs were not *the* central component of Afrikaner cosmology, but merely one among several components that were of equal importance as far as the intellectual system itself was concerned. To return to our earlier architectural analogy, it is misleading to think of Afrikaner racial theory and attitudes as the equivalent of a central vaulting arch in a medieval cathedral; instead, racist attitudes and beliefs were merely one tetrahedron in a fairly compact geodesic dome. They were important to the structure, surely, but no more so than any of the other fundamental Afrikaner beliefs.

Recall here the emphasis upon purity in the covenantal cultural grid, and the way that Afrikaners interpreted purity to include the need to keep alive the Afrikaans language and the necessity of preserving the "true" history of the Afrikaner people from generation to generation. That drive for cultural purity was directed at other white cultures—especially those derived from the British Isles—and was as important a part of the cultural grid as was racism directed against nonwhites.

Another reason that the question of race is so problematic is that it is messy. Whereas one can unhesitatingly describe certain cultural values and institutional practices as specific to Afrikaner culture, the racial attitudes of the Afrikaner were not sharply differentiated from those of other whites in South Africa: they were more overtly expressed, perhaps, and so different in degree, not in kind. Further, because of the ever-loosening imperial authority over South Africa during the first half of the twentieth century, it is even hard to assay to what extent any given piece of racial legislation enacted by the South African parliament was solely a matter of values internal to South African white society, and to what degree it was a perverse product of the last days of the white kingdom's *imperium*.

What is clear is that after the Second Anglo-Boer War systematic legislative discrimination on racial grounds became common. The most overt form of this discrimination was segregation, a practice rooted in nineteenth-century imperial practice, but embraced with enthusiasm by South African legislators in the twentieth century. Although it is a fictive exercise to ascribe solely "rational" reasons to the segregative legislation of the pre-1948 period, the tactical reasons for segregating blacks could be seen as fourfold: (1) to guarantee white control over most agricultural resources; (2) to provide a pool of cheap farm labor; (3) to provide, but only in appropriate quantities, urban and mine workers; and (4) to keep nonwhites out of the skilled mining and urban jobs. These goals were achieved by a series of statutes and by an equally powerful body of administrative practice. The most important pieces of legislation were the 1913 Land Act which set up native reserves and made it impossible for nonwhites to buy land outside these reserves; the 1923 Natives (Urban Areas) Act which introduced the principle of compulsory residential segregation in all towns and cities; the 1937 Native Laws Amendment Act which provided for the removal to rural areas of surplus nonwhite laborers; the 1926 Colour Bar Act which kept nonwhites from the skilled jobs in mining and in other industries; the Apprenticeship Regulations, which blocked entry of nonwhites into the skilled trades.[131]

One could go on. The danger is that one is apt to see the effect of these laws—the economic exploitation of nonwhites—as their sole cause and thus to view the racism as a nasty, but rational, form of economic exploitation. It is more than that. Racism is a set of attitudes and beliefs that influences behavior even when that behavior is economically costly to the oppressor. If there is anything approaching a cultural universal in humankind, it is that throughout history, bands of human beings have feared, hated, and denigrated other bands of humans who have inheritable physical characteristics different from their own.

Where Afrikaner racism of the first half of the twentieth century is different from that of most European-derived nations is in the way that religious texts and theological constructs both shaped and sanctified racist beliefs and practices. The "liberal" reading of the Bible, which posits an equality of all humankind before an omniscient god, was completely overwhelmed by the Afrikaner emphasis on the racist parts of the scriptures. At the demotic level, virtually every farmer and every worker knew the Hebrew scriptures' account of Ham. Every child who attended primary school learned in Bible instruction that "the sons of Noah, that went forth of the ark were Shem, and Ham, and Japheth: and Ham *is* the father of Canaan" (Gen. 9:18). And, when the story of Ham was expounded from the pulpit, it was taught that Ham had committed a sin against the seed, against the purity of the Chosen People, by looking at his father Noah's private parts, when Noah had fallen asleep in his tent: "And Ham, the father of Canaan, saw the nakedness of his father, and told his two brethren without" (Gen. 9:22). His brothers, however, refuse to look at their father's genitals; they respect the seed:

And Shem and Japheth took a garment, and laid *it* upon both their shoulders, and went backward, and covered the nakedness of their father; and their faces *were* backward, and they saw not their father's nakedness. (Gen. 9:23)

When Noah awakes from his drunken slumber, he realizes what has happened:

> And he said, Cursed *be* Canaan; a servant of servants shall he be unto his brethren.
> And he said, Blessed *be* the Lord God of Shem; and Canaan shall be his servant.
> God shall enlarge Japheth and he shall dwell in the tents of Shem; and Canaan shall be his servant. (Gen. 9:25–27)

Since the three sons of Noah, Ham, Shem, and Japheth, were said to be the source of the population of the entire earth, this story when taken literally gave rise to a reading as follows: by virtue of Ham's sins, his descendants are cursed (this is the biblical principle of collective guilt), and they are to be perpetual servants. Who were these descendants? In the Afrikaner reading, they were, first, the people who in the times of the ancient Hebrews were called the Canaanites and, who in modern times are the nonwhite peoples, particularly the African blacks. Japheth, who had seven sons, was taken to be the father of the Gentile nations of whom the Afrikaners were one. Thus, it was a direct working out of the divine plan that made the indigenous inhabitants of southern Africa the servants of the Afrikaner.[132]

For children and for literal-minded adults, this story operated at a level of fact, but it also could be treated by more sophisticated readers as an analogy that revealed the divine wisdom. A person did not have to take the story literally in order to take it seriously. The abstract principle in the tale is clear: it is part of the divine order for one genetic line to serve another, and this is not unjust, it is simply the way the Almighty has arranged things. When this principle of a super-subordinate relationship between genetic lines is combined with the other major genetic dictum of the Hebrew covenant—that mixing of the seed through intermarriage leads to moral impurity—then one has a strong sacralized justification for Afrikaner racial prejudice: strong, that is, for anyone who lived within the Afrikaner cultural matrix.[133]

(10)

I have outlined substantial evidence for the coalescence of an Afrikaner identity in the period 1868–1910. Not only was that identity virtually congruent to the covenantal grid that had been developed by the ancient Hebrews, but it was, in some degree, derived directly from that ancient grid, by way of the holy scriptures. Then, during 1910–48, this covenantal mindset was precipitated into concrete institutional form. The process was by no means complete by 1948, but it was well under way, and the direction of future development was clear.

There are a variety of definitions of apartheid. Apartheid, I would suggest, was what happened when a tribe that embraced the ancient covenantal grid gained control of a modern state, in the context of the economy and society of southern Africa. That occurred in 1948.

4

The Covenantal Culture of
the Ulster-Scots to 1920

(1)

Not all covenantal cultures are fully explicit in the expression of their outlook, especially in the years before the culture gains control of a state. This was the case in Ulster before 1920, when the Partition of Ireland took place.

Here are seven vignettes, some heuristic, others historical, that may help one's reflections on the nature of Presbyterian society in Ulster.

ITEM ONE. Imagine that you are a modern social scientist called upon to witness a debate by a roomful of individuals about whom you know nothing directly. You soon note that they are vocal but that they follow certain procedural courtesies. Everyone is allowed to speak and it is bad form to try to seize the floor before the previous speaker is finished with his or her argument. Decisions about disputed points are made democratically, at least in the sense that everyone present has a vote and that votes take place only according to very strictly observed formal procedures.

The trouble is, most of what these people say makes no sense. As a social scientist, you try very hard to be sympathetic, but often the way individuals in the room react to each other, and the ideas they propound, are, or seem to be 90 degrees, and sometimes 180 degrees, out of line with what you expect. Reluctantly you arrive at the hypothesis that these people are either crazed or neurologically damaged.

Thereafter, everything that you observe about them seems to confirm that hypothesis.

ITEM TWO. Each year on the twelfth of July hundreds of thousands of Orangemen, members of a Protestant fraternal order, march through several designated towns and cities in Ulster. Each Orange lodge is preceded by a banner that is a piece of high folk art, commemorating some aspect of the Protestant experience in Ulster. The most common iconographic reference is to King William of Orange, who in 1690 delivered the Protestants of Ireland from the tyranny of a Catholic absolutist monarch, James II. Eventually, the Orange parade ends at a field where there are speeches and a religious service.

On the twelfth of July 1968, just before the beginning of the present-day Troubles in Northern Ireland, the County Grand Orange Lodge of Belfast marches to its traditional Field at Finaghy. There, after speeches, a service of thanksgiving takes place. A sermon is followed by prayers and just before the closing benediction, thousands of voices join in a hymn that most of the men and women know by heart:

> Guide me, O Thou great Jehovah,
>   Pilgrim through this barren land;
> I am weak, but Thou art mighty,
>   Hold me with Thy powerful hand;
>
> When I tread the verge of Jordan,
>   Bid my anxious fears subside!
> Death of death, and hell's Destruction,
>   Land me safe on Canaan's side![1]

ITEM THREE. It is 6 February 1938 and one of the most boring men in Ireland, D. Lyle Hall, longtime chairman of the education committee of the city of Belfast, has been invited to open a sale of work that marks the centenary of the local Presbyterian church in his native parish of Raloo. It is a lovely rural area north of Belfast. Hall steps forward after being introduced and hitches his thumbs into the pockets of the waistcoat that spans his not-insubstantial stomach. He speaks to his old neighbors, Ulster country folk, in words that he knows they will understand:

You—we—who live on this beautiful hillside and valley surrounded by rich crops in well cultivated fields, with every work of happy interests and comfort all around us, have been singularly blest. If our comforts have depended on our own toil, they have depended even more on the goodness of the Lord over all, who has given us rich soil, seasonable weather, health and strength, and has showered countless blessings on His loyal people.

"Ebenezer," let us cry, "hitherto hath the Lord helped us."[2]

ITEM FOUR. It is 15 December 1985. The Ulsterman best known to the outside world, the Reverend Ian R. K. Paisley is delivering a sermon at the evening service of the Martyrs' Memorial Free Presbyterian Church in Belfast. Paisley is no more a typical Ulster person than Margaret Thatcher is typically English. But both in their day have known how to strike a responsive chord in their listeners. Paisley's sermon, in part, is as follows:

> I was reading . . . the seventh chapter of the prophecy of Micah. In this chapter I realised that there was a description here of the sad and terrible plight into which our land has fallen. In verse two we read "The good man is perished out of the earth, and there is none upright among men. They all lie in wait for blood." . . . As we read on we are told that they do evil with both hands earnestly. There is a dedication today in the doing of evil. There is a revival of evil. There is a resurgence, a renaissance of evil, and it seems that the whole world has become polluted with a confrontation against the truth, righteousness and god-liness of God's law, of God's standards and God's commandments.
>
> Then this old prophet asks "What will I do?" All the props on which I have leaned, the foundations on which I ought to rely, the confidences I ought to have, the supports on which I ought to rest, they are all swept away. On whom will I rely? Where shall I find a sanctuary, a refuge for my soul? He turns and draws his conclusions in verse 7. "Therefore will I look unto the Lord." He lifts up his eyes away from the turmoil, away from the deceit, away from the lying, away from all the programme of confusion, and he lifts up unto the Lord.
>
> That is what we need to do in this day. If ever there was a day that God's people needed to look up and put their confidences in the Lord, it is now.[3]

ITEM FIVE. A young man, expelled from membership in Reverend Dr. Paisley's home church, is talking to a journalist, describing Paisley's methods and mien:

> He has built up a kind of aura around himself that he is something very special—he is the Lord's anointed. He says "the Lord spoke to me, the Lord has shown me"—he particularly uses phrases like that when someone leaves the church. He almost always preaches on the text

"Touch not mine anointed—Do my prophets no harm"—the suggestion being, of course, that he is the Lord's anointed and therefore
you touch him at your peril. He honestly expects God to do it: to deal
with his enemies, to deal with the people who leave the church and turn
against him.[4]

ITEM SIX. In the eighteenth century, even more than in the Reverend
Dr. Paisley's present time, the Lord in Ulster protected his anointed. A
case in point involved the Seceders, a group that broke off in the first half
of the century from the main branch of Ulster Presbyterians. They did so
because of matters that seem small to us (such as whether or not the Bible
should be kissed when taking a legal oath), but which were serious at the
time. Some orthodox Ulster Presbyterians took this secession to be a
major heresy and swore to fight it, violently if necessary. Now with that in
mind, let us consider a memoir left by the Reverend Mr. William Holmes,
a Donegal man who had been educated at Glasgow and ordained into a
Secession church in east Antrim in 1768. One of Holmes's first duties was
to journey to a small kirk at Buckna, between Larne and Ballymena, and
there to preach. That is the background to the following experience, as
recorded by the clergyman:

> On the twenty-ninth day of June, in the year of our Lord 1768, I was
> ordained at Ballyeaston by the Presbytery of Moira and Lisburn, and
> about a quarter of a year after I was appointed by the said Presbytery to
> preach at Buckna. When the time drew on I warned my congregation
> not to expect a sermon next Lord's Day, as I was appointed by my
> Presbytery to preach at Buckna. But lest any occurrence should prevent
> me from preparing a sermon in the end of the week, I resolved to begin
> and prepare it for the new place on Monday. Accordingly I went up to
> my study early on Monday. I took up my Bible with a design to look for
> a text, when the first portion of the Divine Word that struck my eye was
> that in Proverbs XIV.32—"The wicked is driven away in his wicked-
> ness; but the righteous hath hope in his death."
>
> And now all things were ready for my journey to Buckna, when late
> on Saturday evening, William Duncan, one of my hearers, came to my
> place and told me that I must not go to Buckna to-morrow, for he was
> informed by the most unquestionable authority that a number of men
> in that place (among whom was Mr. Francis Moore) had entered into a
> solemn engagement to destroy the life of the first Seceder that would
> preach in the neighbourhood. I was surprised greatly at this intel-
> ligence, but having thought for a moment, I made this reply: "The

appointment of the Presbytery I take to be a call in Providence to perform the duty; and moreover, how shall I answer the question which is put to everyone at next meeting, "Have you, sir, fulfilled your appointment?" I cannot answer it as I should do." "In short," I said to Mr. Duncan, "I am resolved to go and do my duty, and to leave the event to Him Who worketh according to His Will both in heaven and on earth."

Duncan replied: — "Well, I will go with you, and will go and look for more men to go with us."

He did as he said, for next morning at eight o'clock, according to appointment, we set off from my lodging. We were just seven in number, six and myself. Our course was due north, and never was a better day seen than the day on which God sent us to Buckna. We crossed Glenwherry water with great safety; we travelled through the glen and the mountain belonging to it with great ease; we crossed the Black Mire, which separates Glenwherry from the Braid, and now we entered the parish of Buckna, and leaving Slemish, a high conical mountain about a quarter of a mile to our left, we began to descend into the country called Braid. We had not travelled long in this direction when lo! we observed a funeral procession approaching us.

We soon met, as we travelled in contrary directions, and (I remember it as well as this moment) I asked a man who was near me on the outside of the procession what was the name of the person they were carrying to the grave. He immediately answered "Mr. Francis Moore." My company and myself stared at one another, but did not say a word. We soon arrived at the house of James Shaw, where I was to preach, and went in and told him that we had met a funeral not far off from his house. "Yes," said he, "that was a wonderful Providence, for Mr. Francis Moore and more people were bound by solemn oath to have killed our preacher on this day, also many of the people who came to hear him; and God has ordered so that you have met his burial.[5]

ITEM SEVEN. Imagine once again that you are a modern social scientist, this time one who has spent an entire career, from birth through D. Litt. (*hon causa*) living amid a group of Micronesian islanders. Alone among the Pacific islanders, this group has not received a satellite dish from the United States Navy, or a wireless receiver, or any other information from the outside world, save the odd bit of industrial garbage that floats up on the beach.

Now, with very little in the way of western cultural impedimenta, you are placed in a large concrete bowl in some European country. It holds 50,000 people who yell a lot, and in the center of the bowl, in a sacred green space, a group of men run around and perform devotional exercises with a sphere. Sometimes one half of the crowd roars, sometimes the other half, depending upon what is taking place upon the field. No one tells them when to cheer, they just know. So too with the men on the field. Clearly they agree that there are certain things they can and cannot do with the sphere and that there are ways they can and cannot juxtapose themselves to each other. Some actions are sacred, clearly, and others profane. There are rules.

That, anyway, is the social scientific hypothesis that first comes to mind. Of course, it is possible that everyone in Wembley Stadium is crazy, but that clearly is not the case, because, proceeding with the hypothesis that there are rules and that these rules are decipherable, you eventually figure out that in a Football Association cup final there are two opposing teams and that most of the players are prohibited from using their hands to advance the ball and that a team is awarded a single point for a goal. That's how soccer football works.

And that is how the mind of someone trying to gain perspective on the Ulster-Scots should work. One may not like their game, but it is not inchoate or crazy.

My contention is that the Presbyterian culture of Ulster always has had strong rules, and that if one understands the rules, the society always has made sense. One can understand that society's rules only if one recognizes that a major component (and in my view, *the* major component) of the Ulster-Scots mindset has been the conceptual grid that the Presbyterians of Ulster assimilated from the Hebrew scriptures.

My problem in presenting this observation is that, like the rules of a universally understood game, the fundamental conceptual framework of Ulster-Scots society has been so deeply embedded in the mental fabric of everyone who has lived in the culture that only relatively rarely have individuals found it necessary to refer directly to the "Old Testament" grid. No one needs to make the reference, any more than a kid kicking a soccer ball against an alley wall needs to be told that he should not hit the ball with his hands. Therefore, although I will point to some direct influences of the Hebrew scriptures upon Ulster-Scots society, my argument for the scriptures' pervasive influence is largely an indirect argument. It can be reduced to two hypotheses: (1) one cannot understand Ulster Presbyterian society unless one recognizes that the Old Testament grid is central to the culture, and (2) if one does not acknowledge this, then most of what has gone on in that society makes no sense at all, and seems crazy.

The indirectness of this argument should not, however, be taken as an indication of weakness. Of course modern historical writing prefers direct evidence of phenomena to indirect evidence, but this preference should not be taken to self-defeating extremes. It is important to remember, for example, that most of the major scientific discoveries of the modern age (starting with the notion that the earth revolves around the sun, rather than vice versa) are founded primarily on indirect evidence.

(2)

The word "Ulster" has two references. One of these is to the nine counties that made up the historical province of Ulster as shired in the seventeenth century. The second of these is to Northern Ireland, the jurisdiction created in 1920 when Ireland was partitioned. In this latter meaning Ulster consists of all or part of six counties, situated in approximately the northeastern quadrant of Ireland. Thus, when I use "Ulster" in connection with the period before 1920, the historical definition is implied: after 1920, the reference is to the present six counties.[6]

Ulster has always been distinct from the rest of Ireland. Southern Ulster is separated from the rest of the country by a line of drumlins, low mountains, and lakes, reinforced in earlier times by forests. After the Norman conquest Ulster was the province least permeated by foreign influence and most Celtic in its social organization and culture. A line of forests and mountains served as a frontier between the Anglo-Norman culture of the English Pale and the Celtic culture of Ulster. Sporadically, the English tried to subdue the Ulstermen, but they achieved only humiliating defeats and meaningless victories. Aside from a few coastal settlements, most notably Carrickfergus, the Dublin authorities were forced to recognize Ulster as a troublesome native preserve. Long after most of Ireland was at least partially anglicized, the great Celtic princes, especially the O'Neills, headed a vigorous and proud Celtic society.

All this changed radically in the decade after 1603. In that year the last great Celtic prince, Hugh O'Neill, earl of Tyrone, surrendered to Lord Mountjoy, the English lord deputy of Ireland. This event marked a watershed in Irish history: the last of the independent Irish princes was subdued, and the links between Spain, the Counter Reformation, and Ulster, which had so bedeviled Elizabethan statesmen, were broken. England could now settle matters in Ireland permanently, or so it seemed. As the first step in this settlement the English government pardoned both O'Neill and his ally Rory O'Donnell, and allowed the former to keep his English-style title of earl of Tyrone and gave the latter the rank of earl of

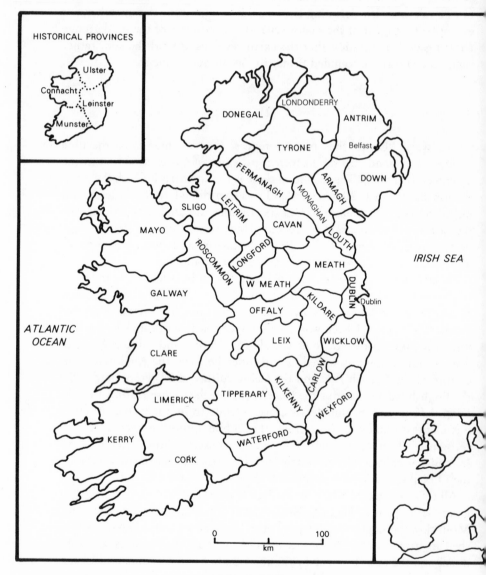

HISTORICAL PROVINCES

Ulster

Connacht

Leinster

Munster

DONEGAL

LONDONDERRY

ANTRIM

TYRONE

Belfast

FERMANAGH

DOWN

ARMAGH

MONAGHAN

SLIGO

LEITRIM

CAVAN

LOUTH

MAYO

ROSCOMMON

LONGFORD

MEATH

IRISH SEA

W MEATH

DUBLIN

Dublin

GALWAY

OFFALY

KILDARE

ATLANTIC
OCEAN

LEIX

WICKLOW

CLARE

CARLOW

KILKENNY

LIMERICK

TIPPERARY

WEXFORD

KERRY

WATERFORD

CORK

0   100
km

Map 2. Irish counties

Tyrconnell. Most of the Irish chiefs were pardoned and allowed to keep their lands, but they, like Tyrone and Tyrconnell, were granted the lands not as Irish chiefs but under new rules that converted them into English-style landlords; the superseding of the Irish system of land tenure by the English system rapidly undercut the Celtic social system.

Then, in August 1607, occurred one of the strangest events in Irish history. Humiliated by the continuing decline of their influence, and fearful of further harassment by the English government, the earls of Tyrone and Tyrconnell and nearly one hundred petty chiefs boarded a boat in Lough Swilly and fled to the Continent. In one brief moment the native Irish leadership of Ulster disappeared, and the province was left open to English manipulation. The English authorities in Dublin were quick to realize the possibilities and treated the earls' departure as evidence of treason. The crown thereupon seized all lands which had been under the control of the departed chiefs. Most of what are now the counties of Armagh, Cavan, Donegal, Fermanagh, Londonderry, and Tyrone were confiscated.

The Dublin and London authorities set to work at once to frame a scheme for the colonization, or "plantation," of Ulster. The scheme, which went into operation in 1610, was uneven and erratic in implementation. It may be summarized as follows. The confiscated lands in the six escheated counties were granted to individuals and groups whose duty it was to form British colonies. The most important single colonizing effort was that made by the City of London Company, which agreed, as a financial speculation, to colonize what is now the county of Londonderry and to rebuild the towns of Coleraine and Derry. Most of the remaining five counties were parceled out to "undertakers," who undertook to colonize a given amount of land and to build villages and fortified enclosures in return for title to their lands. A relatively small amount of land was reserved for Irish natives whose loyalty was certain and who promised to adopt English social and agricultural customs. Originally, the London Company and the other undertakers were required to remove the native Irish from the land under colonization and to bring in British settlers. However, although considerable numbers of English and Scottish colonists were induced to migrate to Ulster, it was economically advantageous for the undertakers to allow large numbers of the native Irish to remain as tenants, intermixed with the Scottish and English immigrants.

Simultaneously, in the counties of Antrim and Down, which had not been affected by the confiscations, an influx of Scottish migrants was taking place. To understand this influx—and indeed to understand the history of Ulster itself—one has to recognize that the British Isles were shaped differently in the sixteenth, seventeenth, and eighteenth centuries than they were later: not physically, but effectively so. In the twentieth century, we have been conditioned to think of lines of travel as being drawn upon land and, hence, the geography of the British Isles is simply the geography of the relevant land masses. Until well into the nineteenth century, things were otherwise. Land travel in most of the British Isles (and especially in Scotland and Ireland) was difficult and in some places virtually impossible. Therefore, marine transport was crucial. The north channel of the Irish Sea was part of a large aquatic basin that joined lowland Scotland, the north of Ireland, the Isle of Man, and the north of England. At the nearest point, Scotland lies only twenty kilometers from the Antrim coast. Therefore, many coastal parts of the north of Ireland were effectively closer to Scotland than they were to Dublin, the Irish capital. Travel to Scotland from most points on the Antrim and Down coast took less than a full day, whereas getting to Dublin required at least three days in the seventeenth and eighteenth centuries, and if any serious haulage was involved, as long as a week. That explains why even in the fourteenth and fifteenth centuries there was a constant traffic across the Hiberno-Scottish maritime basin and why Scottish settlers, some highlanders, some lowlanders, already had settled in Ulster long before the formal plantation of Ulster. The influx became heavy after 1603 when James VI of Scotland assumed the English throne as James I. A number of aggressive Scottish lairds took the opportunity to begin private plantation ventures in Antrim and Down and to a much lesser extent in Monaghan. The two leaders of this movement were Hugh Montgomery and James Hamilton, who acquired 40,000 acres from Con O'Neill by securing a pardon for him on a charge of suspected treason. They then proceeded to gull O'Neill out of most of the remaining 20,000 acres he still held. Into their newly gained land Hamilton and Montgomery introduced lowland Scots as colonists. Other Scots lairds tried similar private ventures, and soon Antrim and Down seemed more Scottish than Irish.

When we aggregate the plantation of Ulster and the immigration of lowland Scots to Antrim and Down it becomes clear that overnight a radical transformation had occurred in the Ulster social structure. Before 1603 Ulster had been a cohesive, independent bastion of Celtic culture. A decade later the province was characterized by a tripartite social division. One segment was the native Irish who had, until 1603, owned almost all the land and who had lived according to political and social customs that antedated the Norman invasions. These people were suddenly trans-

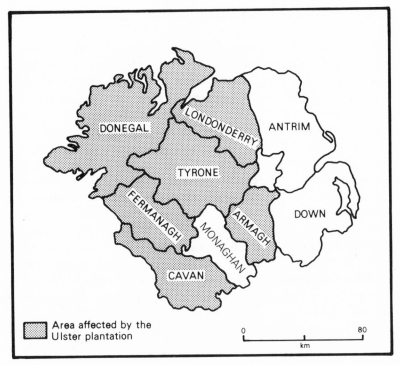

Map 3. The Ulster plantation

formed into the lowest of tenantry. They held only the poorest land. The size of their land holdings was drastically reduced. The native Irish were leaderless, for their chiefs had fled. As the old Celtic social system crumbled, they held desperately to the one remaining badge of their identity, the Roman Catholic faith. The second group was the lowland Scots. The Scots dominated the counties of Antrim and Down, which they independently colonized, and among the planted colonies they were the majority of colonists in Donegal and Tyrone and a portion in Fermanagh and Cavan. The Scots were Presbyterians. The third group was the English. Most of the original undertakers of the planted colonies were English, and therefore the Ulster upper classes were chiefly English in origin. There were, in addition, a considerable number of settlers brought from England who formed the bulk of the colonial population in Fermanagh and Cavan. The great majority of the English colonists were Anglicans. Thus, the early seventeenth century saw the formation of the social structure that characterizes Ulster to the present day. Ethnic (or, if one prefers, national) background became nearly synonymous with religious preference.

In the absence of accurate historical enumerations of population, one must deal with very sketchy estimates of the Scottish and English migrants into Ulster. One point is clear, however, and that is that the English- and Scottish-derived populations grew continuously, right up to the Great Famine of 1846–49. A responsible scholarly estimate places the number of adult Scots and English in Antrim and Down in the early 1620s at roughly 7,500.[7] A muster roll of Antrim and Down, in about 1630 (which would have included only able-bodied males) put the number of English and Scots in those counties at 2,000.[8] Throughout Ulster during the first century of plantation, the Scots greatly exceeded the English. A contemporary estimate for the early 1640s was that there were in Ulster approximately 100,000 Scots and 20,000 English.[9] These contemporary figures may have been an optimistic overestimate by British officials, but certainly by the time of the English Revolution of 1688–89, these totals had been met and surpassed. A. T. Q. Stewart has argued that it was the heavy immigration of the later seventeenth century, not the spectacular plantation schemes of the early century, that laid the permanent foundations of the Ulster colony.[10] Probably, like most migrations of any significance, this infilling of Ulster was characterized by chain migration, especially among the Scots. A pioneering member of a large Scottish lowland family would hear of good land that rented cheaply in, say, south Down, and would take passage on a small trading vessel that was headed to a port near the spot he had heard of. There he would disembark, tramp inland, talk to settlers already present and try to contact his potential landlord or agent, and having struck a deal, would return home to Scotland for supplies, tools, and money. So a new farm would start and soon the original settler would find a cousin or a brother on his doorstep. And so on. This chain migration, combined with the natural population increase that occurred as Ulster-Scots settlers married and raised families, meant that the newcomers' numbers were continuously growing, and much faster than the rate of natural increase of the native Irish population. Sometime in the early eighteenth century, the combined Scots and English population in the areas of plantation equaled and then slightly exceeded that of the native Irish.

The one culturally unique characteristic of the Scots settlers in Ulster was their adherence to Presbyterianism. Thus, as Alan Gailey has convincingly shown, the foundation date of Scottish congregations—which begin with Edward Brice's ministry in Broadisland (the Ballycarry area) and in Islandmagee, County Antrim, in 1613—is an accurate proxy for Scottish cultural penetration in the north of Ireland. Gailey has tallied the foundation of Presbyterian congregations as follows:[11]

Time Period	Cumulative total
1613–1640	13
1641–1660	70
1661–1690	104
1691–1720	148
1721–1740	154

In the middle years of the eighteenth century, schisms within Ulster Presbyterianism inhibited church expansion, and so, after mid-eighteenth century, the proxy no longer works. We must, therefore, jump a considerable gap of time to reach the summation of the Scottish portion of the colonization of the north of Ireland. This summation is provided by the first accurate religious census of Ireland, that of 1834. This enumeration was done according to the diocesan boundaries of the Established Church, and because these are not familiar to most readers the results are best presented in the form of a map.[12] By the 1830s, in the east of Ulster (roughly, the counties of Antrim and Down), Scots-derived individuals were an absolute majority of the population. In the Ulster periphery—counties Donegal, Monaghan, and Cavan—the absolute religious majority was strongly native Irish, although there were in these regions Scottish and English enclaves. In the remaining areas the native Irish outnumbered the incomers, but there were large numbers of British settlers, the exact composition of the colonial population varying sharply by area. The Ulster situation has never been simple, and as a mapping of the various cultural elements makes clear, the situation varied greatly from one place to another.

Nevertheless, certain facts emerge from a survey of the first two centuries of Scottish and English colonization of the north of Ireland. First (and this is often forgotten), the absolute majority of the population in the historical nine counties of Ulster throughout this period (and, indeed, to the present day) remained native Irish by ethnicity and Roman Catholic by religious persuasion. Second, Protestants came to own most of the land in Ulster. This occurred in part through the plantation process and the in-migration of the independent English and Scots. It was also a result of a separate process, the "penal code" of the eighteenth century, which deprived Catholics of most civil rights. Under this snarl of anti-Catholic

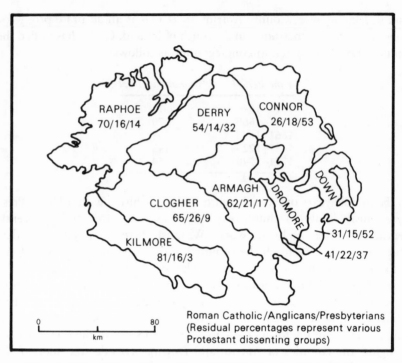

Map 4. Irish religious proportions, 1834, by Church of Ireland dioceses

legislation, it became illegal for Catholics to purchase freehold lands and to pass on intact family holdings of freehold land. Thus, taking Ireland as a whole, the proportion of land owned in perpetuity by Roman Catholics (for which one can read native Irish) declined to the following percentages:[13]

1641	61%
1688	22%
1703	15%
1776	5%

Although in the matter of landownership, the rest of Ireland came to resemble Ulster (in that landownership aggregated in Protestant hands), there was a major difference in the north of Ireland. There, most of the land actually was occupied as well as owned by Protestants—that is, by farmers of Scottish and of English derivation. Scots and English farmers in Ulster displaced the native Irish, pushing them decade by decade off the most desirable pieces of land, to the agricultural margins. Through my reading over the years, I have found a very simple way to predict where the Catholics were in any given area of colonized Ulster from the mid-seventeenth century onward. How high above sea level is any given piece of land and what is the height above sea level of the nearest town? If the difference is more than fifty meters, one is usually dealing with Catholic-held farmland, if less, it is usually Protestant. In Ulster, land quality declines radically as one rises above sea level: excessive moisture prevails, the growing season is shorter, and in any case, cultivating mountainous land is difficult. So, in the planted portions of Ulster, a pattern emerged locale by locale, whereby the native Irish, embittered but unbowed, lived on the heights and looked down on the fertile valleys possessed by the Scottish and English invaders.[14] During the seventeenth century, these colonists, as they built their farmhouses and market towns sometimes literally adopted the practice of the children of Israel. "The builders, every one had his sword girded by his side, and so builded" (Neh. 4:18).

(3)

Presbyterianism was the cultural element that distinguished the Ulster-Scots from the other groups in Ireland, and it was the instrument that kept them distinct.[15] Presbyterianism served as the linchpin of a set of social practices that maintained tribal exclusivity through the limitation of intermarriage with other groups, and it provided for several aspects of social discipline within Ulster-Scots society.[16]

The foundation of Irish Presbyterianism was the set of doctrines usually called Calvinism. The one thing everyone knows about Calvinism is that it was not a lot of fun. Jean Calvin (1509–64), from whom the system derived, was a French reformer who through an unlikely skein of events became the virtual dictator of the "republic" of Geneva from 1541 until his death. In those years, he established a theocratic rule based on what he believed to be "Old Testament" lines. A series of statutes, every bit as detailed as the laws of the Hebrew scriptures, governed almost every aspect of public and private life, and there were prohibitions on dancing, games, and most innocent pleasures. Calvin created a class of religious functionaries, modeled on the Levites of ancient Israel, and he articulated several levels of authority within that caste. He was the patriarch. Anyone who transgressed the austere social code or questioned the authority of the ecclesiastical caste was severely punished. Serious religious opponents of Calvin's regime either were banished or, in several instances, were tortured and executed.

Calvinism would have remained only another sad case of man invoking God, in order to be inhumane to mankind, had not Calvin been a writer of genius on religious questions. Several aspects of the Calvinist theological system were incorporated into the Ulster-Scots demotic religious culture. The first of these was Calvin's doctrine that the holy scriptures alone were the standards of the faith. This implied a rejection of the idea, fundamental to both the Roman Catholic and to the Established Churches of England and Ireland, that tradition served as a companion to the scriptures, and that God's revelation was continuous down through the ages, through the church. Further, Calvin placed a good deal more emphasis than did most Protestant reformers (notably Luther) upon the "Old Testament." Undeniably, Calvin was a believer in the divinity of Jesus Christ, but his Christianity was singularly patriarchal, in the Hebraic sense of the word.

Calvin believed that after the original fall from grace of Adam, there was no such thing as freedom of the human will. From the absence of free will was derived the dogma most characteristic of Calvinism: predestination. According to Calvin, one was justified before God by faith, but whether or not one had faith was determined by the Almighty before the beginning of time. To use another vocabulary: those individuals who were eternally profane and those who were sacred were defined immutably by God's will. The attractiveness of such a doctrine to a group of invading colonists such as the Ulster-Scots is obvious, for one could easily define the natives as immutably profane, and damned, and oneself as predestined to virtue. Finally, within the Calvinist system, divine grace was conceived of as being "inamissible," that is, that it could not be forfeited. Salvation could not be lost no matter how grave one's sins. Thus, if one acted badly, one could be severely punished in this world, but one still remained one of the elect, and therefore inherently distinguished from all of the profane nonelect. Calvinism, therefore, was a perfect tribal religion.[17]

As important as are these specific doctrines for an understanding of Ulster Presbyterianism, the texture and tone of Calvin's writings are equally salient, for Calvin's rhetorical mode, as much as his specific doctrine, largely determined the nature of religious discourse among the Ulster-Scots. The texture of Calvin's rhetoric is best indicated by some short excerpts from his writings. Here, for example, Calvin sets the framework for a discussion of the nature of Christian baptism:

Prototype of baptism in the Old Covenant
These things which we have said both of mortification and of washing were foreshadowed in the people of Israel, who were on this account said by the apostle to have been "baptized in the cloud and in the sea" (I Cor. 10:2). Mortification was symbolized when the Lord, rescuing his people from the domination and cruel bondage of Pharaoh himself and the Egyptian army, who were in hot pursuit and almost at their backs (Ex. 14:26–28). For in the same way he also promises us in baptism and shows us by a sign given that by his power we have been led out and delivered from bondage in Egypt, that is, from the bondage of sin; that our Pharaoh, that is, the devil, has been drowned, although he does not cease to harry us and weary us. As the Egyptian, however, was not cast into the depth of the sea, but, left lying on the shore, still terrified the Israelites by his frightful appearance, yet could not harm them (Ex. 14:30–31), so too this enemy of ours still threatens, brandishes his weapons, is felt, but cannot conquer.[18]

According to Calvin, the scriptures require obedience to kings, even bad ones:

First, I should like my readers to note and carefully observe that providence of God, which the Scriptures with good reason so often recall to us, and its special operation in distributing kingdoms and appointing what kings He pleases. . . . Now it is well enough known what kind of king Nebuchadnezzar was, who conquered Jerusalem—a strong invader and destroyer of others. Nevertheless, the Lord declares in Ezekiel that He has given him the land of Egypt for the service he had done Him in devastating it (Ezek. 29:19–20). And Daniel said to him: "You, O king, are a king of kings, to whom the God of heaven has given the kingdom, powerful, mighty, and glorious; to you, I say, he has given also all lands where the sons of men dwell, beasts of the forest and birds of the air: these he has given into your hand and made you rule over them" (Dan. 2:37–38, cf. Vg.). Again, Daniel says to Nebuchadnezzar's son Belshazzar: "The Most High God gave Nebuchadnezzar, your father, kingship and magnificence, honor and glory; and because of the magnificence that he gave him, all peoples, tribes, and tongues were trembling and fearful before him" (Dan. 5:18–19, cf. Vg.). When we hear that a king has been ordained by God, let us at once call to mind those heavenly edicts with regard to honoring and fearing a king.[19]

Such examples abound in the writings of Calvin. The point here is the style and tone. Even though few laymen actually read Calvin, his message and mode of thought became part of the Ulster-Scots popular culture through the weekly sermons of their clergy. Calvin employs a mode of argument that is much closer to that of rabbinic Judaism than it is to the deductive syllogisms of the Thomists or the Schoolmen; Calvin cares very much about precedent, much more than he cares about logic, and therefore his is an extremely legalistic and even Talmudic style. He rarely begins a major argument without founding it on Hebrew precedents.

Calvinism came to Scotland in large part through the apostalate of John Knox (1513–72). In the early 1550s, Knox made a pilgrimage to Geneva and returned to Scotland a convinced Calvinist. Knox was instrumental in the overthrow of the Scottish monarchy and through his political associations had considerable influence upon the young James VI. Knox championed church governance by "presbytery" rather than by episcopacy, wrote an austere liturgy for the Scottish Church, and produced, among other works, a long treatise articulating the doctrine of predestination. For our purposes Knox can justly be described as the conduit through which Calvinism came to dominate Scottish religious life and thence to be introduced into the north of Ireland.[20] Of course Scotland and the north of Ireland were not the only regions to be influenced by Calvinism, nor was the Scottish kirk the only denomination. The Established Church in Ireland was permanently influenced in its doctrine and in its liturgy (which became notably austere by Anglican standards). Indeed, in the early years of the Presbyterian march into Ulster, the bishops of the Established Church went so far in their accommodation as to induct into Anglican benefices Presbyterian clergymen from Scotland.[21] This period of "prescopacy" came to an end with the reign of Archbishop William Laud, but by then an indigenous Ulster-Scots Presbyterianism already was beginning to flourish.

Calvinism in any context is a very forceful set of ideas. Crucially, Calvinism among the Scots and among the Ulster-Scots was given a spin by another set of ideas, and this spin, like the effect of the rifling in a gun barrel upon a bullet, magnified the intensity and penetration of the original Calvinist concepts. This spin was introduced through the development of an indigenous version of the concept of the covenant. In the sixteenth and seventeenth centuries, a religiopolitical "covenant" was used in Scotland to mobilize radical Protestants against absolutist government and against anything that smacked of "popery." In 1557, various Scottish leaders established a covenant with each other before God, "that we shall with all diligence continually apply our whole power, substance, and our very lives to maintain, set forward, and establish the most blessed

Word of God and his congregation; and shall labour at our possibility to have faithful ministers purely and truly minister Christ's evangel and sacraments to his people."[22] This, the first of the great Scottish covenants, preceded by only two years the Protestant leaders' seizure of Edinburgh and the creation of Scotland as a Presbyterian state. In 1581, amid fears that Roman Catholicism might revive, a statement of faith was framed and required of all parish clergy. It was very strongly Protestant ("We detest and refuse the usurped authority of the Roman Antichrist upon the Scriptures of God, upon the kirk, the civil magistrate, and conscience of men," ran one of its phrases), and it became known as "the King's Confession" because it was signed by James VI of Scotland.[23]

Now, although the theological writings of Jean Calvin had discussed the idea of the covenant, this Scottish enmeshing of covenant thinking with religiopolitical controversy produced something quite new, that is, an emphasis upon the "covenant of works." In other words, righteous actions were required in the social and political realm as well as in the religious world, and these actions volitionally defined the relationship of God and man.[24] The covenantal bond articulated in the King's Confession was no mere antiquarian theology. It lived: the Scottish General Assembly in 1590 engaged in a mass renewal of this religious oath and there were "public bandings" (collective mutual affirmations) of the Presbyterian population during which the oath was reaffirmed.[25] Thus, when later locked in a contest with the monarch over control of the Established Church, the General Assembly put forward in 1638 a "National Covenant" that, among other things, recapitulated completely the King's Confession of 1581. This National Covenant of 1638 professed great loyalty to the temporal monarch, but showed even greater loyalty to the divine monarch:

> We promise and swear by the GREAT NAME OF THE LORD OUR GOD, to continue in the profession and obedience of the foresaid religion; and that we shall defend the same, and resist all those contrary errors and corruptions, according to our vocation, and to the uttermost of that power that God hath put in our hands, all the days of our life.[26]

There is an implicit if-then clause in the National Covenant: if the monarch follows the ways of God, we will be allegiant to him. Otherwise, no.

Gradually, the Scottish Presbyterians slipped into a warlike posture against the king and eventually into open warfare. All this became enmeshed in the events of the English Civil War, a conflict whose physics are so complicated as to defy summary. For our present purposes, the relevant feature is that in 1643 the Scottish parliament affirmed the "Solemn League and Covenant" which advocated the imposition of Presbyterianism not only in Scotland, but in England and Ireland as well.[27] So complex were the social forces of the time that the English parliament, as part of its own fight with the monarchy, actually endorsed this covenant.

Fortunately, the way that the Solemn League and Covenant was introduced into Ulster is well recorded and very revealing. The General Assembly of Scotland appointed four Presbyterian clergymen to take the Covenant to Ireland. One of these envoys kept a diary and it became the basis of a manuscript narrative that was eventually discovered by James Seaton Reid, the first major historian of the Irish Presbyterian Church.[28] The four clerics brought with them to Ulster a bundle of printed copies of the Covenant and reams of blank pieces of paper, intended for the inscription of the names of those who affirmed the document. The emissaries went first to the officers and soldiers of the Scottish army in the north of Ireland. In each locale their concern was initially with gaining the adherence of the military personnel, and thereafter they tried to gain the adhesion of as many of the local Scottish settlers as they could. Not all of the Scottish regiments proved willing to take the oath to support the Solemn League and Covenant, but most did. The Scottish settlers in most areas joined in, but the reluctance of the people of Belfast and of Londonderry was overcome only with effort. The diary of this tour provides a unique insight into the rhetorical methods and intellectual outlook of the lowland Presbyterian clergy and of the Ulster settlers to whom they preached. At each stop on this expedition, the clergy preached from a biblical text, one that they chose not only for its aptness, but because presumably it was familiar to their audience. The biblical text was the ramp for the storming of the Ulster-Scots mind. The texts employed at principal cities were recorded:[29]

Belfast. Isaiah 56:5–7
Even unto them will I give in mine house and within my walls a place and a name better than thy sons and daughters: I will give them an everlasting name, that shall not be cut off.

Also the sons of the stranger that join themselves to the Lord, to be his servants every one that keepeth the sabbath from polluting it, and taketh hold of my covenant;

Even them will I bring to my holy mountain, and make them joyful in my house of prayer: their burnt-offerings and their sacrifices *shall be* accepted upon mine altar; for mine house shall be called an house of prayer for all people.

Antrim and Ballymena. Psalm 102:13

Thou shalt arise, *and* have mercy upon Zion: for the time to favour her, yea, the set time, is come.

Londonderry. 2 Chron. 15:15; Jer. 50:5, and Neh. 9:10

And all Judah rejoiced at the oath: for they had sworn with all their heart, and sought him with their whole desire; and he was found of them: and the Lord gave them rest round about.

They shall ask the way to Zion with their faces thitherward, *saying,* Come, and let us join ourselves to the Lord in a perpetual covenant *that* shall not be forgotten.

And shewedst signs and wonders upon Pharaoh, and on all his servants, and on all the people of his land: for thou knewest that they dealt proudly against them. So didst thou get thee a name, as *it is* this day.

The significant fact here is that the clergy diary does not record any use of "New Testament" texts, and I believe that this is not accidental. In fact, the "New Testament" was of little use in the situation of the Presbyterian clerics. They were promulgating a covenant, trying to gain adherence to it from a group of people who knew their Bible full well. In such a context, not only were the references to the covenantal experiences in the Hebrew scriptures direct and apt, but to refer to the "New Testament," where it is argued that the Abrahamic covenant has been "fulfilled," would have been self-defeating for the clerics. Although they would never consciously have admitted the fact, the clerical envoys to the Ulster-Scots employed the ancient texts because they recognized that, when forced to the bare wiring of their being, the Scottish colonists in Ulster were more a people of the "Old" Testament than of the "New."

After the restoration of 1660, the concept of the covenant ceased to have direct political implication in England and it gradually lost its relevance in Scotland.[30] In 1688–1707, framed by the firm establishment of a Protestant monarchy, and by the union of England and Scotland, the covenant as a formal political concept effectively disappeared in England and Scotland. Nevertheless, two evolutions out of the Scottish covenanting phenomenon have affected events in the north of Ireland from the late seventeenth century to the present day.

One of these is a matter of "high" intellectual history: the development of "contractarian" thought in the Scottish universities and among the followers of John Locke. The "contract theory" that emerged was in fact a secularization of the religiopolitical creed of the Scottish covenants. It posited that individuals give up liberty only by their own consent. Governments come into being by the consent of the governed and for the good of the community. Government undertakes to serve the general good and can be removed for violating this contract within the community. David Miller has convincingly argued that this form of contractarian thinking, although part of the common stock of ideas of Enlightenment Britain, was employed by political leaders of the Ulster-Scots with a rigor unmatched elsewhere in the British Isles. In particular, political loyalism in the north of Ireland came to hold (and, indeed, still holds) a character denominated "conditional loyalty." That is, loyalty is granted to the crown and to the government of the day under a set of unstated contracts which can be revoked if the government is untrue to its responsibility of preserving the just and moral character of the state. Thus, on certain occasions, it is not only morally permissible, but morally mandatory, for loyalists to act in ways that the government considers to be treasonable.[31]

More pervasive than this contractarian thinking, but harder to document directly, are matters of "low," or demotic, intellectual history. Ordinary people have political beliefs but they do not write political treatises; indeed, most of the several generations of Ulster-Scots were born and died without leaving behind a single scrap of paper that the historian can use. Nevertheless, the people, just as much as the political theorists, had ideas of how a proper society should work. These ideas were not percolated-down concepts of Locke or of the illuminates of the Scottish Enlightenment. Instead, there was a traditional knowledge among the Ulster-Scots polity that included, first, knowledge of the various Scottish political covenants, and, second, a deeper acquaintance with the Abrahamic covenant as found in the holy scriptures.

For the Ulster-Scots, the Hebrew scriptures served as an entire cultural cupboard: the scriptures contain direct advice on how to act, they provide analogies applicable to a myriad of situations, and their allusions to ancient peoples and to events provide parallels to experiences in the north of Ireland. From the ancient Israelites the Ulster-Scots learned a particular method of sacralizing politics. And the particular emphasis that comes from covenantal bonding includes a very sharp sense of right and of wrong, of sacred and profane. This meant, among other things, that the Ulster-Scots became one of the hardest people in the world with whom to negotiate. "Whereas the English believe that compromise is the answer to all disputes," A. T. Q. Stewart observes, "Ulstermen believe the opposite."[32]

(4)

Certain characteristics of the Ulster-Scots only make sense if we adopt the hypothesis that the Ulster-Scots historically have operated on a conceptual grid that was, although not identical to the ancient Israelite grid, at least derivative from that ancient framework and, therefore, in many ways similar to it. Emphatically, I am not here suggesting that the Hebrew scriptures were the sole determinant of the culture of the Ulster Presbyterians, but rather that the scripturally derived covenantal thinking was such an essential aspect that it can no more be left out of an analysis of the Ulster-Scots culture than a reagent can be dropped from a chemical equation. Without the recognition that in important ways the Ulster-Scots were an "Old Testament" people, no explanation of their history works.

One characteristic that becomes easier to understand is the extraordinarily sharp us-them disjuncture in Ulster-Scots thinking. Almost every tribal, national, or political group thinks of itself as superior to other groups and defines some rival group as its great enemy. Among religious groups, this distinction frequently is sacralized and becomes coterminous with the distinction between sacred and profane. The nature of Calvinism made this kind of thinking theologically legitimate. When the Calvinistic emphasis upon the "elect" percolated downward from the theologues to the ordinary adherents, it almost inevitably slid "into a form of racism," as Steve Bruce observes. He continues, "Calvinists have tended to suppose that their children have a higher than even chance of being part of the elect and conversely have tended to suppose that people of other races, especially those which have rejected the gospel, are unlikely to be part of the elect."[33] At the grass-roots level, this Calvinistic sense of being of the elect merged with the "Old Testament" saga of the Chosen People. Although the Scots colonists of the north of Ireland did not delude themselves into believing that they were *the* Chosen People, the analogy was strong, and they acted under the conviction that they were *a* Chosen People.

This conviction fits perfectly into the situation in which the Scots found themselves. They held religious beliefs that the native Irish rejected; and thus the native Irish demonstrated that they were not part of the elect. The natives, moreover, were hostile, refusing to readily give up the Promised Land to the colonists. So, like the Hittites and Canaanites, they were evil.

"Congregations could easily identify with Israel," one distinguished Presbyterian historian has observed, "taking possession of the promised land, threatened by the hostility of its fierce inhabitants."[34]

One of the images of a righteous society that runs through the Hebrew scriptures is that of a walled city, well defended against the onslaught of the unrighteous. This coincides precisely with the architectural contours of the Ulster-Scots in the first two centuries of the colony. In the countryside, the bawn, or defended farmhouse, was the characteristic structure:

> The undertaker usually placed his keep-like house at one end of the corners of the bawn wall, the other three corners being defended by circular towers with candle-extinguisher roofs on them. The bawn was entered by a gate surmounted by a baroque gable, if one can accept ancient drawings as witness. The bawns create the effect of being much older than they are, for outside Ulster such defence measures had long before become unnecessary.[35]

What held for isolated farmhouses held on a larger scale for towns. The plantation of Ulster and the subinfeudation of Antrim and Down involved, as conscious policy, the introduction of a fortified urban network. The walled town was a frontier necessity, and city gates were not just ornamental, but were real barriers that could be closed in the face of enemy attack.[36]

Inevitably, the Ulster-Scots, who were aggressive in searching out and settling their Promised Land, were defensive and inward-looking once they had obtained a purchase. Surrounded as they were by hostile natives, the Ulster-Scots assumed something of a corporate personality, not as defined and pervasive as was the corporate personality of ancient Israel, but real nonetheless. Each person within the community was assumed to have a role in protecting the polity against the Canaanites, that is, the Catholics. Community members had to trust one another, and no one else.[37]

This inward-turned aspect of the Ulster-Scots helps to explain why they, like the children of Israel, made no attempt to convert their enemies to righteousness, but instead fought them tooth and nail. Certainly during the seventeenth and eighteenth centuries, the Ulster-Scots made almost no effort to convert the native Irish from Catholicism to Presbyterianism. In part, this follows from the fundamental premise of Calvinism: vulgarly put, the heathen were predestined to be heathen and that was that. Equally important, I think, was the racism that is inherent in the idea of the Ulster-Scots being a Chosen People. They wished to maintain a barrier between themselves and the Irish natives and this would disappear if the Irish converted. Significantly, it has been observed that when in the mid-eighteenth century the "Seceders" within the Presbyterian Church tried to recruit new members they did not direct their effort toward Catholics (or even to Anglicans), but confined their activities to Ulster-Scots.[38]

In many matters, the demotic culture of the Ulster-Scots possessed what Marianne Elliot terms a "disdain for central authority."[39] That is, the covenant mindset implied a distrust of hierarchy and refused to accept any form of revelation—political, social, or religious—passed down from human authorities. In the covenantal grid, each person had direct access to participation in the divine revelation. There might be different forms of involvement (religious leaders, for example, had different roles than did the laity) but the covenant was shared and adhered to by all believers. Now this rejection of central hierarchic authority is not at all the same as an invocation of chaos. Covenantal thinking, whether among the ancient Hebrews or the Ulster-Scots, involves a great deal of religious, social, and political discipline, but that discipline is effectively consensual. Individuals follow certain common patterns because those patterns are part of the covenant and thus must be honored.

To say that the covenantal grid, as interpreted by the Ulster-Scots, led to democracy in religion, society, and politics, is correct as long as one does not mistake what democracy meant in the eighteenth and early nineteenth centuries. The real democracy in the Ulster-Scots outlook was that every individual was directly under divine authority, covenanted to grace. In this system, power did not percolate downward, as in the case of the Catholic and Anglican churches, but rose upward from the level of the individual kirk. Each congregation was governed by a small band of congregation-chosen leaders, and the congregation chose ("called") its own minister. The kirk "session" that governed each church consisted of the minister and of elected lay "elders." This band nested into a larger group, the "presbytery" which consisted of all of the ministers of a given region and of a ruling elder sent by each kirk session. Thus, communication occurred between congregations and the presbytery was able to enforce consensually agreed discipline among the congregations in its ambit. Ultimately, the presbyteries fit into the "synod" which was at once the parliament of the church and its superior court; it too was composed of both laity and clergy.[40]

So, when one hears the commonplace observation that the Ulster-Scots were predisposed by their religion to be democratic in politics, it is true, but not in the sense of "one person, one vote," and not in the sense of direct democracy. What the Ulster-Scots practiced was a form of representative government in religion in which individuals who were covenanted to shared religious values elected leaders who exercised for the whole community the task of religious governance. And thus, when the Ulster-Scots are presented as being advanced politically, it is not that they were proponents of the extreme democracy of the Jacobins, but rather of efficient representative government based on the universal participation of all those who shared certain crucial values.

The Hebrew scriptures are full of instances of indiscipline, and this is inevitable when a people are programmed by the covenantal grid: the corporate nature of covenantal thinking, which gives each person the opportunity to choose to act rightly and, equally, gives every individual an opportunity to go off the rails. Within the Ulster context, this has meant that the Presbyterian Church has been prone to schisms (like its mother church in Scotland).[41] The same thing happened in social and political matters. Within the accepted fundamental rubric that the crown and government must be Protestant, the Ulster-Scots manifested an extraordinarily spiky nature. "The Presbyterian is happiest when being radical" is an apt observation.[42] The covenantal set of mind makes him or her radical. What one can never tell is whether the radicalism will be to the far right or to the far left.

(5)

These observations about the nature of Ulster-Scots society and its biblically based covenantal mindset are not mere abstractions. They characterized a specific band of locales in parts of the north of Ireland. To anchor these observations in one such historical locale, I wish to deal with the area of Ballycarry (often called "Broadisland") and Islandmagee in County Antrim in the late eighteenth and early nineteenth centuries. Ballycarry-Islandmagee is a set of two contiguous communities located about 30 kilometers north of Belfast. The parish that encompasses Ballycarry is approximately 1,850 hectares. It is an inland parish for the most part, although portions of it border on Larne Lough. Islandmagee, its neighbor, in contrast, is surrounded by water on three sides. It is a peninsula of about 2,850 hectares that hooks out into the Belfast Lough and the north channel of the Irish Sea like a rheumatic finger of an old countryman.

These communities are valuable cases, because it was in Ballycarry in 1613 that the Reverend Edward Brice began the first Presbyterian ministry in Ireland. He preached alternately in Ballycarry and in a church in Ballykeel in Islandmagee. These two communities developed very strong Ulster-Scots cultures in the broadest sense. So, although one cannot argue that Ballycarry-Islandmagee is typical of Ulster-Scots communities (I do not believe that there is such a thing as a typical community; attempts by historians to find typical communities are ill-founded and inherently self-defeating), they present something close to a pure type. One sees in them in a very clear fashion characteristics and processes that often were somewhat veiled in communities less close to the epicenter of Ulster-Scots culture. Fortunately, the historical material on the two neighboring locales is singularly good. Both of the communities were studied by the "Ordnance Survey" of the 1830s, the closest thing to an ethnological study of Ireland that was done in the nineteenth century. Ballycarry was the home of a strikingly articulate "weaver poet," one James Orr, and he has left a large body of verse, much of it in the local vernacular. His work is precise and concrete concerning the details of local life. Islandmagee is the only parish in the north of Ireland whose social history has been written by a professional historian, so contextualized details are easy to come by.[43]

One of the most striking things about the two communities was their ethnic purity. The Ordnance surveyor noted that in the Ballycarry area in the late 1830s, "All traces or remains of the aboriginal inhabitants seem to have at the outset been removed, nor is there in the parish at the present moment a member of the Roman Catholic Church nor more than three of the Church of England [the Established Church] holding land, the very few members of either of these churches being confined to servants or labourers who have come from distant parishes.[44] Islandmagee was almost equally pure ethnically. It contained almost no Catholics and the Anglican Church depended for its existence upon the presence of coast guard personnel who were posted on the peninsula. Reflecting on the overall cultural pattern, the Ordinance surveyor of Ballycarry reported that

in character, habits, customs, and in their accent, idioms and dialect the inhabitants of this parish as much resemble the Scotch if not more so than any others in the County Antrim. This may be owing to their limited intercourse with strangers, their comparatively retired situation and their equality as to grade and condition. There are not nor have there been any others of different extraction residing in the parish perhaps since its original colonization by Scottish settlers of the early part of the seventeenth century.[45]

Being Scottish in origin meant that the people were Presbyterian in religion and seriously so. Thus: schism. In 1768 a Secessionist church was set up in Islandmagee.[46] And in 1829 a Trinitarian-Unitarian split in Ballycarry resulted in two congregations.[47] But however given to suspicion of each other's orthodoxy the locals may have been, they were a virtual hoplite phalanx when it came to others' religion. Popery hardly bears mention, so violently were they opposed to it, but here is what they felt about Anglicans: the Ulster-Scots' "hostility to Episcopacy is most decided. They most commonly view the Romish and Established religions as similar and in the same light."[48] (In this attitude they were not in any way unique among Ulster-Scots. The Ordnance surveyor for the parish of Antrim, a community similar to Ballycarry-Islandmagee, reported that "the Presbyterians are very bigoted in their religious and political ideas [being] warmly attached to their own and hostile to any other form of worship, particularly that of the Established Church.")[49] Ballycarry was officially comprehended within the benefice of the prebend of Kilroot and this office was held for a short time by Jonathan Swift. According to a local tradition that is still alive, on only one occasion was Swift able to entice a few Presbyterians to come to his divine service, and so pleased was the mordant champion of Episcopacy with this rare opportunity that he had his sexton nail shut the door from outside, so that the locals had no choice but to listen to his sermon.

As the Ordnance Survey of Ballycarry noted, the people were overwhelmingly of the same social grade and this held true as well for Islandmagee. There were no more than half a dozen gentlemen resident in Ballycarry-Islandmagee and no "middlemen" in the Irish sense of individuals who rented large pieces of land from the freeholder and then rackrented the peasantry. Land tenure for the tenants was reasonably secure and for holdings larger than five acres (and frequently smaller pieces), written leases were the general rule. The relative equality of social status among the inhabitants of Ballycarry-Islandmagee was a social approximation of the configuration of their religious lives. That is, not only was each Ulster-Scot in these communities equal before God in the covenantal way of thinking, but they were pretty nearly equal in the eyes of human-kind.

Most families around Ballycarry made their livings either from farming or from a mixture of small-holding agriculture (one to five acres of potato ground) and weaving. In Islandmagee there were fewer weavers, but many families used the sea, either as a primary source of income or as a supplement. Thus, the economy of these small communities was diversified and also was thoroughly integrated in the cash economy. As for the weavers as an occupational group, there is a considerable literature by Irish social historians on their characteristics and importance (and a much larger literature on English and Scots weavers).[50] Weavers were to Ulster rural societies what printers were to urban centers: shit-kickers. The nature of their craft gave them time to read and even more time to reflect, so they became one of the main conduits through which radical political ideas—as well as rumors, folktales, and querulous arguments—circulated throughout the rural societies where they were resident. The weavers were to the secular culture of the eighteenth- and early nineteenth-century Ulster-Scots what the church elders were to the religious culture. Not surprisingly, many of the weavers—among them James Orr, "the Bard of Ballycarry"—became not only the demotic cultural arbiters of their communities, but sometimes cultural icons.

In considering Ballycarry-Islandmagee in the three decades on either side of the year 1800, one deals with a period when the Scots-derived culture of the north of Ireland had become an indigenous culture of Ireland, independent of (though still in close contact with) the Scottish homeland. There are no standard indicators of cultural maturity among colonial populations, but Alan Gailey of the Ulster Folk Museum has suggested measures that are appropriate for Ulster. For example, until the end of the seventeenth century, most Ulster Presbyterian ministers were born and raised in Scotland.[51] From then onward, almost all Ulster clergy were local men. This development was a key step in cultural maturation.

Near the end of the Napoleonic wars, the further, final stage in the creation of an indigenous religious-cultural leadership took place when the Royal Belfast Academical Institution was formed. In 1814 it began to provide both a secondary school education and the equivalent of the M.A. degree as given by the Scottish universities.[52] Other institutions of secondary and higher education intended for Ulster-Scots (but, in the Presbyterian tradition, not limited to them) followed, and by mid-nineteenth century, the north of Ireland had a full system of educational institutions running from infant schools through university and, for ordinands, through advanced theological training. A study of the matriculants at Scottish universities has shown that after about 1815 the number of Ulster-Scots students (both lay and clerical) seeking higher education in Scotland dropped sharply, because the Ulster-Scots religious and professional leaders had begun to receive their training at home.[53]

One aspect of Ulster-Scots cultural independence from the Scottish homeland was the way in which social discipline was enforced by the community. The thinness of what can be called a police force in Ulster was notable and violence between Ulster-Scots and the native Irish was endemic. Not common, however, was violence or theft within the various local Ulster-Scots communities. Granted, there were the inevitable drunken fights and family feuds, but by the early nineteenth century, even these were being tamped down. "In no district is life or property more secure," reported the Ordnance surveyor for Ballycarry, and he was no enthusiast for things Ulster-Scot. "There is a perfect freedom from crime or outrage and the faction fights between the inhabitants of Ballycarry and those of Islandmagee have long since been given up. The most serious case brought from this parish before the Petty Session rarely can exceed in importance that of a petty assault, a complaint respecting trespass, or a dispute concerning water and even these are of infrequent occurrence."[54] This degree of social discipline was the final stage of a cultural maturation that was achieved through the melding of religious institutions and values, with social practices and values, all within the context of an ethnically homogeneous community.

Most matters of social control were taken care of by an autochthonous system of local law that had nothing to do with the law as set out by the state. This law was based on the church. Take Ballycarry as an example: in the eighteenth century, the parish was divided into districts, and an elder was assigned to each to report on the moral and spiritual welfare of the people. Matters of petty theft, uncivil behavior, and disputes not serious enough to spawn a civil lawsuit were brought to the church authorities. The kirk session operated as a court. Unrepentant sinners could be turned into social pariahs. Those who accepted church discipline were expected to make a full confession before their friends and neighbors and, frequently, to sit in a special place of shame in church, usually a chair that faced the congregation. Depending on the seriousness of the transgression, this humiliation could last for weeks or even months. The most important matters, or at least the most sensational, to come before the church courts concerned sexual behavior. Here is one example from Ballycarry in the eighteenth century. The Ballycarry kirk session had a terrible time deciding whether or not the child of a man who had been accused of adultery should be baptized. The accused offered to purge himself of the charge of adultery by taking an oath before the kirk session. This the session agreed to, but with characteristic gravity told him that he could not take the oath immediately, but must take the oath away and study it for a week and ponder on the consequences of false swearing. Only then was he permitted to take the oath and the baby to be baptized.[55] Fornication and adultery were major matters and one suspects that the details of sins confessed before the full congregation must have been heard with more attentiveness than were the sermons.

That matters of social control were locked into the local economic network is demonstrated by the fact that the two main landlords of the Ballycarry area, one a member of the Established Church, the other a Presbyterian, concerned themselves with congregational matters, going so far in some cases as to pay attention to where the tenants sat in the meeting house. In fact, landlords had the power under their leases to refuse to let a farm to a person who was unfaithful in paying his stipend to the church.[56]

Today, as citizens of a world in which the enforcement of social control is largely left to specialists (police forces, lawyers, and judges), we may find this generalized system, in which the inhabitants controlled each other's behavior, hard to comprehend and oppressive. Perhaps it was oppressive: everyone was watching. But, at minimum, it bespeaks a culture that certainly was cohesive and certainly was convinced that it controlled its own social destiny. Moreover, there were gentler aspects of this system of community social control. In an era before the development of formal methods for taking care of the weak and the poor (Ireland did not even have a functioning Poor Law until the 1830s), the kirk-based society took care of bastards, widows, and the handicapped, not at a high standard of comfort, but humanely.[57]

The demotic culture that evolved in the north of Ireland was similar to that of lowland Scotland but, by the late eighteenth century, independent of it. The independence of this culture became clear with the blooming in the late eighteenth and early nineteenth centuries of a school of popular poets in the north of Ireland. Usually they are called the "weaver poets," although some of them had other occupations, such as schoolmastering. The poets of the "northern Renaissance" were not high artists. Most of them wrote for their own local communities, rather than for a national or even a regional audience. Many of them rejoiced in the title of "Bard" of this town or that, for the title meant that they were the accepted local spokesmen on a variety of topics. Usually, these poets were first published in a local newspaper and then had their work collected in volumes that were printed only when enough money had come forward by way of advance subscriptions. The subscribers in almost every case were the poets' neighbors. The other salient point about the poets of the northern Renaissance is that they were bilingual, as were the communities that they served. Almost all of the poets were able to write in standard English, a tongue understood by their neighbors who, after all, read newspapers avidly. However, the everyday speech of the Ulster-Scots locales was a distinct Ulster variant of Lallans, the language of lowland Scotland. Though not a hard language to master in terms of grammar and orthography, it is very difficult to decipher when rendered in a local dialect. "Their accent, idioms, and phraseology are strictly and disagreeably Scottish, partaking only of the broad and coarse accent and dialect of the southern counties of Scotland," the Ordnance surveyor complained of the Ballycarry inhabitants. "Their manners are dry, blunt, and uncommunicative, wanting in candour and courtesy and, to those unacquainted with them, apparently uncivil."[58] According to linguists, the Lallans dialect spoken in County Antrim by the late eighteenth century had become considerably different from that of the Scottish lowlands because of two influences: through interaction with the native speakers of Gaelic, and, in the towns, the medium of written English, more than the spoken language, had affected the structure of spoken Lallans.[59] Thus James Orr, though enjoying the title "Bard of Ballycarry," could turn out tiresomely correct, slightly inept, formal English lines. Yet, on other occasions, he could describe in wonderfully robust vernacular what happened at the local fair:

> The ginge-bread wife, that's now as drunk's
> An owl; the herds new whistle, O;—
> The bumpkin beau, wi' pouther't funks,
> Like Downs upon a thristle, O—
> Then men o' strength wha bullets pay,
> Or putt in ilka alley, O;
> An' circles warpin' to and frae,
> Mak' a' the spirits rally, O.
>
> The winsome wean, wi' heart fu' light,
> Smiles up, an' seeks a fairin', O:
> The armless beggar craves a mite
> Whare'er he gains a hearin', O,

What tho' they'll waste whate'er we gie
On *sweeties,* an' a *drappie,* O!
We'se gie them something; ae babee
Apiece, wad mak them happy, O.

Now mak'in peace they ply the grog,
Tho' strife like haflin's rises, O—
Now party sangs the maist in vogue
Brust forth frae forty voices, O—
Now sparks, wha scarce dow stagger, try
To dance to dosin' fiddlers, O—
An' now it dauns, an 'hameward hie
The lasses an' their wheedlers, O.[60]

As the nineteenth century wore on, the Ballycarry-Islandmagee dialect was eroded by a combination of the effects of governmentally sponsored mass schooling, which was conducted in the approved national form of English, and the increased ease of physical communication throughout the British Isles. Nevertheless, until roughly the time of World War II, most adults in the area were effectively bilingual, speaking the communal vernacular at home and general English in the world outside. As late as the 1970s, I encountered several older citizens of the Ballycarry-Islandmagee area who maintained this linguistic dualism.

It is worth remembering that at the popular level the Ulster-Scots culture was the most literate in Ireland. The first accurate data that relates literacy and religion are from the year 1861, when the proportions of persons five years of age and upward who could neither read nor write was as follows: Roman Catholic, 45.8 percent; Anglican, 16.0 percent; and Presbyterian, 11.0 percent.[61] In actuality, these differentials had probably decreased rapidly since 1831 (when the national primary educational system was formed), so around the end of the late eighteenth century, the degree to which the literacy of the Ulster-Scots exceeded that of the rest of the population must have been very large indeed.

These people read. The best study yet done of the vernacular reading taste of the Ulster-Scots in the late eighteenth and nineteenth centuries points out that, as one would expect, almost every Presbyterian home possessed a full-sized Bible.[62] After about 1640, the Ulster-Scots switched to the translation made for the English church, which we know as the King James Bible.[63]

Literacy, though, was not simply a matter of reading the Bible, and J. R. R. Adams's study of the books that actually were in the hands of the people of eighteenth- and nineteenth-century Ulster shows that they had a remarkable range of material, from advanced political tracts, to multitudes of chapbooks, to poetry, to near-pornography. A vigorous publishing industry existed in Belfast and in some of the smaller towns of the north of Ireland; it is one of the indications of cultural blindness among bibliographers and cultural historians that these Ulster works are not found in most standard directories of eighteenth-century printed works. In the British Library catalogue one learns almost nothing about the existence of this northern Irish phenomenon.[64]

Just as, in the absence of formal agencies of policing, each Ulster-Scots community established its own means of social control, so in the absence of state agencies of cultural initiation, they created their own institutions. Each community had its own self-created school. That is a commonplace. What is more interesting is the ubiquity in Presbyterian Ulster in the later eighteenth and early nineteenth centuries of "reading societies." These were of several sorts. For example, in Ballycarry in the late 1830s, three reading societies were associated with religious groups: one for the orthodox and one for the Unitarian congregations and one for the Sunday school. Most of the volumes of these three reading societies were "on religious and useful subjects." Another sort of society had broader and more secular interests—history, biography, and novels. There were two such reading groups in Ballycarry. J. R. R. Adams points out that in rural areas of Ulster there was a particularly strong interest in imaginative literature. This is evidenced by local communities supporting their own bards and by the more general phenomenon of a keen interest in written fiction.[65] A third form of reading society was also common among the Ulster-Scots. These groups specialized in circulating serious political works and engaged in formal debates on worthy topics. Such societies were especially common in the late eighteenth century. James Orr memorializes the formal debate in one of these clubs as follows:

> But hark! the question giv'n, we now commence
> The kind debate, and he whose 'lucky hit'
> To silence awes some son of eloquence
> is proud as Fox exulting over Pitt
>
> How fond of order, he who fills the chair!
> How courteous and correct each humbler hind!
> Not one will interrupt, insult, or swear—
> True to the rules that all at entrance sign'd.[66]

What emerges from this survey of Ballycarry-Islandmagee, communities that were in the cockpit of Ulster-Scots culture, is a sense of a small world that by the end of the eighteenth century was part of an independent Ulster-Scots culture, vigorous in its local institutions, and that was, within the context of the times, democratic in its political structure and, with the exception of a handful of landlords, egalitarian in its distribution of wealth.

And radical. We must not forget A. T. Q. Stewart's dictum that the Ulster Presbyterians are inherently radical.

And so we should not be surprised that the people of Ballycarry-Islandmagee, products of this tiny, hard, self-confident world, decided to go to war in 1798 against the governments of Great Britain and of Ireland.

The 1798 Rising remains the most mysterious set of events in the post-Reformation history of Ireland. Granted, modern observers have imposed their own perceptions upon the events of 1798, but more than most aspects of the past, the Rising is sealed away from us. In large part this is because there was no single Irish rising, but rather a series of local risings, each with its own causes, but few with its own scribes, and even fewer with unbiased observers. All that one can say is that for many individuals in many communities, the Rising made sense—but not necessarily for the same reason that it did for people in other communities. Thus the southern Catholics and northern Protestants who came out against the government may not have been fighting the same war, even if they were for a time fighting the same foes.

On 7 June 1798, most of the men of Ballycarry ("to a man" states the local tradition, written down in the 1830s) and many of the men of Islandmagee mustered before Redhall, one of the two large gentry residences in the vicinity.[67] The Islandmagee and Ballycarry men who assembled in front of Redhall knew that the owner, R. G. Ker, Esq., had a supply of firearms. Ker himself had fled, leaving his butler in charge. The rebels forced their way into the house, but when they reached the gunroom found that Ker had removed the firing devices from the arms. Nevertheless, caught up in the martial spirit, many of the rebels shouldered the worthless guns, and these, together with pikes, scythes, pitchforks, makeshift swords, and a few firearms in working order, made up their arsenal. They marched off toward a general muster in Antrim town in fine spirits, because shortly before leaving they had heard the (false) news that Carrickfergus had fallen to their compatriots.

Soon a pattern emerged that was to run through the entire affair: the propensity for prudential disappearance by large numbers of allegedly stalwart rebels. Desertion took many forms. Some rebels stopped by the wayside ostensibly to rest from their night's labors. Others went behind a hedge to answer a call of nature, while still others stopped for provisions—but whatever their methods, by the time the force reached Ballyclare, en route to Antrim, a large number already had deserted. Bitterly, Ballycarry's James Orr later described the scene as leaders and followers matched each other's shamming:

> Now *Leaders*, laith to lea the rigs
> Whase leash they fear'd was broken,
> An' *Privates*, cursin' purse-proud prigs,
> Wha brought 'em balls to sloken;
> Repentant Painites at their pray'rs,
> An dastards crousely craikin',
> Move on, heroic, to the wars
> They mean na to partake in,
>   By night, or day.
> Some fastin' yet, now strave to eat
> The piece, that butter yellow'd;
> An' some, in flocks, drank out cream crocks,
> That wives but little valu'd:
> Some lettin' on their burn to mak',
> The rear-guard, goadin' hasten'd;
> Some hunk'rin' at a lee dyke back,
> Boost houghel on, ere fasten'd
>   Their breeks, that day.

Not surprisingly, the Islandmagee-Ballycarry contingent arrived too late for the battle. It already had been lost. With a few exceptions, the rebel forces scattered. In Orr's vitriolic phrase: "An' rush! the pale-fac'd randies / Took leg, that day."[68]

Yet, although the Ballycarry-Islandmagee rebels certainly were not military victors, neither were they great losers. What happened to the rebels? Sensibly, the military authorities pardoned all those who surrendered their arms, with the exceptions of the leaders, including the weaver-poet James Orr. Of these, none were executed and James Orr, having spent a few years in the United States, returned to become, once again, the recording angel of his community.

How widespread enthusiasm for the 1798 Rising actually was among the Presbyterians of Ulster has long vexed historians and so too have the motives behind the Rising.[69] As far as Ballycarry-Islandmagee is concerned, it is best simply to note that it was easy for a Presbyterian people, living in a rural, ethnically segregated and culturally homogeneous community, to view events in the surrounding world—economic, social, and military—as a threat to their conventional world. In Ballyclare, about twenty kilometers from Ballycarry, in May 1795 a speaker at a radical political gathering had used an analogy that hit home. He compared British policy toward Ireland to Pharaoh's forcing the Israelites to make bricks without straw. "The time of Deliverance is come," he claimed. "A Mighty Salvation is sprung up in France."[70]

(6)

The rhetorical tone of the speaker in Ballyclare and his specific scriptural references draw attention to one aspect of the covenantal grid as embraced by the Ulster-Scots that thus far has gone unmentioned, namely, the prophetic tone that their belief system acquired.

The prophetic books of the Bible are infrequently read in their entirety today, despite their vivid images and arresting turns of phrase. To modern ears the voices are, as one distinguished scholar, Abraham Heschel, has observed, "one octave too high." And, undeniably, some of the prophetic utterances seem to have been produced by men whose auditory and visual hallucinations were as demented as they were divine. Mental imbalance, according to our modern definitions, however, is no reason to reject an ancient prophet. "Ezekiel was one of the greatest spiritual figures of all time," adjudged William Foxwell Albright, one of the most gimlet-eyed of biblical scholars. This greatness was "in spite of his tendency to psychic abnormality—a tendency which he shares with many other spiritual leaders of mankind."[71]

In the history of the Hebrew people, and in the conceptual world of those peoples who later identified themselves with the children of Israel, the prophetic books of the Bible were a codicil to the covenant as articulated in the Pentateuch and associated works. That is, prophecy could only enlarge upon the meaning of the covenant, not alter any of its primary aspects.

In his seminal study of Hebrew prophets, Heschel defines the "classical era of prophecy" as the three centuries before the fall of Jerusalem in 587 B.C. This limits us to Amos, Hosea, Isaiah (chapters 1–39), Micah, Jeremiah, and Habakkuk.[72] However, we should not forget the existence of the minor prophets (Malachi, Haggai, Zephaniah, and others) who, though much cruder rhetorically than the prophets of the classical era, possessed a vigor all their own. Nor should one deny the importance of the text that is least characteristic of the Hebrew scriptures and which, indeed, is the only truly apocalyptic volume in the Hebrew canon, the book of Daniel. The minor prophets and the apocalyptic writings should be kept in mind because the two Gentile nations that most directly integrated into their own culture the Hebrews' covenantal grid—the Ulster Presbyterians and the Afrikaners—paid close mind to these writings.

As a codicil to the patriarchal covenant, the prophetic books operate within a narrow framework and in a fairly standard way. In the first place, the prophetic messages are designed to be unpopular with those at whom they are aimed. That is one sign of authenticity. Paradoxically, although biblical prophecy usually was aimed at a specific audience, the prophecies are for the most part generalizable. They can be applied not just to a specific segment of the Chosen People, but to other peoples and other kingdoms. Although the biblical prophecies were written down (obviously: they are part of the Bible), in the north of Ireland they became part of the oral culture. Adults heard the words of the various Hebrew prophets declaimed from the pulpit—the prophets make wonderful sermon texts—and they took the words home with them, back into a world of long hours of manual labor, of cottages with earthen floors, few windows, and only flickering oil lights during the long winter nights—and there the prophets' words acquired the quality of something that the Ulster-Scots actually had heard.

The message that they heard seemed to apply to their everyday life. For instance, the book of Amos begins with the prophet virtually boxing the compass as he names the peoples and places that Yahweh wants punished: Damascus, the house of Hazael, Tyrus, Edom, Teman, Ammon, Rabbah, Moab, and even Judah:

> Thus saith the Lord; For three transgressions of Judah and for four, I will not turn away *the punishment* thereof, because they have despised the law of the Lord, and have not kept his commandments, and their lies caused them to err, after the which their fathers have walked. (Amos 2:4)

Even Israel is to be punished:

> Thus saith the Lord; As the shepherd taketh out of the mouth of the lion two legs or a piece of an ear; so shall the children of Israel be taken out

that dwell in Samaria in the corner of a bed, and in Damascus *in* a couch. (Amos 3:12)

Such verses suggest that evil is all around, inside and outside of the community of the Chosen People. This is the message that is so easily applied by any Chosen People to their own situation.

All biblical prophecies involve not only denunciations but predictions. These are of three sorts. The first is purely negative: if the path of righteousness is not resumed, then disaster will follow.

Lo, I will bring a nation upon you from far, O house of Israel, saith the Lord: it *is* a mighty nation, it *is* an ancient nation, a nation whose language thou knowest not, neither understandest what they say.

Their quiver *is* as an open sepulchre, they *are* all mighty men.

And they shall eat up thine harvest, and thy bread, *which* thy sons and thy daughters should eat: they shall eat up thy flocks and thine herds; they shall eat up thy vines and thy fig trees: they shall impoverish thy fenced cities, wherein thou trustedst, with the sword. (Jer. 5:15–17)

The second form is positive. If the people who hear the prophecy follow the straight and narrow, at minimum the otherwise-inevitable disaster will not occur. On occasions, the prophet actually promises a direct blessing to the now-obedient people:

And the Lord will create upon every dwelling place a mount Zion, and upon her assemblies, a cloud and smoke by day, and the shining of a flaming fire by night: for upon all the glory *shall* be a defence.

And there shall be a tabernacle for a shadow in the daytime from the heat, and for a place of refuge, and for a covert from storm and from rain. (Isa. 4:5–6)

The third form of prediction is the apocalyptic form, found in full flower only in the book of Daniel, which probably dates from the Maccabean era, the mid-second century B.C. In imagery that at times seems to exceed human imagination, the book of Daniel makes one central point: the end of all human time is approaching and the corrupt present will be replaced by the shining future.

It frequently and correctly has been noted that the prophetic books of the Bible are signposts in the evolution of the Hebrew religion. Sometimes the product of this evolution is referred to as the invention of "ethical monotheism." The observation is valid, so long as one does not take it to an extreme and forget that the covenant, as articulated in the scriptures that discuss the patriarchal period, is a grid that cannot be modified very much without destroying its effectiveness. Thus, it is true that in the books of prophecy one sees evidence of a gradual transformation of the children of Israel from being holders of a monolatrous religion to adherents of a monotheistic faith. Yahweh, who in the patriarchal period is simply the greatest of many gods of the nations, by the book of Daniel has become the only god. Still, Yahweh is very much Israel's own ("the Holy One of Israel" as Isaiah acclaims him, 5:24). In any case, the evolution toward monotheism in the prophetic books is not a characteristic that in any way interfered with the assimilation of the prophetic messages by persons of a Calvinistic cast of mind. Calvinism, with its emphasis upon predestination, is about as far as one can go toward a single Cause and still be within the Christian rubrics.[73]

Although the prophets repeatedly denounce those who have failed to adhere to the law, there is a somewhat greater emphasis in the prophetic books than in the Pentateuch upon virtue as something distinct from mere correct practice. For example, in Isaiah, Yahweh is reported to be tired of mere ritual. "Your new moons and your appointed feasts my soul hateth: they are a trouble unto me; I am weary to bear *them*" (Isa. 1:14). In Micah, the spirit, rather than the letter, of the law is stressed:

> He hath shewed thee, O man, what *is* good; and what doth the Lord require of thee, but to do justly, and to love mercy, and to walk humbly with they God? (Mic. 6:8)

Such thoughts served to smooth out the covenant's harder edges, the extreme emphasis upon law and ritual behavior. Several verses in the prophets suggest that might and right are not related and that a nation should not rely upon physical force (see Isa. 29:19; Mic. 7:16; Zech. 4:6).

There is nothing in this gentling of the covenant's message that would have turned the Ulster-Scots away from their assimilation of the prophetic mode. The preaching of Jesus Christ, with its suggestion to scrap the law entirely and honor its true spirit, could easily be viewed as the logical extension of the spiritual evolution glimpsed in the prophets. Yet this gentling of the prophets is overemphasized in any case, often by those who are uncomfortable with the implications of the patriarchal covenant. And, in fact, for every mention in the prophets of the idea of fulfilling the spirit of the law, dozens of passages demand that it should be strictly upheld. For every instance that the equation of right and might are questioned in the prophets, there are scores of assertions of the patriarchal concept that right is tied to might. Indeed, the idea that the God of righteousness has the right to punish vice is the central idea behind all biblical prophecy: right makes might.

So the Ulster-Scots assimilated the prophetic mode as a codicil to the basic covenantal grid. In a world wherein they were surrounded by evil tribes and in which the central government—whether Dublin or London—was not to be trusted, the prophets spoke volumes. And they still do. That is why, in the sermon quoted at the beginning of this chapter, Reverend Ian R. K. Paisley was being neither antiquarian nor irrelevant when he took the seventh chapter of Micah as his text. It speaks.

Crucially, biblical prophecy not only is a set of specific denunciations and predictions, but it represents a way of using language and thus a way of determining thought. Accordingly, even though the belief in the concrete and direct applicability of biblical prophecy to the Ulster situation declined among the Ulster-Scots in the nineteenth and twentieth centuries (although thousands of devotees there try to find specific parallels to biblical prophecies, they are now a minority), the rhetorical mode of the Bible continues to have an impact. The voice that Ulster politicians have adopted from the 1820s onward (when the Catholic Emancipation campaign, a mass movement led by Daniel O'Connell, terrified them) is a prophetic one. It is no accident that Ulster politicians sound outlandish to the inhabitants of the rest of the British Isles. Their voices are too shrill, their warnings too stark, their vocabulary too vivid, their metaphors too rich. That is because the Ulster-Scot leaders' rhetoric is frequently in the prophetic mode: topological speech and a highly rubricated way of categorizing the social universe are their hallmarks. If the rest of the British Isles listens with slight bewilderment, the Ulster-Scots constituency understands and responds, as much to the *mode* of address as to the actual substantive content. Such is the power of the prophetic voice.

(7)

It is a great paradox about biblical prophecy and, equally, about the Ulster-Scots rhetorical tradition based upon it, that although prophecy deals with the future, it cannot do so creditably unless the prophet spends most of his time talking about the past. It is only after an agreed past has been established and after the symbolic and mythic embodiments of that past have been defined, that a prophet is able to bring his audience with him into the world of the future. Prophetic discourse in the north of Ireland developed certain accepted symbols and myths, and, only after ritually invoking several of these references to the Ulster-Scots past are politicians in the north of Ireland free to talk about their own vision of the future. Stump speeches in Ulster frequently begin at 1641 or at 1690, dates which have such great resonance that mere mention of them is enough to bond an audience.

Of the several symbols and myths established over the years by the Ulster-Scots, the least articulated—because it has been the best understood—has been the land. Steve Bruce, in his brilliant study of present-day Paisleyism, has pointed out that even in the industrial era the heartland of the Ulster mind has been the small farming community:

> Small farmers developed a strong sentimental attachment to the land which is both home and source of income. Where, like the children of Israel, farmers suppose that God gave them the land and let them prosper because they served him faithfully, people link their religion, sense of place, and ethnic identity into a strong attachment to the past.[74]

Most of the Ulster-Scots myths are tied to the land in some way. (I use the term "myth" not to mean an untrue set of views about historical events, but views of the past that take on extraempirical meaning, by virtue of being closely related to the society's views of its collective identity and its special, virtually divine, origin.) Like the deliverance myths in the Hebrew scriptures, these deliverance myths are almost always associated with specific topographical references. "Topography is the key to the Ulster conflict," A. T. Q. Stewart has observed. "Unless you know exactly who lives where, and why, much of it does not make sense. . . . Ulster's troubles arise from the fact that people who live there know this information to the square inch, while strangers know nothing of it."[75] This marrying of specific physical sites with deliverance myths is seen clearly in the story of the siege of Londonderry or, if one prefers, "Derry," in 1689. The siege narrative begins on 7 December 1688 (O.S.) when a group of apprentice boys shut the city's gates in the face of a Jacobite regiment. In the Presbyterian view, King James II of England was a major danger to religious liberty in general and to Presbyterianism in particular, since he was a Roman Catholic and an absolutist monarch. Thus, the Jacobite siege easily can be interpreted as an instance of a virtuous people holding out against a prince of darkness. The actual "siege of Derry" did not begin until 18 April when King James himself was refused entry to the city. So began a time marked by great privation on the part of the defenders of Derry (dogs, cats, tallow, and hides were, in their turn, the only food remaining in the city) and of great hardihood. According to one account, the starving Ulster-Scots resolved, rather than surrender, to eat the Irish soldiers that they killed. So it went until 28 July (O.S.) when ships of King William of Orange (the new Protestant king of England and Ireland) broke through to Derry by way of the River Foyle and saved the faithful defenders.[76] This piece of history makes a perfect myth. It is dramatic in itself and it has a very clear sacred-profane structure.

Moreover, the siege is a reusable template. Oliver MacDonagh has argued that the siege of Derry is the original and most powerful of Protestant myths in Ireland, for it allows the Protestants to see themselves "as an embattled and enduring people."[77] To this observation, Terence Brown adds that "this primal sense of siege has, like nationalist historiography, been infused with millennialism (the assaults may be endless but faith must recurrently be placed in the powers of some eschatalogically prescient prophet)." And as Brown points out, the siege mentality" draws also on a dour blend of the Calvinistic doctrine of election with a Whiggish commitment to a liberty which can only be enjoyed by those possessed of the true faith."[78] In Ulster-Scots thought, there arise dozens of little Derrys. These local deliverance myths reveal how, in smaller battles, some of which were no more than local gang fights, the Chosen People were delivered from their savage native foes. This reliance on an archetypal deliverance myth may sound strange to foreign ears, but is a crucial part of the Ulster-Scots culture.

The other great deliverance, second only to the siege of Derry, involves the image of the king on the white horse. On 1 July 1690 (O.S.), King James II was defeated by William of Orange at the Battle of the Boyne. This marked the end of the Jacobite danger to the Ulster Protestants (James sailed for France three days after the fight), although several secondary battles remained to be fought. Although the Battle of the Boyne was no great military setpiece, it lent itself to striking iconography: in the north of Ireland, it is still common in Protestant districts to see, in large murals painted on the end of rowhouses, a monarch on a white horse leading a victorious army. For the past century the annual marches of the

Orange Order through small towns and through city streets often feature the figure of King William on the banners that precede the marching brethren of each lodge.

King William's status as a primary symbol is not a new development. In the 1790s, an observant Frenchman, the Chevalier de La Tocnaye, traveled throughout Ireland and recorded his impressions. Here is his description of one Ulster town:

> Enniskillen is a pretty little town, situated on an island formed by the great Lough Earne, in a place where it narrows and forms a river of rapid current. This lake is the longest in Ireland, . . . nearly forty miles long, and at many places is from ten to twelve miles wide.
>
> This town boasts of its attachment to King William; it sustained a siege against his father-in-law. I saw on the gate this inscription, which had been placed there recently: "THE GLORIOUS MEMORY OF THE FIRST OF JULY." I do not like these memorials, they serve but to humiliate and anger the vanquished—that is to say, not those who are really wrong, but who happen to be the weakest; it would be more generous and more politic to let the past be the past.[79]

De La Tocnaye was perhaps right philosophically—letting the past become the past in most cases makes for a more peaceful future—but he was unrealistically romantic if he believed that a covenantal culture could ever forget. Covenantal cultures cannot survive without their sense of the past. God's covenant with a Chosen People is defined in certain specific historical moments and if an elect people forgets its past, then it is rejecting the covenant. In preserving their deliverance myths, the Ulster-Scots were doing exactly as the Hebrew scriptures had taught them: preserve the past, or there will be no future.

Two other sets of historical myths are central to the Ulster-Scots prophetic mindset. These are, first, traditions that present the Presbyterian of Ulster as a persecuted minority, and, second, a series of revenge myths.

Of course, British and continental Protestantism already had a rich tradition of martyrology. Woodcuts depicting unflinching Reformers going to their deaths were a standard item in seventeenth- and eighteenth-century Protestant literature. Among the Ulster-Scots, there has long been a tradition of remembering martyrs who died virtuously defending either their religious faith or the freedom of the civil polity. The classic set of events in Ulster-Scots martyrology occurred in 1641–42. In October 1641, a large-scale civil war broke out in Ulster, initiated by the massacre of thousands of Protestants in a conspiracy brought off by the Irish Catholic natives. How many Protestants were killed has long been a matter of conjecture (the impossibly high number of 154,000 was alleged at the time), but certainly several thousand were killed.[80]

These lives were not lost in a military campaign, but in a primitive uprising on the part of the native Irish; Protestant women and children as well as civilian men were killed. In many cases, the Protestant victims were tortured and otherwise abused before being put to death.

Within the Ulster-Scots frame of reference, these victims were martyrs, individuals whose blood had been shed as part of the collective effort to redeem the Promised Land. Immediately, locale by locale, a vivid folklore emerged. Much of this material was collected by governmental investigators after the massacre, and this information became the basic material for a myriad of books on the martyrdom which, in turn, spread the folklore throughout the Presbyterian north. The skein of folk mythology that emerged was riveting and, often, revolting in detail; all of it implicitly made the point that the elect, the Chosen People of Ulster, had suffered mightily at the hands of the evil surrounding tribes. One gains an idea of the influence of this material in J. L. Porter's nineteenth-century life of Henry Cooke, the most powerful figure in Ulster Presbyterianism in the last century (and, many would say, ever). Cook's mother, Porter tells us, "was a woman of remarkable energy and decision of character. She had an insatiable thirst for knowledge, and a memory of extraordinary tenacity. Proud of the struggle of her forefathers in defence of faith and freedom, she never forgot fact or legend connected with their history in Scotland and Ulster. Stories of war and rapine, of flight and defence, were transmitted orally in families from generation to generation."[81]

The impressive point is how long and strong this tradition was. For example, Ernest W. Hamilton, member of parliament for North Tyrone from 1885 to 1892, a staunch anti-Catholic but not a rabid controversialist, produced a book called *The Soul of Ulster,* which included most of the fundamental historical myths of the Ulster-Scots. In 1917, while a major European conflict was occurring, Hamilton's successful book (it was in its second edition) told the Ulster-Scots about real war. He quoted a letter read in the English parliament in December 1641:

All I can tell you is the miserable state we continue under, for the rebels daily increase in men and munition in all parts, except the province of Munster, exercising all manner of cruelties, and striving who can be most barbarously exquisite in tormenting the poor Protestants, cutting

off their ears, fingers and hands, plucking out their eyes, boiling the
hands of little children before their mothers' faces, stripping women
naked and ripping them up.[82]

That was real war, holy war. And as Hamilton wrote in a preface to a
book he published in 1920 on the Irish rebellion of the seventeenth century, "The 1641 massacres are no greater slur on the Irish nation than the
Reign of Terror is on the French nation or Bolshevism on Russia as a
whole. All three represent the temporary ascendancy of the brute element."[83] In point of fact, Hamilton's writings were very moderate by the
standards of Presbyterian martyr literature. They bear note chiefly because they were produced as successful commercial ventures in the twentieth century and indicate the continuing market for this traditional material.[84]

The other important sort of myth that the Ulster-Scots historical memory has kept alive consists of vengeance tales. Unashamedly direct and not
buffered by anything in the way of higher purposes, these tales were much
less likely than any other of the types of myths to find their way into print.
They were very satisfying fireside stories, however, for a people surrounded by enemies. When the vengeance myths entered the public media
it was usually in the form of ballads or in ephemeral literature, such as
tracts and chapbooks. There is, of course, a strong biblical genre of vengeance stories. Of the Ulster-Scots vengeance tales, one will suffice as an
example. It comes from Islandmagee, County Antrim, one of the two
communities where (as discussed earlier) Presbyterianism was first established. According to an Islandmagee oral tradition, in January 1642
(N.S.), in the mist of the then-flaring civil war, the Roman Catholic inhabitants of Islandmagee, already a beleaguered minority, were all thrown
over seaside cliffs, and they crashed to their deaths on the rocks and
shingle beach below. The oral tradition concerning this event went so far
as to suggest that 3,000 Catholics were killed in this way.

Now, the intriguing part of the tradition of this massacre is not that it
was preserved and embroidered by the heirs of the victims (as is usual in
cases of persecution), but by the heirs of the perpetrators. The Islandmagee people kept alive the tradition (the Ordnance surveyor recorded it in the 1830s), and it was assimilated into an Orange folksong
that was alive at mid-twentieth century ("and the Fenians' blood ran
down like water, from Belfast Lough, right to the Irish Sea"). This becomes even more striking when one realizes that in fact the cliffs massacre

at Islandmagee was false historically both in detail and in structure. In the early nineteenth century, the great Ulster antiquary Samuel McSkimin patiently demolished the story: no Catholics were marched over the cliffs and, at most, fifty Catholics were killed in what was one small chapter of the then-widespread civil war between Protestants and Catholics. Later historians have been at pains to disprove the traditional tale and to put the story into proper perspective, but to little effect.[85] I suspect that the reason the tale lived on (as was the case for many similar stories in myriad Ulster-Scots locales) is that, first, it satisfied the need for vengeance felt by any society that finds its world a combat zone. Second, this particular type of revenge tale (not only defeating the Catholics but purging them from the land), fits a very deeply grooved biblical template. It involves purifying the land by removing the remnant of the heathen peoples who previously had held the land. The march of Joshua through the land of Canaan, and his utter destruction of most of the previous inhabitants, was a model familiar to Bible readers, such as the Ulster-Scots. Thus, even vengeance became a sanctioned and sanctified act.

One striking characteristic of the various Ulster-Scots historical myths is how well they fit together as interlocking components of a worldview, one which, moreover, was congruent with the covenantal outlook they derived from the Hebrew scriptures. The adamantine immovability of the Ulster-Scots, so maddening to opponents, so unfathomable to outsiders, in large part derives from their historical experience (as enhulled in their myths), and fits perfectly with their presuppositions about the nature of religious truth, as derived from the Hebrew covenant.

Further, in adopting for much of their public discourse the biblical prophetic mode, the Ulster-Scots employed the perfect rhetorical vehicle for the expression of the union of religious beliefs and collective historical experience. Of course the prophetic mode cannot be used all the time, if for no other reason than that it is tiring, but at moments of crisis, political and religious leaders can adopt the prophetic mode, and their audiences will respond. They always have.

And, equally important, the power of this Ulster-Scots rhetorical mode has remained, only slightly diminished, after most of Ulster society has stopped paying much attention to religious matters in their narrow sense. So deeply embedded is the covenantal wiring in the culture, that even agnostics and atheists among the Ulster-Scots respond to political rhetoric that sounds less like modern political oratory than like the words of Micah or Isaiah.

(8)

What I have just suggested may seem to be academic suicide. As a specialist in nineteenth- and twentieth-century history, I should be arguing that everything important in the world happened after Waterloo. But it did not, certainly not in Ulster. Even after reading nearly all of the scholarly literature on industrialization, urbanization, modernization, and consequent cultural shifts in the north of Ireland, I am impressed with how little fundamental matters changed. Indeed, many of the major societal shifts of the nineteenth and twentieth centuries reinforced, rather than undercut, the Ulster-Scots cultural matrix that had been formed in the seventeenth and eighteenth centuries.

As an example, take industrialization. The common model throughout western European history suggests that the development of an economically specialized, capitalist economy acts to destroy traditional social structures and to replace familial, tribal, and religious allegiances with those of social class. To a small degree, this happened in the north of Ireland (there are trade unions in Ulster, and a labor party has garnered the odd legislative seat over the years), but mostly the influence was in the other direction: industrialization and its attendant forces actually reinforced traditional social structures. This occurred because the north of Ireland, and especially the region around Belfast, was the only part of Ireland to join the world of the British industrial revolution of the nineteenth century. The rest of Ireland remained precapitalist in parts and overwhelmingly agricultural throughout. Thus, there arose an obvious distinction between what Ulster-Scots perceived as the backward and lazy south, the land of the Irish Catholic natives, and their own hard-working, risk-taking, entrepreneurial north. Therefore, the very fact of the industrialization of the northeastern corner of Ireland confirmed the worldview of a people who made very strong tribal and sacred-profane distinctions. This is not a *post hoc* observation: in the years 1912–20, the Protestants of Ulster were violently opposed to their inclusion in an independent Ireland, and in part it was because they believed that they would become the national dray oxen, pulling along the allegedly indolent southern Catholics.[86]

Second, the nature of the urbanization that accompanied the growth of industry in Ulster did not force any change of beliefs: quite the opposite. Urbanization was less abrupt in the north of Ireland than in the rest of the British Isles and, to this day northern Ireland is more rural than is most of the rest of the United Kingdom, but that is not the point. The point is that when the working class in Ulster settled in urban areas, they did so in ethnic enclaves: not quite ghettos, but almost. If, as noted earlier, the prototypical Ulster town was a walled site, now the large cities (Belfast and Londonderry in particular) became cities with internal walls; religion, more than social class, determined neighborhoods.[87]

And, third, serious erosion of ethnic loyalties by class allegiances was precluded by the fact that the spoils of industrialization (jobs, licenses, building permits, and so on) were allocated on a tribal basis. So, instead of identifying their interests with those of Catholic laborers, persons of the Protestant working class were allegiant to their Protestant betters. If an Ulster-Scot could sit in the same church as his foreman, or better yet his factory owner, it was a better form of job security than attending a union meeting with some Catholic riffraff who were competing for the same job; at least so it seemed.[88]

In making these observations, I am not denying that a complex process of change occurred, which historians frequently call "modernization." Nor do I deny that this process affected the society of northern Ireland.[89] Modernization theory (of which there are several variants) is usually posed as an alternative to structural Marxism; yet it works the same way. It presumes that changes in certain fundamental matters (what Marxists in metaphor call "substructure") determine the shape of important aspects of the society (social groups and so on) and eventually determine to a large degree cultural matters ("superstructure"). This sort of schema, in both its Marxist and modernization modes, is quite sensible for most western societies, because it makes culture (in the broadest sense) a dependent variable. In fact, the vexing and amazing characteristic of Ulster-Scots culture is that in the age of modernization it for the most part acted as a force external to, and independent of, the "fundamental" forces that are supposed to buffet it around. Of course changes occurred, but the supposedly revolutionary changes in economics, technology, and social life that took place in the nineteenth and early twentieth centuries only changed the surface vocabulary of the Ulster-Scots culture, and modified the fundamental wiring hardly at all. Indeed, one can argue that the Ulster-Scots conceptual grid had more effect upon modernization than the other way around—in the sense that instead of the Ulster-Scots mindset being forced into the conceptual outlook of the modern industrial world, the Ulster-Scots were able to subordinate most of the complex changes involved in modernization to their own conceptual system.

This point needs to be underscored, for it implies something that holds for each of the three covenantal cultures discussed in this book, Ulster,

South Africa, and Israel: namely, that if one looks at these societies through the lenses that professional historians of today usually have closest to hand, the picture will be strongly distorted. Unlike most societies, covenantal cultures stand traditional historical modes of analysis on end. That is, the social patterns that these societies assume are only tertiarily influenced by economics and are much more determined by belief. In these parts of the world, mind literally overcomes matter.

(9)

Changes, important ones, came to Ulster-Scots covenantal culture, but for the most part they were not shifts derived directly from economic and social factors. Two cultural shifts within the Ulster-Scots cosmology took place simultaneously in the nineteenth century.

One of these was a closing of the distance between the Church of Ireland (the Anglicans) and the Presbyterians. In considerable part this was a purely ideological development. As Peter Brooke has demonstrated, the leading forces in Irish Presbyterianism, and particularly Henry Cooke, its most powerful clergyman, became committed to the concept of some sort of Protestant union. To some, this meant formally merging the two main Protestant churches; to others, it implied not formal union, but simply working together on matters of common interest. The spur for this development was the growing power of the Roman Catholic Church which was recovering rapidly from its disarray during the penal code era of the eighteenth century.[90] The Presbyterian-Anglican rapprochement was not as swift as it might have been, as the Presbyterians in the early nineteenth century still encountered several reminders of the way that the advocates of Episcopacy had treated them in the eighteenth century. Most irritating, however, was the simple fact that the Church of Ireland, by virtue of its being an established church, received greater privileges than did the Presbyterian Church. On this matter, the Presbyterians were in a delicate position, because they wanted their own relative deprivation to stop, but they were not so keen on losing an annual governmental sum given to them for clergy stipends. Many of the Presbyterian leaders were sensitive to the need to subordinate tactics to strategic goals: they did not wish to undercut the position of Protestantism, in the general sense. William Ewart Gladstone, in a measure that rendered the subtleties of Presbyterian strategy an irrelevancy, swept away the privileges of the Anglican Church and from the beginning of 1871 the Anglican Church, like the Presbyterian and the Roman Catholic churches, became a voluntary religious body.[91] From that point onward, nothing really inhibited an alliance of Ulster's two leading Protestant denominations and, as Irish Catholicism and nationalism grew stronger, this Protestant alliance became even firmer.

Simultaneously, the Presbyterians during the nineteenth century became continually more "evangelical." This is a vague term, potentially misleading. Shorn of its late twentieth-century connotations that have come from present-day American "bastard evangelicalism," the term "evangelical" in the 1800s meant that to be "saved," to undergo a sharp conversion experience, implied the abandonment of belief in the need for a disciplined religious polity. Instead, evangelicalism in the British Isles affected all the Protestant churches. In Ireland, it influenced not only the Presbyterians but also the very liturgically disciplined Church of Ireland.[92] Evangelicalism's fruits in Ireland were, first, a greater level of adhesion to existing church organizations as individuals were encouraged to take their religion more seriously and, second, the creation of a wide set of pan-Protestant organizations: Sunday school groups, tract publishers, and so on. These societies were aimed in part at shoring up the faith of the Protestant working class, but also at converting Roman Catholics.

This latter emphasis was new, and it hints at something important about Ulster society. Although it is a commonplace in North American and English historical literature to argue that evangelicalism is a sign of a disrupted and unstable culture that is undergoing stress,[93] in fact a sharply opposite hypothesis better fits the Ulster situation. As Steve Bruce suggests, the Presbyterian settlers only became committed to converting the natives "once their own ethnic identity had become secured and once other differences between competing populations had become firmly established."[94] Certainly, the two conflicting hypotheses cannot be sorted out fully here, but what must be understood is that the rise of evangelicalism in *its Ulster form* should not be taken as an indication of any weakening of the underlying cultural structure of the Ulster-Scots. Instead, it can justifiably be seen as an assertion in a new form of the aggressiveness and vigor of the Ulster-Scots culture.

One reason Ulster evangelicalism is sometimes wrongly read as an indication of social anomie is that it had one flashy moment, the revival of 1859. That event produced a series of sensational anecdotes about various forms of spiritual possession.[95] The 1859 revival probably most affected Presbyterians, but it penetrated all Ulster Protestant denominations, including Methodists and Anglicans.[96] Yet, the striking quality of the revival should not blind one to its near uniqueness. The only other time a mass revival was experienced in Ulster was the so-called Six Mile Water Revival of the 1620s, and there has been no similar experience since 1859.[97] The authorities of the Presbyterian Church neither denounced the revival as a threat to their religious leadership nor did they embrace it, as they would have done had the Presbyterian Church needed to shore up slipping flocks. Instead, the General Assembly of the Presbyterian Church passed a series of resolutions that indicated thankfulness to God for pouring out his spirit, but which warned against extremes. One of the General Assembly resolutions read as follows:

> While the Assembly leaves to ministers to deal in Christian wisdom with individual cases as they arise, the brethern are earnestly reminded of the necessity of guarding, on the one hand, against cherishing undue suspicions of the reality of the work of the Holy Spirit; and on the other, of adopting any course of procedure whereby our people may be led to mistake bodily impressions, or even convictions of sin, for genuine conversion to God.[98]

That is not the voice of a church in trouble, but the calm and confident voice of clergy and lay leaders who knew that however quickly flowed God's river in spate, they, their church, and its attendant demotic culture, would remain.

The change that was occurring in Presbyterianism in Ulster in the nineteenth century has been aptly captured in Peter Brooke's phrase "from Presbyterian to Protestant."[99] Nevertheless, one should not (as Brooke does) view this phenomenon as an indication of the decline of Presbyterianism; rather it demonstrates the dispersion of Ulster-Scots cultural values throughout the entire Protestant population. Granted, during this period, the clergy of the Presbyterian Church lost their role as intellectual leaders of the Ulster-Scots communities, but the Ulster-Scots never had placed clergymen on a pedestal, so in fact the rise of laymen as intellectual leaders was easily accommodated. Granted, also, the edges of the Ulster-Scots communities blurred as new urban communities arose in which Protestant groups were thoroughly intermixed, and as the various irritants that previously had kept Presbyterians and Anglicans apart disappeared. What can easily be missed, however, is that the Ulster-Scots culture was not retreating, much less disappearing. Rather, it was diffusing throughout the larger Protestant community.

Protestants in Ulster who were of English origin and Anglican religion increasingly came under the sway of an Ulster-Scots cultural hegemony. It is no accident that when the Protestants of the north of Ireland were mobilized in 1912, they responded in overwhelming numbers, Anglicans, Methodists, and Presbyterians, to the "Ulster Covenant." They reacted as if touched at some Pavlovian level by a stimulus that they did not recognize consciously, but perceived instinctively. Covenanting was not a vibrant strain in Anglican or Methodist historical experience, so why did the whole Protestant population of Ulster respond to this Ulster-Scots symbol? It was because the entire Ulster Protestant population had, on fundamental matters, come to accept the conceptual framework of the Ulster-Scots.

It is true that one aspect of the standard conceptualization of modernization affected the Ulster-Scots culture in the last century. This was the increasing institutionalization of many activities that had previously been embedded in folk practice. Schooling became increasingly formal; social discipline was enforced less and less frequently by church courts and more often by professional agents of law and order; the responsibility for caring for the weak, sick, and elderly increasingly became a state responsibility. But, once again, an irony arises, for the Presbyterians were successful in gaining control in many locales of these institutions and thus of bending modern state institutions to their own template. In the crucial matter of mass education, for example, they fought the founders of the Irish system of national education and succeeded in gaining control of elementary schools in Presbyterian areas.[100]

I think that a case can be made that the Ulster-Scots were more anti-Catholic at the end of the nineteenth century than at the beginning— largely because of the forces of modernization (which, recall, are supposed to reduce, not increase, tribal loyalties). Perpetual urban rioting, which began in Belfast in the 1850s, for example, actually sharpened the anti-Catholicism of the Ulster-Scots, who before industrialization had lived mostly in rural areas, some of which had few Catholics, and no one of which had the huge frictional Catholic-Protestant interface that Belfast possessed. Equally, the rise of nationalist politics in the nineteenth century, which accompanied the escape of the Irish Catholic majority from the agricultural subsistence world and its entry into capitalist agriculture, brought about a reaction in Ulster much stronger than anything that had occurred since 1690. Ultimately, Ulster became the small state called "Northern Ireland" because the Protestants of the north refused to live within the borders of a Catholic state and were willing to go to war to prevent such an occurrence.

Whether or not the Protestants of Ulster were right or wrong in their political decisions is not here to be debated. What is clear is that one of the fruits of "modernization," nationalism (in this case Irish Catholic nationalism) reinforced a particular sense of identity among the Protestant population of Ulster, the cultural and political leaders of whom were preponderantly Presbyterian in religious heritage and Ulster-Scots in ethnicity. The state that, by a series of bizarre ironies, emerged in the north of Ireland in 1920 was a devolved government under the watchful eye of the London authorities. That state—Northern Ireland—was a semisacralized entity. It was founded morally on the terms of the Ulster Covenant, and pragmatically on the promise that it would be a Protestant state for a Protestant people, a Chosen People.

5

Zionism and the Land of Israel to 1948

(1)

"It is debatable whether there is a history of Zionism beyond 1948," Walter Laqueur wrote.[1] Zionism of course has many definitions, but, as Laqueur implies, it is most useful to view it as the preparation for the emergence of the state of Israel. Once that state was in existence, an entire national culture was created. Although titular Zionist organizations continue to exist, their role changed radically after 1948. No longer did they follow the pillar of cloud by day and the pillar of fire by night; now they supported a geographically defined and geopolitically specific Zion.

Because the emergence of the modern state of Israel is so dramatic—it rises from beneath the seas of world politics like a giant underwater Krakatau—there is a great danger of describing its creation as the result of forces that were unseen at the time, but now are obvious to the omniscience of historians. Indeed, because so many of the historians of Israel have been bonded religiously or culturally to the new state, the emergence of Israel often takes on a teleological aspect. In contrast, I am struck with how improbable and attenuated were the contingent series of events that eventually produced the Israeli state and how unlikely one would have been to predict the actual course of events if one had taken a stance, say, at the beginning of World War I.[2]

More than is the case with most nations, the creation of Israel is full of ironies. Not the least of these is that until the late 1930s most people of the Jewish diaspora were unresponsive to the conception of the land of Israel as a functioning state, and the great majority of religious Jews were opposed. Within the context of this book, an obvious irony is that although the state of Israel eventually evolved into a covenantal state, this development was decades behind similar developments among the Ulster Presbyterians and the Afrikaners. That, though, is only natural, for paradoxically, until the late nineteenth century, enthusiasm for the creation of a Jewish homeland in the ancient Middle East was more widespread among Bible-reading Protestants—especially those of the British Isles—than among diaspora Jewry. And not only Protestants. In 1799 Napoleon Bonaparte (hardly a Bible-reading Protestant) tried to rally support for his military ventures by proposing a Jewish state. "Rightful Heirs of Palestine!" he proclaimed, "Hasten! Now is the moment which may not return for thousands of years, to claim the restoration of your rights among the population of the universe which has been shamefully withheld from you for thousands of years, your political existence as a nation among the nations."[3]

To be sure, even before the word "Zionism" came into favor in the 1880s, there were Jewish theorists of nationality, such as Heinrich Graetz, Moses Hess, Peretz Smolenskin, and Moshe Leib Lilienblum.[4] Their arguments for the existence of a Jewish nationality laid the groundwork for what eventually became Zionism and this holds true whether one sees Jewish nationalism as the revival of ancient Hebrew tribalism or, as Amos Elon suggests, as a Jewish imitation of the various nationalisms that swept Eastern Europe in the second half of the nineteenth century.[5]

This brings us face to face with a strange aspect of the conventional (indeed, virtually official) history of Zionism, namely that the First Aliyah (that is, the first wave of immigrants) began in 1882 and was East European in origin. Actually, modern scholarship has established that there was significant immigration into Eretz Israel (the land of Israel) from the middle of the eighteenth century onward. But these immigrants did not become part of the eventual Israeli establishment: they were Moroccan and Italian Jews, who arrived in the summer of 1741, Hassidim who first arrived in 1746 and kept trickling in thereafter, and Yemenite Jews who caravaned into Eretz Israel in 1882 before the officially recognized First Aliyah began.[6] Further, because of the tension (not to say hatred) that emerged between Jews in Palestine and the British authorities in the mandate in the 1930s and 1940s, the fact that British efforts between 1827 and 1839 increased the Jewish population of Jerusalem by ten times (from about 550 to 5,500) is usually ignored. (This effort was stimulated by the belief that the return of the Jews to Jerusalem would hasten the Second Coming of Jesus Christ.)[7]

Yet no matter when one places the beginning of Zionism—1741, 1746, 1827, or 1882—its success still is an improbable phenomenon. Some circumstances, however, were favorable. For example, from the late eighteenth through the nineteenth century, the European portions of diaspora Jewry (roughly, the Ashkenazim), underwent the first element in the equation called the "European demographic transition." From about 1780 to about 1914, social and family structures characterized by high birth rates and almost equally high death rates changed to the present-day Western European situation, with low birth and death rates. Ashkenazi Jewry, however, experienced the sharply declining death rates (due mostly to improved health measures), but their birth rates remained high instead of falling. As a result, Ashkenazi numbers grew rapidly, from approximately 2 million in 1800 to 7 million in 1880. In contrast, the other major segment of diaspora Jewry, the Sephardim, concentrated in the most economically backward portions of the Mediterranean basin and in parts of Africa and Asia, did not experience any part of this demographic transition. Thus, their numbers only grew from one-half a million in 1800 to approximately three-quarters of a million in 1880. The Ashkenazi population explosion continued right up to World War I, when there were roughly 13 million Jews in the world, overwhelmingly Ashkenazi.[8]

During the nineteenth century, European governments engaged in (but in most cases never completed) a process that is usually called "Jewish emancipation." What emancipation meant varied greatly from country to country, and ranged from the reduction (and in some cases the removal) of restrictions on Jewish entry into the professions, reduction or abolition of residential segregation, and granting the right to vote and to sit in civil legislative assemblies. The emancipation process was very uneven and although legal barriers were reduced, social prejudices continued to restrict enjoyment of basic civil liberties. Nevertheless, in many European countries, Jews as a group became much more outward-looking and active in the political life of their respective countries, and they benefited materially from this aspect of nineteenth-century European liberalism.

Concurrent with the reduction of restrictions on Jews in several European countries, European Jewry itself changed. The usual term for this is "secularization" and reference often is made to the late eighteenth- and nineteenth-century Jewish equivalent of the European Enlightenment of the eighteenth century. Intellectual and social energies that previously had been enclosed within the rabbinic tradition now burst forth and produced a virtual Jewish cultural renaissance in Western Europe. As was the case of emancipation, the process of cultural vitalization had its lag-and-lead sectors, with Jews in the Germanies being the van.

Lagging far behind Europe as far as the Jews were concerned was Russia. In the last quarter of the nineteenth century, about 5 million Jews were under czarist rule.[9] They were limited to the "Pale of settlement" which ran between the Black Sea and the Baltic. Russian policy during the nineteenth century vacillated wildly, from active persecution to semi-toleration, but always it was unpredictable. The lives of the individual Jews, lodged in *shtetlen*, villages and regional market centers that often were mostly Jewish and Yiddish-speaking, were not necessarily terrible, but they were fundamentally insecure.[10] The vulnerability of Russian Jewry—which is to say, of most of the world's Jewish population—became clear in 1881 when a series of pogroms began. Mobs, tolerated by the police (and in some cases incited by them) burned and plundered Jewish settlements. Uncounted murders took place, and thereafter new anti-Semitic laws were introduced. Jews in the tens of thousands were forced to move as the Pale was redefined. Right up to the Russian Revolution of 1917, Russian Jewry was continuously persecuted.

The immediate result was a massive exodus not only from Russia but from nearby East European countries. This exodus totally redrew the map of the Jewish diaspora, for it is estimated that between 1882 and 1914, nearly 3 million Jews emigrated from Russia alone.[11]

This exodus brought some Russian and East European Jews to the land of Israel. They are memorialized in the historical canon as the First Aliyah (1882–1904) and Second Aliyah (1904–14). Between 1882 and 1918, the Jewish population of what was then Palestine rose to 60,000.[12] This is not an insignificant number, but if one considers that in the same period nearly 3 million emigrants left Russia (plus others from Eastern Europe and Germany) it is clear that at most only about 1 percent of the exodus saw Eretz Israel as a homeland. Most went to a Promised Land, indeed, but that land was the United States of America.

Although there is something of a "golden age" myth about Jewish settlements in Palestine under the Ottoman empire (that is, before 1917), recent research has shown that there was strong Arab antagonism to such settlements and life was anything but easy. From 1882 onward, Jewish entry was restricted into Palestine (very inefficiently enforced by Ottoman officials, to be sure) and from 1892 onward, Jewish land purchase was limited. During the decade before the First World War, Arab objections to Jewish immigration became more focused. Some objections stemmed from local patriotism that defined Palestine as only for Arabs. At a higher level of abstraction, Arab leaders began to understand that the Jews eventually intended to have a state of their own. Even if this state were comprehended within a larger entity (such as the Ottoman empire), they realized that the Jews would not be loyal to an Arab and Islamic empire.[13] Even though the inefficiency of the tottering Ottoman empire made possible Jewish immigration into Palestine and the Jews' acquisition of land and the creation of their own communities, the difficulties of the early years should not be ignored. The years 1882–1917 were just as fraught with tension as the post 1917-era. In fact, as one scholar has noted, "Every bit of land which passed into the control of the Jews, at least until 1947, was in the possession of someone else before they acquired it, and in order to transfer the land to Jewish control, the collectivity [of Jewish settlers] had to pay an economic, political, and social price which was high by any criterion."[14]

(2)

Thus, on the verge of World War I, a prescient observer probably would have concluded that Jewish settlement in Eretz Israel was an interesting idea and an expedient attempt to solve the problems of Russian and Eastern European Jewry, but one with at most marginal long-range importance: a historical curiosity in the making.

That such an expectation would have been markedly wrong stemmed from four factors. First, despite the fact that the vast majority of diaspora migrants did not choose to settle in Eretz Israel, an institutional network developed as a basis for the long-term evolution of Zionism. Second, a mythology of the Land of Israel was created—or re-created—and this acted both as a romantic magnet to later generations of diaspora Jews and as an ethical and moral justification of Jewish actions into the Holy Land. Third, the magic of language was invoked. Although the predominant languages among Jews in Eretz Israel in the first four decades of the twentieth century were Yiddish and German, the revivification of Hebrew as the private language of Jewish culture in Israel was a major bond. And, fourth, the Jewish settlers in Palestine caught a historical wave, the fall of the Ottoman empire and its replacement in much of the Middle East by the British.

Immediately after the 1881 pogroms began, an organization known as

Hibbat Zion (Lovers of Zion) came into being in Russia. By 1889, the Lovers of Zion had founded twenty-two rural settlements in Palestine, involving 5,000 colonists. The colonists were not terribly good farmers (the Lovers of Zion were drawn mostly from university students, an elite that had little acquaintance with manual labor), and they were saved from starvation by the financial support of Baron Rothschild of Paris. The methods that the Lovers of Zion employed were essentially furtive. They smuggled settlers into Palestine without Ottoman approval.[15]

In contrast, the World Zionist Organization, founded in 1897, was created as a public instrument. It is impossible to think of this body without immediately mentioning its founder, Theodor Herzl (1860–1904), one of the most compelling, but seemingly least likely figures in modern Jewish history.[16] Herzl was a cultivated, dilettantish Viennese Jew, who knew neither Yiddish nor Hebrew and had little experience of Jewish religious customs. A qualified lawyer, he preferred to spend life as a playwright and author of witty newspaper sketches. These ill-paying vocations were made possible by his marriage to a rich woman who, in later years, came to loathe the very idea of Zionism. A fashion plate, Herzl in his younger years alternated between trembling (and apparently unfulfilled) passions for ten- and twelve-year-old girls and visits to prostitutes, from whom he contracted a social disease, probably gonorrhea. How could such a person become a patriarchal figure, the modern Abraham of Zionist history?

A partial, but misleadingly rational, answer is found in his publication in 1896 of a classic document, *Der Judenstaat* ("The Jewish State"), which argued that the only answer to growing anti-Semitism in Eastern and Western Europe was for the Jews to have their own state. But even though Herzl believed his own prescription and, from the mid-1890s onward, spent his life propagating the idea, it seems incongruous that he became a talismanic figure to so many Russian and East European Jews. His followers were not the haute bourgeoisie of French, German, and Austrian Jewry, but the ill-dressed and badly educated, nearly dispossessed eastern Ashkenazi. Part of his hold on them was that he was not as they were. His position was very much like that of the Irish Protestant landlord, Charles Stewart Parnell, among the Irish Catholic peasantry: he was the darling of the masses not merely for the nationalism he shared with them, but for the social style, the arrogance, and the demeanor, which he did not. That Herzl could demand that the delegates to the world Zionist conference wear formal attire was not functional and not even sensible, but it worked; he made them adhere to his standards and they loved him for it. (One has to be somewhat awed by his choice of the ceremonial music for the second meeting of the World Zionist Organization in 1898: that of the arch-anti-Semite Wagner.) When Herzl died in 1904 at the age of forty-four, a Byronesque figure departed the world stage. What he left behind, however, was permanent: an organization that eventually touched all the separate national groups of the Jewish diaspora.[17]

One of the curious things about early Zionism, and especially about Herzl himself, is that although the need for a Jewish homeland was broadcast, exactly where that land should be was very much an open question. In a classic essay published in 1896, "The Jewish Question," Herzl declaimed the need for the creation of a Jewish state, but as for its location, this is as specific as he became: "Let them give us sovereignty over a part of the globe that is large enough for our just national needs, and we will take care of everything else."[18]

In thinking about the various territories that could serve as a Jewish homeland, the early Zionists were clearly and unambiguously nineteenth-century European imperialists. "European supremacy had planted in the minds of even the most deprived of those who shared in it, the idea that any territory outside Europe was open to European occupation," Maxine Rodinson has shrewdly noted. "It was a matter of finding an empty territory—empty not necessarily in the sense of actual absence of inhabitants, but rather of a kind of cultural barrenness."[19]

One possible location for the new Promised Land was Argentina. In the wake of the great Jewish exodus from Russia and Eastern Europe, the Jewish Colonization Association, masterminded by Baron Maurice de Hirsh, had raised roughly 10 million pounds sterling in gold (expressed in nineteenth-century rates; several times that amount in modern currency) and had acquired 1.5 million acres of good land. By the 1890s, 6,000 Jews had settled on the land and by the time of World War II, 30,000 colonists were living in Argentina. The Argentinian venture was well organized, but it remained a logical and pragmatic option—it never caught the Zionist imagination.[20] Later, a minor attempt at Jewish colonization was made in San Domingo and as late as the early 1940s places such as British Guiana, Madagascar, and Alaska were seriously canvassed as possible national homelands.[21]

Other than Palestine, British East Africa (Uganda) was the only possibility that ever seriously attracted Zionist leaders. In 1903, the United Kingdom offered territory in British East Africa and Herzl was inclined to accept, in part, because pogroms had started anew in Russia, and in part because he believed the best form of Zionism was the quickest. Solutions to the immediate problems of Russia and East European Jews were foremost in his mind. In contrast, most of the Russian Zionists who attended the sixth congress of the World Zionist Organization were skeptical. Central in their ranks was Chaim Weizmann, destined eventually to take up Herzl's mantle. Weizmann's initial opposition to the Uganda homeland was founded on practical considerations. He met with well-informed British officials and statesmen and came to the conclusion that the native inhabitants of Uganda were too pugnacious to be dealt with easily and that local British settlers would be almost equally difficult. Further, all the best land already had been taken by colonists from the British Isles.[22] However, in public, Weizmann's stand, and that of his associates, was more principled, namely that nothing should divert the Zionist organization from settling the Holy Land, no matter how long this took. The debate on the Uganda proposal was one of the pivotal movements in modern Jewish history and had the Zionist movement turned toward British East Africa as a solution to Europe's "Jewish problem," the course of modern world history (including the fate of European Jewry in World War II) probably would have been radically different—but not necessarily trouble-free, for a major black-Jewish confrontation well might have followed.

The debate on the Uganda proposals (more precisely, the debate was on whether or not to investigate the British offer, but that was a technicality; if negotiations were begun, the internal momentum of the negotiating process would have presumed acceptance) began with Herzl delivering an address that stressed the desperate situation of the Russian Jews and the need for immediate palliation of their condition. He gave this speech against a backdrop of a large map of Uganda—which replaced the map of Palestine that traditionally was behind the rostrum. A remarkably ugly debate followed and in it three facts became clear: the "religious Zionists" strongly favored Uganda over Palestine (an irony that serves as a reminder that the relationship between religious belief and Zionism is anything but a straightforward affair), that most Russian Zionists opposed Uganda, and that Herzl's prestige was such that he could swing the vote. When the vote was taken, 275 delegates voted to entertain the Ugandan offer, 175 against, and roughly 100 abstained. Had this been the parliament of a functioning state, the decision would have been made. The World Zionist Organization was not a parliament, however, but a pressure group that required substantial unity in order for it to be effective. Thus, when a majority of the Russian Zionists withdrew from the assembly hall, Herzl immediately recognized the threat. To maintain unity, he invited them to return and assured them of his unswerving devotion to Palestine as the true homeland. Thus, nothing came of the Uganda offer.[23]

Palestine, therefore, would be Eretz Israel. But what the land of Israel meant to Zionists in the first half of the twentieth century is a conundrum. The meaning of "the Land" was contradictory, metaphorical, and even if one could perform the equivalent of an axial tomography of every inaccessible part of the Zionists' psyche, it still would resist complete analysis. Note, for instance, the several fundamental paradoxes of what the land meant in relation to various forms of Jewish belief. Many of the early Zionist leaders, and, indeed, the political leaders of the first decade of the Israeli state, were individuals who, in Conor Cruise O'Brien's words, "had broken, or thought they had broken, with the Jewish religion."[24] Thus, the idea that the force that moved the Zionist state to the old Holy Land was nothing other than a revival of ancient Jewish nationalism is so simplistic as to be trivial.[25] Theodor Herzl, after visiting the Wailing Wall in 1898, responded not with affirmation, but with revulsion. "What superstition and fanaticism on every side!"[26] And Sigmund Freud, who briefly contemplated settling in Palestine, wrote in 1930 to Albert Einstein, "I can muster no sympathy whatever for the misguided piety that makes a national religion from a piece of the wall of Herod, and for its sake challenges the feelings of the local natives."[27] Most of the leaders of orthodox Judaism were opposed to Zionism and to its plan to settle in the land of Israel. To most of the orthodox faithful, Zionism was the worst heresy to come out of the nineteenth century.[28] They were waiting for the Messiah. Manifestly, devotion to traditional Jewish belief did not necessarily produce approval of the idea of actually settling in Eretz Israel, any more than rejection of those traditional beliefs implied opposition.

Nevertheless, in an important sector of world Jewry "the Land" became a central concept, a transcendental belief that triggered a historical memory (if not religious sentiments) in some of the most cold-eyed secular Jews. Chaim Weizmann, the German-trained scientist and religiously nonobservant president of the World Zionist Organization in the generation after Herzl, illustrated the way that the bond with the land became essentially a religious experience in itself. "The renaissance of the Jewish nation is bound up with Palestine," he declared. "The choice made by destiny cannot be undone. Palestine is the Jewish people's birthplace and it gave birth to no other. It owes its place in history to the Jews and to no other people. The Jews as a people and Palestine as a country, ceased to be truly creative when the bond between them was severed. But the hope of renewing that bond has kept the Jewish people alive, and meantime Palestine remained desolate."[29]

A similar example of the mystical power of the land and the transformation of this power into a moral imperative is found in the testimony of Weizmann's bitter rival, the avowedly agnostic David Ben-Gurion. The land of Israel "always had been, and will remain, our country. We are here as of right."[30] Ben-Gurion repeated this refrain throughout his life: "We are here as of right." In making that statement he asserted what he believed to be a historical fact, a geographic description, and a statement of morality, all revolving around the transcendant land. It was not necessary that the mystical and historical connection with the land be made by most Jews, just that it galvanize some. Equally, the land did not have to win all its converts quickly, for the concept could lie dormant, like a seed, until the conditions were right for its growth.

Much the same held for the Hebrew language. In the first half of the twentieth century, the first language of most settlers in the land of Israel was Yiddish. German was the most widely used second language, and there was considerable use of English as well. Yiddish would seem to have been the natural language for Eretz Israel, except that it was the tongue of the Ashkenazim and thus unacceptable to the Sephardim. A telling early illustration of the linguistic problem in Eretz Israel occurred in 1883 in a secondary school funded by a French Jewish society. In the school the majority of the students were from the Sephardic community, but to complete the enrollment, pupils from the Ashkenazic community also had to be attracted. The Ashkenazic parents refused to permit their children to attend an institution in which teaching was in Ladino or Arabic, the dominant tongues among the Sephardim, and the Sephardic parents would not accept Yiddish. The pragmatic solution: employ Hebrew.[31] Although unfamiliar as an everyday tongue to both groups, it had one advantage, namely that neither group would veto its use.

But more than pragmatism was involved in the revival of Hebrew. The promulgation of a distinct national language occurred in most European nations in the nineteenth century. Linguistic nationalism in European culture sometimes involved the revivification of tongues that had been nearly lost (as in the Celtic language revivals in Ireland and in Wales). In other instances, purification of existing national tongues was demanded (the French codification of linguistic purity is well known). And in still other instances, the glorification of a single tongue was used to bring together otherwise distinct political entities (the German language was used as a unifying theme to bring together the nineteenth-century German principalities). But in every case, there was an argument that the particular tongue fit the particular people. The ideas of a unique match of a language and a people were not scientific linguistic statements, but romantic ones, frequently semimystical in their intensity. The revival of Hebrew followed this pattern. During the nineteenth century, Hebrew was broadened from a solely ecclesiastical tongue into a written language of high culture, and then into an everyday demotic language. This was a minority movement within diaspora Jewry, but it raised the possibility of religious language of Judaism becoming the secular tongue of Eretz Israel.

Within the land of Israel, the founding father of the Hebrew revival was Eliezer Yitzhak Perlmann, a Russian emigré with a French education who was the first Zionist settler to change his name to Hebrew (to Ben Yehuda). From his arrival in Eretz Israel in 1882 the modern Hebrew language movement is dated.[32] Ben Yehuda and his allies and successors had many of the unlovable qualities of fanatics and some of the risible ones (the renaming of things, especially of people, was a passion and so successful was the movement in this regard that it was wryly suggested that a directory entitled "Who Was Who" should be published).[33] But their passion was undeniable and, ultimately, unstoppable. The so-called war of the language focused on the projected Technicon in Haifa in 1913–14. The question was whether German or Hebrew would be the language of instruction. In fact, the question turned into a referendum on whether or not Hebrew would become the official language of Eretz Israel. The national teachers' union (very pro-Hebrew) went on strike; simultaneously, the issue was argued in Zionist centers throughout the diaspora. The Hebrew advocates won a complete victory. From that time onward, Hebrew was the official language of Zionism,[34] in spite of the fact that most settlers knew little of the language. The Holy Land now had its holy language.

When World War I began, the land of Israel was part of the tottering Ottoman empire; when it ended, it was part of the British. In terms of world geopolitics, that change propelled the land of Israel from the sixteenth century into the twentieth. For convenience, the years from 1917 to 1948 in Zionist history can be termed the Yishuv era. (*Yishuv* means a settlement but often the term is used to speak of the Jewish community and its organizations in Eretz Israel.) Because in the mid-1940s Zionists and the British authorities in Palestine came into conflict, it has become a commonplace to bad-mouth those Zionist leaders (and most particularly Chaim Weizmann) who used the British imperial connection as a lever with which to pry the Zionist enterprise away from the dead weight of the Ottoman world. Actually, Weizmann and his Anglophilic colleagues seized a unique moment in world politics, and had they not done so, it is hard to imagine Israel's ever having become a viable state.

This fleeting movement had two aspects. One of these was that as the Great War progressed, it became obvious that the French and the British would be carving up the Middle East between themselves. The French were far from hospitable to the idea of Zionism and had they obtained control of Jerusalem or of other major sectors of Palestine, the Zionist enterprise in Eretz Israel would have been greatly hindered, perhaps permanently blocked. Second, not only were the British in general more open to Zionism, but during 1916 David Lloyd George had come to the prime ministership. A Welsh nonconformist in religion, he was an examplar of that strong strand in conservative Protestant opinion that read the Bible seriously, was fascinated by ancient Hebrew culture, and was predisposed to support Zionism. This was a major stroke of good fortune for the Zionists, the more so because Lloyd George appointed as his foreign secretary Arthur James Balfour. Balfour, under the influence of Lionel Rothschild, had become an enthusiast for Hebraic culture and was committed, at least intellectually, to the rebuilding of Zion as a Jewish homeland.[35]

That granted, it is true that the Balfour Declaration of 1917, negotiated between the British authorities and the Zionist leaders, was typical of the legal instruments uttered by Lloyd George's government: it was said that David Lloyd George was the only person in the world who could write on three sides of a piece of paper at once. The Balfour Declaration was a single sentence.

Entire books have been written dealing with this gnomic utterance.[36] At minimum, it gave a British *pratique* for a Jewish homeland in Palestine and simultaneously seemed to reduce the existing Arab communities to a residual status: "non-Jewish." However, the declaration also attempted to protect the civil and religious rights of those same Arabs. It appears that the British statesmen of the Balfour era foresaw the day that the Jews would become a majority in Palestine and this was acceptable to them, provided Palestinian civil rights were respected. That this was the case is indicated in a discussion that took place between Arthur Meighen, prime minister of Canada, and Winston Churchill, then colonial secretary, in 1921. When Meighen asked if the British policy of encouraging a Jewish national homeland implied giving Jews control over the government, Churchill replied: "If, in the course of many years they become a majority

Foreign Office,
November 2nd, 1917.

Dear Lord Rothschild,

I have much pleasure in conveying to you, on behalf of His Majesty's Government, the following declaration of sympathy with Jewish Zionist aspirations which has been submitted to, and approved by, the Cabinet

"His Majesty's Government view with favour the establishment in Palestine of a national home for the Jewish people, and will use their best endeavours to facilitate the achievement of this object, it being clearly understood that nothing shall be done which may prejudice the civil and religious rights of existing non-Jewish communities in Palestine, or the rights and political status enjoyed by Jews in any other country"

I should be grateful if you would bring this declaration to the knowledge of the Zionist Federation.

Figure 2. The Balfour Declaration

in the country, they naturally would take it over." Meighen wondered, "Pro rata with the Arab?" and Churchill affirmed, "Pro rata with the Arab. We made an equal pledge that we would not turn the Arab off his land or invade his political and social right."[37]

That the eventual Zionist control of Palestine and the maintenance of Arab political and social rights were potentially incompatible was not something that the United Kingdom government intended to face. A well-informed journalist, after having spent a long period in Palestine in the Balfour era, came to this conclusion about British intentions: "The Balfour Declaration seemed to promise the Jews everything and seemed to reserve everything for the Arabs, at one time and with one twist of the pen. I was to learn in Palestine that it had actually given the Jews little, had reserved little for the Arabs, and had achieved one certain purpose only: the installation of the British as the governing power in the country."[38]

That judgment is perhaps a trifle cynical, for it underrates how much the Zionist cause gained in the first fifteen years of the British mandate by the substitution of British permissiveness for the obstinacy of the Ottoman rulers. Under the treaty of Versailles, the former German colonies and most of the old Ottoman empire were converted into "mandates." The arrangement for the Palestine mandate was singular among these, however, for it decreed that the chief purpose of Britain as mandatory power should be the establishment of a national home for the Jewish people. The British administration of Palestine was to work with a "Jewish Agency" on matters such as immigration and settlement in the Jewish homeland.[39] The World Zionist Organization became the agency, *pro tem*, until the formal Jewish Agency for Palestine was established in 1929. All this was a huge step from the semisurreptitious Jewish settlement movement under the Ottoman empire. The Jewish homeland became an internationally recognized concept by the Balfour Declaration of 1917, by the San Remo Agreement of 1920, and by the League of Nations Council in 1922.

(3)

We must recognize that during the years between the two world wars there was nothing approaching uniformity in the Zionist ranks. The range of opinion and parties in Eretz Israel can only in part be arranged on a conventional left-right spectrum, for the left-right axis was intersected at several points by a spectacular array of religiously determined factions.

Probably the largest Zionist group within the Palestine mandate was Mapai, whose identity was closely associated with David Ben-Gurion. This group pushed for a collectivist state, and emphasized cooperative economic activities and working-class solidarity, but was not strictly Marxist. Two smaller parties, Hashomer Hatzair and Left Poalei Zion tried to blend orthodox Marxism and Zionism. In the center of the spectrum was the General Zionist party under Chaim Weizmann. This group split in 1935 into the basically liberal General Zionists A, led by Weizmann, and the General Zionists B who became strongly antilabor, antisocialist, and pro-free enterprise. A far right wing, the Revisionist party founded in 1925 by Vladimir Jabotinsky, was a highly aggressive body, given to talk of military methods and territorial aggrandizement as the prescription for Zionism's future.

This escarpment of political belief, ranging from hard-line Marxist to rabid Revisionists, was intersected by various religious parties. The largest of these was the Mizrachi movement (an abbreviation for "Merkaz Ruhani," meaning spiritual center), whose origins were in the Lovers of Zion Movement of the 1880s. Mizrachi leaders formed a Zionist beachhead among the usually anti-Zionist orthodox, and they presented the rebirth of Israel as a divine and celestial event. Israel was to be a Jewish homeland governed by the Torah. A second religious group, the ultraorthodox Agudat Israel (the "Federation of Israel," usually referred to as "Aguda"), had roots outside of Palestine. It was established in 1912 among East European Hassidim. During the 1920s and 1930s, Aguda, which had a significant following within Eretz Israel, maintained the unusual position of refusing to belong either to the World Zionist Organization or to have anything to do with political Zionism within the land of Israel. This was based on the belief that the Jewish people must wait patiently in the Promised Land for the Messiah and that political Zionism in all its forms was a corruption of this religious duty. Further, the Aguda leaders refused in principle to consort with any political group that allowed women to vote.[40]

These were just the main groups. There were so many more that the equivalent of an *Audubon Guide* would be required to identify all the species and variants of interwar Zionism. Yet, just as the great biannual journeys of the migratory birds have scores and scores of species within their ranks, but nevertheless have a common direction, so the Zionists in Israel, despite their multifarious speciation, were engaged in a common enterprise. They were all part of the colonization of Palestine by Jewish settlers.

Notice those words: "colonization" and "settler." They are terms that now make politically aware citizens of western democracies shudder. Today's dualistic way of thinking opposes in concept settler to indigene, colonization to resistance, and vice to virtue. Colonial enterprises and settler societies are automatically taken to be bad, irredeemably so. Because of these present-day connotations, Israeli spokespeople go to great lengths to avoid using these words, and their opponents use them whenever possible.

But we must accept a simple set of facts: the Zionists of the Yishuv were indeed settlers and they engaged in a collective act of colonization. They said this themselves in literally thousands of documents and public statements in which the words "settler" and "colonist" were not meant in any obscure or technical or metaphorical or archaic sense. Martin Buber repeated the story of the early Zionist leader Max Nordau's (1849–1923) discovery that there were Arabs in Palestine. He rushed excitedly to Theordor Herzl and exclaimed, "I didn't know that! If that is the case then we are doing an injustice."[41] But Nordau's double naiveté—ignorance of the Arab presence and refusal to commit injustice as a condition of one's own existence—was not characteristic of the Yishuv. Instead, a pragmatic and unapologetic attitude prevailed. For example, when the sixteenth congress of the World Zionist Organization established the Jewish Agency in 1929 to administer the settlement of the homeland, it issued this resolution:

Colonisation Policy

1. The Congress declares that it must for all time be the fixed policy of the Jewish Agency to use every effort to ensure the development and expansion of the Jewish agricultural colonisation in Palestine to the furthest possible limit in accordance with the principles laid down by Congress for cooperation in the Jewish Agency.[42]

That was in rural areas. Concerning urban locales, the Zionist authorities talked just as freely of "colonies," "settlers," and "colonization."[43] Those were the words of the mainstream organizations. From the Revisionist right, things were expressed even more clearly. Jabotinsky himself wrote:

Colonisation has its own explanation, integral and inescapable, and understood by every Jew and Arab with his wits about him. Colonisation can have only one goal. For the Palestinian Arabs this goal is inadmissible. This is the nature of things. To change that nature is impossible.[44]

There is no doubt that from at least 1917 onward, the movement by Zionists to the land of Israel was a self-conscious work of colonization and that its intention was to create a settler society. That, however, does not automatically mean that the colonial enterprise entailed the ruthlessness of the European conquest of the Americas, Australasia, and Africa. Granted, a significant number of Arabs in Palestine were strenuously opposed to the Zionists' efforts. Al-Fatah, founded in Paris in 1911 became operational in Palestine after World War I as a doubly anticolonial movement: it was both anti-British and anti-Zionist. Arab nationalism, although considerably behind that of Zionism, became more active after World War I. In 1929 and again in 1936–39, as clashes between Arabs and Jews proliferated, these faction fights were called "pogroms" by the Jews and "massacres" by the Arabs.[45]

For the outsider viewing the Zionist colonization efforts, the key question is, What methods were used? Two aspects, land and population, are crucial. As Baruch Kimmerling notes in his detailed study of Zionist land acquisition in Palestine, the Zionist immigrants of the early twentieth century had an unpleasant surprise. Whereas, as Herzl suggested, they had thought that they were a people without land who were going to inhabit a land without people, the reality was very different. The local population was much larger in number than the early Zionists had estimated. Moreover, all of the arable land was owned by someone. The Palestinians had a sharply developed sense of land ownership, both individual and collective, and even the uninhabitable tracts were owned by someone, either the Ottomon government, or, later the British crown.[46] Thus, the Jewish colonists had no real alternative: because they could not conquer the Arabs (nor would the British have allowed them to do so), and because they could not take over land by state compulsion (they did not as yet control a state), they had to acquire land by purchase. In 1910 the Zionists paid roughly the equivalent of 20 U.S. dollars per rural acre (approximately the going rate for rural land in the United States), but by 1944 they were paying the equivalent of $1,050 per rural acre (meanwhile rural land values in the United States had risen only to $45).[47] The Zionists paid heavily for the land they acquired, especially considering that much of the land was swamp, barren, or otherwise marginal. Neither on the matter of price nor on freedom of contract (no Arab landowner was forced to sell; transactions were voluntary) were there grounds for complaint by the Arab sellers.

Nor was the total amount of land purchased by the Jewish colonizers very worrying. A United Kingdom royal commission indicated that in

1935 Jews owned only about 5 percent of the total rural and urban land area of Palestine and that they held about 12 percent of the mandate's cultivatable land.[48] By 1948, the Jews' percentage of the total rural and urban land area was only 6.6 percent,[49] so that their proportion of the cultivatable land cannot have risen even to 15 percent. The progress of Jewish land acquisition was so slow that even by the most generous of extrapolations, it would have been past the middle of the twenty-first century before the Zionists would have held even half of the land of Palestine.

Nevertheless, certain aspects of the land acquisition process upset many Arabs and not only the relatively small band of Arab nationalists. One reason was that although Jewish purchase of land put a good deal of money in Arab hands, the benefits were not well distributed. In the years 1901–27, 68 percent of the land purchased by Jews was from absentee landlords, and a further 20 percent from local owners of large estates. In 1928–36, most of the land was bought from absentees—44 percent from owners who lived in Palestine and 36 percent from Arabs living outside of the mandate.[50] Not only did the Arab tenants of small holdings receive no benefit from the sums paid to their former absentee landlords, but they actually were directly injured: they lost their leases and were replaced by Jewish settlers. The eviction of thousands of Arab peasant farmers and their families, though economically profitable to the large Arab land-owners, created a rolling series of bitter waves in the Arab proletariat.

Second, there was the matter of the Jewish National Fund and its purchase of land. In addition to private purchases by individuals or small groups of Jewish settlers, the Jewish National Fund as a collective entity bought land. The JNF was formed at the fifth World Zionist Congress in 1901 and began purchasing land in Eretz Israel in 1905. In 1920, the World Zionist Organization voted to establish an "immigration and colo-nisation fund" and at least one-fifth of these monies were to go to the JNF. Thus, in 1921, the JNF was able to begin an extensive land acquisition program. By 1948, the JNF was the largest nongovernmental land-owner in Palestine. In that year it held nearly 54 percent of all Jewish-owned land.[51] In one sense, this was not much—roughly 3.5 percent of the mandate—but it frightened the Arabs, because, unlike the case of private purchase, once the land was placed by the Jewish National Fund in its land bank, it disappeared as far as the Arabs were concerned. The JNF was committed to holding all land it acquired in perpetuity, as the in-alienable property of the Jewish people. Its lands could not be transferred into individual hands, only rented (to Jews only). Such land could never return to Arab ownership. Thus, whereas in theory, private land purchase by individual Jews was reversible—there was no legal impediment to a piece of ground being sold in future to an Arab—this was impossible if the JNF gained control of tracts of land. In practical terms, purchase by the JNF removed the land from Arab Palestine.

The Jewish National Fund's collective trusteeship of land can be seen as one early and important step in the creation of a corporate personality by the settlers of Eretz Israel. As we have learned, this is one of the crucial preconditions for the establishment of a covenantal culture. But this level of cultural development within the Jewish community was largely hidden from the Arabs. What they saw was the Zionist policy of physically demonstrating Jewish suzerainty over JNF lands. The Jews immediately fenced off the land, breaking up traditional landmarks and field patterns, and erected highly visible watchtowers, flagpoles, and boundary markers. These acts were part of a systematic policy of rubbing salt in the Arab wounds. Zionist authorities argued that it was a necessary cruelty, as unless the Jews seized complete physical control over the lands that they purchased, the Arabs might someday try to resume control of them.[52]

A complementary aspect of the Zionist colonization program was demographic. The Zionists wished to build a settler population that would, in the first instance, be large enough to create a self-enclosed Jewish economy and society within Palestine, and, eventually, to become the controlling numerical majority in the land. This could not happen by natural increase, for although the settlers of the Yishuv had a high fertility rate, so did the indigenous Arabs. Immigration was the only answer.

The British authorities in Palestine drew up estimates of the population of the mandate for 1920 and 1936; the results are shown in the table.[53]

	1920		1936	
	Number	*Percent*	*Number*	*Percent*
Jews	66,574	9.9	370,483	27.7
Moslems	521,403	77.4	848,342	63.5
Christians	77,801	11.6	106,474	8.0
Others	7,415	1.1	11,219	0.8
	673,193	100.0	1,336,518	100.0

So, through immigration, the Jews in Palestine were increasing rapidly in absolute numbers and they were also becoming a larger and larger proportion of the total population. Both Zionists and Arab nationalists foresaw the day when Jews would be a majority in the mandate.

In the mid-1930s, a perceptive journalist wrote that "the opposition to Zionism, so far as I can tell—the only reasonable opposition anyhow—is based upon the fact that Zionism proposes to settle or colonize a country that is already inhabited by another people."[54] We have already seen how Zionist colonizers rationalized this process: possession of the land, Eretz Israel, and the consequent dispossession of the indigenous Arabs, was justified on the basis of the historical tie of the Jews with this particular land. Some Zionists phrased this justification solely in modern-sounding historical phrases, while others referred directly to the ancient covenant. But though the Zionist covenantal and historical arguments had plangency in the worldwide Jewish community, these arguments did not have much resonance with those outside the community. Only a strand of Protestants—Bible-reading, low church, or nonconformist—was convinced by these historical and covenantal references. Nor did the argument that the Jewish colonization was fundamentally different from that of the English, French, Dutch, and Germans because the Jews did not set out from a single national homebase to conquer Palestine have much influence; it was transparently a case of special pleading. Thus, for presentation to a wider world, the Zionist authorities had to develop a set of moral justifications for their colonization of Palestine that would not depend on biblical or historical precedents, or on obvious self-interest.

The fascinating thing about the justifications put forward for the primacy of Jewish rights over those of the Palestinian Arabs is that the arguments were generic. That is, they were the same arguments employed in previous centuries (with tailoring for local circumstances) by the Australian colonists concerning the aborigine; the Canadian settlers about native Canadians; the American frontier expansionists about the Amerindians; the Afrikaners concerning the Xhosa and Zulu; the British, French, German, Portuguese, and Belgians about black Africans. The same canonical justifications were used by all European imperialists when explaining why it was all right for the colonists to bash the indigene. (That there are both factual and logical objections to be made to each of the arguments is not here at issue; nor is the fact that some of the arguments contradict each other. The arguments themselves were real, whatever their validity.)

One of the primary Zionist arguments was that the Palestinian Arabs were not really a people. The Palestinians, Zionists argued, were part of a much larger group distributed throughout the Middle East. This group was said to have many homelands, so the Palestinian Arabs could not have any particular tie to Palestine. And an emotional and historical tie to a particular piece of land was one of the requirements of a modern nation-state. Thus, in 1929, David Ben-Gurion could compare the Jews and the Arabs concerning their respective senses of place: "Jerusalem is not the same thing to the Arabs as it is to the Jews. The Arab inhabits many great lands. . . . But for the Jewish people—in every generation and place of dispersion—Palestine is the one and only country with which its national destiny has been tied."[55]

Frequently, Zionists presented Palestinians as backward. Presumably, this meant they had a lower level of rights than people (such as the Jews) who came from more advanced cultures. In 1923, Vladimir Jabotinsky articulated the classic Revisionist Zionist view of the Palestinian Arabs:

Any native people—it's all the same whether they are civilized or savage—views their country as their national home, of which they will always be the complete master. They will not voluntarily allow, not only a new master, but even a new partner. And so it is for the Arabs. . . . Culturally they are 500 years behind us, spiritually they do not have our endurance and our strength of will. . . . They look upon Palestine with the same instinctive love and true fervour that any Aztec looked upon his Mexico or any Sioux looked upon his prairie.[56]

From the pacifist end of the Zionist political spectrum, Martin Buber noted the pervasiveness of the viewpoint that Jabotinsky articulated. In 1926 Buber commented,

We must have a sympathetic knowledge of our neighbours, which can only be acquired by the study of their language and traditions, and above all, by decisively discarding the invidious feeling of superiority. . . . When I say things like that to people who live in Palestine, they generally respond by describing the uncivilized character of the Arabs.[57]

In 1929, he wrote:

A few years ago I spoke about the Arab question with the director of a great cultural institution of the Yishuv. The man spoke to approximately this effect: "You know me, and you know that I am no chauvinist, but—they are an inferior race."

Buber, in his commentary, added wryly: "We are spoken of in similar terms in several parts of Europe."[58]

The idea that the Palestinians were backward rolled into another argument, one that was promoted energetically in Western Europe and the United States. Zionists maintained that since the Arabs were not productive, they were not really being dispossessed. As David Ben-Gurion declared in 1924: "We do not recognize the right of Arabs to rule the country, since Palestine is still undeveloped and awaits its builders."[59] Even Martin Buber, one of the least strident of Zionists, felt that this was a valid argument. Zionist "right rests on proved fact," he said in 1929. "After thousands of years in which the country was a wasteland, we have transformed it into a settled country, where it was open to us to do so, by years of labour."[60] Just after the end of World War II, Ben-Gurion declared with characteristic vigor: "We didn't merely buy the land, we re-created the land."[61]

From this position it was possible to posit another point: not only were the Arabs not being dispossessed, but the whole process of Zionist colonization was good for them.[62] In 1930, the Jewish Agency for Palestine published a pamphlet titled *Financial Aspects of Jewish Reconstruction in Palestine: How the Arabs Have Benefitted through Jewish Immigration.* By virtue of Jewish land purchase, "the Arabs have obtained as a gift, and without any productive work on their own part, a capital reserve of 30 to 50 million pounds or more."[63] Jewish settlements were good for the Arabs, because they paid wages to the Arab peasantry. Thus, Palestinian peasants "who lived within the radius affected by Jewish settlements" had been able "to make themselves independent of the usurers to whom they were in debt. Not only so . . . they began to buy land themselves and to transform themselves more and more into 'free peasants on their own soil.'"[64] The pamphlet claimed that the only Arabs adversely affected by Jewish immigration were employers who exploited the cheap labor of the peasant, and the rack-renting landlords, the moneylenders, and the Arab land speculators.[65] David Ben-Gurion, as leader of the socialist wing of the Zionist movement, went so far as to argue that the "historic mission" of the Jewish workers' movement in Palestine was "to stand at the vanguard of the movement of liberation and revival of Near Eastern peoples."[66] Jewish colonization, therefore, was presented as a movement for the liberation of the Palestinian peasant.

Zionist colonization policy in the interwar years was like a four-sided citadel, three sides of which we have already surveyed: land acquisition, immigration, and propaganda. The fourth was the development of a segregated labor system. When the Jewish Agency was created in 1929, by the World Zionist Organization, the labor policy was clearly stated: "The

Congress affirms that the employment of Jewish labour for all branches of Jewish production in Eretz Israel is an indispensable condition for the growth of the Jewish Yishuv and for the realisation of Zionist aims."[67]

In practice, this meant that Jewish firms and agricultural enterprises should hire Arabs only when Jews were not available and then only for the lowest jobs. Curiously, this ideology of economic segregation was most clearly articulated in the branch of the Zionist movement that one would least have expected: the socialist wing. The evolution of the thinking of the leader of Zionist secularism, David Ben-Gurion, is revealing. In the early 1900s, he had accepted the employment of Arabs as a practical necessity, but in 1907 he called for lands owned by the Jewish National Fund to be worked exclusively by Jews. In the subsequent decade he deepened his commitment to segregation, so that by 1920 he was insisting that Jews employ only Jewish workers.[68] This was not always possible in actual practice, since there were not enough Jewish settlers to take the worst jobs. In 1920 the Histadrut was founded, and in 1920 Ben-Gurion became its head: this was a trade union, but much more. It became one of the major channels of investment money for Zionist enterprises and also a direct employer of labor.[69] Occasionally, the Histadrut supported Arab labor strikes (such as the strike of the Haifa boatmen in 1932), but in its day-to-day operations it worked toward a segregated employment market in which Jews had the best jobs and virtually full employment, and in which the Arabs were used as a surplus labor pool to be employed only when no Jew would take a given job. This policy was successful. We should not, however, perceive it as unusual. It is one of the archetypal ways that settlers in colonial societies had used indigenous labour. At moments in their histories, South Africa and Northern Ireland have provided similar examples.

(4)

The "Arab revolt" of 1936–39 marked the end of the era of easy colonization. Among the side effects of the revolt was that it jogged the British into paying more attention to what was happening in Palestine. A series of United Kingdom investigations—the Palestine royal commission (the Peel Commission of 1937); the Palestine partition commission (the Woodhead Commission of 1938); and four separate governmental white papers, of July 1937, December 1937, November 1938, and May 1939—yielded contradictory policy recommendations. Yet the conclusion was

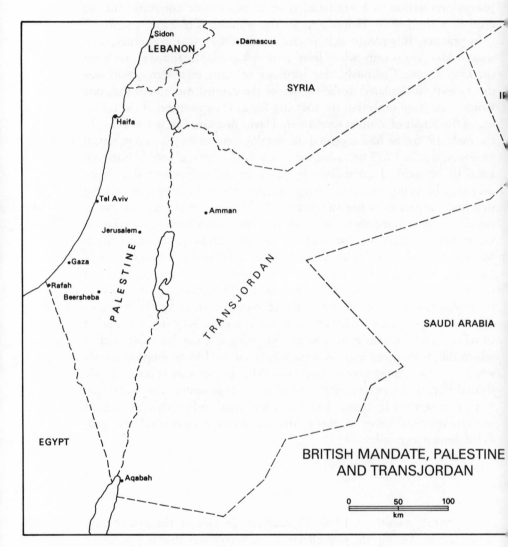

Map 5. The British mandate, Palestine, and Transjordan

unavoidable: British self-interest precluded letting things ride as they had done in the past. The fundamental problem was that British and Jewish self-interests began to diverge. The United Kingdom government, while more sympathetic to Zionism than any other major European government, had important interests in the Middle East, interests that required amity with the Arabs. Oil and trade routes (especially the Suez Canal) were central. Both the Peel and Woodhead commissions tried to harmonize matters by suggesting some sort of partition of Palestine.[70]

Among Zionists, the concept of partition brought forward two questions. What were the rightful boundaries of Eretz Israel? What pragmatic, and presumably temporary, reduction of these boundaries could be accepted? Strangely, the first question was still unanswered by 1936 and to this very day there is no general agreement.[71] Given that the Zionist's primary self-justification for claiming the land of Israel is a historical one, the biblical mentions of the Holy Land are pivotal. The first mention of the Land of Israel as a covenanted possession of the children of Israel is found in Genesis 15:18:

In the same day the Lord made a covenant with Abram, saying, Unto thy seed have I given this land, from the river of Egypt unto the great river, the river Euphrates.

Some scholars believe that this reference probably includes most of modern Jordan, Syria, Saudi Arabia, Kuwait, and Iraq. Others say that it includes present-day Israel, the present state of Jordan, the Sinai, and a strip of eastern Syria. Manifestly, the reference is wanting as a surveyor's description because it gives only three of the four boundaries—the Nile (and here some scholars say that the "river of Egypt" is not the Nile but a wadi on the north coast of Sinai), the Euphrates, and, presumably, the Mediterranean Sea—needed to enclose the land. Accordingly, Zionist scholars have looked with more favor upon Numbers 34:3–12 (repeated, with minor modifications, in Ezek. 47:15–20). The book of Numbers is much more precise and provides the full perimeters of the Land of Israel. These borders enclose a much smaller area than in the promise to Abram, but they still encompass much of the Middle East. There are three basic ways of reading the geographic information given in the book of Numbers. These vary because, although the description of the Land of Israel gives precise place names as coordinates, many of these places have vanished over the years; further, in some instances the place names have been transposed from one site to another. In the actual course of history, the ancient Israelites never conquered the entire land described in Numbers. Even the Davidic kingdom fell short. The ebb and flow of the various Hebrew kingdoms centered around Jerusalem and what is now the Israeli-controlled west bank of the Jordan River.

In 1917–19, leading Zionist scholars and policymakers conflated a map from a combination of their reading of the scriptures and their inference of modern military realities. Since the British controlled both Palestine and Transjordan, all that the Zionists asked for was Palestine and a small piece of Transjordan. Presumably the great imperial power could affect this bit of geopolitical gerrymandering easily!

No, not if the British were to keep peace with the Arab world. Unrest in 1936 among the Palestinian Arabs made the British uncomfortably aware that under the Balfour Declaration they had promised to protect Arab rights as well as to foster a Jewish homeland. Thus, the Peel Commission brought forward in 1937 a partition plan to split Palestine into Jewish and Arab sectors, with a proposed neutral zone around Jerusalem and Bethlehem. One might have expected the proposed division of Eretz Israel to have produced a universal cry that the Holy Land was being desecrated, but it did not. In fact, the Peel partition plan coincided with the thinking of one notable group of Yishuv leaders, gathered around David Ben-Gurion.[72] In the late 1920s and early 1930s, Ben-Gurion had taken up the idea of having separate "autonomes" or "cantons" for Jews and Arabs within the Palestine mandate. Each would have internal self-rule and this form of government would be a halfway house to a full state. When the Peel Commission suggested in 1937 that Arabs and Jews be physically separated through population transfer (a transfer of roughly 100,000 Arabs and of 1,250 Jewish settlers), Ben-Gurion favored it. In his diary he wrote, "The compulsory transfer of the Arabs from the valleys of the proposed Jewish state could give us something which we never had, even when we stood on our own during the days of the First and Second Temples," namely, a Galilee almost totally free of non-Jews. For the first time in history, there would be a "a real Jewish state."[73]

Since the partitionists among the Zionists eventually won, it is crucial to realize that the argument for partition was a pragmatic one: partition would create a manageable Jewish homeland in the shortest possible time. One must emphasize that acceptance of partition did not in the mind of any of its proponents imply a limitation on the ultimate land claims of the future state of Israel. As Ben-Gurion said in 1937:

> The acceptance of partition does not commit us to renounce Transjor-
> dan; one does not demand from anybody to give us his vision. We shall

accept a state in the boundaries fixed today, but the boundaries of Zionist aspirations are the concern of the Jewish people and no external factor will be able to limit them.[74]

(5)

How long the borders proposed for the Jewish homeland in the 1930s would have lasted before Zionist energies pushed beyond them in the continuing drive to redeem Eretz Israel is a very uncertain speculation. What is certain is that in the late 1930s time stopped, as in the book of Daniel, and then, following a virtual apocalypse, a new Dispensation began. It is impossible for a historian to take even the most distant view of the holocaust without being dazed and feeling beyond one's depth. It is one of those events after which nothing is ever again the same.[75]

As far as Zionism was concerned, the holocaust recast temporarily the moral balance sheet of the western world. In noting that, however, I am not accepting the judgment of Earl Berger in *The Covenant and the Sword* that "Zionism was a failure until Hitler came to power."[76] Berger underrates the vitality of Zionism and turns a persecutor into a benefactor. But the holocaust made the world listen. Before World War II, the testimony of Chaim Weizmann before the joint U.S.-British Committee on Palestine would not have been creditable. "The Jewish State is the only guarantee of survival," he asserted in 1947. He coldly dealt with the simplistic sentiment that the Zionists should get along with the Arabs by pointing out that he had heard an Arab say, " 'Why don't the Palestinian Jews join their brethren in Europe?' I do not know whether they meant they should join them in the cemeteries or in the concentration camps," he replied.[77] The same moral high ground permitted David Ben-Gurion to lecture the Anglo-American commission in impassioned terms:

> When we say "Jewish independence" or a "Jewish State" we mean a Jewish country, Jewish soil; we mean Jewish labour, we mean Jewish economy, Jewish agriculture, Jewish industry, Jewish sea. We mean Jewish language, school, culture. We mean Jewish safety, security, independence, complete independence, as for any other free people.[78]

Before the holocaust, the western world would not have listened. After the holocaust, it did.

The Second World War confirmed a trend that had been in train since World War I, the decline of the British empire. The rise of the United States to world prepotency coincided with a shift in the balance of power in the world Jewish community. American Jewry became a "third force" in Jewish affairs, of equal importance to European Jewry (which lost 6 million members during the holocaust years) and to the colonists of the Yishuv. Far from all American Jews were in favor of Zionism—there was a sharply anti-Zionist segment as well as a large number of noncommitted people.[79] But as knowledge of the holocaust became widespread, the majority became pro-Zionist and pressured the American government in favor of the quick establishment of an independent Jewish homeland. Unlike the British, the Americans had few long-standing relationships with the Arab world and at that time were independent of the need for Arab petroleum. When the United States took the Zionist side, it totally changed the physics of world politics as far as Eretz Israel was concerned.

The key date in the replacement of the British with the Americans in the Zionist scheme of things was 1942. A meeting was held at the Biltmore Hotel in New York and there the Anglophilic and gradualist regime of Chaim Weizmann was replaced by the Anglophobic and impatient headship of David Ben-Gurion.[80] The "Biltmore programme" implied a new logic for world Zionism. The establishment of a Jewish state as quickly as possible was the primary goal, and America was the force to be employed. Therefore, American Zionists did not try very hard to change the rigid U.S. immigration policy—for there was the possibility that many of the holocaust survivors would have chosen the United States rather than Palestine as the Promised Land—but concentrated on obtaining U.S. support for creation of the new Middle Eastern state.[81] A further implication of the new logic was that Great Britain was defined as an enemy of Zionism and thus a terrorist campaign began against the British in the mandate, conducted by at least two different Zionist guerrilla groups, Irgun, and Haganah, neither of which thought much more of the other than they did of the British.[82]

In February 1947, the United Kingdom, tired of being caught between the Zionists and the Arabs, handed over the whole problem to the United Nations. In late November 1947, the General Assembly, with the support of President Harry Truman, endorsed a plan for the partition of Palestine into Jewish and Palestinian Arab states, with Jerusalem as an international zone. About 55 percent of what had been the Palestinian mandate under the British was allocated to the new state of Israel. With a mixture of prudence and cowardice, the United Nations plan avoided any reference to population shifts, this fundamental question being too hot a topic.[83] Considering that before World War II, the Zionists had only managed to purchase less than 7 percent of Palestine, this was a great victory indeed. (And, as a consequence of the 1947–48 war, no Palestinian state materialized.)

With United Nations approval, the state of Israel became an independent nation on 14 May 1948 and was immediately recognized by both the United States and the Soviet Union.

Thus ended Zionism, successfully, its task completed. Organizations with the name "Zionist" in their title continue to exist, but that is misleading. Zionism ended on 14 May 1948, and thereafter a new state was in existence. Hope was replaced by reality. The new state of Israel held land consecrated by the history and the religious beliefs of the Jewish people; the same state employed the ancient sacred language, Hebrew, as its everyday official tongue; and, most important, the citizenry at once began to develop a corporate personality. All this occurred within a state that in theory was secular. Yet, as we shall see, the state became so sacralized that the ancient covenant was thereby reaffirmed. That, however, was still in the future.

Part III

THE COVENANT
AND THE STATE

6

Northern Ireland: A Protestant State for a Protestant People, 1920–1969

(1)

I f there ever was a state that no one wanted, it was Northern Ireland: not the British, who had tried to rid themselves of all of Ireland during three attempts at passing "home rule" measures; not the Irish nationalists, who wanted control over the entire island of Ireland; and least of all the Ulster Protestants, who wished to remain an integral part of the United Kingdom of Great Britain and Ireland. Unlike the southern nationalism of which Yeats sang, the northern state was not a terrible beauty, but a terrible embarrassment. Ulster (to use the contemporary synonym for Northern Ireland, even though in fact the territory of Northern Ireland encompassed only six of the original nine counties of Ulster) came into existence in 1920. Because a large majority of Northern Ireland's inhabitants were Protestants, the new state was freed from the restraints of pluralism and was able to work out laws and institutional practices based upon the attitudes and assumptions that had prevailed in the north before 1920, but which had been suppressed by Ulster's having been part of the larger polity that was Ireland. As such, Northern Ireland is the first of our series of three case studies of what happens when a convenantal culture assumes control of a modern state.

The fundamental irony is that Northern Ireland, which, of all the regions of the United Kingdom least wanted home rule, was the only one to receive it. This becomes a little more understandable when one recognizes that Ulster "unionism" (which in Irish politics refers not to trade unions but to those who wish to maintain the union with Great Britain) was itself affected by some very paradoxical behavior on the part of Irish nationalists. A. T. Q. Stewart touched the nub of the issue when he wrote that "in the long run the one decisive factor in partition" of northern and southern Ireland

> is not the weakness of Irish nationalism, nor the guile of unionists, nor the chicanery of British statesmanship. It is the simple determination of Protestants in north-east Ireland not to become a minority in a Catholic Ireland. It is towards weakening this determination that all the efforts of nationalism ought in theory to have been aimed. Instead they have been largely directed to strengthening it in every possible way.[1]

Applying Stewart's perspective to the formative years of the Ulster state, 1886–1920, it is clear that the Irish nationalists said and did things that—however unconsciously—were bound to frighten the Ulster Protestants. Thus they affirmed everything that the Protestants believed about the Catholics and about Irish nationalism, and thereby produced the Protestant's violent refusal to live within an independent Catholic Ireland. To someone imbued with a covenantal frame of mind, the response to cultural and political attack was automatic. Instinctively the Protestants drew closer together and adopted hard-shell defensive postures, for the assaults by the nationalists confirmed everything they had always known about the Canaanites who still were abroad in the land.

Ulster Protestant fears of living in a nationalist Ireland were threefold: they expected the new nation to be industrially backward and, in all probability, economically isolationist; they feared an onslaught upon their own culture; and they believed that in a nationalist-dominated Ireland, the Roman Catholic Church would directly reduce Protestant civil liberties. If one examines these three fears, one sees that they were not entirely chimerical.

First, note that an important strand in Irish nationalist thinking was that Ireland should become economically self-sufficient, and recall that the northeast part of Ireland was the only region that had undergone the British industrial revolution of the nineteenth century. Hence, nationalistic propaganda about self-sufficiency ("Sinn Fein," the name of the leading Irish independence pressure group, means Ourselves-Alone, and implied, among other things, economic isolation), presented Ulster Protestants with the prospect of severe economic setbacks. They did not want to sever their ties with industrial Britain, nor did they want to become economic beasts of burden forced to carry the economically primitive remainder of the country. The second concern, given the information available to Ulster Protestants about nationalist cultural intentions, was also very real. The Irish drive to revive the Gaelic language and culture and, wherever possible, to push out the English language and its attendant culture, was hardly the sort of thing to appeal to people who had been raised on the King James Bible, on Bunyan, and on Shakespeare. The third great fear, that Catholics would assail Protestant civil liberties, was fueled directly by the actions of the Catholic authorities. During the second half of the nineteenth century and the early twentieth centuries, the Catholic Church in Ireland and throughout the world had become increasingly aggressive on certain matters of concern to Protestants, notably education, mixed marriages, and church-state relations. Moreover, one school of nationalist thought equated Irish nationalism with Irish Catholicism, a blend made all the more repugnant to the British-oriented unionists when cultural nationalists added the Gaelic revival program to the equation.

One clear articulation (among many) of these Protestant fears was published in 1912 by the Presbyterian Church in Ireland, following a convention called to discuss the possibility of home rule for Ireland. The convention resolved

That we, the members of this great convention, representing the overwhelming majority of Irish Presbyterians . . . hereby record our unalterable opposition to all such proposals . . .

We are confident that, among other disastrous results, under Home Rule,

— our religious and civil liberties would be greatly imperilled;
— our industrial and agricultural interests would be seriously crippled . . .
— In view of the long-continued action of the Roman Catholic hierarchy in the direction of denominationalising education in Ireland, the children of such minorities would be deprived in all the provinces of Ireland of places of instruction which they might frequent, as they do now, without danger to their faith.

We call upon the Government . . . and should the Government fail us, we would earnestly appeal to our co-religionists of all shades of political opinion in Great Britain to save us while there is yet time from such overwhelming calamity. . . . We appeal to them to remember that we Presbyterians are now in Ireland because three centuries ago our forefathers were "planted" in Ulster by the English government in order that, by their loyalty and industry they might secure the peace and prosperity of our province and promote the mutual welfare of both countries . . .

Our Scottish forefathers, in their struggles for religious freedom and civil rights, cast their burden on the Lord Omnipotent, who gave them signal victory. Facing as we do dangers similar to theirs, we shall follow in their footsteps and emulate their faith. In the profound belief that God reigns, we commit our cause in all confidence to Him. . .[2]

Home rule for Ireland bills were introduced in 1886 and 1893 and they were blocked, the second after having passed the House of Commons, by the House of Lords. Though unsuccessful, these attempts made the Ulster Protestants hyperdefensive, for the question inevitably arose—what happens if a home rule bill actually passes through the United Kingdom Houses of Commons and Lords? This specter took palpable form in 1912, when a third home rule bill was introduced, for changes in the United Kingdom's constitutional structure had reduced the House of Lords veto to a mere three-year delaying power. In 1912, the government was strongly committed to riding the bill through, no matter how serious the Ulster political opposition.[3]

By mid-1912, it was obvious to the Ulster Protestant leaders that the third home rule bill would become law. The Ulster Protestants thereupon decided to go beyond conventional political behavior and engage in paramilitary tactics. As early as September 1911, 50,000 men representing the Orange Order and the unionist clubs had marched past the home of the Protestant leader Captain James Craig in a show of solidarity against home rule. In September 1912 virtually the entire adult male Protestant population of Ulster signed "Ulster's Solemn League and Covenant" (the women signed a separate "Declaration") which was consciously redolent of Scottish covenanting antecedents. This was a distinctly treasonable document in that its signers swore to use all means necessary to defeat the "conspiracy" to set up a home rule parliament in Ireland. That this document, which is the nodal point around which all subsequent Ulster history revolves, was a distinctly Presbyterian artifact is yet another indication of the real (but frequently unrecognized) cultural hegemony that the Ulster-Scots held over the entire Protestant population of the north of Ireland.

Throughout the Protestant area of Ulster, groups were formed to hold regular military drills, using firearms whenever available. Early in 1913

Ulster's
Solemn League and Covenant.

Being convinced in our consciences that Home Rule would be disastrous to the material well-being of Ulster as well as of the whole of Ireland, subversive of our civil and religious freedom, destructive of our citizenship and perilous to the unity of the Empire, we, whose names are underwritten, men of Ulster, loyal subjects of His Gracious Majesty King George V., humbly relying on the God whom our fathers in days of stress and trial confidently trusted, do hereby pledge ourselves in solemn Covenant throughout this our time of threatened calamity to stand by one another in defending for ourselves and our children our cherished position of equal citizenship in the United Kingdom and in using all means which may be found necessary to defeat the present conspiracy to set up a Home Rule Parliament in Ireland. ¶ And in the event of such a Parliament being forced upon us we further solemnly and mutually pledge ourselves to refuse to recognise its authority. ¶ In sure confidence that God will defend the right we hereto subscribe our names. ¶ And further, we individually declare that we have not already signed this Covenant.

The above was signed by me at ....
"Ulster Day," Saturday, 28th September, 1912.

God Save the King.

Figure 3. The Ulster Covenant

these disparate paramilitary bodies were welded into a single organization as the Ulster Volunteer Force. The Volunteers were successful in buying arms abroad and in smuggling them into the country. By late April 1914, Ulster was an armed camp, its Protestant citizens pledged to frustrate the will of the United Kingdom parliament at whatever the cost. The unionists' plan of action, should home rule be thrust upon them, was for the Ulster Volunteer Force to seize control of the province. All United Kingdom military barracks, ammunition, and equipment were to be captured. The existing civilian administration was to be replaced by a provincial government headed by members of the Ulster Unionist Council.[4]

In these circumstances, the United Kingdom government might have been expected to move sharply against the Ulster unionists. They dared not, however, because in March 1914, the "Curragh mutiny" of the military forces in Ireland had shown that they could not be counted on to march on Ulster. Effectively this meant that the United Kingdom's prime minister, Herbert Asquith, had to find a compromise settlement. But was there common ground? If Asquith allowed the home rule bill to become law (as scheduled for 1914), there almost certainly would be a civil insurrection in Ulster, one that probably could not be put down militarily. And if he broke his promise to the Irish nationalists to complete the home rule transaction, then the south probably would flare into guerilla warfare. Ironically (in a situation already heavy with irony), the great European war temporarily prevented the domestic war. When war was declared in Europe, a measure was passed to suspend the Home Rule Act until the end of the war; the unionists were promised that the home rule measure would not come into effect until an amending bill dealing with Ulster was hammered out.

As we know now, Protestant Ulster had won, although ultimately it won something that it did not really want. During World War I, Irish nationalism passed from a constitutional to a paramilitary mode (the Easter Rising of 1916 was the signal event in this process), so home rule ceased to be a realistic solution to the demands of nationalist Ireland. However, the Home Rule Act of 1914 was now on the books, and there was still that promise to be fulfilled, to work out something under home rule rubrics to suit the northern Protestants. Thus, David Lloyd George negotiated a set of agreements that eventually resulted in the Government of Ireland Act of 1920, usually called the Partition Act. This act was a mixture of realism and hypocrisy: in essence it was the Home Rule Act of 1914 bisected. It provided for two home rule parliaments to be set up in

Ireland, one for the six northeastern counties, the other for the rest of the country, both to be under the supervision of London government, and both to belong to a "council of Ireland." At any future date the council could be replaced by a united Irish parliament through the passage of identical affirming acts by the parliaments of Northern and Southern Ireland. Of course most of these provisions were fictitious. The southern Irish nationalists were well beyond playing the constitutional game and were unwilling to recognize the partition of Ireland in any form. So the only parts of the act that came into actual practice were the provisions for establishing a local home rule parliament for the six northeastern counties of Ulster. In 1921, Sir James Craig, head of the northern government, wrote to David Lloyd George, "As a final settlement and supreme sacrifice in the interests of peace the Government of Ireland Act, 1920, was accepted by Northern Ireland although not asked for by her representatives."[5]

(2)

Because the state that they controlled had been thrust upon them, rather than obtained by a long and holy quest, the Ulster Protestants never ascribed to their state the fully sacralized character that one expects in covenanting cultures (and as was clearly developed in both South Africa and Israel, discussed later). Yet this should not obscure the fact that the Ulster state owed its existence to the covenantal bonding, under Presbyterian forms, of the Ulster Protestants, a bonding so strong that the imperial leaders in the United Kingdom knew they could not dissolve it. Nor should we forget that the new state assumed a sectarian character dictated by the religious adhesion and attendant social configurations of Ulster society. Ulster did not have a state church, but the Ulster Protestant churches had something approaching a church state.

Throughout 1920–69, Northern Ireland was the most religious region of the United Kingdom, and, as secularization occurred rapidly in twentieth-century Britain, the unusual salience of religion in Ulster life became more striking with each passing year. A study of group relations in Northern Ireland using data generated in the late 1950s concluded that the "church attendance percentage for Northern Ireland is probably higher than in England at the beginning of the century, and for Protestants may well be four to six times as high as the present figure for England."

(Weekly attendance in Ulster was nearly 60 percent for Presbyterians, between 45 and 50 percent for Anglicans and well above 90 percent for Roman Catholics.)[6]

In 1968 and 1969, just at the end of the period of unchallenged Protestant control of Northern Ireland, the Independent Television Authority, as part of its marketing research, conducted an extensive survey comparing religious attitudes in Northern Ireland and Great Britain. This fairly sophisticated survey indicated not only the valence of religious beliefs, but also how strongly they were held. Fifty-seven percent of Ulster adults showed strong patterns of religious commitment, in contrast to 22 percent in Great Britain. This finding had notable corollaries in a wide variety of areas. For example, nearly three-quarters (74 percent) of Ulster people of all denominations said that it was "very important that their country was a Christian one." Fewer than half (48 percent) of British people felt the same way. When respondents were asked how important religious beliefs were in their everyday life, over three-quarters (76 percent) of Northern Ireland's adults said, "a great deal," or "a lot," while less than half (45 percent) of adults in Great Britain had equally strong attachments. One of the more interesting differences was that the Ulster people had a much stronger tendency to follow the Yahwistic tradition and to believe in a personified God than did people on the British mainland.[7] The responses revealed that Ulster society was undoubtedly more deeply permeated by religious ways of thinking than the rest of the United Kingdom, which helps explain why the Northern Ireland government, a devolved and miniaturized version of the United Kingdom government, operated according to rules determined by a regional political culture very different from that of Great Britain.

In reflecting on the place of religion in the political culture of Northern Ireland in the period of unchallenged Protestant control, we must not fall into the belief that religion caused everything. Obviously, it did not, but what religion did not dominate, it tinctured. Similarly, one should not jump to the opposite extreme and conclude that just because there was a good deal of vocally expressed irreligion in Ulster formal religion was only a veneer over more fundamental cultural and social forces. Actually, in the period under examination there was a high degree of what one may call "religion by surrogates." Frank Wright has documented this phenomenon, which was especially common among urban working-class Protestants. "There are many, even in the non-church-going communities, who, despite not being convinced believers themselves, nonetheless have an anxiety about their unbelief. They recognize that, in some sense, the things they value depend upon *some* people believing." In Wright's view, it would be wrong to see this as "a calculative concern for religion based upon political motives." That notion, says Wright, "seems to me to run rather easily over the often very real reverance for the 'open Bible.' "[8] And this explains, Wright argues, why even those urban working-class Protestants who had given up orthodox religion in the sense of attending church regularly, still followed religious leadership—even when they themselves no longer believed.

It is easy to forget the demographic fact that among the Northern Ireland population, the Roman Catholics were the single largest denomination—33.5 percent in 1926, 34.9 percent in 1961, to take two representative dates. The two other major denominations were Protestant: Presbyterians, 31.4 percent and 29.0 percent and Anglicans, 27.0 percent and 24.2 percent, at the same respective dates.[9] As noted earlier, however, the Presbyterians were clearly dominant in shaping the collective outlook of Protestant Ulster. This was in part because the actual buildings of their headquarters and, more important, their spiritual home—were in Belfast, whereas the Anglicans (the Church of Ireland) were centred in Dublin and tried to maintain an all-Ireland perspective. A considerable minority of Anglicans were in the south of Ireland, while the Presbyterians had only a few scattered congregations there. Therefore, the Anglican Church had to cultivate political relationships with the successive governments of southern Ireland. This prevented the development of a vigorous unionist ideology among Anglicans which would be consonant with the political values of the Protestant people of Northern Ireland. Further, certain class factors in Northern Ireland buttressed the Presbyterians' dominance. Simply put, Ulster's upper class (mostly old landowning families) and the urban working class tended to be Anglican, and were disunited in terms of social relations. On the other hand, the class most politically active in Ulster and most culturally homogeneous, the middle class in the countryside and in the cities, was largely Presbyterian.[10] Most important, the Presbyterians, with their covenantal cultural system, had a way of thinking, a cultural code, that both united them and gave them a way of integrating other northern Protestants into their way of thinking—without requiring religious conversion on the part of other Protestants. The latter point is telling, because changing one's religion in Ulster, even between Protestant denominations, is not something done lightly. Therefore, what in generalized terms was described as a Protestant state for a

Protestant people was, in fact, a covenantal state, shaped for and by Presbyterians and for those who (like most Ulster Protestants) thought like them.

The social universe in which the Protestant state operated from the 1920s onward was one of simple, stark dualism. Nearly everything in the society—business firms, schools, clubs, political parties, and many urban neighborhoods—was signposted, in a way obvious to locals if not always to outsiders, indicating whether they were Protestant or Catholic. These were not like the "Whites Only" or "Coloured Only" signs of South Africa of the apartheid era, for someone of the other side could gain entry, but it was always clear who was in charge. Someone who "dug with the wrong foot" would at least be uncomfortable with the cool welcome in a public bar that belonged to the other side. A Catholic in a Protestant working-class neighborhood or a Protestant in a working-class Catholic district stood a strong chance of being harassed and physically abused. Even in places where the two sides met on an open basis—for example, at internationally organized service clubs, such as Rotary—everyone who was a regular knew what sort everyone else was. Even people who were genuinely tolerant had to keep a mental file on the religious persuasion of their acquaintances, if for no other reason than to avoid giving offense on social occasions.

Within the larger cities, the working-class districts were traditionally demarcated as being either Protestant or Catholic. In Derry and in Belfast, the history of these borders went back at least a century and to locals they bulked as large as the Maginot Line. In Northern Ireland, most middle-class areas were religiously integrated, but because of the favored economic position of the Protestant population, they were mostly Protestant. Rural areas were less sharply segregated, but individual pieces of land were often clearly labeled in local knowledge as being either Protestant or Catholic. One only has to look at property advertisements of, say, 1920–40, in newspapers such as the Belfast *Newsletter* (a Protestant paper) or the *Irish News* (a Catholic paper), to realize that both groups were extremely sensitive about property transfer and would often offer to sell only to their coreligionists. In rural areas, both groups employed their own real estate auctioneers, who were expected to know the religion of everyone who might bid, and if someone from the wrong side bid highest, the auctioneer would announce that the reserve price had not been met and then asked for sealed bids by post. Manifestly, such practices were not universally enforced, because land did change hands between Protestants and Catholics, but the inhibitions on the transfer were real.

Even when not territorially segregated, Protestants and Catholics in Northern Ireland lived in separate social universes. In the years 1920–69, no schools beneath the university level were religiously integrated. In law, nothing stopped a Protestant child attending a Catholic school, or a Catholic child a state (de facto Protestant) school, but that happened so rarely that the children of Ulster can be described as having existed in a religiously segregated educational environment.

Social practice tended to be differentiated denominationally. Rugby, cricket, and girls' field hockey long were identified as predominantly Protestant games, while various Gaelic games (hurling, camogie, Gaelic football) were almost exclusively Catholic. Although it seems quaint to outsiders, a great deal of tension existed in this period on what it was proper to do on a Sunday: Catholics tended to go in for leisure amusement once their religious duties were done, while Protestants had a more severe Sabbatarian streak. Thus arose such a trivial (but typical) fracas as the attempt in 1958 of the Portadown Borough Council, a thoroughly Protestant group, to withhold a "seven day license" from three Catholic churches that wanted to hold dances on Sunday evenings. Never mind that few, if any, Protestant youths would be attending these dances, Sabbath-breaking could not be condoned. (The case took more than two years to wind through borough council and then the courts, which eventually decided to let the Catholics dance on Sunday.)[11]

The one thing that disturbed both sides more than anything else was intermarriage. There were some inhibitions on Protestants marrying those of other Protestant denominations, but nothing like the penalty that a Protestant-Catholic marriage elicited. The authorities of the Roman Catholic Church, it must be emphasized, were just as adamant as the Protestants on the prohibition. It is no surprise that Protestant-Catholic marriages were few. Indeed, one social scientist who studied rural Ulster society in the 1940s came to the conclusion that intermarriage between Catholics and Protestants was so rare that "they can be considered as two endogamous societies."[12]

What this all adds up to is quite simple. Given the dualistic nature of the Ulster society and the character of the covenantal cultural grid of the dominant group in Ulster's Protestant culture, the Presbyterians, it was inevitable that the state of Northern Ireland would institutionalize strong patterns of discrimination by Protestants against Roman Catholics. How could it have been otherwise? Had the leaders of the new state been nonjudgmental and nondiscriminatory, they would have been untrue to the culture that supported the state. The Ulster state had grown organ-ically out of the covenanting mindset in general, and was based on the Ulster Covenant of 1912 in particular. Anyone who has made a covenant with God and with fellow believers can be nonjudgmental only by breaking those vows. To be true to its God, a covenantal society is constrained to act in ways that appear, to outsiders, to be unjust to others.

The covenantal commitment to tilting the state in favor of their own tribe was reinforced by the Protestant's perpetual anxiety about "the enemy." For example, Protestants feared that Catholics would "outbreed" them and thus eventually become a majority within Northern Ireland. Eventually—say in the middle of the twenty-first century—this may come to pass, but in 1920–69, the relative size of the Catholic population was stable, at about one-third of the total Ulster populace. Another form of Protestant anxiety involves what has been called the "Lundy fixation."[13] During a late-seventeenth-century siege of Londonderry, the governor, Robert Lundy, was willing to negotiate with the Catholics. To this day, "Don't be a Lundy" is a phrase that makes Protestant leaders turn away from compromise. The ultimate Protestant fear was of being cast into a united Ireland with a Catholic majority. This point was graphically made by Barritt and Carter's collection of the lead editorials in the main Protestant newspaper, the Belfast *Newsletter*, which appeared before each general election. Here is a sampling:

> (1929) The issue is whether a Unionist Government shall continue to control affairs, safeguard the interests, and help to shape the destiny of Northern Ireland . . .
>
> (1933) The issue at stake in this contest must be apparent to all. Do the Ulster people still value their birthright?
>
> (1938) Lord Craigavon's purpose in this election is to show that Ulster stands precisely where it did in relation to the Free State or rather that its people's attachment to Great Britain and Empire is as strong as ever . . .
>
> (1945) From whatever angle the General Election in Northern Ireland be regarded, the Constitutional question emerges as the governing issue.
>
> (1949) Today Ulster people go to the poll on an issue which admits of no compromise—whether they are to continue in Union with Great Britain or to be absorbed into an Irish Republic.[14]

And so on, right through the 1960s. At each moment of potential political vulnerability, the Protestants of Ulster reaffirmed that they stood behind the Covenant of 1912, and the state that, in 1920, had been founded in Protestant Ulster.

(3)

On the surface, the state that was created in Northern Ireland by the Partition Act of 1920 was not remarkable. It had a threefold foundation, involving constitutional arrangements, financial relations with Great Britain, and a boundary settlement with the south of Ireland.

The basic principle underpinning the constitution of the Northern Ireland regime was the principle of devolution. Northern Ireland was not a sovereign state and it had powers and responsibilities only in matters specifically defined and delegated by the government in London. The division of powers between "Stormont" (the colloquial name for the Ulster administration, based at Stormont Castle, near Belfast) and London was between matters of local concern and those of concern to regions other than Ulster. Parliament in London legislated on matters affecting the entire United Kingdom, including Ulster. Northern Ireland had twelve members in the London parliament, but most of the daily government of Ulster was determined by policies set by the Stormont parliament. The Stormont parliament was a scaled-down version of the United Kingdom parliament. It was bicameral: the fifty-two members of the House of Commons were elected directly and the members of the Senate were chosen by the party in power in the lower house. In practice, the Senate had few powers and membership was a reward to Unionist party stalwarts. The Ulster cabinet was a regional replica of the United Kingdom cabinet, having, in a normal year, ten members plus the attorney general and eight parliamentary secretaries. Thus, roughly one-third of the membership of the parliament of Northern Ireland was in receipt of official salaries, a situation that made for unusually tight discipline.[15]

The financial relations between Great Britain and Northern Ireland were extremely complicated and the details were never open to full public scrutiny, but the most important fact was this: the government of Northern Ireland received a sizable subsidy from the United Kingdom government so that the citizens of Northern Ireland payed less for the same level of social and governmental services than did the British. In the late 1960s this subsidy amounted to at least 80 pounds annually for every inhabitant of Northern Ireland. This was not intended when the Government of Ireland Act of 1920 was framed, during a time of economic optimism.

Then it was believed that Northern Ireland would be able to bear its proportionate share of the United Kingdom's financial obligations. By the mid-1920s, however, it was clear that Northern Ireland would be unable to do so, and from then on Ulster was an economically depressed area compared to the rest of the United Kingdom (although well off compared to the rest of Ireland). Within the United Kingdom context, Northern Ireland's social and welfare services (which were kept at a par with the rest of the United Kingdom's) were relatively high and its tax revenues comparatively low. Hence, the subsidy from London.[16]

The third building block upon which the Ulster government rested was a settlement of the question of territory—the "border question" as it was known by contemporaries. The amount of territory under its control is crucial to any state, and in the case of a settler society, such as Protestant Ulster, doubly so. Besides the territory's economic significance, the land had taken on almost mythological significance: Protestants saw it as having been redeemed as a result of its occupation by the covenanting society. The Government of Ireland Act of 1920 had defined the six counties that were to constitute Northern Ireland, but in 1920 it was still unclear whether or not the United Kingdom government intended partition to be permanent. In late 1921, during the course of the negotiations of the Anglo-Irish treaty (to end the war between Irish nationalists and the United Kingdom government), the British representatives suggested that provisions be made for a "boundary commission" to revise the Northern Ireland territory in accordance with the wishes of the inhabitants. (This assumed, correctly, that the Ulster unionists would remain adamant in their refusal to join the south.) As finally enacted, the Anglo-Irish treaty of 1922 contained a provision that if the parliament of Northern Ireland decided not to join the newly created Irish Free State, a boundary commission would be appointed consisting of three people, one chosen by the Free State government, one by the Northern Ireland government, and one by the United Kingdom, the latter being automatically named chairman.

The boundary commission convened in 1924. The British appointed as their representative Mr. Justice Feetham of the supreme court of South Africa, a jurist with wide experience in dominion affairs. The Irish Free State appointed Professor Eoin MacNeill, its minister of education. The Northern Ireland government, faced with the possibility of losing some territory, refused to appoint a member. Thus, the United Kingdom government (now under the Labourite Ramsay MacDonald) responded by appointing an Ulster Protestant and longtime friend of the Ulster leader James Craig, Joseph R. Fisher, to represent northern interests. The commission met regularly throughout the autumn of 1925 and conducted careful examination of whether various locales—parishes and in some cases mere townlands—should be moved north or south. Apparently the commission was ready to report in November 1925 and planned to make only minor changes in the border, including not only transfers from Ulster to southern Ireland, but also transfers of small Protestant pockets in eastern Donegal to the northern government. Just before the commission reported, however, the London *Morning Post* published a map, which had been leaked to the press. It showed these border changes, and suddenly there was a public outcry in the south of Ireland. Professor MacNeill resigned from the commission and once the Free State representative was gone, the commission was dismantled. Its investigation was now totally disregarded and classified as secret. In the wake of this debacle, the three governments—Northern Ireland, the Irish Free State, and the United Kingdom—signed an agreement ratifying the existing boundaries. The six counties were not reduced and, to the vexation of Irish nationalists, Northern Ireland remained an economic and governmental unit of viable size.[17]

That the state of Northern Ireland was expected by the Ulster majority to favor Protestants and to discriminate against Catholics was axiomatic. However, it must be emphasized that discrimination in Ulster society was not uniform. Discrimination occurred at certain points for the tactically important maintenance of the majority position, especially on matters related to control of political machinery of the state. But even in matters of electoral discrimination, the practice was very specific in its application. To understand how this surgically sharp discrimination worked, one must recognize two ground rules. The first is that there were, in Ulster politics, only two real parties, and although these had secular names—"unionist" and "nationalist" were the most common—the parties actually were simply Protestants and Catholics. The nonsectarian Labour party had a small success in Belfast, and there were nationalist splinter parties, but basically all voting was tribal. And second, one must realize that tribal discrimination could occur at three levels of government: elections for seats in the Westminster (United Kingdom) parliament, elections for seats in the regional (Stormont) parliament, and local government elections, for towns and borough councils and county councils.[18]

The thirteen Ulster members of the United Kingdom parliament (reduced to twelve when seats for the universities were abolished in the United Kingdom in 1949) were elected under the same franchise rules, and under the same system of single-seat constituencies as in the rest of the United Kingdom. The constituency boundaries were set by United Kingdom statues and reviewed by the national electoral boundary commission, a group with no vested interest in the Ulster scene. Nevertheless, a person sensitized to matters of discrimination might point to a typical election, 1931, for example, in which eleven of the thirteen seats were won by Protestants. That person might conclude that gross discrimination was occurring, since Roman Catholics made up roughly one-third of the Northern Ireland population. In reality, however, these results were a product of the United Kingdom's system of single-seat constituencies, rather than of any electoral maneuvering by Protestants. As long as single-seat constituencies were the rule, and as long as the Catholic population was dispersed throughout the larger population, Catholics were inevitably underrepresented at Westminster. Indeed, the two largest constituencies for Westminster elections were south Antrim and north Down, both Protestant areas, which is just the opposite of what the situation would have been if gerrymandering had taken place. In point of fact, the United Kingdom elections were treated with indifference by Ulster voters of both sides. In 1931, for example, there were only four contested seats and only 135,000 votes were cast out of an electorate of about 785,000.[19]

Nor was the provincial electoral system the site of significant discriminatory social management, although it was less scrupulously fair than was the United Kingdom electoral system. The brute demographic facts of Ulster life meant that Protestants (in the form of the Unionist party) would control the provincial parliament. At first, elections for the Stormont parliament were held on the basis of proportional representation, which, in principle, was fair to small minority groups but did not affect in practice the overall Protestant-Catholic electoral balance. In 1929, proportional representation was replaced by single-seat constituencies in order to stop the development of right-wing Protestant splinter parties. In terms of the Protestant-Catholic split, the single-seat system produced results almost exactly identical to those of the proportional representation system, namely that eleven or twelve seats out of fifty-two went to Catholics.

Where the real electoral discrimination took place was at the local level. Ulster's system of local government was similar to that of England. It rested on a prepartition statute, the Local Government (Ireland) Act of 1898. To take a representative point in time, there were in the mid-1930s, six administrative counties, two county boroughs (Londonderry and Belfast), two boroughs, thirty urban districts, and thirty-two rural districts—seventy-two units in all, each headed by an elected council. These councils were powerful because they controlled thousands of local jobs (from road sweepers to town clerks, to chief administrative officers of county boroughs), and they controlled access to most of Ulster's public housing. It was here, at the local level, that it was not only profitable to discriminate actively against Catholics, but also necessary—for unlike the province as a whole, the Catholics were a potential electoral majority in a considerable number of local government areas. Thus, the system was shamelessly rigged to maintain Protestant control. This was achieved, in the first instance, by permitting plural voting for elected councils. Owners of businesses (more often Protestants than Catholics) received an additional vote. Second, universal suffrage was not granted in local elections: one had to be a rate payer, meaning a property-tax payer (and not, for instance, living at home with one's parents). A larger proportion of Catholics than Protestants were excluded by this rule, given the Catholics' generally lower economic position. And, third, local electoral boundaries were drawn to maximize Protestant power. In theory, local electoral boundaries were established under the principle that the valuation of property in a given area was as important in establishing the electoral boundaries as was the number of people in the district. This is a plausible principle, but in practice Catholics were lumped together into any district that they were sure to control (thus causing them to waste votes) and Protestants were spread into thin (but sure) electoral majorities in other districts. The classic case of gerrymandering occurred in Derry. In that city there were three wards containing a total electoral population of roughly 14,300 Catholics and 8,700 Protestants. Yet the unionists controlled the city council by the simple expedient of placing most of the Catholics in a single ward. A similar situation held for the County Fermanagh council.

Finally, one should mention that a marked degree of electoral corruption was permitted in close elections. Today older Protestant residents of Derry nostalgically recall the great "jumble sale" elections of the past— when they donned one set of clothes, impersonated a long-dead Protestant elector, and then came back to party headquarters to put on another costume and go out and vote again. And yet again.

Housing and jobs were well worth controlling. In the years between the end of World War II and 1969, roughly 100,000 new houses were built in Northern Ireland—three-eighths by private enterprise, one-quarter by the Northern Ireland Housing Trust (a provincewide body that was largely nondiscriminatory in its operation), and three-eighths by local government bodies. The overwhelming evidence is that whichever religious side controlled a local council very heavily favored its own coreligionists in allocating the new housing units. That point must be underscored: in 1969 Roman Catholics controlled eleven local government units and they discriminated just as heavily against Protestants as Protestants did against Catholics; the only difference was that Protestants were more apt to be in power.[20] It is on this matter—housing—that the convoluted and systemic nature of discrimination under the northern state becomes clear. Recall that to vote in local elections one had to be a rate payer. Thus, if one allocated a house to a person from the other side, one was also creating a voter, one almost certain to vote for his or her own tribe. Therefore, the realities of the electoral system meant that local authorities had to discriminate (even if, by some stretch of the imagination they did not want to do so). Providing housing for someone of the other religion was to put oneself out of political office.

Of course, as part of maintaining the faith with their coreligionists, Protestants engaged in employment discrimination against Catholics in all economic sectors (as did Catholics against Protestants when they were in a position to do so). To do otherwise would have been to be faithless. Job discrimination both at entry and on promotion was virtually universal in all private businesses owned within Ulster, but accurate statistical evidence is impossible to obtain. What one can obtain, however, is public sector employment data. For example, if we examine the senior level of the Stormont civil service (from staff officers up through permanent secretaries) we find that in 1927, 94 percent of the posts were held by Protestants. Between 1927 and 1959, the number of provincial civil servants increased 300 percent, yet in 1959, 94 percent of the senior levels still were Protestant.[21] This cadre, enormously powerful, was charged with the day-to-day administration of the government. Here the real power of the state resided. (Tellingly, the Ministry of Home Affairs, which controlled security for Northern Ireland, had not a single Catholic at the rank of principal or above in 1959). A mid-1950s study indicated that if one took all grades above custodial level, roughly 12 percent of the Northern Ireland civil service was Roman Catholic.[22] As one would expect, at the local level almost all senior jobs and most lower ones were alloted on a sectarian basis.

What was the overall result of the Protestants of Ulster keeping faith with each other, as under the covenant? In the first place, vertical (religious and tribal) alignments carried much more weight in determining personal loyalties than did class alignments. Protestants garnered for themselves most, but far from all, of the positions that controlled employment and economic activity. And, as a group, Protestants were slightly better off economically than were Catholics. A study conducted in the late 1960s found that Catholics had an average family income level of approximately 15 percent less than that of Protestants.[23] That is a significant difference, but not great when compared to, say, the difference in white and black family incomes in the United States.

At the risk of becoming too ethereal, I would suggest that the chief way in which the covenanting mentality of the Ulster state bore down on the northern Catholics was in reminding them, day after day, in matters more symbolically humiliating than economically painful, that the state was not theirs. What the Protestants communicated so well was that for "us," the Protestants, Ulster is ours, the land, the state, and what-we-have-we-hold. Symbolic activities, such as flying the Union Jack over the Belfast shipyards, and singing "The Queen" at public events became charged with significance. Such acts reminded the Catholics who was in charge and that even if they were doing well economically (and many of them were better off than many Protestants), it was in a land ruled by the other tribe.

Control of the system of justice and of the police, in such a charged atmosphere becomes something more than mere security considerations. From 1922 on, a series of special and emergency powers acts suspended in part and under certain circumstances the normal civil liberties and normal legal rights of those thought to be engaged in antistate activities. Twelve percent of the Royal Ulster Constabulary, in 1969 numbering around 3,000 members, was Catholic. Actually, one-third of the places were reserved for Catholics, but the force was perceived as so sectarian that Catholic recruitment was difficult. Catholic distrust of the system of justice was particularly keen since the 1920s, when a group of volunteer constables (usually called "B-Specials") was formed entirely from among Protestants. This militia gave armed Protestants quasi-police powers. As important as individual cases of intimidation, false arrests, and unjust imprisonment may have been, I think that of greater weight was the fact that this system affected everyone. One did not have to be convicted, or even detained or questioned, to be continually reminded of the reality that was represented by every policeman and every B-Special one encountered. Their very presence brought home the reality of the Protestant state.[24]

As I mentioned earlier, the state of Northern Ireland never became a sacralized entity, but certain rituals produced a continuity of covenantal commitment. The original event, of course, had been the 1912 signing of the Ulster Covenant (by men) and the Declaration (by women), by almost the entire adult Protestant population of Ulster. In the eyes of its adherents, this covenant was later immersed in the sacrificial blood of thousands of Ulstermen, shed at the Battle of the Somme. True to their professed willingness to die for the United Kingdom, the overwhelming majority of the Ulster Volunteer Force had enlisted in the army to fight in Europe. On the first day of July 1916, the Ulster division was ordered to advance on half a dozen strongly held German trenches. On the dawn of the attack their padre read to them these words: "Thou shalt not be afraid for the terror by night nor the arrow which flieth by day. A thousand shall fall by thy side, and ten thousand at thy right hand, but it shall not come nigh thee." And then, after a heavy bombardment, they were sent forward. An English officer of the time was struck by their bravery and their ancient Protestant cry, "No surrender." The Ulstermen took the German trenches and then it was discovered that the allied officers had blundered terribly. On neither flank had there been a parallel advance, and now the men were surrounded on three sides. The full casualty lists were published at home in Northern Ireland just before the traditional Protestant holiday, the twelfth of July, whose celebrations were canceled that year.[25] By sealing the covenant with their blood, the Ulster Volunteer Force morally legitimated Ulster's claim not to be included in a Catholic state. In the years that followed, the Orange celebrations of 12 July contained the traditional visual and rhetorical references to 1690, to the battles of Derry, Enniskillen, and the Boyne, but now also to the Somme, to the Covenant, and to blood sacrifice.

7

The High Noon of
Apartheid, 1948–1969

(1)

The term "apartheid" became part of the vocabulary of Afrikaner thought in the 1940s.[1] Dan O'Meara finds its first official usage in the Afrikaner economic movement in May 1943 in an editorial on economic segregation.[2] In September 1943 the word was used in a speech by D. F. Malan, point man on many Afrikaner issues and, in 1948, prime minister of South Africa. Irving Hexham finds that "apartheid" was used as early as 1914 by Dopper theologians within the context of arguments for preserving the unique Dopper way of life.[3] Whatever the precise date of its introduction as a term, apartheid in practice was the completion of a process that gradually and inexorably had occurred in Afrikaner society. Anyone who has observed one of those crystal-growing exercises so beloved of primary school science classes will have a feel for this: apartheid grew so gradually that one cannot point to its origin at any particular moment, but like the forming crystals, the process was continuous. If one takes readings at intervals, the progress is unmistakable and, after 1948, apartheid becomes full blown, the visible institutional incarnation of the values and beliefs of Afrikaner culture, society, and economy.

The one major way in which the Afrikaner people of the early twentieth century differed from their ancient Hebrew models was that they did not have the power to make laws themselves. The Afrikaner's covenantal cultural grid implied a great deal of concern with the sacred and the

203

profane and with right and wrong behavior. The rules of right conduct were formulated in churches and in schools. A covenantal society requires more than voluntary discipline, however. Such societies require the freedom to create a full *halachah,* and this the Afrikaner *volk* acquired in 1948.

The general election of 1948 was won by the Herenigde Nasionale party (usually called the National party or the Nationalists), with an absolute parliamentary majority although they did not receive as many votes as did the United party: 79 seats in a House of Assembly of 159 members. This victory in itself did not cause a major reorientation in South African history, but it was the external ratification of a long sequence of internal shifts and intensifications within the society, and especially within Afrikaner culture. Whether the accession to power of the proponents of the "purified" version of Afrikaner nationalism could have occurred somewhat earlier (Dunbar Moodie suggests that had there been a general election in 1941, the Nationalists would have had a good chance of victory),[4] or whether their victory could have been staved off for a few years after 1948 is immaterial. The physics of South African white society made their victory virtually inevitable. The reason is found in two related phenomena. First, the "purified" version of Afrikaner nationalism, as set forth by the National party, not only served the economic interests of Afrikaner community but also, as Hermann Giliomee notes, addressed through a strategy of ethnic mobilization the "cultural and psychosocial fears and needs of the *Volk.*"[5] And, second, simple demography guaranteed that once the Afrikaner *volk* adhered to a single political party, that party would be dominant. Not only were there more people of Afrikaner than of British Isles origin in the Union of South Africa—the ratio was roughly 60 to 40—but the Afrikaners had a markedly higher birth rate.[6] Undeniably, there were technical reasons why the Nationalists had their breakthrough in 1948—most important was the redrawing of constituency boundaries before the 1948 elections in a way that led the Nationalists to "waste" fewer votes than did their opponents—but the central point of the election victory should not be lost.[7]

The National party achieved victory by forging a movement that simultaneously cut across classes and was ethnically specific. The way this movement mobilized voters is enlightening. In the first place, Afrikaner workers deserted the Labor party and joined the Nationalists in the Witswatersrand constituencies. In the second place, large numbers of Transvaal farmers abandoned the United party and turned to the National party.[8] Undoubtedly each of these groups, the workers and the farmers, believed that their own economic interests would be better served by voting Nationalist than by following the other parties, but in doing so, they were not joining a class-oriented movement, but one whose very raison d'être was to repudiate class divisions. It was an Afrikaner party: that is, an ethnic interest group. As Jeffrey Butler notes, any useful analysis of the election must "explain why it was the Afrikaner farmers, not all farmers, who deserted the United Party in 1948."[9] In fact, ethnic mobilization had overcome all other factors in South African political life. So intense was the mobilization that South Africa became, if not a one-party state, a state in which from henceforth only one party had a chance of victory. The Nationalists won a plurality of votes and 94 seats in the general election of 1953 (of 159 seats in the Assembly), 105 in 1958, and 126 in 1961. When the Assembly was increased to 166 members in 1966, they took 126 seats and 118 in 1970.[10] If it is true, as the political proverb has it, that the time between any two general elections is a lifetime, the National party's hold on power has seemed to be for an eternity.

And eternity was very much part of the vocabulary of the Afrikaners as they carved apartheid into law. The South African state was put on earth to preserve intact a line of divinely ordered historical development, a line that ran from the creation to the end of human history. This belief, along with the belief that Afrikaner culture was one of the pure bastions of western civilization, was widely held by the Afrikaner population. When, in the early 1960s, a team of social scientists conducted a survey of white attitudes in the Transvaal, they noted in the introduction to their study that "South Africa believed that she would" through apartheid "safeguard the essentials of the civilisation which whites had brought to the continent three centuries ago and which they had developed in line with the main cultural stream of the Western world."[11] This sense of continuity with the central values of western civilization was more stridently expressed in a lead article in *Die Volksblad* in 1946. "World affairs, moving at a furious pace, have brought our people to a second moment of crisis in which everything is at stake. We stand before a second Blood River. . . . Western civilisation has destroyed itself in a titanic struggle . . . and with it the Divinely ordained divisions between East and West and between the white men and the coloured races." Here in South Africa "is the setting of the final trial of strength between Christendom and heathendom."[12] D. F. Malan, prime minister of South Africa from June 1948 to November 1954, said in 1942 that "it is through the will of God that the Afrikaner

People exists at all. In His wisdom He determined that on the southern point of Africa, the dark continent, a People should be born who would be the bearer of Christian culture and civilization."[13]

Although Malan's victory in 1948 meant for many Afrikaners that (in a widely quoted phrase of the time) "from now on a Kaffir is a Kaffir again,"[14] there was also a good deal of talk, much of it serious and some of it doubtlessly sincere, about apartheid being part of a divine plan of the white man's trusteeship for the black. Trusteeship was necessary because the blacks were like children. And there was a spiritual trust involved. "Because we understand the soul of Africa, we have a noble task and calling towards Africa," B. J. Vorster averred in 1967. He added, "But I also make bold to say that Africa understands us."[15]

The Dutch Reformed clergy continually worked on the trusteeship theme in the 1950s and 1960s, but they were always on the edge of uncomfortable contradictions. On the one hand, the clergy strongly favored racial segregation and economic discrimination against nonwhites: in 1963 more than 40 percent of the clergy of the three main Dutch Reformed churches were members of the Afrikaner Broederbond or its youth affiliates.[16] Yet, on the other hand, they had to deal with Christianity's doctrine of the equality of all persons before the Almighty. Much ingenious theology was the result, of the sort that reminds one of the suggestion that the real purpose of most theology is to make excuses for the behavior of both God and man.

For example, in November 1953, the Federal Missionary Council of the Dutch Reformed Churches convened a council of church leaders at the Voortrekker Memorial Hall in Pretoria to discuss "the application of Christian principles in our multiracial land." There they heard the moderator of the NHK churches in the Transvaal, C. B. Brink, explain that the development of separate nations and races was the work of God and that the Reformed churches' practice of apartheid within religious institutions rested both upon practical considerations and upon matters of principle.[17] These practical and principled considerations were articulated in detail in 1957 when a report of an ad hoc commission on race relations was adopted by the Federal Council of Dutch Reformed Churches in South Africa. This document propounded an explanation of the views of the mainline Reformed churches to critics overseas. Two justifications for supporting political apartheid and practicing religious apartheid were presented. The first rationale was historical. The Dutch Reformed churches, the document said, had always given serious attention to preaching to "the heathen," that is, nonwhites, and during the nineteenth century, sponsored several missions that preached to nonwhites in their own tongues. Historically, a "natural separation" occurred between the races. In 1857 the NGK synod had agreed that (1) although it was "desirable and scriptural that our members from the heathen be received and absorbed into our existing congregation," nevertheless "where this measure, owing to the weakness of some," was unacceptable, the heathen were to worship in a separate building or institution. Thereafter, "weakness" won. Throughout South Africa, individual congregations became either white or nonwhite, and during the last quarter of the nineteenth century and first half of the twentieth, separate Reformed denominations for nonwhites evolved.[18]

But was Afrikaner tradition compatible with biblical principle? Yes, the churches argued in the same document. Although the Almighty had created a spiritual unity in all humankind, God had simultaneously established racial diversity:

> The Dutch Reformed Church accepts the unity of the human race, which is not annulled by its diversity. At the same time the Dutch Reformed Church accepts the natural diversity of the human race, which is not annulled by its unity.[19]

The proof texts for this argument were Genesis 1 and 2, Genesis 3:10, and Acts 17:26. Doctrinal unity "does not mean that the one true Church cannot be embodied in separate independent Churches. . . . The natural diversity and the different spheres of influence and relationships of authority which God has ordained are in no way broken down by this unity in Christ, but are rather restored and sanctified."[20]

These lines of reasoning were frequently reaffirmed. In October 1966 the General Synod of the NGK produced a document titled *Human Relations in South Africa,* in which it argued that "ethnic diversity is in agreement with God's will," and that to blur by racial mixing the distinctiveness and character of various groups was sinful. Particularly sinful were marriages between nonwhites and whites. "Mixing must be resisted with every resource as wrong and sinful, and such a development must be opposed in principle."[21]

A parallel set of contradictions was involved in the repeated assertion that the emerging apartheid order was erected by the sort of self-sacrificing nationalist patriots who, in other contexts, were soon to be called freedom fighters. Afrikaner nationalists depicted their ascession to power as the casting off of the last shackles of United Kingdom imperialism. Viewing this process from a skeptical distance, Conor Cruise O'Brien has noted: "The fact that a genuine national-liberation movement should invent the ideology of apartheid and erect its institutions, should not surprise us. . . . People fight for freedom, but what some of them win is power."[22]

Most paradoxical (but again, not surprising) is that the establishment of apartheid was so meticulously legal. At every point, enactments were highly detailed, specifying precisely what was permitted and what was not. Admittedly, a sacred-profane distinction runs through all societies, but in covenantal cultures this dualism takes the characteristic form of legalistic thinking, in which fine shades of difference are defined in law. In such cultures, law acquires a transcendental aura of its own. As T. R. H. Davenport remarks, "The dominant South African assumption, which seems to be rooted in history, is that law made by a properly constituted authority, carries its own legitimacy, whatever its content."[23] This ethico-legal stance leads to a paradox: "respect" for the law continues to be elicited, even when the purpose of the law (as in the case of apartheid) is to remove or reduce the legal rights of those who are the law's subjects. Thus, laws are upheld, even if their substantive content destroys the ethical basis upon which the laws are presumed to have been made.

(2)

Despite all its legalism, apartheid was not a legal code, but rather a matrix of overlapping strands, some at cross purposes with each other. (In both its tone and messiness, the apartheid legislation bears comparison to the anti-Catholic "penal code" enacted in eighteenth-century Ireland.) Nor did the apartheid system appear fully formed. It evolved in these years in two phases. The first was the era of "doctrinaire and negative apartheid" of the administrations of D. F. Malan (1948–54) and J. G. Strijdom (1954–58), and the second was the period of "separate development" initiated by H. F. Verwoerd (1958–66). The changing facets of apartheid being noted, it is useful to accept the conventional distinction between petit, or *petty apartheid,* and territorial, or *grand apartheid.* As long as one realizes that these terms are aids to discussion, not sharply drawn legal categories, the distinctions are helpful. Petty apartheid comprised all the niggling rules that regulated the social and economic interaction of the major racial groups when they came into contact with each other in daily life. Grand apartheid involved the territorial regulation of nonwhite groups, usually limiting them to certain areas and allowing them in other locales only under stringent conditions. Many individual statutes involved both aspects of apartheid.[24]

Before either sort of apartheid could be fully articulated, an elaborate system of racial classification to encompass everyone within South Africa had to be created. This was established by the Population Registration Act of 1950.[25] Every person was classified as being white or some sort of nonwhite: either "coloured" or "native." (After 1951, "native" became "Bantu" and in 1978 "black" was substituted.) The "native" component was further broken down according to tribal or ethnic group. Within the "coloured" category, Asians were distinguished from those of part-white ancestry, and this latter group usually is what is meant by "coloureds." The everyday administration of this act had a grotesquely Kafka-like filigree. For example, people of Chinese ancestry, who had once been a disliked unskilled-labor pool, were classified as nonwhite, but the Japanese, whose post-World War II trade with South Africa became increasingly important, were honorary whites. The chief problem, of course, was to determine who was white. In administrative practice, a white person was defined either as one who was obviously white in appearance and was not generally accepted as a coloured person, or as a person who was generally accepted as white and was "not in appearance obviously not a white person." There was a bizarre spin on these definitions, however: the white category did not include anyone who voluntarily admitted that he or she was by descent either native or coloured— "unless it is proved that the admission is not based on fact."[26] This meant that a white person who for some reason wished to declare him or herself "coloured" (for example, to contract a marriage with a "coloured" person) could not do so. The reminiscences of lawyers who specialized in cases under the law are replete with stories of "coloured" people who wished to be "upgraded" to white, by convincing functionaries to declare their grandparents or great-grandparents posthumously white. Strange as was South Africa's effort at establishing a nationwide taxonomy, it had a certain mad logic to it: the Chosen must be distinguished from the Canaanites, and this classificatory exercise was the basis upon which all subsequent apartheid legislation was built.

But note: so worried were the Afrikaner leaders about one particular issue that they actually passed stringent legislation on it *before* completing their full system of racial categories. They passed two measures to try to stop racial interbreeding. The first was the Prohibition of Mixed Marriages Act of 1949.[27] But the problem that the act dealt with was more theological than actual. The number of formal marriages (as distinct from common-law relationships) between whites and nonwhites was small: between 1943 and 1946, for example, there were fewer than 100 mixed marriages per year contracted in South Africa.[28] The dominant social conventions would have kept these incidences low, yet the issue was central to Afrikaner culture. It is traditional among the psychoanalytically informed to explain such legislation as the result of deep-seated white fears of the allegedly sexually superior black; or, more specifically, white males' fear of superior black males. There may be something in the suggestion. Within the context of the present discussion, however, it can also be seen as an expression of the concern with purity, and with the necessity for endogamy. We must recognize the horror of "mixing" that covenantal cultures inherit directly from the Hebrew scriptures. Indeed, if one compares the prohibition of mixing in South African law with the biblical injunctions that were discussed in chapter 2, the use of the scriptures as South African precedents is obvious.[29] As H. F. Verwoerd declared in 1948, reaffirming a document of 1942 called "The Policy of Apartheid," the National party accepted the "Christian trusteeship" of the European race in regard to the non-European races, "but it is emphatically opposed to any mixture of blood between the European and the non-European races."[30]

Maintaining the purity of the sacrament of marriage was one aspect of the biblical fixation on keeping the "seed" pure. A second facet was the Immorality Act of 1950 which, for the purpose of regulating sexual intercourse, divided the population of South Africa into whites and nonwhites.[31] This act amended a 1927 statute that had prohibited actual carnal intercourse between a white person and a "Bantu." This older statute, adopted in imperial days, had been an attempt to stamp out black prostitution. In the apartheid era things changed. By the simple expedient of deleting the word "Bantu" and introducing the term "nonwhite person," the antiprostitution measure was transformed into a general antimiscegenation statute.[32] In actual practice, the law was used chiefly to break up whites and "coloureds" living together in common-law marriage.[33] Like the Mixed Marriage Act, the Immorality Act of 1950 was passed even before the racial taxonomy system was articulated. Prohibiting the pollution of the white seed mattered.

Another invasive side of petty apartheid was most clearly encapsulated by the Reservation of Separate Amenities Act of 1953.[34] The act allowed anyone who legally controlled public premises to maintain separate facilities for whites and nonwhites, including buses, libraries, parks, trains, water fountains, toilets, bars, restaurants, almost every public facility. It permitted local municipalities to develop detailed rules as to who could use what facilities and when. These measures were not compulsory, but they were nearly universal. At the height of the era of petty apartheid, public park benches in many towns were for "whites only" or for "non-Europeans" only; telephone booths in white residential areas bore "whites-only" stencils, and it is reported that in a whites-only amusement park in Durban the coin-operated weighing machine had "whites-only" stenciled on it. Taxicabs in the era of high apartheid were either white or nonwhite, and so too were railway carriages, buses, and ambulances (the later provision brought apartheid to a sometimes-mortal extreme).[35] A crucial part of the Separate Amenities legislation was what it did not include: there was no provision that the separate facilities had to be equal. In fact, the 1953 act removed the power of the courts to declare such segregation in amenities invalid on the basis of the provision having been made on a separate-but-unequal basis.

Of greater long-term significance were the acts that controlled the economic interaction of the races. Long-standing apprenticeship and job-entry restrictions, which reduced nonwhite access to the skilled trades, were expanded in 1951 and 1956. In 1953, blacks were prohibited from conducting labor strikes.[36] The economic impediments to nonwhite acquisition of skills, capital, and economic bargaining power were of greater moment than the rest of the petty apartheid system because they were a long-term mortmain on South African society. Whereas a whites-only municipal park could be racially integrated at the stroke of a legislative pen, it would require at least a generation (and probably more) to make up the deficit in modern economic skills that the job-restriction system visited upon the nonwhite population. And this is doubly true, because the black educational system that emerged under apartheid—sometimes called "Bantu education"—was designed to keep the blacks out of the white economic world, except as exploitable labor.

Here the theology of Afrikaner Christian Nationalism was crucial. Remember that the Dutch Reformed Church held that racial diversity was divinely designed and also that the evil of racial mixing should be minimized, and, further, that the Afrikaner political elite was emotionally committed to "mother tongue" education for its own children. Therefore, the National party could suggest that the native groups should be educated in their own mother tongue and that the goal of "native" schooling should be to preserve the cultural identity—and thus the cultural separation of those peoples. Since there could be no common life of white and nonwhite, education was not intended to prepare blacks for a common economic life with whites. The Bantu Education Act of 1953 was thus a charter for the systematic educational retardation of the bulk of the nonwhite population of South Africa.[37]

In 1962, the former director of education in the province of Natal, Dr. W. G. McConkey, issued an indictment of "Bantu education." He concluded by looking at the highest levels attained:

> Children in the upper primary school—the select minority who have survived the lower primary school and who will supply the leaders of the future—spend six hours a week on these subjects! tree planting and soil conservation (two hours), gardening (two hours), and handwork A, which in most cases boils down to planting reeds and grasses and making useless articles out of scraps of waste wire, old boxes, beads and so on. Children so trained can be guaranteed non-competitive![38]

At the top end of the education system, a 1959 act—ironically called the Extension of University Education Act—introduced segregation into South African universities, with the clear intention of making provision for university education not only separate, but heavily unequal.[39]

That was petty apartheid. In the matter of grand apartheid, the foundation stone was the Group Areas Act of 1950.[40] The act was of particular consequence, as it completed the system of territorial segregation by limiting "coloured" and Asian residence in cities. Under the statute, separate areas in towns and cities were to be created for the various racial groups. At first this division was among whites, blacks, and coloured, but later legislation also segregated the Chinese, Indian, and Malay in larger urban areas. When this legislation of the early 1950s was combined with the pre-1948 statutes which created rural reserves for the blacks, the pattern was clear: the entire country was demarcated into precise regions with complex regulations as to who could and who could not be there.

This measure encompassed a series of earlier acts designed to keep blacks out of cities and certainly it implied territorial segregation of the races. In one of his first speeches in the Senate, H. F. Verwoerd in 1948 quoted a letter from J. G. Strijdom to a Mr. Brill, written in 1942, as containing the pure milk of the Afrikaner view:

> As far as territorial segregation is concerned, "total segregation," . . . would have been the ideal solution but in practice it is incapable of being carried out, because quite apart from all the other difficulties, our own people, our farmers and thousands, and ten of

thousands of others, who use the services of the Natives and coloured people as labour, would never agree to it. For that reason, as far as "territorial segregation" is concerned, we have adopted as a policy mainly the following:

(1) That Natives should not be allowed to own land among white people, but that so far as the ownership of land is concerned they should be confined to the various Native reserves;

(2) that Natives and coloured people in our towns and villages should not live in European residential areas, but that there should be separate residential areas for them, that is to say, separate Native and coloured villages; and

(3) that in our factories, etc., Europeans and non-Europeans should not be allowed to work among one another, but separately, and that certain sorts of work should be reserved for the Europeans.[41]

But, as M. C. de Wet Nel, minister of Bantu administration and development, observed in 1960, apartheid in its actual development became something more than mere segregation. It was a more comprehensive system aimed at regulating relations of all sorts between the various groups and, in de Wet Nel's view, at allowing blacks "self-determination."[42]

That is a curious term, and it points to a development that took place during the 1950s under the leadership of a racial think-tank at Stellenbosch University, the South African Bureau of Racial Affairs (SABRA). Although formally independent, this group of professors, intellectuals, and policy savants was tied in at the highest levels to the Broederbond and to the National party. They were visionaries who wished to take apartheid to its logical extreme and to establish virtually complete regulation of race relations by confining most blacks to separate "homelands" (variants: Bantustans; black states). These leaders were influential in shaping the report of the Tomlinson Commission of 1954, which declared that there could be no compromise or middle way in racial relations: there had to be either complete integration or "separate development" of black groups. In line with that vision, the SABRA theoreticians argued that considerable economic resources should be poured into the black homelands to allow them to become genuinely self-sufficient.[43] This became the theory of "separate development" that the Verwoerd administration (1958–66) espoused, but when put in practice, precious little development money went to the black homelands. They became rural slums.

These rural slums became a major problem for the South African government in implementing grand apartheid. (Eventually the ten homelands of various sorts turned into six homelands and four pseudoindependent "self-governing states": Ciskei, Transkei, Venda, and Bophuthatswana.) They were too poor to be self-supporting; the homelands existed mostly on the remittances sent back home to their families by workers in the mines and factories, and in domestic service. Agricultural productivity on the various forms of reserves fell continually as a result of overpopulation and underinvestment. Young blacks preferred life in urban slums to the rural subsistence sector, and they drifted to the cities. In response, a government measure of 1952 made it an offense for adult blacks to remain in an urban area longer than seventy-two hours unless they could prove fifteen years of legal residence in the urban area or could show that they had worked in the area for the same employer for ten years, or had been granted permission to remain in the area by a labor bureau.[44] This law, combined with a change in the pass laws that required all blacks over the age of sixteen to carry an identity card, was supposed to keep the blacks on their reserved rural lands.[45] "Separate development" in no way made staying in the rural hinterlands more attractive.

(3)

Amid all of this social engineering, where did whites of British Isles extraction stand? How did apartheid affect them? There is no doubt that as a group the Anglo-Celtic population was less "reactionary" and more "liberal" in the sense of not being so keen on apartheid as the Afrikaner population. This was clearly established by an independent (nongovernmental) survey conducted in 1964.[46] On the whole, the Anglo-Celts held slightly less strong racial attitudes and were more apt to be racial integrationists. But this finding should not be overstated. The British Isles group's record on race relations was very far from being unblemished. In Natal, for example, where there was a British Isles majority among the whites, rural racial segregation had been introduced in some degree in the nineteenth century, and indeed, Durban had pioneered urban segregation. And there is some truth in the Afrikaner's belief that the Anglo-Celts were willing to accept the economic benefits of apartheid, even if they were unwilling to accept the public responsibility for enforcing it.

However, I think that the chief reason that the Anglo-Celtic population kept its distance from apartheid had nothing to do with their alleged liberalism, and everything to do with a crucial characteristic of the apartheid system: in the high noon of apartheid, the system was not only about race, but about culture; not only about keeping whites and nonwhites apart, but also about keeping Afrikaans-speakers and English-speakers culturally separate. At its mildest, this took the form of D. F. Malan's belief that the relationships between the Afrikaans-speakers and the English-speakers should be like that in Switzerland among the speakers of French, German, and Italian: they should be separate nations within a single overarching South African state.[47]

But, in fact, apartheid was also about forcing Afrikaner cultural values upon the Anglo-Celts and about transferring power from the Anglophones to the Afrikaans-speaking population. This is too often forgotten. The system of apartheid in the years 1948–69 was as concerned with the dangers to Afrikanerdom posed by Anglophones as it was with the threats from blacks. That concern is demonstrated in a speech given by Dr. Piet Meyer, head of the Afrikaner Broederbond. Delivered in Bloemfontein in 1966 after the assassination, by a deranged white parliamentary messenger, of H. F. Verwoerd, a strong Broederbonder and prime minister of South Africa from September 1958 to September 1966, Meyer's speech was intended to be a confidential assessment of what had been done and what was yet to be done concerning relations between Afrikaners and people of British Isles origins. Meyer's first and most basic proposition was that the future of the two white groups was bound closely together, but that the future depended upon "the survival of the Afrikaner nation as an indigenous, separate, and independent Western cultural community in Africa."[48]

Meyer noted that when Afrikaans and English-language cultural forms were integrated, the result worked almost entirely to perpetuate the worldview carried in the English language. He claimed that 200,000 Afrikaners had anglicized completely (he did not say in what period of time but he probably meant between the end of World War II and 1966). "This tendency is increasing, not decreasing," he warned. There was, he admitted, some traffic the other way, but "English-speakers who have completely Afrikanerized are mainly English *plattelanders* and impoverished city-dwellers. The Afrikaners who have been totally Anglicized, however, came predominantly from our highest and middle income groups." This had to stop. The goal "must be the complete political nationalisation and the growing cultural Afrikanerisation of the English-speaker in our country." However—this was crucial—"The aim to nationalise the English-speaker politically will only be of permanent value in ensuring the survival of the Afrikaner nation, if it goes hand-in-hand with the predominant Afrikanerisation of our country's economy. . . . And there is not much time left to achieve this. . . . The next step is not another economic national congress, but *well-planned confidential economic action*, which is possible and practicable" (italics mine). As for cultural goals, "The Afrikanerisation of the English-speaker is in its essence an education task—it must begin in our schools." Ultimately, Meyer declared, English-language schools must be stopped from inducting children into "English and contemporary Western cultural life." When properly controlled, the English-language schools would Afrikanerize the Anglo-Celts. "The Afrikanerisation of the English-speakers of our country thus means in essence that the English-speaker has to make the Afrikaans world-view his own; that he will integrate his ideals and life-style with those of the Afrikaner; that he will adopt Afrikaans history as his own; that he will accept Afrikaans as his national language, alongside English as the international community language."[49]

That was what Afrikaner cultural and political leaders were saying in private gatherings. Publicly, what was obvious to citizens of British Isles background was that after 1948 they were locked out of the spoils of state power. The Nationalists used patronage plums with an overt enthusiasm that would have made even Sir Robert Walpole wince. English-speakers were turfed out of important posts and replaced by loyal Nationalists. The Nationalists introduced a requirement for bilingualism as a prerequisite for obtainment of the higher positions in the civil service. On the surface, this requirement made perfect sense, since the country had two official languages, but to introduce it on short notice and without providing facilities for the acquisition of the second language meant only one thing: only Afrikaners would receive civil service patronage. By 1966, 71 percent of whites in the civil service were Afrikaans-speaking, and the corresponding numbers for police were 87 percent and for prison service 98.5 percent.[50]

How far the Afrikaner community progressed in its attempt to gain control of the South African economy can only be the subject of speculation: financial reporting requirements are not strict in South Africa; furthermore, given the interplay of multinational corporations in the economy, such results would be hard to interpret. It is clear, however, that the Nationalist party used the considerable powers of the state to channel funds to Afrikaner businesses. In the financial field, governmental accounts went to Afrikaner institutions, such as the Volkskas Bank, which between 1948 and 1958 saw a four and three-quarters multiplication of its overall deposits.[51] Governmental funds for industrial development went much more frequently to Afrikaner than to non-Afrikaner firms.

This, combined with the fact that Afrikaner private investment became increasingly significant as the entire Afrikaner community became wealthier, facilitated the rise of some very large Afrikaner firms. For example, in 1963, the second largest mining finance house—General Mining and Finance Corporation—was under the control of committed Afrikaner nationalists, as was the second largest conglomerate in the country, the Sanlam group.[52] Similarly, in the field of trade union organization, the power of Anglophones was reduced. This occurred, in part through the Suppression of Communism Act of 1950 which was employed against organizers in the trade union movement who brought English-inspired radicalism to the shop floor, especially in the Garment Workers Union. In other unions, the pre-1948 attempts at taking over the leadership continued and in some cases, where this failed, rival Afrikaner unions were formed.[53]

The overall result of the Afrikaners' employment of the control of the state to reduce the economic and social position of the Anglo-Celtic population was clearly indicated by a study conducted in 1974. It revealed that, excluding farming (an occupation where there were many more Afrikaners than Anglo-Celts), the proportional distribution of the occupations of Afrikaans-speakers and of English-speakers was very similar; differences were minor.[54] A defender of the apartheid system could well argue that as far as relations with English-speakers were concerned, one of the chief fruits of apartheid was that at last the Afrikaners had gotten their fair share.

(4)

Nonetheless, the developments most revealing of the inner soul of the apartheid system occurred not in the counting houses, but in the schools. In many ways, the schools of any society can be used as a cultural litmus paper, and this is certainly true in South Africa. One of the beliefs running universally through the entire range of Afrikaner cultural, political, and religious organizations was that the future of Afrikanerdom lay in its children and that if the children were not inducted into the *volk* culture, then any gains that the Afrikaners as an ethnic group might make in the economic or political spheres would be transient, mere writing upon water.

In 1948, the Institute for Christian National Education, in concert with the Federation of Afrikaner Cultural groups, published a report on

"Christian National" education. Although not a government document, is the closest thing in existence to a statement of Afrikaner educational goals at the moment the Nationalists assumed power.[55] The value system that underlay this report was deeply anti-Anglophone. Section 1 of Article 8 stated,

> We believe that there must be at least two sorts of schools for primary and secondary education: one for children of Afrikaans-speaking parents with their communal creed and language, with only Afrikaans as medium: and the other for the children of English-speaking parents with English as medium.

This was phrased elsewhere in the emotional terms of "mother-tongue":

> We believe that the mother-tongue is the basis of all teaching and education and that the mother-tongue should be the most important secular subject in school. It must also be the only medium in the teaching of all other subjects, except in the case of other modern languages. (Article 5, section 3)

What should the mother-tongue encompass?

> We believe that the teaching and education of children of white parents should occur on the basis of the life and world view of the parents. For Afrikaans-speaking children this means that they must be educated on the basis of the Christian-National life and world view of our nation. . . . The Christian basis of this life and world view is grounded on the Holy Scriptures and expressed in the Creed of our three Afrikaans Churches. By the national principle we understand love for everything that is our own, with special mention of our country, our language, our history and our culture. (Article 1)

In the Afrikaner's covenantal cultural grid, two subjects were especially prominent:

> *Geography.* We believe that every nation is rooted in its own soil which is allotted to it by the Creator. Every citizen of our country must have a sound knowledge of our land . . . and this knowledge must be communicated in such a way that the pupil will love our own soil, also in comparison and contrast with other countries. (Article 6, section 5)
> *History.* We believe that history must be taught in the light of the divine revelation and must be seen as the fulfillment of God's decree

(*raadsplan*) for the world and humanity. . . . We believe that God has willed separate nations and peoples, and has given each separate nation and peoples its particular vocation and task and gifts. . . . We believe that next to the mother-tongue, the patriotic (*vaderlandse*) history of the nation is the great means of cultivating love of one's own. (Article 6, section 6)

The blueprint, then, was quite specific: to reduce as much as possible the mixing of Afrikaner and non-Afrikaner white children and to use the schools to inculcate the covenantal cultural system, through the teaching of the *volk* view of history, geography, and religion. All these subjects should be taught through the mother-tongue, Afrikaans.

In attempting to achieve these ends, the Afrikaner cultural leaders had a good deal going for them in the years after World War II. Demography helped greatly. A rough rule of thumb is that from the middle 1930s onward, the Afrikaans-speakers formed roughly three-fifths of the white population. Before World War II nearly 90 percent of the unilingual Anglophones lived in cities, and more than half of the unilingual Afrikaans-speakers lived in the countryside. Each of these groups could easily support single-medium schools. The problem was that, before World War II, there were not enough Afrikaans-speakers to warrant Afrikaans-only schools in many urban areas. Here a massive demographic shift helped the proponents of Christian National education for Afrikaans children. The Afrikaners moved to the cities in large numbers so that by 1960 well over three-quarters of the unilingual Afrikaans-speakers were urbanites and the proportion was growing constantly, to nearly nine-tenths in 1974.[56] Therefore, in nearly every town and city (outside of certain parts of Natal) it became possible to gather enough children to run an Afrikaans primary school. In the cities, not only were there enough children for a purely Afrikaans system, but in the more populous cities—Johannesburg, Pretoria, and Cape Town in particular—large Afrikaans-only high schools were established.[57] Hence, both in the countryside and in the cities it was possible to operate a network of schools in which the two main white cultural groups were segregated from each other.

After 1948, the advocates of Afrikaner covenantal education ("Christian National" schools, in the vocabulary of the time) had strong allies within the educational service. This is a difficult thing to put one's finger on directly, but we know that the Broederbond had within its ranks a large number of educationalists. In 1972 the Broederbond had 1,236 members in the teaching profession below university level: 647 classroom teachers, 468 headmasters, and 121 school inspectors. This was in addition to 171 university professors and 176 university lecturers, 24 rectors of universities and teacher training colleges, and, notably, the directors of education in each of the four provinces, as well as the chairman of the National Education Advisory Council.[58] Given the extremely ardent attitude of Broederbonders on the matter of education, their members certainly influenced the school system in the way that they conducted individual classes in history, geography, civics, and religion; in the way that, as headmasters, they managed their individual schools; and in the way that, as inspectors, higher administrators, and directors of provincial educational systems, they tilted practice toward the Afrikaner covenantal viewpoint. Writing in 1977, Ernst G. Malherbe, who was probably better informed about educational developments in South Africa than anyone else of his time, noted that schools which previously had been dual-language and attended both by English- and by Afrikaans-speaking children had been split into single-medium schools "under Broederbond pressure during the last three decades."[59] That is, since the Nationalists came to power in 1948.

In the post-1948 era, the rule was that the "mother-tongue" of the child's home had to be used as the exclusive educational medium up to standard 8, except in Natal where parents still had a choice. Thus, a study conducted in 1967 by the South African Human Sciences Research Council found that at the standard 6 level (roughly, age thirteen), only 2 percent of the children received instruction through both languages, and at the standard 8 level, only 4 percent were being instructed through both media.[60] Thus, by the late 1960s, the degree of segregation among whites that had been specified by the Christian National Education blueprint of 1948 had been nearly achieved. This situation was ratified by the National Education Policy Act of 1967.[61] In the debate on that measure, an English-speaking member made the following observation: "Under this Bill apartheid is being applied among the white race. The other races in this country are separated on the grounds of colour; now the white race is going to be separated on the ground of language difference."[62] Going to be? It already was.

This separation of white children according to ethnic origin was not an exercise in segregation for its own sake, but for a purpose: to preserve pure and intact the Afrikaner *volk* culture. With the non-Afrikaner children removed from Afrikaner schools, the entire curriculum now was framed to inculcate the covenantal cultural system.

Measuring the actual effects of schools—as distinct from the intentions of their administrators and teachers—is notoriously difficult. Fortunately, however, two studies indicate what actually was occurring in the schools. A content analysis of the history books and syllabuses used in Transvaal high schools was conducted in the late 1950s and early 1960s by F. E. Auerbach.[63] A second study, by J. M. du Preez, analyzed the "master symbols" used in South African education.[64] This later work was published in 1984, but it dealt with the curriculum formed in the heyday of Christian National doctrine. Auerbach's earlier study began by noting that "when [the Columbia University expert] Professor Joseph Lauwerys made his first visit to South Africa in 1958, he said on several occasions that South Africa was the only country he knew that used its educational system to divide its people."[65] In elucidating this observation, Auerbach engaged in two exercises: he compared English and Afrikaner versions of the same school texts, and he compared entire history syllabuses in the two school systems in the Transvaal. He concluded that the Afrikaner curriculum placed greater emphasis upon local issues, whereas the English-language system operated within an international perspective. On sensitive issues—such as the historical forces that yielded a Great Trek—there were major differences of interpretation. Even when textbooks were translated from one language to another, changes in individual wordings sharply shifted the meaning of the pages at hand. Most important, the Afrikaner books and syllabuses taught an attitude of loyalty to the *volk;* the English-language ones did not. As a synedoche of this, Auerbach pointed to the "Code of Honour" that was printed in the 1965 version of the standard "Pupil's Study Diary." In the English version, the pupil vowed "to serve my country and *its* people at all times"—"its" being inclusive and implying devotion to the welfare of all groups within South Africa. In the Afrikaans version of the same Honor Code, the student promised to strive "always and at all times to serve my country and *my* volk"—a promise that excludes all save the Afrikaner.[66]

J. M. du Preez's study, *Africana Afrikaner,* exhibited in detail the salient characteristics of the Afrikaner half of the culturally partitioned educational curriculum. She found that an entire set of distinct symbols ran through the school texts used in government-funded Afrikaans-language schools. Du Preez analyzed fifty-three textbooks used in the secondary schools (standards 6 through 10) in history, geography, Afrikaans literature, and English literature. Because the South African school system (particularly the Afrikaans-language portion) is so much more standardized than that of most western countries—studies have shown that roughly 95 percent of teaching and study time is devoted to textbooks—the texts themselves are a reliable guide to what finally ends up in the childrens' minds.[67] Du Preez's analysis indicates that behind the various specific facts and skills that are taught, there existed within Afrikaner schools a latent curriculum of twelve "master symbols." These were bedrock beliefs that the schools transmitted: they constitute the control beliefs that one generation of Afrikaners passed on to the next. The twelve symbols were (1) legal authority may not be questioned; (2) whites are superior to blacks, who are fundamentally inferior; blacks are a threat to whites; (3) the Afrikaner nation has an exclusive relationship with God; (4) South Africa rightfully belongs to the Afrikaner; (5) South Africa is an agricultural nation and the Afrikaners are a farming people; (6) South Africa is an afflicted dry country; (7) South Africa and the Afrikaner are isolated; (8) the Afrikaner is militarily ingenious and strong; (9) the Afrikaner is threatened by everything un-Afrikaans, including all other population groups; (10) world opinion is important to South Africa; (11) South Africa is the leading nation in Africa; and (12) the Afrikaner has a God-given task in Africa.[68]

Obviously, only a few of these beliefs could be shared with English-speaking South Africans. Undeniably, from 1948 on, the Afrikaans-speaking children of South Africa were raised under a policy of cultural separation vis-à-vis English-speaking children that was almost as sharp in its cleavage as was the policy of physical apartheid vis-à-vis the nonwhites.

In view of my contention that a covenantal grid congruent with that of the Hebrew Pentateuch was the conceptual basis of Afrikaner culture from the late nineteenth century until the recent past, Du Preez's analysis of three powerful features of the Afrikaner mindset are significant here. On the "laager" tendencies of the Afrikaner, du Preez concludes that

> the Afrikaner still tends towards a laager mentality when he feels threatened.
> Only White Afrikaners are allowed within this laager in which one finds the last bastion of Christian civilization in Africa. By keeping himself separate the Afrikaner will avert racial mixing and maintain purity of race.
> The laager concept ties in with the isolation of the Afrikaner, for it implies definite exclusion of all who are not inside the laager.

Under the heading "Reliving the Day of the Covenant," du Preez writes,

> The Battle of Blood River is considered the most important event in the history of the Afrikaner for that event justifies his presence in Africa.

At Blood River God demonstrated to the Afrikaner that his presence in Africa is by Divine Will, that he will receive Divine protection against the heathens. The Covenant is confirmation of the special relationship that exists between God and his people.

Du Preez notes the dominance of the Old Testament in Afrikaner thinking:

The Afrikaner identifies with the Jewish people of the Old Testament. The History textbooks and Afrikaans setworks in particular are written in the idiom of the Old Testament, e.g. the mission of the chosen (*uitverkore*) people; the epic journey through the desert (*wildernis*), all sorts of trials and tribulations; the heathens who are exterminated, the preservation of a pure White nation; the Covenant that binds the people to God; judges (national leaders) and other symbols or master symbols.[69]

Peter Lambley, a psychologist who trained and practiced in South Africa in the era of high apartheid, explained how the schools and the Afrikaner social system worked together in the socialization of the Afrikaner child, who like children in other cultures, is brought up with certain cultural values and perspectives, but with one outstanding difference:

Unlike other children, the Afrikaans child finds these same [Afrikaner] values expressed uniformly at every level of his society. Thus he is taught that he is superior, Godly, a descendant of brave men and women who fought for their beliefs and values, that the English tried to take his birthright away and that the African is simply waiting his chance to do the same. He is encouraged to be watchful, lest he be overwhelmed. At school he hears this from *all* his teachers, he reads it in his school books. At home, his parents reiterate the same values.

Lambley continues,

When the Afrikaner child grows up, if he is male, he goes into the army, which is completely Afrikaans-orientated, then on to an Afrikaans university and joins an Afrikaans professional group, practices in an Afrikaans suburb or town, joins Afrikaner charities and service organizations and can in fact find Afrikaans organisations to fulfill his every need. There is an Afrikaans Automobile Association Club [and] Afrikaans banks, building societies, insurance groups, everything.[70]

Everything. Self-sufficient, self-referential, self-protecting: that is the nature of covenantal cultural systems. In South Africa, only the Afrikaners, and not the English-speaking whites, could be part of the inner circle of the covenant, even though the Anglo-Celts could benefit economically from the apartheid system that the Afrikaner covenant produced.

(5)

During the high period of apartheid, a stegasaurus-like foreign policy emerged: the South African government was adamantly assertive of its own sovereignty, insensitive to most external attacks, slow moving, and not swift to react. But for all that, the state's foreign policy was not stupid. When South Africa told the United Nations to mind its own business, when it dropped out of UNESCO, when it laughed at the preachments of the World Council of Churches, it was following a foreign policy perfectly congruent with its own domestic policy—of circling the wagons and treating everyone outside as hostile. Given the covenantal frame of mind, this policy was especially productive domestically. The covenanting mindset holds that the godly shall always be under attack from the ungodly and the impure, and that compromise with the Canaanites is always wrong. By refusing to compromise on anything, by virtually inviting the international community to condemn it, the South African government produced a warrant of its own value: only the righteous are denounced and attacked by the unrighteous. Hence, by sometimes intentionally exciting international pressure and by, at minimum, being publicly indifferent to it, the South African government solidified the loyalty of the Afrikaner population to the state.

One of the most righteous cards played by the South African government was the imperial one. Kicking at the symbols of the old empire was especially useful, for it allowed the government to claim that South Africa, in common with most emergent African states, was breaking away from the confining chrysalis of imperialist rule. And anything anti-United Kingdom went down very well with the Afrikaner *volk*. Hence, in 1957, the prime minister announced that "The Queen" would no longer have status as one of South Africa's two national anthems, and, further, that the Union Jack would no longer have any official standing. One flag, one anthem, no reminders of empire, no truckling to the sensitivities of the Anglo-Celtic population.

Of greater consequence was the announcement in late January 1960 by Prime Minister Verwoerd of a referendum on whether or not South Africa should become a republic, a republic within the British Commonwealth, but a republic nonetheless. Given that roughly four-tenths of the electorate was composed of people of British Isles ethnicity and that these voters were overwhelmingly, though not universally, opposed to the republican concept, the referendum promised to be a very near thing. The government's pro-republican position was helped immensely by a visit from the British prime minister, Harold Macmillan, which took place just a fortnight after the referendum was announced. In the most irritatingly patrician manner, Macmillan lectured a combined sitting of both houses of the South African parliament about the "wind of change" that was blowing across the South African continent. He suggested that apartheid was not countenanced either by the London government or by the international community. Undoubtedly Macmillan was correct in his assessment of the shifting geopolitics of the African continent, but he could hardly have done more for the Nationalist party. When the referendum was held in October 1960, the vote in favour of the republic was 52 percent to 48 percent. This meant that between 80 and 90 percent of the Afrikaner electorate voted for the republic. Cannily, Prime Minister Verwoerd did not directly interpret the referendum as a repudiation of the British Commonwealth. South Africa applied for continued membership in the Commonwealth, as a republic. However, when several member-states of the Commonwealth threatened to withdraw if South Africa were to be permitted membership, Verwoerd took the high road and, for the sake of international amity, withdrew. Thus, on 31 May 1961, South Africa became a republic and a lone one, free at last of the entanglements of the old empire. The two Anglo-Boer wars had been refought, and this time the Afrikaners had won, without a shot being fired.[71]

If unbending truculence on the international scene is one well-known facet of the apartheid regime at its height, a less well-known facet concerned the nature of the state. Compared to the pre-World War II situation, after 1948 the state was much more active in every aspect of economic and social life. The central government not only engaged in new activities, but the state itself became more centralized. In 1960 an estimated 30 percent of economically active whites were in public sector employment, and by 1966 this figure had grown to 35 percent.[72] This does not include employment in publicly owned corporations, which would have added between 5 and 15 percent to the grand total of people dependent on state-initiated economic activity.[73] For those whose ethnicity made them eligible for the largesse of the state, the apogee of apartheid was a very good time indeed.

The growth of the state's power inevitably involved the articulation of systems of social control. Increasingly, the state engaged in juridicially and legislatively sanctioned terrorism. The 1950 Suppression of Communism Act not only banned the Communist party, but outlawed any group that aimed at bringing about political, social, industrial, or economic change by unlawful acts of any sort. Hence, the African National Congress was prosecuted under the act. An amendment to the criminal code in 1953 provided prison terms of up to three years and/or public whipping for any person who violated a law in protest against any other law: thus was outlawed peaceful civil disobedience. A 1963 statute permitted senior police officers to arrest and incarcerate anyone without warrant, if the person was thought to be guilty of any act under the Suppression of Communism Act. The "offender" could be held at police pleasure for ninety days without habeas corpus or trial of any sort. This detention was extended to 180 days in 1965. And, in 1967, the Terrorism Act permitted the indefinite (which is to say, perpetual) detention of anyone believed by a senior police officer to be either a terrorist or to have knowledge of terrorism. The price of maintaining apartheid, obviously, was the surrender to the state of many (and for some people, almost all) civil liberties.[74]

Yet, for the Afrikaner community, these prices were easy to bear. They were doing well. In 1969, the Republic of South Africa was the most militarily powerful nation on the continent of Africa. It had by far the most advanced economy, and it seemed to have the most stable of African political systems. Without blasphemy, even the most pious Dopper could say that for them, by God, apartheid worked.

8

Israel: A Singular State, 1948–1967

(1)

T he state that came into existence in mid-May 1948, was destined
to be singular. Of course, no state is identical in all details to any
other, but Israel was to be radically different. That this was to be
the case is made clear by portions of the new nation's Declaration of
Independence, dated 14 May 1948, effective at midnight on the fifteenth.
The declaration concluded with these words:

> WE CALL upon the Jewish people throughout the Diaspora to join forces
> with us in immigration and construction and to be at our right hand in
> the great endeavor to fulfill the age-old longing for the redemption of
> Israel.
>
> WITH TRUST IN THE ROCK OF ISRAEL, we set our hands in witness to
> this Proclamation, at this session of the Provisional Council of State, on
> the soil of the homeland, in the city of Tel Aviv, this Sabbath eve, the
> fifth day of Iyyar, 5708, the fourteenth day of May, nineteen hundred
> and forty-eight.[1]

Because the state of Israel was shaped so as to receive the approval of the
United Nations and of the major postwar international powers, its
creators used words that the outside world wanted to hear. Israel would
be a state that was "democratic" and "secular" and some political scien-

tists of the time even used the world "pluralistic," although the term was not yet in everyday usage.

Yet, when one looks behind these words, which were part of the standard vocabulary of western political science, it is obvious that they meant something quite different in the Israeli context than they did in most western countries. This is not to claim bad faith on the part of the founders of the state of Israel (a more sincerely idealistic group of human beings is hard to find), but it is to note that the realities of life in Israel quickly gave to these words operational meanings that had nothing to do with the abstractions of western political theory. The closer one looks, the more singular Israel becomes.

A prime singularity of the new Israeli state was that it was at once the tightest of little islands—surrounded by hostile Arab countries, it immediately became a maximum security state—and yet one that had a world-girdling sense of itself. This sense arose because Israel defined itself as the homeland for the world's Jewish population. And this was not merely a theoretical relationship. Any Jew, anywhere in the world, had an absolute right to emigrate to Israel and to become an Israeli citizen. Immediately, complex arguments arose around the question of "who is a Jew." These questions will be discussed later, but here the point is that, alone among modern states, Israel had an extraterritorial population whose members had a right not merely to residence but to citizenship at any time they pleased. These rights were bedrock provisions of the state of Israel and, unlike, for example, the right of the holders of the British Commonwealth passports to reside in Great Britain, the privilege could not be revoked without destroying the moral basis of the state.

Thus, if he or she wished, every diaspora Jew was a quasi citizen of Israel. These quasi citizens were woven into the Israeli state by institutions as well as by emotions. For example, the World Jewish Congress, and several other pro-Israel organizations, raised immense amounts of money for the new state and in return obtained positions on the various Israeli governmental agencies that spent these monies. The main conduit for charitable money into Israel was the Jewish Agency, which was a functioning part of the Israeli state. Diaspora Jews held positions on its boards of control. In 1972, the Jewish Agency funded 63 percent of Israel's health and welfare services, 21 percent of primary and secondary education, and 87 percent of higher education, and this was done almost entirely with funds raised abroad. Most of the money spent by the government of Israel's Ministry of Immigrant Absorption came from the Jewish Agency, which insisted on a direct influence on the day-to-day operation of the ministry. Thus, non-Israelis (especially American Jews) had a considerable operational influence on Israeli state activities.[2]

When Israeli officials used the word "secular" to describe their new state, they were far from agreeing among themselves on what they meant by the word. Only a small phalanx used the term in the way that political scientists and constitutional lawyers in the west used it. A tiny band of political activists, self-designated as "the Canaanites," believed that Israel should be a secular state in the sense that, say, France was. This "Canaanism" was associated with the followers of Yonathon Ratosh (1909–81) and the movement had some political piquancy, if no real influence, in the late 1940s and 1950s. "Canaanism" was not anti-Zionism ("anti-Zionist" is a smear term within Israeli political life), but it was non-Zionist. The "Canaanites" held that Israel should be a totally new nation, free of association with diaspora Jewry, unalloyed with Jewish religion, and clear of Jewish debts to history. The country should be run, they argued, on completely secular lines. As James Diamond has shown in his study of the movement, "It is easy to see why Canaanism never had a chance. Ultimately, it represented a metamorphosis of Jewish identity into something that had no defined historical precedent or definable content. . . . Secularism as the upshot of modernity and the Emancipation could be appropriated by Jews as individuals but there was as yet no way for Jews to do this meaningfully as a collective entity without some recourse to the Jewish past and the Jewish religion."[3] How many Israelis held tenets of "Canaanism" or a similar position in the early days of the state of Israel is impossible to determine, but a social science survey conducted in the late 1970s found that only about 6 percent of Israelis believed that Jewishness and Israeliness should not be associated; that is, only 6 percent believed in something akin to secularism.[4]

At the other end of the spectrum, a significant proportion of the Israeli population not only rejected the idea of secularism, but they went about as far as one can go in the opposite direction. Not only did they believe that being an Israeli and being Jewish were coterminous conditions, but these individuals desired a virtual theocracy. At present, such groups usually are labeled as the "religious right" but in conventional political terms they have been neither right nor left wing, believing as they do that all acts of the state should be determined by the nature of Israel's covenant with Yahweh. The classic articulation of this position was the closely reasoned argument of Rabbi Meir Bar-Ilan who, in 1922, had asked, "What kind of life shall we create in Eretz Israel?" In his article, he pointed out that the idea of "church" and "state" as being separate entities was entirely a Gentile construct. "Our case is different," he asserted. "Our Torah and traditions are not man-made constitutions, but God's own law. . . . We have no 'church' that is not also concerned with matters of state, just as we have no state that is not concerned with 'church' matters—in Jewish life these are not two separate spheres."[5] The proportion of the Israeli polity that in the early days of the state agreed with these ideas is unknown, but in the 1970s, roughly 15 percent of the populace held similar theocratic beliefs.[6]

Thus, roughly (very roughly) four-fifths of the Israeli polity probably defined the state as something between the extreme secularism of the "Canaanists" and the theocracy of ancient Israel that the extremely religious Zionists desired. These included large numbers of nonobservant Israelis, who, though not given to practicing traditional religion, were nonetheless willing to honor the historical and traditional aspects of Jewish life, and also included the majority of observant Israelis who, unlike the ultraorthodox, did not want a theocracy. Most Israelis accepted that there was an association of Jewishness and Israeliness, but even on that point the strands of belief were bewilderingly complex. It was not at all unusual to find agnostics and atheists who averred that Israel was a secular state, and yet who invoked a panoply of traditional Jewish symbols. Labor Zionists (David Ben-Gurion and Golda Meier are the best known of those who straddled the line between agnosticism and atheism), were particularly given to attaching traditional religious symbols to the state of Israel and thus raising the state itself to transcendent status.

A historical analogy can help us understand what the broad center of Israeli society believed about the relationship of religion and the state. On paper, the United States in the nineteenth century was one of the most radically secular states in existence. There was no established religion and church and state were sharply separated. Yet, if one had asked most Americans of the time, "Is this a Christian country?" they would have replied, "Of course it is." The state school systems taught Christian (albeit not specifically denominational) morality. Christian prayers and "New Testament" biblical prayers were part of the publicly funded curriculum. Official government functions—those of courts and legislatures, for example—began with Christian prayers. Most legal oaths were taken on the Christian Bible; and the overwhelming majority of the American population was at least nominally Christian. So, American citizens in the midst of the nineteenth century could describe themselves as citizens of a state that was at once Christian and secular, and would see nothing incompatible in these two conditions. Similarly, Israelis in the 1940s and 1950s could describe their state as being both Jewish and secular and not see these as contradictory assertions.

At its creation, the international community was keen on Israel's being a "democratic" state, in the sense of it being a liberal democracy along western lines. This meant that it would also be a "pluralistic" society, in that minority groups would not be suppressed but would be allowed to articulate their views publicly and to participate without handicap in the political process. In actual practice, however, democracy was limited from the beginning. Full rights as citizens in reality (as distinct from theory) were not extended to non-Jews (this is discussed in detail later). One of the greatest practical limitations on democracy in the early days of Israel was that, as Yehezkel Dror of Hebrew University has argued, the Jews had little experience with state building, especially democracies. "The greatness of the Jews has been in building moral systems," he argues. "We view history as the unfolding of morality. The Chinese and the Europeans regard it as the development of statecraft. There's a big difference. We don't have a history of statecraft."[7] To the extent that the citizens of the new state shared a common political culture, it was, as Shlomo Avineri has suggested, "quintessentially Eastern European." "If Israel is—or has ever been—related to Europe, it was to this Europe that it was related: our roots were in Warsaw and Vienna, in Prague and Odessa, in Bessarabia and Lithuania."[8] And whatever else those places were, they were not breeding grounds of pluralistic and liberal democracies.

(2)

The first task of this new and unique state was to carry forward the mission of colonization that had been the purpose of Zionism and now was the task of Israeli nationalism. "The Land" had to be made secure and the hostile inhabitants of Eretz Israel removed or thoroughly subordinated. These goals were achieved in a two-stage process that was successful beyond almost everyone's expectations. The first Jewish citizens spent the years 1948 and 1949 denuding Israel of most of its Palestinian Arabs and, simultaneously, winning more land in a war with the Arab countries bordering the new nation. The second phase, which began in earnest in 1950, may be denominated "domestic imperialism" (to use a phrase from British history). The Israelis systematically deprived the Palestinian Arabs of their lands, segregated their places of residence, and developed a dual economy and severe restrictions on the civil liberties and civil rights of the indigenous population.

In April 1948, David Ben-Gurion decided to take a step forward in the "redemption" of the land. Knowing that the British mandate in Palestine would end on 14 May, and believing that the pieces of Palestine that were scheduled to be ceded to Israel were too small and too scattered, he ordered an offensive. His army, the Haganah, took Haifa, Safed, Acre, and Jaffa even before the Declaration of Independence was published.[9] Technically, these actions were against the British, but in reality they were an attack on the Palestinian Arabs. Ben-Gurion concentrated on gaining control over the area allocated by the United Nations partition plan, but lands that the UN intended to allocate to the Palestinians were also seized by the Haganah. Thus began what later historians may well point to as the Hundred Years War of the twentieth and twenty-first centuries. The Arab states that bordered Israel declared war on 15 May 1948. The Arab-Israeli war of 1948–49 resulted in a massive victory for the Israelis. Under the United Nations plan for the partition of Palestine, Israel had been promised roughly 55 percent of the old Palestinian mandate and had faced the prospect of having a Palestinian Arab state as a neighbor. By the end of the 1948–49 war, the Israelis held about 80 percent of Palestine and their territorial acquisitions had made the creation of a Palestinian Arab state a virtual impossibility.[10] A series of peace treaties with most (but not all) of the Arab states yielded a hair-trigger truce.[11] The Israeli government, one must emphasize, made no ideological commitments to live permanently within the truce boundaries, advantageous though these boundaries were *pro tem*.[12]

Even more important than the acquisition of land by Israel as a result of this first Arab-Israeli war was the massive shift of population (almost all of it Arab) that accompanied the conflict. There is a controversial literature on this stage of the Arab depopulation of Israel; it boils down to one question: in fleeing Israel, were the Palestinian Arabs pushed, or did they jump? That is, did the new Israeli state effect a pogrom against the Palestinians? Or did the Arabs voluntarily abandon their homes in Eretz Israel with the intention of eventually returning as members of a victorious pan-Arab army?[13] What is clear is that the number of Arabs in Israel was drastically reduced. Before hostilities began, roughly 700,000 Arabs lived within the territory that was to become the state of Israel; by the autumn of 1948, only 156,000 Arabs remained within the borders of the new state.[14] Thus, as one authority noted, "The large Arab population which had threatened to swamp a Jewish state under a democratic regime fled to the neighbouring Arab countries, leaving a manageable ten percent minority within the state."[15] The reduction of the Palestinian Arabs from their position as an awkward majority to a "manageable minority" was a qualitative as well as a quantitative process. The Arab urban elite, the economic and political leadership of the Palestinian culture, was almost totally destroyed. With the exception of Nazareth, only a small remnant remained.[16] What was left for the most part was a leaderless Arab rural proletariat.

Some Palestinian Arabs did return to Israel after the 1949 armistice, but their numbers were more than offset by the flow of new Jewish immigrants. The year 1949 was the peak period in this era for immigration to Israel, when almost 240,000 Jews arrived. Between the creation of the state of Israel in May 1948 and the end of the calendar year 1951, over 686,000 Jewish immigrants were admitted.[17] The result was that in 1951 the Jewish population of Israel was 1,404,000 and Jews constituted 89 percent of the total population.[18]

These developments permit us to formulate what was to become the reccurring tactical question in the continuing process of the colonization of Eretz Israel. Is it better to have a relatively limited land area, within which the non-Jewish population is a small and easily manageable minority? Or is it better to continue to expand the territory of the state and thereby to risk having to govern a much larger and much less tractable Palestinian Arab population? From 1949 onward, something akin to an equation in natural law obtained: for each increment in "the Land" that Israel "redeemed" from the surrounding Arab states, it lost a quantum of control over the Arabs within the state's borders. So, in a manner that a medieval philosopher would have approved, too much ambition in acquiring territory inevitably would produce its own punishment. The point when that equation would become painfully manifest, however, was still in the future.

For the moment, the authorities who directed the Israeli state in the 1950s and 1960s focused their attention on the development of a system for controlling the Arabs within Israel. The primary tool in this program was the confiscation of as much of the land that remained in the hands of Palestinian Arabs as could be taken without causing outright rebellion. For Israelis this process had the dual attractiveness of "redeeming" an ever-increasing portion of Eretz Israel from the modern equivalent of the Philistines and Amalekites, while simultaneously making the country more secure militarily. Crucially, the ideological spine of the land acquisition program was unchanged since the Yishuv era: the land of Israel was considered to be the joint possession of the Israeli people, an attribute of their corporate personality. Thus, almost all of the lands taken from Arabs after May 1948 went either into the hands of the Jewish National Fund or into the control of the state of Israel. Very little found its way into private ownership.

Early in the first Arab-Israeli war, the highest level of Israeli government had outlined a land acquisition policy that would preclude the Palestinian Arabs who had abandoned their lands and dwellings from returning to them. The Abandoned Areas Ordinance of 24 June 1948, a temporary measure, permitted the state of Israel to expropriate and to confiscate any "abandoned area."[19] A "Custodian for Enemy Property" was named and land that this officer seized eventually was transferred to the Development Authority of the state and then either to the Jewish National Fund or to state title.[20] In 1949, the Emergency Land Requisition Law gave the government the right to expropriate land whenever a state-appointed "competent authority" determined that the land was "required for the defense of the State, the security of the people, to resettle retired soldiers or men disabled while on active service."[21] All Arab lands, not just those abandoned during the 1948–49 war, came under the purview of this law.

The key piece of legislation in the de-Arabization of Israel was the Absentees' Property Law of 1950. It was written in anticipation of the possibility that a significant number of Palestinians who had fled during the first Arab-Israeli conflict would return to Israel and demand to exercise their property rights. To prevent this, the 1950 act declared that all "absentees" had abandoned their property in Israel, and that virtually every Palestinian Arab who had at any time left Israeli territory during the 1948–49 war was an absentee. An absentee was defined as

a Palestinian citizen and [who] left his ordinary place of residence in Palestine
(a) for a place outside Palestine before the 1st September 1948; or
(b) for a place in Palestine held at the time by forces which sought to prevent the establishment of the State of Israel or which fought against it after establishment.[22]

The next step was to pass on to the Development Authority (for eventual transfer to the state of Israel or to the Jewish National Fund) these abandoned and now-confiscated lands. Later, an act of 1953 validated all the ad hoc cases of Arab land confiscation that had occurred at any time since 15 May 1948.[23]

Another measure pressed down on those unaffected by any of the preceding acts. In 1948, the Prescription Law was enacted, aimed at the remaining Arab landowners. It declared that in order for land titles to be considered valid, they had to be proved not (as previously had been the case under Ottoman law) by ten years of unchallenged possession, but by at least fifteen years' possession and in some cases twenty-five. This meant that Arab landowners had to prove an unchallenged land title back into the days of the British mandate for Palestine. Because a modern system of land registration had not existed under the mandate (and because most potential witnesses had fled from Israel), establishing ownership of long-held family lands was very difficult.[24]

A more efficient (indeed, the primary) tool for taking the lands of Arabs who had not become "absentees" under the various expropriation acts, was Article 125 of the "Defence Regulations (Emergency) 1945" as set out under the British mandate and incorporated into Israeli law. These regulations empowered military authorities to declare as closed (save to persons with military authorization) locales of importance to national security. These usually were areas near the borders of Israel. During the 1948–49 war, twelve entire Arab villages and their surrounding lands were declared closed (and eventually seized).[25] After the 1948–49 war was over, Israeli authorities continued to use these defense regulations to confiscate Arab lands that could not be taken by other means. The process was, first, to declare an area "closed." Palestinians would then be denied permission to enter it and soon their farms turned to weeds and dust. Then, under the Cultivation of Waste Lands Ordinance of 1948, the Ministry of Agriculture would issue certificates stating that the lands were uncultivated. The owners were notified that unless they farmed the lands immediately, the tracts would be expropriated. Since the military authorities still kept the lands "closed," the Palestinian Arabs soon became former owners. The state of Israel or the Jewish National Fund became the owners of the lands, which were then rented to Jewish farmers.[26]

Observers of the de-Arabization of Eretz Israel may have major differences in their evaluations of the ethical correctness of the process, and minor differences about its exact extent, but the overall outlines are clear and unarguable, and, indeed, they are well documented in Israeli sources. As a base line, recall chapter 5's point: on the eve of the creation of the state of Israel, Jews owned only 6.6 percent of Palestine (this entity being somewhat larger than the eventual state of Israel). And then consider that a well-informed American scholar, Stanley B. Greenberg, could write in 1980 that "virtually all the land of Israel is now owned by the government or the Jewish National Fund."[27] That is the fundamental, unquestionable dimension of the process.

Part of the process of putting the land of Israel into collective Jewish ownership involved wiping out the Palestinian Arab villages and settlements, because they were potential sites of resistance. In 1945, there were 452 predominantly Arab villages in Israel. According to Arab sources, 385 of them were destroyed between 1948 and 1967; Israeli sources state that 362 villages were destroyed. In essence, the two sources agree: even if one takes the official Israeli estimates, 86 percent of the Palestinian Arab villages that existed at the time of the British mandate disappeared within twenty years.[28] In 1962, the Israeli Land Authority's annual report gave the following distribution of land in Israel: state and Development Authority, 75.07 percent; Jewish National Fund, 17.62 percent; and private ownership, 7.31 percent.[29] Of the 7.31 percent of Israeli land in private hands, roughly half—approximately 3.5 percent—was held by Arabs.[30] Even this figure underestimates the degree to which the Palestinians had been dispossessed: almost all Arab agricultural lands in the valleys and on the coastal plain were confiscated, so that the Palestinians were reduced to living on patches of hill, swamp, and desert. In the 1970s, more than half the land cultivated by Palestinian Arabs was in the Negev desert.[31]

Some might argue that the land seized by various legal devices did not disappear from Israel and that in theory the Palestinian Arabs still might have access to it. But Israel continued and expanded upon the policy that prevailed before 1948: thus, in the case of lands owned by the JNF and, now, in addition, by the state of Israel and by the Development Authority, land transfer, either by sale or in any other manner to private or collective ownership that was not Jewish was legally prohibited.[32] Therefore, the nearly 93 percent of Israel that was collectively owned by the JNF, the state, and the Development Authority was available only by rental. And here a sharply discriminatory policy operated. The standard lease for Jewish settlers was forty-nine years; that for Palestinians usually was only a single year.[33] This left Palestinian Arab farmers living in perpetual uncertainty and greatly hindered their chances of making economic progress. Capital investment in a farm, orchard, or market garden makes little sense to someone who can be evicted after a single crop year.

Although the process of seizure of Arab lands and displacement of the Palestinian Arabs was unique to Israel, the process had some striking parallels to the displacement of the Irish Catholics in Ulster during the seventeenth and eighteenth centuries. The Protestant seizure of large portions of Ulster followed the flight of the native Catholic leadership during the wars of 1688–89. Subsequent confiscations in Ireland (involving the whole country, not just Ulster) were predicated upon the need for what would today be called "national security." The Irish Catholic portion of the ownership of land in Ireland was reduced to roughly 5 percent in 1775 (compared to about 3.5 percent ownership by Arabs in Israel). Legal structures enforced a dual land-rental system: Catholics under the eighteenth-century penal code could not purchase freehold land and could rent it for a maximum of thirty-one years, and usually much less; no restrictions affected Protestants. Of course there were important differences between the two situations, which are further divided by centuries, but the similarities may haunt not merely the past of both countries, but the future.

Because most Palestinian Arabs lived in rural areas, the seizure of the bulk of their lands effectively removed them as an economic threat to the Jewish settlers in Israel. However, there remained the question of how this rural Arab proletariat, and the remaining urban Arabs, would relate to the Israeli economy. Here the policy again was based on a pre-1948 precedent: now the state and quasi-state institutions created a dual labor market, not unlike that established by custom in Northern Ireland in the years 1920–69, and by law in South Africa in the years 1948–69. As in those other two cases, the ideology behind Israel's creation of a dual labor market was explained by idealistic premises, in this case the concept of "Jewish labor." One of the early tenets of Zionism had been the "productivization" of the Jewish people. In Europe, the Jews had been primarily small merchants, artisans, and speculators. As a group they had had little to do with primary production, especially agriculture, and not much more to do with urban manual labor. The socialist wing of the Zionist movement believed that for Eretz Israel to be truly redeemed, the working of the soil and the carrying out of everyday toil would have to be done by the colonists themselves. For this principle to succeed, the Jewish economy in Israel had to become a closed loop. And, assuming that the Arabs were not totally eliminated from the new land, it followed, therefore, that there would be two economies in Eretz Israel, one Arab, the other Jewish.[34]

In practice, the two economies within Israel could not be totally segregated. What developed is best described as a "single economy, characterized by a dual labor market." One segment of this dual labor market, the Jewish sector, enjoyed full employment in most years and included almost all the professional, technical, and skilled posts. The other, the Palestinian Arab sector, had (with very minor exceptions), the lowest paid posts and high unemployment. The line between the two labor markets was in part established by informal mechanisms (Jewish employers were under strong moral suasion to adopt a Jews-first hiring policy) and in part formal. This dual labor market was also perpetuated institutionally by the system of labor exchanges, whose main function was to protect Jewish workers from Palestinian competition. A network of labor exchanges (that is, employment bureaus) existed for Jews from the very first days of the state; only a single Arab exchange, in Nazareth, came into operation in 1949. Others were later created, but in 1958, for example, only three of these bureaus were in rural areas where the majority of the Arab workers lived.[35] In practice, the Arab labor exchanges were designed to act as a control valve on Arab urban employment. During the 1950s Arab workers could travel to take jobs in security-tight locales (which meant most of Israel) only if they had travel permits. These were allocated through the Arab labor exchanges and usually given to the local Arab headman, who distributed them as he wished.[36]

Since the state of Israel had a strong socialist component, one would expect to have found some commitment to working-class unity, and, at least in the labor union movement, a degree of economic integration of Jews and Arabs. But here cultural allegiance overcame socialist orthodoxy. In the face of some pressure to permit Arabs to join the Histadrut (the Israeli labor federation), in January 1952, the government ruled "no." A little more than a year later, in May 1953, Arabs were allowed to affiliate with various Histadrut insurance and benevolent schemes, but not to join the union federation directly.[37] In 1956, non-Palestinian Arabs who had served in the Israeli army were granted full union rights (a boon to the tiny syncretistic Druze tribe, who were part Christian, part Muslim, and part Jewish). Finally, in 1959, Arabs were allowed to join the Histadrut, but at the same time the Zionist nature of the labor federation was affirmed. In that year, 6,500 Arabs became members of Histadrut-affiliated trade unions, and by 1969 the figure was approximately 31,250.[38]

In assessing the impact of the dual labor policy, one must remember that the early days of the state of Israel were hardly lush. Jews within Israel did not live a soft life. In the first decade, the actual income difference between Jews and Arabs was much less than one might expect. In 1955, the ratio (expressed in terms of income per head) was 2.75:1, and given that the Arabs had a larger proportion of children and old people in their population, the actual difference was less. The differential is significant, but by the standards of what was happening elsewhere in the world—say, in North Africa where the difference between European settlers and indigene was about nine-to-one—it was not very sharp.[39] The real effect was in the future. As the Israeli economy became more and more sophisticated, the Arab workers became a source of surplus labor that could be tapped whenever there were jobs that no Israeli wished to take. Thus, when the economic boom of 1955–64 worked its way through the labor market, the employment of Arabs in the Jewish economic sector increased dramatically. It is estimated that in 1950 only 3 percent of the total number of employed Arabs were working in the Jewish sector. In 1961, this figure was 12 percent.[40] What this says is that as the Israeli economy developed, most Arabs still were segregated in the Arab economic sector (88 percent of them in 1961), but during good times they could be shunted into the Jewish sector easily. Ironically, despite the employment opportunities for Arabs that the flourishing Israeli economy provided, it created a sort of infernal machine: because Palestinians could enter the quickly advancing Jewish economic sector only at the bottom, the gap between the income of the Jews (who increasingly held technologically sophisticated employment) and the Arabs in the manual and unskilled jobs, continually widened. Thus, the dual labor market created more and more discontent, even in times when it increased Arab employment.

How to keep the Palestinian Arabs from revolting? In the 1950s and early 1960s, this was much easier than it would be later. At that time the Palestinians were only slightly more than 10 percent of the population of Israel and, moreover, they had the bitter memory of their recent and total defeat. Israel's Declaration of Independence of 14 May 1948 had called on "the sons of the Arab people dwelling in Israel to keep the peace and to play their part in building the state on the basis of full and equal citizenship." The declaration had affirmed the "complete equality of social and political rights for all its citizens without distinction of creed, race, or sex." But keeping the Palestinian Arabs subdued and giving them full civil rights in the Jewish state were incompatible tasks. From the first day of its existence until August 1959, Israel was under a military government that gave the "military governors" of the sectors into which the country was divided virtually unlimited powers to suspend civil rights. In 1959, David Ben-Gurion eased some of the travel restrictions that applied to Arabs, and the introduction of civilian law was begun, a process that was completed in November 1966.[41]

However, for most of the period covered in this chapter, the Palestinian Arabs remained under military, rather than civilian, law. The actual rules were those determined by the "Defence Regulations (Emergency) 1945" framed by the British mandate authorities and assimilated by the Israeli state. The country was divided into military sectors and a military governor, appointed by the Israeli minister of defense, was in charge of each sector. For "security" reasons, by a simple administrative order, the military governor could subject any person to police surveillance, refuse him access to his property, prohibit him from having contact with any individual or group of individuals, and prohibit any activity deemed dangerous to state security (such as Palestinian journalists writing about land confiscation). An individual could be "detained" (that is, imprisoned) at any time for security reasons and kept locked up as long as the military governor wished, without any charge or any explanation. The military governor had the right to deport persons from Israel, and if the governor of a locale even suspected that a bomb had been thrown from a certain house or piece of property, he had the right to confiscate the property and, if he wished, to destroy it.[42]

"Security"—that magic word of the second half of the twentieth century—was behind the military rule. Perhaps the reasons for such security measures were sufficient, but there is no doubt that in practice the rules impinged only rarely on Jews and almost entirely upon Palestinians. It can be argued in justification of this situation that security threats came from Arabs and not Jews, but this is structurally the same argument that was used throughout the nineteenth and twentieth centuries to justify the use of state violence to suppress colonized or otherwise disadvantaged groups who objected to their treatment. Until the mid-1960s, the Arabs had effectively no civil rights. In 1959, when the government debated whether or not to begin to ease the military controls, a revealing argument for keeping them was put forward by Yigal Allon, the senior governmental official specializing in control of the Arab population. He argued that it was necessary to keep the system of military administration, first, to maintain "efficient control over the Arab population and its movements in order to prevent organization and hostile military activity by Arab citizens of the state"; second, to prevent "the unwanted movement of Arabs into certain delicate areas such as divided Jerusalem, the Negev, and especially Eilat"; third, to maintain "a legal basis for actions taken against treasonous assemblies and so that traitors can be punished"; fourth, to retain "a basis to prevent and deter hostile political actions and organisations"; and finally to enforce "separation between the Arab population and new settlements."[43]

In contrast, many Israelis saw the military administration as unnecessary and immoral. The state controller of Israel published a report on the use of the 1945 defense regulations as a means of controlling the Arab civilian population. He concluded that "there is something improper about this law, which was drafted with the intention of its being applicable to all the inhabitants of the country, whereas in fact it is only enforced against some of them."[44]

Israel, from virtually its first day, had made effective propaganda by describing itself as "the only democracy in the Middle East." The state of Israel was highly democratic for Jews, but for no one else. Under the defense regulations, it was impossible for Palestinians to form political parties that reflected their actual beliefs: since their beliefs were anti-Zionist, by definition their parties would have been punishable as treasonous by the military governors. Yet Arab citizens of Israel had the franchise and, because of the fragmented character of Israeli politics, their votes were coveted. From the viewpoint of the various Jewish parties, the trick was to seduce the Arabs away from their nonparticipation (after all, every one of the major parties in Israel was pro-Zionist, so Arabs were not all that keen on electoral politics), but without going so far as to open themselves to the charge of being pro-Arab. In 1948–69, none of the mainline Israeli parties opened their ranks to Arab members, but some kept lists of "affiliated Arabs" who voted for the party but were not given any right to influence it directly. Significantly, even the Mapai (renamed the Labor party in 1973) did not admit Arabs to membership in this period; that did not occur until 1976 and then only 4,000 to 5,000 Arabs joined. As late as the end of the 1960s, the only party to which Arabs had full access was Rakah—the New Israeli Communist party—an anti-Zionist, far-left splinter group that was completely cut off from political influence.[45]

Given their political powerlessness, it is perhaps not surprising that the Palestinians were denied access to many (probably most) social welfare benefits provided by the state. The Palestinians of course were not eligible for the settlement services and housing subsidies available to new Jewish immigrants. More important, the Arabs were cut off from other benefits (family welfare provisions, for example) that were limited to individuals and to families of people who had served in the Israeli armed forces. This was a particularly unctuous bit of business. All young Israelis (with exemptions for certain religious students) were liable to conscription for national service. Certain small minority groups were also permitted to serve (Christians, Bedouin Moslems, Druze and Circassian males) and from the mid-1950s onward they were subject to conscription. Most

Moslem Arabs—and most especially Palestinians—were not permitted to enlist even if by some wild twist of ambition they had wished to do so.[46] Because most social welfare benefits in Israel were related in one form or another to "veterans' benefits," this became yet another device to discriminate between the two main populations.

Occasionally, the attempts to filter state benefits had comic side effects. In 1949, David Ben-Gurion, worried that the Arabs would outbreed the Israelis and thus at some date in the future become a majority within Israel, set up a cash-bearing motherhood award (for once, army service was not a prerequisite). The award was given to every woman who bore her tenth child. Ben-Gurion, however, had neglected to include any stipulation that Arabs need not apply, and during the 1950s many Arab women applied for and received the award. In 1959, when this disquieting fact became known, the motherhood award was quietly abolished.[47]

Although economic, security, and political issues necessarily are discussed separately, this should not blind us to the fact that in everyday life they were not detached from each other and that their effect was cumulative and self-reinforcing. The cumulative impact of the Israeli government upon the lives of the Palestinian Arabs was substantially the same as was the impact of apartheid upon the lives of the nonwhites of South Africa: a dual labor market operated, restrictions on place of residence and work applied, homes and villages were destroyed and almost all the decent agricultural land of the country was seized, strict "pass" or "travel permit" laws were enforced, there was no access to the political process except as collaborators with the regime, civil rights were severely restricted, and access to state welfare programs was greatly reduced for the minority. Yet Israel's system in one crucial aspect was different from South Africa's. Unlike the South Africans who refused to dissemble, the Israelis decided "to stand up and lie like white men" (in P. J. O'Rourke's corrosive phrase).[48] The appropriation of Palestinian lands and the economic, social, and often residential segregation of the indigene was never labeled as such.[49] Always "redemption," or "security," or similar words were employed.

The differences between South Africa and Israel in this period were not limited to their contrasting willingness to admit what they were doing. The two nations were at different stages in their collective evolution. The South Africans had "redeemed" their land from nonwhites long before 1948, but at that date the Israelis were just beginning to deal with the Palestinians. More important, by 1948, South Africa was a fully formed covenantal culture, whereas at that time Israel was not even close to being a single cohesive society. Indeed, the massive migration of Jews from all over the world made Eretz Israel much less cohesive in 1948 than it had been in the 1930s. The limited number of central beliefs that the variegated settlers to Israel held in common—that they had in some way been chosen to "redeem the Land" and to displace the modern equivalent of the Philistines and Canaanites—became in themselves a source of bonding. It is no accident that these central points whereon the citizens of the new Israel agreed were bedrock ideas from the books of Moses.

(3)

But, in the early days of their state, did the Israelis need a common enemy (the Arabs) and a common goal (redemption of the land and suppression of the Palestinians) to bond them together? That, like so many hypothetical questions is impossible to answer directly, but it is obvious that the Israeli authorities were worried that their polity could shatter into myriad pieces. The best evidence of this anxiety is found in the strenuous efforts that they took to form a synthetic unity among Israeli citizens. What any percipient observer of Israeli communal life saw in, say, the early 1950s was this: a particularly bizarre mixture of multi-party politics and proportional representation, which made a clear political majority in the Knesset unlikely and political instability commonplace even during the era of the Mapai-Labor domination; the absence of a common "political culture," and, for most of Israel's citizens, little or no experience with the institution of liberal democracy; a population that was drawn from all over the world, and who shared no common culture, save a sense of being Jewish, a feeling that was not the same thing to all people; a deep split between those in Israel whose background was European Jewry and those whose roots were in the Middle East or North Africa; and almost irreconcilable tensions between the various groups of observant Jews and their secular, or secularized, coreligionists.

So, the authorities of the new state faced a heroic task: nothing less than the creation of a new cultural entity, Israel. Moreover, this had to be done in such a way as not to alienate diaspora Jewry who provided so much of the financing for the new state. One of the words most commonly found in official usage in the 1950s and 1960s (and one which, with the arrival of the Soviet Jews in the early 1990s has once again become prominent) is "absorption." The flood of immigrants had to be absorbed and integrated into a single nation-state. The size of the migrant influx in relationship to the pre-1948 population was staggering. The population of Israel roughly quadrupled between 1948 and 1969. In 1949, one out of every two Jews living in Israel had only arrived in that year.[50] As late as 1972, immigrants made up 53 percent of the Jewish citizenry of Israel.[51]

Indoctrination of the new immigrants with the values of the new culture and with their duties as citizens would have been difficult in any case; it was made more difficult by an ethnocultural chasm within world Jewry. Although the Zionist movement in the Yishuv era had been directed and populated chiefly by Ashkenazic colonists, after 1948 the great influxes of new settlers were from North Africa and the Middle East. (These immigrants were referred to loosely as the "Orientals.") By the late 1970s, approximately 55 percent of Israel's population was of Oriental background.[52]

"Immigration was the reverse of homogenous," was the restrained understatement of a quasi-official survey published in 1961 by the Israel Digest. This report continued:

Jews of all lands, in all stages of culture and development, talking a torrent of discrepant languages, and trailing the habits of their exiles were housed together higgedly-piggledy: Western Jews, Oriental Jews *with a development lag of centuries* [italics mine], Jews until recently cave-dwellers in the Atlas Mountains. It is not difficult to conceive the tensions, frictions, and hardships that all endured.[53]

Note the phrase "a development lag of centuries" concerning the Oriental Jews. It reveals the attitude of the Ashkenazic establishment toward the African and Asian newcomers. As much as was possible, the Orientals were pushed into agricultural and manual labor and were shunted into the new "development towns."[54]

In the short run, the absorption officials did what they could: provided temporary housing (often in tents), immediate medical attention, resettlement in areas where manual and agricultural laborers were needed, and subventions to help in acquiring permanent housing. But the difficult long-range question was beyond their purview. How does one make a nation out of such disparate elements? The answer was that—consciously or unconsciously—Israeli society turned itself into a massive and efficient agent of self-indoctrination. That sounds tautological, but it is not: Israel, more than any other nation of which I have any historical knowledge, created itself. The Israelis created a set of institutions and nursed a set of beliefs by which they eventually convinced themselves that they were indeed a single nation. Many, probably most, members of diaspora Jewry carried a conviction of being part of a single people, but becoming in Israel a single nation, with all that implied, was something very different. Once having convinced themselves of this national unity, in fact, they actually were united as Israelis. This ongoing process was nowhere near completion before the start of the 1967 war.

Take the army. During the great flood of immigrants in the later 1940s and early 1950s, the Israeli Defense Force (IDF) often was the chief agent of cultural integration. The government allowed many soldiers to do their compulsory military service as tutors to newcomers in the development villages. Because the areas where most of the newcomers settled were under the close scrutiny of the various military governors, the social control in many new settlements initially was by the IDF. Much more important, however, was the fact that at age eighteen every Jewish male and female (with the exception of most Yeshiva students) became liable to conscription. For the nation's youth, therefore, the army became the great integrator. Not only were Sephardic and Ashkenazic young people taught to work and to fight side by side, but the IDF did a good deal of teaching: it taught trades to the unskilled, Hebrew to those who did not know it, and it indoctrinated everyone in the loyalty required by the new state. The IDF had extremely high morale. By virtue of its defeat of the Arab nations in 1948–49, it had a developing mythology of its own. According to its historian, the Israeli army had as its operating motto "Few against Many." It viewed itself as a tiny band, defending Eretz Israel against an outside world full of enemies. The centrality of the IDF to Israeli life was made manifest by two facts: the military was far and away the largest governmental agency in terms of budget and staff, and from 1948 to 63 David Ben-Gurion was both prime minister and minister of defense.[55]

The Israeli army adopted as its everyday language a tongue that in the first decades of the new state was spoken only haltingly by most of its recruits: Hebrew. Thus, in the early years, military training was also an immersion course in the official language of the new nation. "Hebrew worked because the new army spoke it," one observer has suggested. And, conversely, "the army worked because it spoke Hebrew."[56]

What held for the army carried over, with somewhat less intensity, into the larger society. The state (spearheaded by the enthusiasm of David Ben-Gurion) pressed hard on the language issue. Most state-aided schools used Hebrew as the primary language of instruction; officials in governmental agencies were urged to do their everyday work in Hebrew; considerable pressure was exerted on immigrants to adopt "real" Hebrew names. Thus, the very process of dealing with government, of acting as a citizen, became part of a process of linguistic acculturation, and the language acquired was a bonding agent, a tongue that had belonged solely to the Jews. It was estimated that in 1954 about 60 percent of the Jewish population of Israel used Hebrew as their first language and that, as of 1957, nineteen out of every twenty Israeli Jews could carry on their daily business in Hebrew.[57] Considering that Hebrew had not been a language of government for nearly 2,000 years, this revival was astounding.

Charles S. Liebman has suggested that in its first two decades Israel was characterized by "statism," by which he means that "the centrality and legitimacy of the state as a focus of loyalty" exceeded that of any other private or public institution.[58] David Ben-Gurion, who as much as anyone promoted statism, believed this was necessary because of the nature of Jewish history. "Exile has planted into us distrust of all government, because we were not in control of our own fate."[59] To keep the people of Israel from falling into the Jewish habit of opposition to the government, the "primacy of the state" (Ben-Gurion's phase) had to be established. To him, this meant that the state of Israel could not be just another government, but that it had to be a model state, a moral beacon to other nations.[60]

Now a state with a moral purpose can hardly be a modern secular state, so it was natural that Israeli leaders elicited fervent loyalty to the state by couching its description in religiously based languages and symbols.[61] The use of traditional language and symbols has been employed by representatives of the entire political spectrum, from the Revisionists and their political descendant, Likud, to the left-wing establishment, Mapai-Labor. The only Israeli politicians who have not used this religiously derived symbol system as the foundation of their political rhetoric have been the two minorities at opposite ends of the spectrum: the self-consciously secular ("the Canaanites" and their heirs) and the religious groups so hyperorthodox that they refuse to recognize any political government in the land of Israel. Take Menachem Begin's rhetoric as an example of the use of religious symbolism.[62] Here is Begin—whose roots were Revisionist, whose military background was the guerrilla movement Irgun, and whose own religious position at the time was nonobservant—appealing in his role as commander in chief of the Irgun in 1946 to diaspora Jewry:

> A new generation has arisen in Israel, a generation which draws super-human strength from the mother land, hallowed from ancient days with the blood of the brave and the holy.

. . . .

Here in this country the eyes of the masses and even the eyes of the leaders have been opened to see that there is only one alternative before us and none other, either to fight and *be redeemed* or to live in the status quo and *be destroyed.*

. . . .

The hour of redemption is near! Take on strength! Rise to the aid of fighting Zion! Rise to the struggle of the nation![63]

This rhetorical strain continued throughout Begin's career.[64]

The key point is that the symbols he employed and the metaphors he exploited were essentially the same as those found in the speeches and writings of Begin's left-leaning opponent, the doyen of the Labor party, David Ben-Gurion. Labor Zionism drew heavily on the biblical theme of the return to Israel and the redemption of the Promised Land, and often the mission of creating a model society was presented in Messianic terms. Ben-Gurion began his own book on the history of Israel ("a personal history," he called it with characteristic modesty) this way: "From the moment of their appearance on the stage of history, the Jewish people have been more than a political entity. Without grasping their unique spiritual and moral character and historical mission it is impossible to understand the history of the Jewish nation."[65] He argued that "Moses, our Teacher, said two things that are no less true today than they were three thousand and three hundred years ago. He, the greatest of our Prophets said, 'Ye shall be a peculiar treasure unto me above all people.' (Exodus 19:5) And he repeated this in saying 'The Lord thy God hath chosen thee to be an official people unto himself above all people that are upon the face of the earth'" (Deut. 7:6).[66] In a letter to General Charles de Gaulle written in December 1967, Ben-Gurion remarked, "When I appeared in Jerusalem in 1936 before the Royal Commission, I said 'the Bible is our mandate.' It was from the Bible that we drew the power to survive in a hostile world and to retain our faith that we would return to our Homeland and that peace would reign on earth."[67] Ben-Gurion, though he thought of himself as a nonbeliever, simply could not talk about Israel without using a vocabulary redolent of faith and traditional religious symbols that were eons away from the stark Bauhaus-like vocabulary of modern secular political democracy. Well might an orthodox rabbi comment in exasperation that "for Mr. Ben-Gurion we are a Chosen People—chosen by a God that he doesn't believe in, for reasons he denies, in a book he doesn't accept."[68]

It has been argued that one of the chief tasks of the state of Israel in its first two decades was to create a set of agreed-upon symbols and myths. In the years when the Labor Zionists were the largest political party, these symbols were in essence verbs—that is, actions or the human embodiment of these actions: redemption and working of the land; military heroism, exile and return; the pioneers who began Zionist colonization; and labor itself in the sense of the holy work.[69] These symbols were used in nearly every civil ceremony, in school lessons, in homilies delivered by management to workers, in speeches of military commanders to troops.

Even more striking was the articulation and refinement of a set of "myths" (Charles Liebman and Eliezer Don-Yehiya use "myth" in the sense of belief-stories and make no judgment as to the accuracy or inaccuracy of the factual component of these stories, and that is a sensible approach). In the early days of the state of Israel, two myths were raised to centrality, that of Masada and that of the fall of Tel Hai. Neither of these events had been important in Jewish tradition. Both involved heroic human sacrifice. At Masada, in 73 A.D., the last survivors of a Jewish movement of resistance to Roman rule were surrounded by a Roman legion. The Jews chose suicide rather than accept enslavement. This situation—being surrounded in a desert stronghold by Gentile enemies—fit closely to the perceived position of Jewish settlers during the Yishuv and in the early state period. The phrase "Masada will not fall again" was made into an oath, a promise to die rather than give in to the enemies of the present day.

A second myth is that of Tel Hai (a settlement in Galilee) which fell in 1920 before Arab attack. In that battle, one Yosef Trumpeldor, fought heroically and died. His last words were reported to be "it is good to die for our country." Another defender invoked an oath: "No settlement is to be deserted, nothing built is to be relinquished." The message for modern Israel was dramatic: the motifs of blood sacrifice, redemption of the land, holding fast in the face of the surrounding enemy, all came together. David Ben-Gurion was especially fond of the Tel Hai story and declared his generation to be the "comrades of Trumpeldor."[70]

As it became clear in the 1950s that the state of Israel would be successful and that there would not be another Masada or Tel Hai, a new layer of myths was added, like another layer of pigment added to an oil painting. "We are living in the days of the Messiah," David Ben-Gurion himself declared.[71] By this he meant that through the Jewish "redemption of the land" and the creation of a model state and society, all humanity would be redeemed. This was an overarching myth. Beneath it were articulated various submyths. For instance, around the figure of the *sabra* (the

native-born Israeli) arose a collection of attributes not unlike those ascribed to demigods in classical mythology: the *sabra* was portrayed as
having no fear, no material appetites, no obsequiousness before the unclean Arab or Gentile. Similarly, in the 1950s and 1960s, the Israeli
Defence Force was virtually deified, and those who had fought in 1948–
49 were singled out as larger-than-life figures. This was a healing myth,
for it brought under one loyalty the two military factions, Irgun and
Haganah who, in the years 1945–48, had been close to engaging in a civil
war against each other. The IDF mythology was tied neatly into the
virtual canonization (were there such a thing in Jewish tradition) of Theodor Herzl. His bodily remains were transferred to a mountain in Jerusalem, which was named after him, and the date of his death was declared
"State Day" or "IDF Day" by the Knesset. Curiously, the holocaust (in
this case a mythic set of events based on a very real historical reality), only
began to receive much attention in the late 1950s. It was not until 1959
that Holocaust Day was fixed as a permanent day of observance. The
reason the holocaust received so little attention in the early days of the
state of Israel was that it memorialized the kind of behavior that the Israeli
myth makers wanted to obliterate: supine martyrdom before a Gentile
enemy. Israel was to be the antidote for the holocaust, and it was not until
the late 1950s that the authorities felt secure enough to encourage the
ritual celebration of this great tragedy.[72]

What all the myth making added up to within the kaleidoscopically
complex pattern of the early Israeli state can hardly be pinned down with
precision. Everything changed, so much was awhirl. Although I do not
find their argument completely convincing, it has been suggested by the
distinguished scholars Charles Liebman and Eliezer Don-Yehiya that
what was evolving was a "civil religion." This idea bears serious consider-
ation. Civil religion (as distinct from traditional Jewish religion) was
created in modern Israel. It was, Liebman and Don-Yehiya suggest, an
entire "meaning system," one that employed both traditional symbols
and newly formed ones; but instead of relating all these symbols to a
transcendant power (as does traditional religion), it referred primarily to
a corporate entity, in this case the corporate personality of the Israeli
people as embodied in the Israeli state.[73]

This interpretation seems to me to be less than completely satisfying
(not dead-wrong, just not quite on target) because it suggests that the
state authorities (and especially the Labor Zionists under Ben-Gurion,
who were the largest political party in these years), consciously used both
the new and the traditional religious symbols for their own ends. The

argument assumes that they knew what they were doing, that they controlled things. Perhaps that is how matters appeared to the ruling elite—the leaders of government always like to think that they are in charge, but as often as not they are fooling themselves. I do not think that the Israeli leaders ever had anything approaching full control over the symbols they invoked or the myths they elaborated. When Ben-Gurion and his state makers played with the motifs of the Messianic return, of the redemption of the land, of blood sacrifice (as in Masada and Tel Hai), they were dealing with ideas that they couldn't control. It would be easier to keep a nuclear explosion in a bell jar than to "use" these concepts in support of a secular state. What was occurring in Israel's first two decades was the start of a process that I think is still being played out: the wiring of Israeli society with certain lines of cultural commonality that spread throughout all of the society; we are witnessing the gradual, but ineluctably accelerating, reintroduction of a covenantal worldview to the people of Israel.

(4)

That Israel desperately needed a common cultural-ideological grid that could be accepted by almost all (but, realistically, never by everyone) of its religious and political groups is clearly shown by the way that politicians and judges tiptoed through the minefield of familial-religious law. So volatile were matters that dealt with family and religion that a fundamental compromise had to be reached *before* the state of Israel came into existence; otherwise the new state well might have shredded itself in its first two or three years. In 1947 closed-door negotiations resulted in what usually is called the "status quo agreement." The formal signatories of what can be accurately described as a peace treaty within Zionism were David Ben-Gurion, who led the Zionist Labor party, headed the Jewish Agency, and was the odds-on favorite to become the first prime minister of Israel; Isaac Gruenbaum, from the "General Zionist Organization," an ad hoc front representative of diaspora Jewry and of the financial underpinnings of the Zionist cause; and Rabbi I. L. Fishman, of Mizrachi, representing religious Zionists. The concordat that they signed, dated 19 June 1947, set down some basic rules for life in the new Israel:

(a) *Sabbath.* It is clear that the legal day of rest in the Jewish State should be the Sabbath, with Christians and members of other faiths naturally being granted the right to rest on their own festive day of the week.

(b) *Dietary laws*. All necessary measures should be taken to guarantee that in every State Kitchen intended for Jews the food will be Kosher.
(c) *Marriage*. All members of the Executive appreciate the gravity of the problem and its great difficulties, and on the part of all bodies represented by the Executive of the Agency everything possible will be done to satisfy in this respect the profound need of adherents of the faith, so as to prevent the division of the House of Israel into two parts.
(d) *Education*. The full autonomy of every "trend" in education will be guaranteed . . . there will be no interference on the part of the Government with the religious conviction and the religious conscience of any section in Israel.[74]

The keys to understanding this agreement are threefold. Initially, one must realize that it was in effect the foundation stone of the Israeli constitution, antedating the Declaration of Independence. The outside world focused on the independence declaration and the United Nations went along with the conceit that Israel would be a secular state, choosing to ignore the religious commitments the new state made prior to its coming into existence. Second, although the document is often called the "status quo agreement," it was nothing of the sort. It did not confirm existing rules, but rather laid down precepts where none had previously existed. Under the British mandate in Palestine there had not been any privileging of the religious sector by the state, merely a legislated respect for the freedom of private conscience. This 1947 agreement introduced a totally new situation, in which the state yielded control over certain central civil functions to Jewish religious authorities. And, third, one should note that the religious establishment that assimilated these powers while the state of Israel was being formed was not representative of worldwide Jewry. The rabbinate so empowered was exclusively orthodox. Thus, the largest groups in diaspora Jewry (North American Jews, most of whom were reformed or conservative) were excluded (and, many would say intentionally derogated).

As for the specific matters involved in the 1947 concordat, the honoring of the Sabbath and the dietary laws were not central to society, however important they were to observant Jews. Every modernized society has at least one day of rest each week, and the Sabbath was accepted by virtually every Jew. The only difficulty was that the ultraorthodox groups felt that *all* Jews should be required to keep strict Sabbath. On occasion, small-scale rioting, stone throwing, and harassment were practiced by these groups, aimed at their fellow Jews who did such things as attend the cinema on the holy day. (And there was a political crisis in 1969 when

Sabbath television finally was permitted.) Dietary matters, such as Kosher field kitchens for the Israeli army, were no great imposition on anyone. (Indeed, Kosher food can only have been an improvement on the meals ordinarily served to soldiers.) During the 1950s and 1960s, pressure by orthodox religious authorities forced hotels and restaurants (many of which did not wish to go to the expense of keeping Kosher kitchens), to do so. The orthodox won by refusing to grant "certificates of correctness" to those hotels and restaurants that did not accept their rules, and without this certificate, tourists business (especially from American tourists) disappeared. It was a victory, too, for the rabbinate when it won the banning of non-Kosher food on ships of the Israeli steamship line. But all these were essentially minor matters.[75]

What really counted was that the 1947 concordat delivered into the hands of the orthodox rabbinate total control over matters relating to family law, which is to say control over the very heart of society. Under the concordat as refined by the Rabbinical Courts Jurisdiction (marriage and divorce) Law of 1953, there is no such thing as a civil marriage. Further (considering only the Jewish majority), not only was the definition of a valid marital union defined solely in religious terms, marriage was defined by the orthodox religious sector. Marriages performed by a conservative or reform rabbi, say, in New York, would be valid if the couple were Americans at the time of the ceremony; they could emigrate to Israel as a legally married couple. However, the requirement that marriage of persons who are "nationals or residents of the State [of Israel] shall be under the exclusive jurisdiction of rabbinical control" in the 1953 law meant that if, for example, an Israeli man and woman were married in New York by a reformed or conservative rabbi and the couple moved to Israel, then their union was invalid and all the children born under the union would be denied Jewish status by the rabbinate. Under orthodox religious law, such offspring have had severe problems when they assert that they are Jewish.

The orthodox rabbinate's control of marital unions meant that in Israel there could be no such thing as a valid "mixed marriage" involving Jews, as orthodox law prohibited this. Such a rule does not fit with the pluralism that a modern democratic state is said to encourage; instead it honors the ancient concept of keeping the Jewish "seed" pure. Similarly, just as the rabbinate controlled the making of marriage, so it was given control over the dissolution. The rules for religious divorce were complex, but from the standpoint of divorce in most western countries, the awkward point was that rabbinical law made it impossible for a woman to be divorced from her husband, no matter how abusive or dangerous he had been, unless he agreed to grant a dissolution of the marriage.[76]

The orthodox rabbinate's control over family law gave them the dominant word in what was the major unresolved question in Israeli society in its first two decades, namely "Who is a Jew?" It was a demographic certainty that by controlling the rules of family formation, the orthodox eventually would gain hegemony over the entire society on the issue of who-is-a-Jew, as eventually most Israelis would be *sabra* and they could marry only by orthodox rules, so that their offspring would be canonically correct Jews. But problems arose in the short run because so many diaspora Jews wished to migrate to Israel. Many of these, the orthodox rabbinate believed, were not "real" Jews because they had experienced the full set of religious rituals. Here was potential trouble. The Law of Return of 1950 gave the right to settle in Israel to all Jews, and, further, the Law of Citizenship gave anyone who immigrated to Israel under the Law of Return the right to be an Israeli citizen. When the Law of Return and the Law of Citizenship were debated in the Knesset, David Ben-Gurion explained matters this way:

> The Law of Return has nothing to do with immigration laws. It is the law of perpetuity of Jewish history; this law asserts the principle of sovereignty by force of which the state of Israel was established. . . .
>   The Citizenship Law completes the Law of Return and states that by force of the fact of immigration to Israel the Jew becomes a citizen in the fatherland.[77]

The statute was a secular act, however much it might be a product of the long and unbroken skein of Jewish history. The minister of immigration (later, the minister of the interior) was charged with deciding who was a Jew, but was given no guidance on how to do so.[78]

Hard cases arose. The first one of importance was the Rufeisen case of 1958. Oswald Rufeisen was a Polish Jew, born in 1922. He had received a Jewish education and been active as a youth in the Zionist movement. He intended to emigrate to Eretz Israel, but World War II intervened. He was a resistance leader, twice imprisoned by the Nazis, and he was credited with saving numbers of Jewish lives. In 1942 he hid in a Christian monastery and there became a convert. At war's end, he became a Carmelite monk. He still had strong loyalties to Eretz Israel, however, and he still considered himself to be a Jew. So, in 1957 he applied for an immigrant's certificate under the Law of Return and for an identity card (all inhabitants of Israel being required to carry such a card) that denominated him as a Jew. Thence the conflict: for the first time, it transpired that governmental and religious definitions of Judaism were in conflict. Under halachic law, anyone born of a Jewish mother (and both Rufeisen's parents were Jewish) was Jewish. The minister of the interior, however, refused to permit Rufeisen to be registered as a Jew or to claim status under the Law of Return. The case went to the supreme court which backed up the official interpretation in a judgment rendered in 1962. The supreme court stated that although according to religious law Rufeisen remained a Jew, for the purposes of the secular Law of Return and for purposes of population registration, he was not. Thus, it was possible for a person to be ruled Jewish by the rabbinate, but not accepted as Jewish by the state.[79]

Usually, however, the fissure between state and rabbinical authorities ran in the other direction: most often, the state was more liberal in assigning Jewishness to individuals than were the religious leaders. In late June 1958, two cabinet ministers from the religious parties in the Labor-dominated coalition resigned. This occurred because the minister of the interior, for the purposes of the Registration of Population Act of 1949, as amended (under which all residents of Israel must be registered according to religious affiliation), had made a decision against religious precedents. The issue in this case was how to register children of mixed marriages, especially those in which the father was Jewish, but not the mother. Under rabbinical law, such children were not Jewish and therefore they would be excluded from most of the benefits of the state of Israel, even if they were permitted residency. Of course, the children could be forced by their Jewish parent to undergo formal conversions, but many parents found this to be offensive to their own moral principles. The orthodox view was that until the non-Jewish mother converted to Judaism (thus making the children post facto Jewish), or the children were induced to convert formally, the youngsters were not Jewish. The minister of the interior ruled otherwise—the children were Jewish—and after a very nasty Knesset debate his actions were upheld. A compromise, cobbled together in 1960, put off for a time the moment of truth. The compromise was that until a child came of legal age, and at that time chose his or her own religion, no final religious determination under the Registration of Population Act was to be made.[80]

But the possibility that a person could be ruled Jewish by the state, yet rejected by the religious establishment reappeared, this time in the Schalit case. This case, which went to court in the later 1960s and was decided early in 1970, involved an Israeli naval officer who married a Scottish Gentile. She was the granddaughter of Sir Patrick Geddes who had helped Chaim Weizmann plan the creation of the Hebrew University. When a daughter was born to this couple in 1967, they tried to have her registered as nonreligious, but as belonging to the Jewish nation. The supreme court ruled, in a five-to-four vote, that the child could be denominated under the Registration of Population Act as Jewish.[81] This decision voided the 1960 compromise, because under this ruling, a permanent determination of the Jewishness of a child of a mixed marriage could be made before the youth reached legal age. Therefore, there now existed two axes of incompatibility: the state could rule (as in the Rufeisen case) that someone was not Jewish, even though the rabbinical authorities said that person was; and (as in the Schalit case) the rabbinate could decide that someone was not Jewish, but the state could determine that, for its purposes, he or she was.

Discussion of these matters, which arose under the "status quo agreement" of 1947, is not a matter of mere casuistry. They illustrate a central point about the nature of Israeli society. In 1948, and in the early years of the state, there simply was no agreed Israeli identity. It had to be created. Rifts had to be obscured. That is why the development of an agreed set of symbols, a shared system of myths, and a common vocabulary of historical references were so essential to the state's survival. And it is why Israel's having enemies was so valuable, for they helped to make one out of many.

(5)

One might have expected that the educational system would have been useful in bringing together the disparate strands of Israeli society. But in fact, the primary and secondary schools of Israel were largely de facto segregated even among Jews (Arabs and Christians were totally separated). This intra-Jewish segregation occurred in two forms, by religious practice and by ethnicity. Consider, first, religion. Before statehood, the 1947 concordat, that almost-invisible cornerstone of the Israeli constitution, had guaranteed the perpetuation of "every trend" in education. Like most words employed in Israeli politics, "trend" had a special meaning. When the state of Israel was founded, nearly every primary and secondary school was affiliated with some political or religious or special interest agency. For convenience, these were categorized as being "religious," "general," or "workers" schools, but these terms mask their great diversity and their exclusivity, especially in the religious sphere. The state authorities faced an almost insurmountable task in trying to fit all of these schools into a semblance of a single educational system. And at best it could only be a semblance, for the "status quo agreement" of 1947 meant that a single national school system was impossible. The only thing that almost all of the schools were willing to accept was that Hebrew should be the primary language. In 1949, the Knesset passed a Compulsory Education Act that abolished tuition fees in government schools and required school attendance from ages five to fourteen. That flooded the various "trends" with children and gave the state sufficient leverage to pass, in 1953, a major State Education Law that set up two types of government schools and one category of "recognized" nonstate school. The government sector's schools were divided into two sorts, "state schools" which were not distinctive of any form of Judaism, and "state religious schools." Each sort was almost entirely funded by the state. "Recognized" schools, such as those run by the ultraorthodox parties, received only partial state support, but they were generally free from governmental interference. In the school year 1960–61, 68.3 percent of Jewish children in primary and secondary schools were in "state schools"; 25.4 percent attended "state religious schools"; and 6.3 percent went to "recognized schools."[82] In addition, a small number of ultrareligious schools refused to have anything whatsoever to do with the state.)

Matters of education were a controversial topic in Israel's first two decades. No one, however, would have denied that the "state schools" gave a markedly different education than did the variety of "state religious schools," despite the government's attempt to prescribe a common central curriculum. In the 1960s, a study revealed that roughly one-quarter of the time in "state schools" was given over to what can be described as Jewish religion and culture—Hebrew, Bible, and Jewish tradition—whereas almost half of the time in "state religious schools" was spent on these topics, and 56 percent of the time in "recognized schools."[83] There was more to the difference than merely the amount of time spent on various subjects, however. The "state schools" tended to teach a "secular" or "literary" interpretation of Jewish tradition and the Bible, whereas the "state religious schools" taught these subjects as divinely inspired texts and as holy traditions. The result was that the state school system was not training up one nation of young Israelis, but several.

This would have been divisive in any case, but the religious-state division of schools was cross-cut by the great ethnic divide in Israeli society, between "Europeans" and "Orientals." These distinctions overlapped, but it was not the same thing as the older Ashkenazim-Sephardim split. "Oriental" Jews were those with origins in North Africa, the Middle East, and some parts of Asia. Most "Orientals" were Sephardic, although only some of the Sephardim were Oriental; others were European. For the purposes of understanding Israel's social stratigraphy, the key question was whether people came from societies that had experienced modernization (as had virtually all the Ashkenazim and those Sephardim from Spanish and Portuguese backgrounds), or whether they had not. "Oriental," though undoubtedly a term of prejudice, described a common background in traditional, not-yet-modernized, non-European societies.

Orientals were very badly served, indeed. Here is a summation of the situation by a well-informed outsider:

> The attitude of the Israeli establishment toward the Oriental Jews, in the fifties and sixties, and even later, might be defined as benevolent but pessimistic paternalism, strongly affected by negative racial attitudes and stereotypes, mitigated by the sense of a common Jewish bond. The negative attitudes applied in their full force to the adults, and especially the elderly among the Oriental immigrants. These were "the generation of the desert" and there was no hope for them.
>
> For the children, there was some hope, but how much and how soon was open to question.[84]

A study conducted in the late 1960s revealed that "although there is no deliberate policy of school segregation, many schools are in fact segregated or semi-segregated."[85] For example, in Tel Aviv (a city with a greater degree of mixing of Oriental and European Jews than most urban areas), fourteen of the twenty-eight elementary schools were de facto segregated.[86] The tendency to Ashkenazim-Sephardim segregation was exacerbated by economic factors. Oriental children tended to be shoved into the nonacademic streams of the schools. (The academic stream in Israel, as in almost every place else in the world, was as much a reflection of economic privilege as of academic ability.) The result was that, in the late 1960s, only 5 percent of the students enrolled in secondary schools and in higher education were of non-European background.[87] In 1964–65, approximately 8 percent of university students were Oriental Jews. The proportion had risen to a bit over 16 percent in 1969.[88]

Whatever the schools of Israel did to build a single communal identity (and in teaching Hebrew and in enforcing a core curriculum, some progress was made) was probably offset by the structural characteristics of the school system. Ethnic and religious divisions were perpetuated, and, one suspects, in many cases exacerbated.

(6)

Thus, once again, one becomes aware of how important it was for the Israelis to have enemies. If the Arabs had not existed, they would have had to have been invented.

During 1949–54, the bordering Arab states came to a consensus that Israel was not to be recognized as a legitimate nation nor would they deal with Israel in any kind of an international bargain. They would not cooperate with Israel, but they were unable to cooperate with each other.[89] They began to overcome their fragmentation in 1954. In late February 1954, Gamal Abdul Nasser came to power in Egypt and dedicated himself to building an anti-Israel coalition. In September 1955, Egypt made a major arms deal with the Czechs, who were acting as conduits for the Soviets. In October, Egypt and Syria signed a treaty that was supposed to be a mutal defense pact, but which had clear offensive implications. In late December, Saudi Arabia joined Egypt and Syria in an alliance and five months later Egypt and Jordan agreed to unify their military forces.

Israel well could have been in deep trouble, but Nasser overreached himself. Not only did he deny the Israelis access to the Suez Canal (this, though against international law, had been done since the foundation of the Israeli state), but now he prevented Israeli access to the Gulf of Aqaba. This he might have gotten away with, but in July 1956 he nationalized the Suez Canal, which had been built by a British-French consortium. Thus, suddenly, the big players were arrayed against Egypt, and by the physics of international politics, on the same side as Israel.

David Ben-Gurion's most recent biographer has revealed that at this point in 1956 Ben-Gurion had grandiose plans for the expansion of Israeli territory. He submitted to Guy Mollet, the French prime minister, a plan for reshaping the Middle East in the interests of Israel, France, and Great Britain. Besides the removal of Nasser, Ben-Gurion's plan included the dismemberment of Lebanon (its southern portions going to Israel, its east to Syria, and the rest to be formed into a Christian state) and the partition of Jordan. The West Bank of Jordan would be annexed by Israel and the East Bank by Iraq.[90] When, in late October 1956, Egypt, Jordan, and

Syria set up a joint military command for the publicly declared purpose of a "war of destruction" against Israel, the French, British, and Israelis attacked. The Anglo-French force took the Suez Canal easily and the Israelis conquered the entire Sinai peninsula and Gaza.

The Israelis concluded this war with a great piece of strategic wisdom: they did not keep the territories that they captured, although historically Gaza and Sinai were considered (at least by some scholars) as part of Eretz Israel. The reasons for this self-denial were partly geopolitical— when the British and the French went home, Israel was exposed militarily and partly the result of U.S. pressure. But there was another factor. David Ben-Gurion had toured some of the Palestinian Arab refugee camps in Sinai and Gaza and he was shaken by an obvious fact: the Palestinians had not fled. "No, this time they won't run away," was his observation.[91] In contrast to the 1948–49 war, the Palestinians did not leave their homes when they were defeated. Therefore, if the Israelis wished to take over large pieces of Palestinian territory, they had a limited number of alternatives: to effect the "transfer" (meaning expulsion) of the Palestinian population, to segregate and suppress the newly conquered Palestinians within Israel, or somehow to try to incorporate them as citizens of Israel with the attendant danger that the Palestinian population might one day outnumber the Jews. Surveying the risks of each of these alternatives, Ben-Gurion said "no" to each. He decided that it was better to have a small, more homogenous, and more governable Israel.

In the short run, Ben-Gurion seemed wrong. By the mid-1960s, Nasser was rearmed and reorganized and in May 1967 he placed troops in the Sinai.[92] Iraq and Jordan mustered their forces on Israel's other flank. In response, on 5 June 1967, the Israelis launched their own air offensive and effectively wiped out the Egyptian and Syrian air forces. By 10 June, Israel had taken the Arab portions of Jerusalem, the West Bank, the Gaza Strip, the Golan Heights, and had driven all the way across the Sinai to the Suez Canal. At the conclusion of the "Six Day War," the Israeli government announced (on 12 June 1967) that it would not withdraw to the armistice line which had been established after the 1948–49 war.

With that announcement began the history of present-day Israel.

Part IV

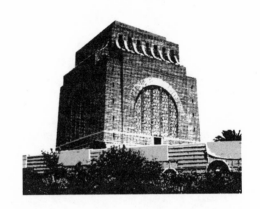

THE COVENANT
IN RECENT TIMES

9

A Covenant Comes Apart:
Ulster, 1969 to the Present

(1)

Once a covenantal culture has gained control of a state, is it possible to wean it away from its mindset? Or is an Armageddon the only way?

Messy as the history of Northern Ireland has been, as a case study in the covenanting worldview it is extremely valuable, for it is largely played out. That statement may come as a surprise but it is a fact nonetheless. In 1969 no one would have predicted that the state of Northern Ireland would disappear and that the belief systems of the Ulster Protestants (and, particularly of the Ulster Presbyterians) would have come apart so quickly. There is a lot of history yet to come in Northern Ireland, but unlike the past century, it will not be primarily of a serious Bible-reading, covenantally bound people, not that of a collectivity whose outlook was formed centrally by the Hebrew scriptures.

So, although the recent history of Northern Ireland is not a happy one, it should make the observer mildly optimistic about western society's ability to regenerate itself. A middle road does exist between simply acquiescing to the dictatorship of the covenant and "reforming" covenantal states by marching through their world like General Sherman marched through the American south, leaving behind a band of scorched earth. The middle path is not thorn-free, but it is passable.

(2)

Today several fragments of the covenantal culture still survive in Northern Ireland, and though ever-decreasing in import, they probably will endure for a generation or two. But the Protestants of Northern Ireland as a group are no longer a covenantal society. In order to understand how, between 1969 and the early 1990s, this critical change occurred, one must take a big eraser to the blackboard and clear away the most common misconceptions about Northern Ireland that are found in the international popular press. In so doing, one erases several plausible, but false, explanations of why Ulster's covenantal culture has come undone.[1]

The first of these false explanations is that terrorism has played a controlling part in shaping events. Actually, Northern Ireland is a case study in the ineffectiveness of guerrilla warfare against the modern western state, even when it is carried on by a group such as the "Provos,"—the Provisional Irish Republican Army, an underground guerrilla organization, whose activities are highly sectarian, but whose public ideology is merely ecumenical Marxist terrorism. If one takes the death toll of all sorts of caused by the Troubles—that is, by events since 1969—and even if one includes in that total combat deaths of professional military personnel in Northern Ireland, then one finds the following results: from 14 August 1969 (when the first United Kingdom troops were deployed on Ulster's streets) until the twentieth anniversary of that day, the death toll was 2,755. That is a significant number of human beings, and no one should underestimate the pain and grief involved in each case. However, to claim hysterically, as one recent Ulster journalist did, that this death rate is comparable to that of the United States during the Civil War, is to turn tragedy into a subject of ridicule.[2] The Troubles-caused annual average mortality of 137.75 in a population of roughly 1.5 million is not very high. This point was made in 1974, just after the peak of the Troubles (1972 was the worst year, with 467 persons killed) by a statistics professor at the Queen's University of Belfast, writing in *Nature* Magazine. David Bates analyzed the Troubles as one would any epidemic, in terms of the mortality rate induced among the general population. Taking the years 1969–74 (a period in which the average annual number of deaths was 190, higher than the overall average from 1969 to the present), he found that the Troubles-induced death rate was lower than the murder rate in most American cities. The table shows the murder rate for some major U.S. cities in 1970.

City	Deaths per 100,000 population
Cleveland	36.1
Detroit	32.7
Dallas	28.7
Chicago	24.1
Philadelphia	18.1

Northern Ireland's Troubles-induced death rate was only 12.4 per 100,000 population, which is to say that Northern Ireland, even with a low-grade civil war going on, was safer than most American cities. The average murder rate in U.S. cities of 250,000 population and above in 1970 was 17.5 per 100,000 population. Bates also pointed out that if one added the Troubles-induced death rate to the motor vehicle death rate in Northern Ireland, even that sum would not equal the American death rate from motor vehicle accidents alone.[3] And since his calculations were made, the Troubles death rate has dropped markedly, while the U.S. homicide rates have risen. Life in Northern Ireland, even with a terrorist campaign in progress, is not as dangerous as life in the United States, ostensibly a nation at peace.[4]

But in a guerrilla war, deaths are not spread evenly; perhaps the loyalist (that is, Protestant) population has endured all the suffering and consequently has been broken. Not true. Of the 1,811 civilian (that is, non-security force) deaths in the period 1969–88, for whom it was possible to obtain information on religious affiliation, slightly over 35 percent were Protestant.[5] This percentage would increase somewhat if one included all casualties in the Ulster Defence Regiment, which was over 90 percent Protestant in 1978. A study of 1977 indicated that if one included every death, save those of United Kingdom troops from outside of Northern Ireland, 42 percent of the Troubles deaths up to that point were Protestant.[6] Accepting, then, that roughly four-tenths of the deaths have been Protestant over the two-plus decades of the Troubles, this should be compared to the Protestant proportion of the Ulster population, namely six-tenths. Therefore, the Troubles-induced deaths, far from being concentrated upon Protestants, have fallen mostly upon Roman Catholics.

P. J. O'Rourke, who is not nearly so big a jerk as he pretends to be, got it right when in the late 1980s he reported for *Rolling Stone* on his trip to Northern Ireland:

> The phase was coined in 1973 by a British official trying to be British about Northern Ireland. Home Secretary Reginald Maudling said that

the violence had reached "an acceptable level." *Acceptable level of violence.* It's like the air-quality index in an American city. During the week I spent in Ulster, a Connecticut-sized province with a population smaller than metropolitan Philadelphia's, that's what the violence level was—acceptable. Not excellent, the way it was in 1972, 1916, 1798, and 1690, but fair to middling.[7]

The level of terrorism that prevails in Northern Ireland is not nearly enough to break any cohesive culture, let alone that of the Ulster Protestants.

Nor is the level of support for anti-Protestant terrorism and for republican revolution high enough in the Catholic population to shake the Ulster Protestants very much. Beginning in 1983, Sinn Fein, the political front for the Provisional Irish Republican Army began to participate in elections. In 1985 Sinn Fein received 11.8 percent of the votes in local council elections. In 1987, this share was 11.4 percent, which means that Sinn Fein received slightly less than one-third of the Roman Catholic votes.[8] Similarly, in the voting for the Northern Ireland members of the United Kingdom parliament, Sinn Fein received 13.4 percent of the votes in 1983. This fell to 11.4 percent in 1987.[9] In the elections for Northern Ireland's seats in the European parliament, Sinn Fein's share dropped from 13.3 percent in 1984 to 9.2 percent in 1989, indicating that some of Sinn Fein's early popularity had stemmed from the novelty of the Provos adopting the ballot box alongside the Armalite.[10] Tellingly, not only was the terrorist-front party rejected by most Catholics in Northern Ireland, but when it ran in the Irish Republic during the European elections in 1989, it received only a derisory 1.2 percent of the vote. In August 1989, the former *taoiseach* of the Republic of Ireland, Garret Fitzgerald, surveyed recent history and observed that twenty years of Provisional IRA activity had only achieved a shift in the policy of the government of the Republic of Ireland away from the unification of Ireland and to a unity of purpose with the British government.[11]

If there is one lesson taught by the history of Northern Ireland since the Troubles began, it is that the modern European state can effectively contain even a highly dedicated guerrilla movement, through the admixture of money and suppression. The money has not been lavish, but, clearly, it has been well spent. As discussed in chapter 6, since the mid-1920s, Northern Ireland has been weaker economically than the rest of the United Kingdom and therefore has received significant economic and social welfare subventions from the mainland. During the 1970s and 1980s these were between 100 and 200 pounds per year for every man, woman, and child in the province (estimates vary). In the 1980s, after the United Kingdom joined the European Economic Community, EEC funds for regional economic development flowed to London, for use in Ulster. If these funds are fully passed on (it is impossible to know if they actually will be), European aid to Ulster during the first half of the 1990s will be roughly 70 pounds for every inhabitant of Northern Ireland.[12]

Those funds are general. More effectively focused have been programs that directly combat terrorism and buy political loyalty. For instance, early in the Troubles, the Northern Ireland authorities introduced a program of compensation for terrorist damages done to individuals and businesses. This fund now runs between 40 and 50 million pounds a year.[13] It means that all the bars that are blown up and the cars and houses burned through terrorism or political vandalism are simply replaced, in the same way that cars and houses are replaced by ordinary accident or fire insurance in most western countries.

Crucially, as the economy of Northern Ireland has come under attack by the guerrillas, the United Kingdom government has responded with economic offensives as a way to undermine terrorist appeal. In 1968, 26.0 percent of all employees in the Northern Ireland economy were employed in the public sector. This had risen to 44.7 percent by 1982[14] and probably has risen to nearly 50 percent since then. A reasonable estimate is that 87,000 new public service jobs were created between 1968 and 1982. Roughly 15,000 of these were directly related to the Troubles—prison staff, and increased police force and civilian security personnel—but the remaining 62,000 were distributed throughout nonsecurity activities.[15] In all probability, the effects have been twofold. First, the 15,000 security jobs probably went overwhelmingly to Ulster Protestants: a few were taken up by Roman Catholics, but Catholics who accept such posts are at high risk of assassination by terrorists. And, second, most of the remaining 62,000 other governmental jobs probably went to Roman Catholics. No direct figures on this phenomenon are available, but it is known that (1) before 1969 the Stormont government virtually locked Catholics out of middle- and upper-echelon governmental positions, and (2) since 1972 the United Kingdom authorities have worked strenuously to place Catholics in governmental jobs, and whenever possible into positions of authority. The most reasonable conclusion is that the great bulk of the nonsecurity jobs have gone to Catholics. So the former policy gives pay packets and pistols to Protestants and the latter has created a large cohort of Catholic governmental employees who have a long-term investment in seeing that some version of the Ulster civil service continues to exist.

If the modern welfare state cannily seduces the members of the terrorists' potential constituency with jobs, it simultaneously uses physical force to break those who will not be bought. If all the commentaries written on the various security methods that have been employed in Northern Ireland since the Troubles began were collected in one place, they would form a small mountain. The fact is, though, that however inefficient any given piece of security activity may have been, the overall policy when combined with the spending program, has worked.

Security measures in Ulster have had two aspects: force and enforcement. The forces are various. The most visible force, because it stands out against the British and Irish tradition of law enforcement by civilians, is the military. In the wake of serious rioting in mid-1969, United Kingdom regular army troops were sent to Northern Ireland. Previously there had been a garrison of roughly 2,000 soldiers in Ulster. This rose to 7,000 in 1970. The numbers have fluctuated since then, from a high of 21,000 in 1972 down to 9,000 in 1985 and then back to about 10,000 in early 1990. These regular army units are augmented by various military units whose exact size and mission are kept secret: the Special Air Services (the U.K. equivalent of the Green Berets) and units from MI5 and MI6 (the equivalent of the American FBI and CIA). The other major military force is the Ulster Defence Regiment, a local militia created in 1970 in response to Catholic complaints about the sectarian nature of the "B-Specials." The UDR is a well-trained, mostly full-time force. In 1988, it had 6,300 full-time members. The UDR has tried to recruit Catholics, but figures for 1978 revealed that only 3 percent of the force was Catholic. The primarily civilian force is the Royal Ulster Constabulary, which had more than 8,100 full-time police and 1,650 reservists in its ranks in 1988. The RUC is only about 10 percent Catholic, despite strenuous efforts to recruit more Catholic members.[16]

Behind these forces there developed a singular system of legal enforcement. Given that the aim of guerrilla warfare is to break down a state's control over its citizenry, it is hardly surprising that terrorism during the Troubles exceeded the capabilities of the normal apparatus of justice. A number of extraordinary measures have been employed to keep civil order, but two stand out. The first of these was the massively ill-timed attempt at interning terrorist suspects without trial. This was inaugurated on 9 August 1971, when the army and police arrested 342 men and, then within six months, a total of 2,537 people. The measures were aimed chiefly at Catholics and the primary result was to unify temporarily the Catholic population behind the Provisional IRA. Ultimately, internment caused more problems for the security forces than it solved. Although under present legislation (the Northern Ireland Emergency provisions Acts of 1973 and 1975 and the Prevention of Terrorism Acts, 1974), power of internment is still extant, those in authority are at present unwilling to use this power.

The second extraordinary measure of enforcement is the system of "Diplock courts," created under the Emergency Provisions Acts, 1973 and 1975, which suspends jury trials and modifies the usual rules of evidence in certain cases (such as in instances when the chief witness is a police informant).[17] Suspension of juries probably is necessary in terrorist cases: such jurors are vulnerable to extreme forms of intimidation and the lives not only of the jurors, but also their families and relatives, are at risk. Nevertheless, the Star Chamber tone assumed by most of the major terrorist trials has undercut general faith in the justice system. Certainly the conviction rate is suspiciously high: of the 596 defendants who appeared before Diplock courts by 1986, 567 were convicted.[18] Despite these two extraordinary measures, however, the enforcement system did not greatly undercut the Protestant political culture—the chief unionist complaint about the security forces and about the justice system was not that they were too harsh, but too soft.

Neither did economic developments break the Protestants' spirits. One of the facile and misleading interpretations of the Troubles is to note the broken glass and the troops on patrol and to point to the ubiquitous private security firms, and then to add up the supposed "costs" of the Troubles. Inevitably, it is then concluded that the Troubles have been costly to Northern Ireland. Now, it is true that there have been significant relocations of individuals because of the Troubles—the actual rehousing of as many as 60,000 persons in Belfast during the early 1970s—and individuals have suffered considerable financial loss. Nevertheless, when the economy is examined as a collective entity, the losses on the communal balance sheet are not great. For example, the Troubles have almost killed the tourist industry, but, on the other hand, the Troubles have created a private security industry every bit as big. In one of the most persuasive analyses of the Ulster economy since 1969, N. J. Gibson of the New University of Ulster has shown that the Troubles have had no direct aggregate impact whatsoever.

What is his evidence? First, if one looks at Northern Ireland, Wales, the north of England, and Great Britain generally, as economic units, they have moved almost in perfect synch from the mid-1960s onward. This holds for unemployment figures and for rates of economic growth. On both of these indicators, Northern Ireland has been the worst-off region, but that is the way things were before the Troubles began. The fact that Northern Ireland did not follow a different economic trajectory than other parts of the British Isles, and that it did not become relatively worse off after the Troubles, dictates a prima facie case that the Troubles had little or, probably, no impact. Gibson's second point is that the major changes that have occurred since the Troubles began—especially reductions in the manufacturing proportion of the Ulster economy and the compensating rise in public sector activity—began a full decade before the Troubles started. The governmental policy of increasing public sector employment spoke directly to the terrorist problem, but it would have occurred in any case for purely economic reasons.[19]

It seems difficult to accept that such a long guerrilla campaign against the state has had so little economic effect. How can that be? Although Gibson does not make much of this point, one reason relates to something discovered during the postwar assessment of military activity in World War II: within a certain threshold, communal stress and even war frequently give meaning to individuals in a society and energize their activities. Two classic studies conducted by the OSS (the predecessor of the CIA) after World War II revealed that in German and Japanese cities, economic activity and civilian morale actually increased because of bombing. Economically, most societies work a good deal below their capacity (and certainly this was true of Northern Ireland in the late 1960s), so that any loss is quickly made up. Indeed, disruption frequently gingers managers and workers out of their old ruts and makes their firms more productive. Only when a city is virtually flattened does military attack reduce economic activity, and Northern Ireland never has come near that threshold. A second, more important reason for Northern Ireland's being economically unscathed by the Troubles is that (as mentioned earlier) the United Kingdom welfare state has replaced the losses in the manufacturing (and tourist) sectors with public sector activity. Gibson notes that the long-range effects of the weakening of the private sector may be serious, but in the short run (which is to say, over the past two decades), it is hard to see any great costs. Undeniably, the Northern Ireland economy is a mess. Its unemployment rate was 14 percent in the early 1990s and had been as high as 23.1 percent in the mid-1980s, twice the U.K. average. Generally the Ulster economy is the worst in the United

Kingdom, and almost as bad is that of the Republic of Ireland. But it would have been that way in any case, Troubles or not.

Finally, it might be suggested that perhaps there were psychological costs of the Troubles and that these have been strong enough to undercut the Protestant worldview. Again, no. At various times during the Troubles, media reports have made much of three alleged indicators of psychiatric stress in Northern Ireland: the level of tranquilizer prescriptions, the incidence of psychiatric hospitalization, and the seemingly inevitable harm to children as a result of growing up in an environment of conflict. Take the first item. In mid-1984 *Newsweek* suggested that the Ulster population anesthetized itself. The story's assertion was based on the fact that prescriptions for tranquilizers such as Valium had tripled in the previous ten years and were used at a rate 20 percent higher than the rest of the United Kingdom. Here, obviously, was an empirical indication of psychological distortion on a significant scale and clearly ascribable to the Troubles. Except . . . except for some inconvenient facts. Although Valium and Librium were used more in Northern Ireland than in Great Britain, sleeping pills, hypnotics, and antidepressants were much less used, so that what one had here was merely a substitution effect, not an indication of greater usage. Moreover, the use of tranquilizers, while high relative to most European countries, nevertheless was lower than that of both Iceland and Denmark, a fact that calls into question the reliability of using drug dosages as an indication of violence-induced psychological problems. And in any case, once reports on the dangerous side effects of tranquilizers became known in the 1980s, use dropped markedly in Northern Ireland, which suggests that tranquilizers were and had been part of a rational program of stress control, not an indication of any widespread psychological breakdown. Similarly, despite the common assumptions about psychiatric referrals and hospitalization, figures for these do not indicate any increase because of the Troubles. In fact, studies (admittedly these are sketchy) imply that the onset of the Troubles actually reduced the incidence of depressive illnesses, especially among males in the areas directly affected by violence. In the country areas around Belfast, where there was little or no direct violence, the number of referrals went up slightly. The most thorough review yet conducted of the studies of the psychological effects of the Troubles concludes that the mental health of most adults was not affected adversely by living in Northern Ireland during the Troubles. The greatest cause of psychological problems has been found to be the economy, especially the high unemployment rate.[20]

But surely the children of Ulster have been psychologically scarred? Again, no, not as a group. Although there have been terrible individual traumas, as a group the children of Northern Ireland have not gone to pieces. Familial authority structures are still very strong and the children, studies show, are much more morally conservative than their counterparts elsewhere in the United Kingdom. Almost all of the serious research studies agree that the Troubles have not had catastrophic impacts on children. The problems of Northern Ireland's children are those of any deprived society, especially one that has a high proportion of working-class children and a perpetual background of economic vulnerability. It is true that when the children of Ulster grow up they frequently emigrate, either to Great Britain or overseas, but that is inevitable given economic conditions. And it is part of a pattern that has continued unbroken since the mid-eighteenth century when Ulster's young people started leaving in large numbers for the New World.[21]

(3)

If none of the seemingly obvious effects of the present Troubles have significantly undercut, much less destroyed, the underpinnings of the covenantal mindset of the Ulster Protestants (and, particularly, of the Presbyterians), nevertheless something ultimately fatal has been happening to the covenantal outlook.

This process is complicated, but at heart it is quite simple: the covenant has become unlocked. Recall that a vital characteristic of the covenantal way of organizing the world is that each piece dovetails nicely with every other piece and that the whole structure locks together, like a building constructed of old-fashioned mortise and tenon joints. Such structures have great integrity, but if one component cracks, the entire structure is vulnerable. Once a single joint is dismantled and can no longer carry stress, the force is shifted to the other joints and in turn they pull apart and eventually the whole structure comes down. That is what has been happening among the Protestants of Northern Ireland since 1969. The process is not yet complete, but it is irreversible.

The key to this course of events is the Ulster "civil rights" movement of the 1960s, which was actually a movement for civic justice that developed within the context of the expansion of the welfare state after World War II. In fact, in Northern Ireland, Catholics had most of the basic civil rights—votes (though some voting restrictions existed on the local level), state-paid education, the rights of movement and assembly—long before the movement began. Their decision to call their struggle a civil rights movement was a shrewd, but intentionally misleading propaganda coup. What the Catholics did not have was civic *justice*. That is, in the matters of public employment, public housing, and in the siting and control of public amenities, they were sharply discriminated against, especially by agencies of local government. Thus they pushed for their fair share.[22]

The ideal of justice is the one concept that can most effectively undercut the rule of laws. An inherent part of the covenantal worldview is a legalistic way of thinking and an ingrained belief that laws are to be obeyed, not questioned. This goes all the way back to the very foundation of covenantal thought, the Pentateuch, where the justification of the legal code is not that it is right, but that it has been given by Yahweh and therefore is to be obeyed. Covenantal societies inevitably develop a casuistic industry, one of whose purposes is to explain that the laws are not merely there by divine *force majeure* but that, incidentally, they also happen to be right. These arguments are dangerous, though, for they open the possibility that any given law may not be consonant with justice and, therefore, that such a law must either be changed or ignored. That possibility in turn entails the corrosive further possibility that the law itself, considered as an entity, may not be consonant with justice. And that is one of the things that happened in Northern Ireland. The civil rights movement in Northern Ireland convinced the outside world that law, as it existed in Northern Ireland, was corrupt. Simultaneously, a significant minority of Protestants (mostly among the middle class, the leaders of Ulster society) came to agree that possibly, just possibly, this interpretation was correct. Although most Protestants resisted the view that their laws were incompatible with justice, for the first time they had to defend their views and even this process was unsettling. Thus began the first small stress fracture in the covenantal mindset and it rapidly deepened.

The initial event in the sequence that led to the violence was the election in 1963 of Captain Terence O'Neill as prime minister of Northern Ireland. There was nothing in O'Neill's background to suggest that he would unwittingly set off sectarian clashes. He seemed an ordinary unionist politician, if a cut above the standard in education and background. A direct descendant of Sir Arthur Chichester, who was in charge of the plantation of Ulster under James I, O'Neill was related to a number of influential politicians in modern Ulster. He was educated at Eton and then served in the Irish Guards. After the Second World War he entered

Northern Ireland's parliament, serving from 1946 to 1948 on the back bench and then from 1948 to 1956 in a series of junior ministries. In 1956 he received his first senior appointment as minister of home affairs and soon thereafter transferred to the Ministry of Finance, a position he held until 1963. In that year he became, somewhat to the surprise of most observers, Northern Ireland's fourth prime minister. Seemingly, another loyal, trustworthy, colorless unionist party stalwart had become head of the government.

When O'Neill took over as prime minister, Northern Ireland was in a state of equilibrium. On the surface, community relations were improving and overt sectarian strife was not in evidence. But this tranquillity, it later became clear, was not attributable to the fact that community relationships were noticeably improving but that the opposing forces were quite evenly balanced and there was no specific issue to set off hostilities. O'Neill entered the picture and began making moves that would improve conditions for the Roman Catholics. Undoubtedly he was chiefly motivated by idealism, but also by long-term political expediency, since he foresaw a coming increase in the electoral strength of the Catholic population. O'Neill's recognition of the necessity of alleviating many Catholic grievances was not coupled with an understanding of the fears of the average Protestant. His meeting with Sean Lemass, then *taoiseach* of southern Ireland, in January 1965 raised Protestant anxieties about his commitment to the union with England. O'Neill's refusal to ban the 1966 celebration of the fiftieth anniversary of the 1916 Easter Rising led to a permanent estrangement of the Protestant right wing. As time passed, O'Neill's support within the Unionist party declined, and to compensate for this loss he appealed over the head of the party to the electorate. (In September 1966 an attempt to overthrow him was made at a Unionist party meeting; it failed chiefly because there was no acceptable alternative leader.)

Given the delicate balance of forces within Northern Ireland it probably would have been impossible for anyone to improve the Catholics' condition without setting off a reaction among Protestant conservatives. Certainly that is what occurred when on 22 November 1968, O'Neill announced a five-point reform plan under which his government undertook to (1) develop arrangements whereby the allocation of public housing would be carried out on a nondiscriminatory basis, the primary criterion for allocation being the need of the applicant; (2) establish procedures for investigating and alleviating citizens' grievances; (3) introduce an economic development plan for Londonderry; (4) reform local electoral procedures, specifically by 1971, to revise the local government structure and abolish the business vote in local elections; and (5) allow the Special Powers Acts to lapse as soon as possible without hazard to the public safety. Unfortunately, the reform program only intensified the right-wing Protestant backlash against O'Neill. Also, while the Catholics were pleased with the reforms, O'Neill's suggestions created what has been called in the American context a "revolution of rising expectations." That is, even though the Catholics' position was being bettered, the improvement stimulated demands for even greater governmental reforms, with the result that instead of being pacified by the reforms, many Catholic leaders were energized.

If Captain O'Neill was primarily responsible for the changing governmental position on Catholic grievances, the Civil Rights Association was the chief agency for changing popular opinion among the Catholic population. In 1964 the Campaign for Social Justice in Northern Ireland was founded to protest against anti-Catholic discrimination, mainly in housing. Next, in February 1967, the Northern Ireland Civil Rights Association was formed to press the Catholic cause in more general terms. In viewing the Civil Rights Association's early history it is necessary to understand three points. The first is that the association was not publicly concerned with the basic constitutional arrangements under which Northern Ireland was governed. The association's leaders seemed at that time to accept the union with Britain because it was a tie that the majority of the people in Northern Ireland wished to maintain. Hence, one should not equate the original Civil Rights Association with the nationalist movements of the past. The association's goal was to give Catholics full membership in the political, economic, and social system of Northern Ireland as a constituent of the United Kingdom. Second, although members of the Irish Republican Army had an interest in the Civil Rights Association from its beginning, their position was a subordinate one. The men of the IRA did not assume positions of public leadership, although they accepted the association's activities as likely to be contributory in the long run to their own cause. Third, although the association worked to overcome discrimination against Roman Catholics, it was a secular organization over which the authorities of the Catholic church had no direct influence. The Civil Rights Association, therefore, was something totally new to Ulster, an attempt to build a mass movement on the principle of social justice, independent of the old nationalist propaganda machine and independent of the Roman Catholic clerical authorities.

To return to the narrative, the specific sequence leading to the first significant outbreak of violence began in June 1968 when the local authorities in Caledon, County Tyrone, evicted a Catholic tenant from a council house and allocated it to an unmarried Protestant girl. On 20 June, Austin Currie, a nationalist member of the Northern Ireland parliament occupied the house in order to publicize this and similar injustices to Catholics in the allocation of local government housing units. Next, the Civil Rights Association staged a march from Coalisland to Dungannon on 24 August to dramatize the situation. This was the association's first mass demonstration. About 2,500 people took part. Then the association agreed to join a march instigated by left-wing activists in Derry to call attention to the Catholic grievances in that community. The march, set for 5 October, was to follow the path through Derry traditionally taken by Protestant Orange Order processions. Fearing violence, the minister for home affairs, William Craig, prohibited the procession. The organizers decided to march anyway. Clashes occurred between police and demonstrators. It was later judged that the police had used unnecessary force. Following the conflict between police and civil rights demonstrators, hooligan elements in the Londonderry population who had nothing to do with the movement, rioted, with attendant looting and damage to property.

In direct response to the police brutality in Derry a group was founded, based in Queen's University but not restricted to university students, called People's Democracy. The organization had no specific membership requirements or constitution and was soon to lapse into obscurity. But for the moment it was vibrant, its program an amalgam of various radical viewpoints. Demands ranged from "one man, one vote," at the local level to worker control of all branches of industry. More important than the group's specific demands were its methods: unlike the Civil Rights Association the People's Democracy did not bind itself to nonviolent methods. At first the group had wide support among the Queen's University student body but this support waned as the People's Democracy became increasingly radical. The core members of People's Democracy decided that they should join the Civil Rights Association. Whether or not this was an attempt to take over control of the association is unclear, but the effects were unmistakable: the Civil Rights Association was moved toward greater activism. It became at once more radical in its demands and at the same time more aggressive in addressing Catholic grievances. It moved from demanding Catholic equality to demanding Catholic power. As the Civil Rights Association was becoming more militant, the moderates in the association were becoming uneasy and some were leaving the organization altogether.

Recall at this point that November 1968 was the time when Prime Minister O'Neill introduced his five proposals. These proposals were the working-out of ideas he had prior to the rioting, but it was natural that they would be interpreted by Protestants and Catholics alike as a response to the October disruptions. To many Protestants, therefore, the proposed reforms seemed like a surrender in the face of violence. To the Catholic militants the reforms seemed to validate their activist policy. These conclusions were reinforced by O'Neill's dismissal of William Craig as the minister for home affairs in December 1968. Craig was responsible for the maintenance of civil order and had come to view the civil rights movement as a front for revolutionary republican activities.

Meanwhile in Londonderry, after the 5 October riots, a moderate group was trying to stabilize civil rights activities. This was the Derry Citizens' Action Committee headed by John Hume. (Derry and Londonderry are synonymous, but ideological twists sometimes accompany the use of one or the other term.) Ivan Cooper was a leading member of the executive committee. Both Hume and Cooper were among the original leaders of the Civil Rights Association and in creating the new Derry organization they were committed to pressing Catholic grievances, but only by nonviolent means. Sit-downs and marches were conducted during the last quarter of 1968, but always with discipline and without either creating or provoking violence. If this group had been able to maintain complete control of civil rights activities in Derry, peace would probably have been preserved. The People's Democracy, however, decided to organize a Belfast-to-Londonderry march for early January 1969. The Derry Citizens' Action Committee objected (as did Edward McAteer, leader of the Nationalist party) because the march would almost certainly lead to violence. The People's Democracy persisted, and finally the Civil Rights Association gave its support to the march, although this support was only nominal.

The Belfast-Derry march, which lasted from the first to the fourth of January 1969, inflamed sectarian passions. The marchers were met by a hostile crowd at Burntollet Bridge, and the police did not protect the marchers. More than a dozen persons were injured, and several were taken to the hospital. But the real trouble came in Derry itself. Counterdemonstrators clashed with the marchers there. A number of Derry citizens joined the marchers and replied in kind to the stone throwing and other aggressive acts of the counterdemonstrators. These clashes set off further serious riots in Londonderry. By 4 January, violence had already become the keynote for Northern Ireland in 1969.

In February 1969 Prime Minister O'Neill, realizing that Derry was a powder keg, appointed the Londonderry Commission as he had promised in his reform program of the previous year. This body superseded the former unionist-controlled city council, whose corruption and discrimination had been a major Catholic grievance. Urgent steps were taken to expedite a major housing program for Derry. Nevertheless, in mid-April further riots stemming from civil rights activities were only narrowly averted.

With each incident the members of the Unionist party were becoming less and less happy with Prime Minister O'Neill's apparent inability to maintain civil order and increasingly suspicious of his apparent truckling to Catholic pressures. The only reason O'Neill was kept in office was that there was no alternative leader. The chief rival, Brian Faulkner, did not command enough support to upset O'Neill. But then Major James Chichester-Clark became a viable rival by the simple expedient of resigning from the cabinet. His ostensible reason for resigning was that O'Neill's "one man, one vote" policy, announced on 23 April 1969, was pushing reform too fast, a reason that would appeal to the hard-line dissidents in the Unionist party. On 28 April, O'Neill resigned, and on 1 May 1969 the unionist members of parliament met and by a vote of seventeen to sixteen awarded Chichester-Clark the prime ministership.

But a new prime minister did not bring Northern Ireland peace. The beginning of a summer of turmoil was signaled by the twelfth of July parades of the Orange Order. These traditional parades are highly inflammatory to the Catholic population since the marchers are affirming their Protestant solidarity against the alleged Catholic threat. Usually the Catholics stayed at home, but in Derry the Orange parade was followed by street fighting and by looting and arson by Catholic hooligans. On subsequent days pitched battles between the police and Catholics took place, and fighting also erupted between the police and Protestant mobs that were trying to attack the Catholic sector of Derry. Similar flareups occurred in several smaller towns in Ulster. But the real trouble was not unleashed until 2 August 1969 when Protestant and Catholic mobs clashed in Belfast. These clashes reccurred night after night, while barricades were thrown up for protection by each side. The police were unable to control the rioting and arson and appeared to have been anything but impartial in their efforts to restore order. Sectarian violence, which had dwindled momentarily in Derry, was rekindled on 12 August when the Apprentice Boys of Derry, a Protestant fraternal order, held their annual parade. Finally, the United Kingdom, realizing that the Stormont government had lost control of the situation, sent in troops. The troops arrived on 14–15 August and were concentrated chiefly in Belfast and Londonderry. The very day the troops arrived the rioting claimed its first fatality.

Significantly, the arrival of United Kingdom troops was considered a victory by the Catholics, for the British were believed to be more impartial in protecting lives and property than were the Protestant-dominated Royal Ulster Constabulary and the B-Specials. Moreover, the necessity of United Kingdom intervention was a judgment of incompetence against the Ulster government, so in this instance pragmatic considerations overcame the traditional nationalist opposition to having British troops on Irish soil; the United Kingdom soldiers were hailed as allies by the Catholics. The British, however, were not immediately able to restore order. Severe rioting continued in Londonderry and Belfast. By the end of the first week in September the death toll was up to nine, and only in the second half of October were the troops able to quiet the province.

The introduction of United Kingdom troops signaled the beginning of the intervention by the London government in the internal affairs of Ulster on an unprecedented scale. In mid-August, Major Chichester-Clark was summoned to 10 Downing Street by Prime Minister Harold Wilson. A seven-point declaration was issued jointly by the two men on 19 August. Predictably, the declaration reaffirmed the commitment of the British government to maintain Northern Ireland as part of the United Kingdom and affirmed the right of Northern Ireland to jurisdiction in its own domestic affairs. The real message followed: "The United Kingdom government have ultimate responsibility for the protection of those who live in Northern Ireland." The declaration affirmed that "every citizen of Northern Ireland is entitled to the same equality of treatment and freedom from discrimination as obtains in the rest of the United Kingdom, irrespective of political views or religion. In their further meetings the two Governments will be guided by these mutually accepted principles."[23] Behind the words of this declaration was a simple relationship: the United Kingdom government had told the Northern Ireland government to put its house in order and to alleviate Catholic grievances, or London would take command. Officials of the Ulster government bravely maintained that there had been no diminution of the powers of the Northern Ireland government, but the claim rang hollow.

As if to underline the superior-subordinate relationship of Great Britain and Ulster, James Callaghan, home secretary in the London government and the man with direct responsibility for Ulster affairs in the United Kingdom cabinet, visited Northern Ireland on 27–29 August. His welcome in most Catholic areas was close to triumphal. More important, two meetings of the Northern Ireland cabinet were conducted with Callaghan present, and from those meetings emerged a statement by the Ulster government affirming the necessity of maintaining "the momentum of reform." It was agreed by the Northern Ireland ministers that effective action was needed in the following five fields: (1) equal opportunity for all public employment without regard to religious or political considerations; (2) protection against incitement of hatred and intimidation for all citizens; (3) guaranteed fairness in public housing, with need the only criterion; (4) effective procedures for investigating grievances against public bodies; and (5) fair electoral laws. To emphasize the urgency of these goals the prime minister of Northern Ireland stated that he would appoint a governmental minister with special responsibilities for communal affairs. Now it should be noted that this forward-looking program was presented by Major Chichester-Clark, who a scant five months before had overthrown Captain O'Neill as prime minister because O'Neill was proceeding too quickly along reforming lines. Clearly the United Kingdom government must have been dictating the Northern Ireland cabinet's new policy. To keep the Ulstermen to their pledges, arrangements were made for joint working parties composed of officials of the Northern Ireland and United Kingdom governments to examine the Ulster government's actions in the major reform areas.

Naturally the Protestant militants were furious at the series of "betrayals" by the London and Stormont governments. but were the Catholics correspondingly gratified? On the surface it appears they should have been, for by early 1970 they had been granted all of their demands: in November 1969 a permanent ombudsman had been appointed to protect any citizen with a valid grievance; in December 1969 a commission was established to investigate complaints against local governmental authorities; the Londonderry City Council, long a unionist bastion, had been abolished; the hated B-Specials were dissolved; "one man, one vote" legislation was passed, effective in the local elections of 1972; a Community Relations Board was created and a minister of community relations was appointed; and the government promised that the allocation of housing was to be taken from local governments and placed in the hands of a new Central Housing Authority which operated on a nondiscriminatory points system developed in England (the act became law in February 1971). Thus, within three short years, 1968–70, the aims of the Civil Rights Association had been obtained.

Seemingly as a harbinger of better days, the old fragmented unproductive gaggle of nationalist political sects came together in the autumn of 1970 to form the Social Democratic and Labor Party (SDLP). This party gained the allegiance of most leading Catholic politicians and, although it refused to become an official opposition, promised to promote efficiently the Catholic interest in Northern Ireland politics. Some optimists thought that the era of two-party politics was, at last, dawning in Ulster.

So, the first half of 1971 was sometimes hopeful. The resignation in March of Chichester-Clark under Protestant dissatisfaction with his alleged failure to move effectively against rioters and terrorists was not disruptive, for he was replaced as prime minister by Brian Faulkner, generally accepted at the time as the most able unionist politician. In June, Faulkner made the extraordinary offer (for a unionist politician) of seats for the SDLP opposition on three new functional policy committees, for social, environment, and industrial services. Two of these bodies were to be chaired by opposition members of parliament. Potentially, a major break-point in Northern Irish history had been reached. On 7 July 1971, interparty talks were held at Stormont, and it was clear that the opposition was seriously interested in the proposal. But then, on 8 July, two rioters were shot dead by the British Army in Derry under questionable circumstances (the question was whether they were merely rioting or intent on killing British soldiers). Thereupon the SDLP, afraid of being outflanked by the IRA, veered sharply and announced that it would withdraw completely from Stormont unless a full inquiry was conducted at once under conditions acceptable to the SDLP. Soon the opposition, now withdrawn from Stormont, was meeting in various "alternative assemblies." Almost overnight the Catholic representatives had gone from prospective partners in governing Ulster to self-defined political exiles.

If Faulkner's constructive initiative offered both communities their best brief hope, the introduction of internment of suspected IRA terrorists without trial on 9 August 1971 was disastrous for everyone. Four weeks of sectarian rioting followed the beginning of internment, and for six months violence levels remained high. Thus, in March 1972, United Kingdom Prime Minister Edward Heath made three proposals to the Northern Ireland government: that internment be phased out, that full responsibility for law and order be transferred to Westminster, and that periodic plebiscites on the border issue be conducted—this last was tied

to a promise that there would be no change in the border without majority consent of Northern Ireland's people. Apparently Prime Minister
Faulkner was willing to accept the first and third demands but not the
second. Heath insisted, Faulkner's government resigned, and on 24
March Heath announced that the Stormont government was being "temporarily" suspended and that Northern Ireland was to be directly governed from London.

(4)

One should not lose sight of how surprising and confusing the events of
1969–72 were for Protestants as well as for Catholics. Much of the street
violence of those years had nothing to do with programmatic beliefs, but
instead was the action of panicked, frightened people, seeking an escape
in action, however mindless, from their own sense of confusion and helplessness.[24]

The civil rights movement had led, indirectly, to the Protestant state
disappearing from the face of the earth. From 24 March 1972 onward,
Northern Ireland has existed only as an administrative region of the
United Kingdom. A secretary of state for Northern Ireland sits in the
London cabinet and a team of London-appointed ministers has assumed
all major governmental portfolios. Since March 1972, all major deci-
sions concerning the governance of Northern Ireland have been made by
London-appointed officials. This is not exactly a colonial situation, as
Ulster has several seats in the United Kingdom parliament (increased from
twelve to seventeen since 1983).

But if not a complete throwback to the high days of the British Raj, the
situation is a long way from everyday parliamentary democracy as practiced elsewhere in the British Isles. Therefore, successive U.K. governments, both Conservative and Labour, have tried to establish forums or
provincial representative bodies that would be acceptable to both religious communities. Success has been limited. The first such effort was
made in the early days of direct rule. A locally recruited "advisory committee" was to be set up to advise the U.K. officials. The Protestants
boycotted the committee and it had no influence. Next, the Conservative
government of Edward Heath brought in the Constitution Act, 1973,
which empowered a seventy-eight member assembly to semigovern
Northern Ireland. The scheme was fairly canny. Activities that throughout
modern history have been religiously divisive—police, courts, security—

were to be left in London's hands, but most other governmental matters were to be transferred to Ulster politicians if—and it was a very big "if"—a Protestant-Catholic coalition were prepared to take the reigns of power. This was a very shrewd idea, for it played upon the desire of politicians to have power (why else, after all, are they politicians?), and it almost worked. An election was held for assembly seats in June 1973. By the beginning of January 1974 a coalition of one Protestant party (the Official Unionist party), one Catholic party (the SDLP), and one ecumenical party (Alliance) had formed a coalition. Breakaway Protestants in the assembly, however, were able effectively to impede business even though they had only a minority position. Then, when Brian Faulkner tried to convince his own party of the value of the "Sunningdale Agreement" for cross-border cooperation on security matters and for a "council of Ireland" that potentially was a future all-Ireland parliament, his Official Unionist party turned on him and he was voted out of the leadership. Meanwhile, outside of the assembly, Protestants were coalescing against what they viewed as a conspiracy to lead them into an all-Ireland state. In mid-May 1974, a massive Protestant general strike effectively closed down the economy of the entire province. At that month's end, the remaining unionist members of the power-sharing executive resigned and the power-sharing assembly idea collapsed. Direct rule returned.[25]

A third effort was made. The United Kingdom government called a constitutional convention aimed at defining a political settlement to the Ulster problem in July 1974. So, once again, seventy-eight representatives were elected, but this time they had no administrative powers, just the task of negotiating among themselves a viable constitution. Predictably, the project failed and it was given an official burial in March 1976, full-scale talks between the main Protestant and Catholic parties having lasted roughly one hour. A fourth attempt, between October 1979 and late March 1980, involved an invitation from the Northern Ireland secretary to the two main parties in Ulster to attend a constitutional conference. The Official Unionists refused to attend, and Ian Paisley's right-wing Democratic Unionist party was even less keen, so the whole exercise went nowhere. Direct rule continued.

Rather more creative was a fifth effort, the attempt at "rolling devolution." This concept began with the establishment of a seventy-eight seat assembly, with the intention of giving to it progressively more and more powers. This assembly was established in 1982 and it merely became a kennel, full of heavy snarling and backbiting. The Protestant groups would not join in the power sharing that was required by London as a prerequisite to granting real power to the assembly. The Catholic parties believed that the assembly did not have a sufficient "Irish dimension." At one time or another, most of the major parties boycotted the assembly— while Paisley's Democratic Unionist party stayed within and used the half-empty assembly chamber as a barracking ground for their own style of politics. Finally, in June 1986, this assembly was dissolved. Direct rule continued.

Markedly different was the sixth attempt. This was the Anglo-Irish Agreement (AIA), which for the most part was negotiated over the heads of the Ulster politicians by the London and Dublin administrations. It was signed in November 1985 at Hillsborough, County Down, by the U.K. prime minister Margaret Thatcher, and by the Irish *taoiseach*, Garret Fitzgerald. The pivot of the agreement was a "conference" of ministers of the Irish Republic and of the United Kingdom which would meet regularly to discuss Ulster affairs. Although final authority over Northern Ireland remained in the hands of the London government, the fact that the Dublin government was now being regularly consulted implied that the government of the Republic of Ireland had a legitimate interest in the governance of the north. This, in turn, opened the possibility of the reunification of Ireland at some time in the future. The result was years of Protestant protest against the "AIA," ranging from marches to 400,000-signature petitions to the boycotting of local government bodies to a one-day general strike. Yet the British government did not move: Margaret Thatcher was no Edward Heath. She bent not in the Protestant gale and the consultative bodies created under the Anglo-Irish Agreement are the one post-1972 governmental experiment that has not been scuttled. Formal talks on security and trade at a ministerial level are held every six months and less formal meetings at shorter intervals. Still, all this occurs only within the context of direct rule. In late 1990, the secretary of state for Northern Ireland, Peter Brooke, announced a new "peace initiative." For a time, representatives of the major Protestant and Catholic parties actually negotiated with each other, but by late spring 1991 the talks broke down, and Brooke's peace initiative joined the long skein of good ideas whose time had not yet come.

Despite two decades of constitutional confusion, there are three things that the Protestant community can infer with certainty. First, unless there is a massive tactical blunder on the part of the United Kingdom government (such as simply pulling out of Northern Ireland and allowing a civil war and a sanguinary repartition of Ulster to occur in a manner similar to what happened on the Indian subcontinent after the Raj retired), the

Protestants of Ulster will never again be in sole charge of their own state. Second, unless they are willing to share power with the Catholics, they will not even be able to participate in a devolved government with limited powers. And, third, some kind of institutional cooperation between the north and the south of Ireland can be taken as a permanent part of any future constitutional development.

The fact that they have almost no hope of ever again controlling their own state has at last hit home to the Ulster Protestants. Polls conducted in the late 1980s showed that most Protestants in Northern Ireland had come to prefer complete integration into the United Kingdom to any form of devolution.[26] That is, they had given up hope of establishing a state that could protect their cultural identity.

Having in 1972 lost control over their own state, the Ulster Protestants automatically surrendered control over the construction of laws. Law-making is one of the most important prerogatives of any covenantal society and loss of lawmaking powers sharply reduces the ability of the society to draw clear lines between tribal member and outsider, between the sacred and the profane. Now, it is true that in the three decades before the great events of 1912–14, the Ulster Protestants did not have the power to enforce their own morality and their own tribal discriminations in law, but undeniably the covenantal worldview was strongly ascendant in Ulster Protestant society. This implies, true enough, that a culture does not have to have control over the apparatus of secular law to enforce and propagate its own morality and ideology. Yet the years 1886–1914 and those of 1972–92 are not comparable, for in the earlier period, the informal mechanisms of Ulster covenantal society were in full force: church discipline, ubiquitous male Orange Lodge membership, adherence to a single political party. Things were much different in the 1970s and thereafter. The half-century existence of the Ulster Protestant state, 1920–72, had bred a dependence on state mechanisms for the articulation and enforcement of discipline and, consequently, the old informal mechanisms of social control and cohesion had atrophied. Therefore, when the state disappeared so quickly in 1972, the Protestants were handicapped, with only weak and attenuated voluntary associations to fall back on. They show no signs of being able to repair that loss.

(5)

But have not the setbacks and humiliations experienced since the start of the Troubles by the Protestants unified them and thus reinforced their old covenantal instincts? At moments this seemed to be the case, but actually, no.

On two occasions, the Protestants seemed to speak with one voice: during the general strike of 1974 and in their reaction to the Anglo-Irish Agreement of 1985. The 1974 strike is the stuff of Irish legends and to anyone who was there at the time it was both frightening and awe-inspiring. The province was almost totally shut down. An ad hoc body, the Ulster Workers' Council (UWC), attacked the power-sharing political assembly with a mixture of technical brilliance and crude ruthlessness. The UWC realized that power supplies were the key to everyday life in the province and in May 1974 they took control of electrical generating facilities and then cut power to major factories. In sequence, the Protestants in major factories in the Belfast area went on strike and these strikers then closed down other businesses. A virtually paramilitary infrastructure sealed most of the main roads in the province and anyone who went about his or her business without permission from the strike officials was liable to serious bodily harm. Catholics, wisely, stayed home. Thus was successfully effected a complete general strike of the sort that one associates with European syndicalism, rather than with Ulster conservatism. The response of the London government was to back down. The power-sharing assembly was aborted and unionist victory was declared.

In contrast, as mentioned earlier, the almost universal Protestant condemnation of the Anglo-Irish Agreement of 1985 has had no success. In early March 1986 a one-day general strike was called and rioting and intimidation and power cuts occurred, but the majority of Ulster Protestants lacked the stomach for an extended general strike. Instead, the Protestants took to fairly conventional political methods: a 400,000-person petition against the AIA was signed and, more creatively, all the Protestant members of the Northern Ireland assembly resigned their seats and thus forced by-elections to be called and these they used as a provincewide referendum on the AIA. They won, overwhelmingly but, predictably, Margaret Thatcher, whose brass neck and deaf ears served her well in so many circumstances, ignored them.

The Ulster Protestants' present-day problems pose a very simple question: what are they to do when their viewpoint is ignored? The Protestants' instincts for covenantal loyalty to "the British" are still there, but, as Frank Wright notes, "their allegiance to Britain has always been conditional upon Britain leaving Ulster alone."[27] When "the British" interfere continually in Northern Ireland, and show no signs of bending in the face of traditional Protestant political methods (as employed in the classic case of the massive shows of solidarity at the signing of the Ulster Covenant in 1912), then it leads to ideological confusion. As Sarah Nelson noted in her study of Protestant paramilitaries, in the 1970s "many Protestants found their political world collapsing around them. Their beliefs, their very political and social system were in question on a world stage, while each political reform (culminating with the suspension of Stormont) seemed to remove another plank from the structure they were defending. . . . How did they make it tolerable or comprehensible, and how did it affect their political behaviour?"[28] Transposed into the late 1980s and early 1990s, Nelson's questions yield this response: Protestants in Ulster no longer belong to a single covenantal culture; one portion of Protestant society thinks that the answer is to try harder, to believe more fervently and to act more determinedly; another segment has decided that the covenant is dead and gone, that it's with Edward Carson in the grave.

"It's a bit of a cliche," according to one wry observer, "to point out that the Ulster unionists are like the Bourbons, who after the French Revolution and the Napoleonic Wars had 'learnt nothing and forgotten nothing.' "[29] But in fact, a large segment of middle-class Protestant Ulster has learned a great deal, and as a consequence, they have moved away from all save the most minor forms of political commitment. They may vote, but that is simply a listless ritual. David Miller noted that the beginnings of the "middle-class Protestant disillusion with the contractarian political culture" predated 1969,[30] but there is no question that the progress of this disillusion has accelerated, almost logarithmically since 1969. There still are many middle-class Protestant politicians in Ulster, but their ascendancy has declined. At the same time, the old rural Protestant upper class has receded from politics. The situation today contrasts very sharply with that which appertained at the high point of Ulster covenanting society, the years just before World War I: then a commitment to unionism was equally evident in all strata of society in Protestant Ulster. The covenant subsumed class difference.

No longer.

This is easily demonstrated by examining election results. Until the advent of direct rule, splinter unionist parties received a maximum of little more than 10 percent of the Protestant vote. The table shows what happened among unionists after direct rule.[31] If anything, these figures understate the degree of Protestant disunity, because from 1973 onward, the nonsectarian Alliance party drew a significant proportion of middle-class Protestant voters, at times probably in excess of 10 percent of all Protestant voters.

Election	Ulster (Official) Unionist party (%)	Democratic Unionist party (%)	Other Unionist parties (%)
1969 Stormont Parliament	90.7	—	9.3
1970 Westminster Parliament	92.3	—	7.7
1973 Local government	73.1	7.6	19.3
1973 Assembly	47.3	17.5	35.2
1974 Westminster Parliament	50.3	12.8	36.9
1974 Westminster Parliament	58.8	13.7	27.5
1975 Constitutional Assembly	41.3	23.7	35.0
1977 Local government	58.3	25.0	16.7
1979 Westminster Parliament	62.0	17.3	20.7
1979 European Parliament	37.1	50.5	12.4
1981 Local government	46.3	46.4	7.3
1982 Assembly	50.0	38.7	11.3
1983 Westminster Parliament	59.6	35.1	5.3
1984 European Parliament	37.1	57.9	5.0
1985 Local government	51.8	42.7	5.5
1987 Westminster Parliament	68.9	21.3	9.8
1989 Local government	63.8	36.2	—
1989 European Parliament	41.8	58.2	—

The splits among the Protestants are in some degree ideological. It has been said that "the classic unionist uncertainty lies in being unsure of what is more important—being British or being Protestant,"[32] and each of the political parties has answered the question differently—while constantly asserting, if not really believing, that it is possible to be both. This ideological quandary in future will only be increased, since one of the projects of the Conservative party on the mainland for the 1990s is to organize Ulster branches of its own (previously the Tories have let the Ulster unionists hold the field).

Yet, the split is more than merely ideological. Since 1969, and especially since 1972, serious social class differences have emerged within Ulster Protestantism. The covenant no longer binds everyone together. "One of the major and most visible effects of direct rule," Sarah Nelson noted, "was that it stirred a new class consciousness both among members of Protestant paramilitaries and workers' groups, and among residents of loyalist working class areas."[33] The main above-ground Protestant military group, the Ulster Defence Association, has been almost entirely working class in membership and leadership. The 1974 general strike was planned and led by what, in other contexts, is called the "aristocracy of the working class"—trained technicians, shop stewards, workers in the skilled trades. Ian Paisley's Democratic Unionist party has a large lower-middle class element, a shopkeepers' bourgeoisie, but members of the executive and professional class, the high bourgeoisie, are rare. As far as can be determined, the several now-illegal violent Protestant paramilitary groups—the Ulster Volunteer Force and the various bands of sectarian killers that adopt names such as the Red Hand Commandos—are working class, almost entirely. It is true that there still is a good deal of deference to middle-class politicians on the part of the Protestant working class, but it is a fast-eroding residual. That is the real point: everything, all the old unities, are slowly coming undone.

As a group, Ulster Protestants are highly aware politically and they can read the electoral handwriting on the wall just as clearly as King Belshazzar could read the words "Mene, Mene, Tekel Upharsin," which announced that his kingdom had been weighed in the balance and that its days were numbered (Dan. 5:25–28). The decline in the unionist share of the overall number of votes cast (see table) is simultaneously a record of the past and a prediction of a somber future.[34]

Election	Unionist (%)
1969 Stormont Parliament	67.4
1970 Westminster Parliament	58.8
1973 Local government	56.6
1973 Assembly	61.9
1974 Westminster Parliament	64.2
1974 Westminster Parliament	62.1
1975 Constitutional Assembly	62.5
1977 Local government	50.8
1979 Westminster Parliament	59.0
1979 European Parliament	59.0
1981 Local government	57.3
1982 Assembly	59.4
1983 Westminster Parliament	57.0
1984 European Parliament	58.0
1985 Local government	56.9
1987 Westminster Parliament	54.9
1989 Local government	49.2
1989 European Parliament	51.4

Of course there is a good deal of vibration on the trend line, but the overall direction is unmistakable. What any sensible Ulster Protestant can see is a time, just beyond the horizon, when the majority in Northern Ireland will vote nonunionist.

Behind the electoral fear is another specter, one that has haunted Ulster Presbyterians since at least the time of the First World War: that they will be swamped by a rising tide of Catholic population. Since about World War I, Catholics have had markedly larger families than have Protestants (before that time, family size was roughly equal). Until the late 1960s, however, the Catholic emigration rate was so much higher than that of the Protestants that the religious balance was stable. When the Protestant state controlled governmental jobs and also the placement of governmental contracts with private firms, it could guarantee this stability, by forcing Catholic emigration through economic deprivation. As noted earlier, however, since 1969, a massive number of governmental jobs have been established and most of these have gone to Catholics (whose unemployment rate nevertheless is still higher than that of Protestants). Moreover, in the future, it appears that job discrimination in the private sector will become more difficult to practice. In 1983, the Fair Employment Agency was established to deal with religious discrimination in employment, but its powers were distinctly weak. In late 1988, however, the Department of Economic Development, which has a good deal of influence in the spending of large sums of government money, required that all private firms with twenty-five or more employees would have to monitor the religious composition of their work force and to develop plans to correct both gender-based and religious-based discrimination. This will not produce a perfectly level playing field, but it undoubtedly will reduce the pro-Protestant tilt. In turn, that will mean fewer Catholics will need to leave Ulster for economic reasons, and thus that the demographic impact of higher Catholic marital fertility will be even greater.[35]

When, exactly, the Roman Catholic population of Northern Ireland will exceed that of the Protestants is impossible to predict with any accuracy, for there are so many imponderables (including the question of whether or not there has been systematic undercounting of Catholics, and to what degree). The trend, though, is clearly shown by looking at primary school numbers, a useful surrogate for the differential birth rate, since compulsory attendance laws require all children to enroll in school. In 1924, Roman Catholics were 34.8 percent of the total on the rolls, in 1951, 45.5 percent, and in 1968, 51.0 percent.[36] In 1982 in the secondary schools, Catholics were 60.5 percent (this slightly understates the Catholic proportions of the youth population because of economic gradients).[37] Thus, by the mid-twenty-first century Roman Catholics will constitute a majority in Northern Ireland—providing that its borders are not redrawn.

As one section after another of the covenantal system has come unlocked and slowly pulled part, one might expect religious constructs to be brought forward to buttress the points of stress. Religion, after all, is the bedrock of the covenantal cultural system. Yet, since the Troubles began, covenantal concepts have become less and less discussed. In part this is because the mainline Protestant churches, from the 1920s onward, became increasingly "liberal" and their professional leadership less committed to covenantal thinking. Although far from theologically radical by the standards of international Protestantism, the Presbyterians, Anglicans, and Methodists of the 1960s and thereafter have been positively wet by the historical standards of Ulster covenanting thought.

The explanations for the altered stance of the mainline churches is complex, but simple processes are at work. In the first place, the clergy and the bishops of the Church of Ireland (the Anglicans) broke free of the Ulster Protestant covenanting tradition even before the Troubles began. The Church of Ireland has its headquarters in Dublin and, ecclesiastically, the church is an all-Ireland body. As a church, it does not recognize the border between the north and the south. That did not matter much in the old pre-1920 days, because "southern unionism" was strong, and thus the fact that the Anglican Church in the north was under the cultural hegemony of the Presbyterians was peripheral, since they all were unionists together. However, by the 1960s, the Anglicans in the Republic of Ireland no longer were unionists. They had accepted and were allegiant to the reality of the Republic and saw little reason to identify with the northern unionists. Thus, the Anglican clergy and bishops in the north of Ireland either had to abandon their acceptance of the covenantal mindset that had bound them to the majority Protestant culture in the north, or they had to abandon their solidarity with the rest of the Anglican communion in Ireland. Some went one way, some the other, but in both cases, their influence waned.

Meanwhile, the leaders of the Presbyterians and the Methodist churches had undergone their own transformation. The theological education of the ministers of both churches changed considerably in the 1950s and 1960s and they had dropped rock-ribbed covenantal thinking (this was especially important among the Presbyterians because of their central place in the Ulster cultural milieu). Their clergy in the 1960s were strongly influenced by the worldwide ecumenical movement. Therefore, although occasionally one finds flashes of the old covenantal outlook among church leaders—as when, in 1970, the Presbyterians pulled out of the liberal World Council of Churches on the grounds that some of its budget went to the support of terrorist groups, and when in 1985 the then-moderator of the church strongly denounced the Anglo-Irish Agreement—but mostly, from 1969 onward, the Protestant churches have been ecumenical in spirit and irenic in attitude. One could fill a small room with the printed statements of the leaders of the various Protestant churches that call, not for the old message of stand-firm-and-God-will-protect, but for forgiveness, toleration, and the condemnation of violence of all sorts. Thus, after the Anglo-Irish Agreement was signed in 1985, the Methodists issued a document that criticized parts of the agreement, but distinctly welcomed it. The Anglican clergy and bishops did nothing,[38] and, strikingly, in 1987, when the then-moderator of the Presbyterian Church in Ireland, Dr. John Thompson, left office, he described the campaign against the Anglo-Irish Agreement as "counter-productive and morally questionable."[39] The fact that the clerical leaders of the mainline Protestant churches abandoned the covenantal worldview would not have been fatal, had Northern Ireland as a state continued to exist. But once direct rule was invoked, the churches were needed to shore up the Ulster Protestant ideational structure and they were as a broken reed.

As early as four years into the Troubles, Frank Wright noted "the declining influence of Protestant religion among nominal Protestants."[40] The penumbra of church influence among nonchurchgoers that had typified Ulster was fast fading. But even within the group that still attended regularly to religion, there was a problem: the mainline church leaders and the bulk of their laity were going in rapidly different ideological directions. The bulk of the laity maintained the covenantal mindset and refused to yield an inch, whereas the clergy pushed for accommodation and compromise—which is to say, for an abandonment of the Ulster covenant.[41] Therefore, the covenantal outlook was undercut in two ways: some of the laity followed their clergy into "liberal" views, while others left the mainline church or continued attending church, but stopped listening to their religious leaders. Either way, the old connections between laity and clergy, between secular and sacred, which had undergirded the covenant, were broken. One result of this situation was the rise of various new denominations such as Ian Paisley's Free Presbyterian Church, and the increase in radically independent groups such as the Baptists, and the establishment of "parachurches," small, often locally organized groups that meet in home or village halls.[42]

What has happened in religious circles has also occurred, albeit on a larger scale, in the political realm. Considered as an entity, the Ulster covenanting culture has been losing force, losing unity, and throwing off "holy fragments," both religious and political, like a small planet that is breaking apart. These holy fragments—such as Ian Paisley's Democratic Unionist party which combines hard-line politics with old-time religion—are cohesive, but their cohesiveness is bought at the cost of their influence being unavoidably circumscribed. In the early 1990s, the Democratic Unionist party was the second largest Protestant party (behind the Official Unionist party). The Democratic Unionist party is cohesive not only because Paisley is a remarkably charismatic figure, but because (as of 1986) 80 percent of its professional politicians are members of his church.[43] The Free Presbyterian Church, however, has only approximately 10,000 adherents.[44] Its members are noted for their commitment, both financially and ideologically, but the very thing that makes Paisley's church successful as a fragment means that it is virtually impossible for it as a political party to enfold more than a minority of the Ulster Protestant population: the monarchical managerial style Paisley employs and the aggressive, indeed vitriolic, denunciation of anyone who veers from the True Faith, be it political or theological, limits its appeal. There are other fragments that try to keep the true faith—for example, the Ulster Volunteer Force, a terrorist group that claims to encapsulate and preserve the true essence of Ulster's heroic past—but each of the present-day Ulster fragments maintains its ideological cohesion only by being small, exclusive, and, ultimately, unimportant. The only way that any of these groups can keep themselves together is to stay rigorously out of touch with reality—in particular the reality of their own dwindling significance.

This insignificance stems from context: if the Ulster covenantal community has broken into fragments, a small world falling apart, it has done so within a galactic system that is expanding rapidly. The international backdrop to the Troubles has been the ongoing creation of Europe as a single entity. Northern Ireland has always been situated on the cusp between two sovereign states, southern Ireland and Great Britain, but under the Single European Act, effective in 1993, Ulster has become part of a much larger solar system, one whose center is Brussels and wherein in matters of economics, labor mobility, and transfer of capital, there is no Britain, no Ulster, no Republic of Ireland, just a single, massive capitalist system.[45]

The crucial characteristic shared by what are now merely the holy fragments of Ulster's once-united covenantal culture is that they are red-hot and volatile. It will take more than a single generation for them to cool down and during the waiting period, a miscue by British, Irish, or European authorities could make them coalesce once again: If that happens, an implosion of fierce proportions could occur, as in the process of nuclear fusion.

Patience, a long view, and a steady hand are the only way.

10

A World Unhinged: Afrikaners and Apartheid, 1969 to the Present

(1)

The Day of the Covenant (or Day of the Vow) on 16 December 1988, was the 150th anniversary of the oath taking that preceded the Afrikaners' sanguinary victory at the Battle of Blood River, and it was the 50th anniversary of the single greatest outpouring of *volk* enthusiasm and unity in their history, the political-mystical-cultural up-welling that accompanied the centenary commemoration on 16 December 1938. It should have been a great day.

Something was very wrong, however. Unlike the centennial celebration of 1938, which surprised even the organizers by setting off a spontaneous wave of nationwide enthusiasm, the 1988 celebrations were lifeless, the response far below expectations. As in 1938, trains of ox-wagons and teams of costumed drivers repeated the steps of the Voortrekkers, but this time they excited more curiosity than enthusiasm. English-language South Africa ignored the event and even the Afrikaans-language papers gave it little attention. In Pretoria, 40,000 people were estimated to have attended at the Voortrekker monument, not a small crowd, but well below half the attendance of fifty years before.[1]

Whereas the celebrations of 1938 had been an affirmation of Afrikaner unity, those of 1988 revealed disunion. A rival ox-wagon performance was organized by the political right wing, an amalgam of cultural tradi-tionalists, biblical fundamentalists, and not-an-inch apartheid supporters. Thus, at the Voortrekker monument, the religious establishment and the National party had its commemorations and forty-five kilometers away the Conservative party and its right-wing outriders held rival services.[2]

Comparison of a 1938 and 1988 celebrations is like a cardiologist's comparing a patient's cardiograms over a period of time and seeing the onset of sclerosis, arhythmia, and clear dysfunction. But only a clairvoyant could have foreseen that within two years of that 150th anniversary of the Day of the Covenant, the Afrikaner establishment would have publicly abandoned the ideological faith of their fathers and begun to take apart the apartheid state as part of the transition to a new constitution, and, inevitably, a new social order.

The events visible to the world outside South Africa were as follows. In August 1989 President P. W. Botha was forced by the cabinet of his National party government to resign. He had suffered a stroke some months previously and had been impaired in the conduct of his duties, but the revolt went deeper than that; the majority in the cabinet believed that the government had to come to terms with South Africa's black majority, and had no stomach for Botha's increasingly uncompromising policies. Botha's successor, F. W. de Klerk, won a narrow general election victory in September 1989 and then on 2 February 1990 lifted the ban on the African National Congress and began a systematic release of political prisoners. This was extended by the "Pretoria Minute" of 6 August 1990, which returned the Communist party to legal status and promised further lifting of security measures and a "negotiated peaceful settlement" with the ANC. Along the way, de Klerk promised the abolition of all forms of petty apartheid and abolition of the land- and group-areas acts upon which grand apartheid was based. These things were in fact achieved by the middle of 1991: a virtual revolution, most Afrikaners felt.

(2)

Whether or not South African society will escape from the prison of apartheid without a bloodbath is impossible to foretell, and I do not believe the situation will be stable until at least the beginning of the twenty-first century. The history of revolutions suggests that the Girondists often are merely forerunners of the Jacobins, that recalcitrant royalists sometimes upset peaceful transitions, and that, frequently, jacquerie is one of the bitter fruits of freedom. What is certain is that de Klerk's initiatives of 1990 formally marked the end of Afrikaner society as a *volk* and as a united Chosen People, covenanted to each other and to their God.

Thus, we confront a momentous historical question: What were the dimensions and characteristics of the changes that on the surface appeared to be so sudden and dramatic? One of the most helpful sources in detailing the *sub rosa* changes in Afrikaner society from the 1960s to the late 1980s comes from the field of political science. In the mid-1960s, the high era of apartheid, a German-born political scientist, Heribert Adam, studied in considerable depth the attitudes and beliefs of almost 350 elite white South Africans: members of parliament, higher civil servants, and leading businessmen.[3] A similar, but more analytic study was done by a South African team led by Hendrik W. van der Merwe.[4] The latter work, conducted in 1968 and 1969, was founded on personal interviews with more than 900 members of the white ruling elite. From the work of Adam and of van der Merwe, then, one can draw a base line of the beliefs of Afrikaans-speaking leaders when Verwoerdian apartheid was at its height.[5] More recently, two American political scientists, Kate Manzo and Patrick McGowan, shrewdly recognized the potential such a base line offered. They designed a study of Afrikaner leaders comparable to those done in the 1960s, which, when combined with those earlier studies, gives an accurate indication of the direction and extent of the changing beliefs of the Afrikaner establishment.[6] Their study, which involved responses from more than 430 Afrikaner leaders, has two characteristics that make it particularly useful. One of these is timing. Their data were collected in the second half of 1988, that is, before the drastic political initiatives of 1990 (and, coincidentally, just at the time that the symptomatic event, the 150th anniversary of the Great Trek, was in train). Thus, Manzo and McGowan's material is untainted by the events of 1990 and, since it was collected before those events, it provides an unrivaled window into the beliefs of the Afrikaner establishment on the eve of their great political adventure. Second, the Manzo and McGowan study is a fine example of the value of what might be called good old-fashioned mindless empiricism. That is, the authors did not let their own quite strong ideological commitments bend their research. The questions were open and neutral; the results are open to interpretation by everyone from Stalinists to members of the Afrikaner Weerstandsbeweging (the militant Afrikaner Resistance Movement), but they stand independent of any of these frameworks.[7]

Manifestly, and undeniably, the beliefs (and thus the implied ideology)

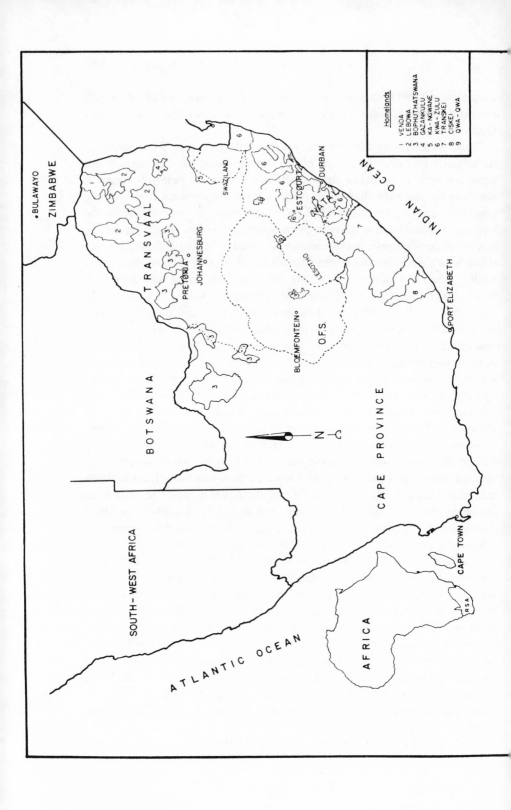

of the Afrikaner establishment changed greatly between the middle 1960s and the late 1980s. My own interpretation of these changes is as follows. The most notable change was that, by 1988, nearly half of the Afrikaner elite had abandoned the belief that the division of humankind into different national (read: racial) groups was an expression of God's will.[8] The level of continuing adherence to this belief may seem high by international standards, but in the context of the South African educational and religious system, which had inculcated the belief from the cradle on, it is a major degree of apostasy. Since the ultimate underpinning of apartheid was supposed to be divine sanction, this loss of faith is tantamount to a great flood destroying the walls of a medieval walled fortress. Thereafter, everything else crumbles, although not everything collapses at the same rate.

Congruent with this shift was the growth of the opinion of roughly half of the elite sample—52 percent—that grand apartheid (that is, territorial separate development) was a bad idea.[9] This contrasts with virtually unanimous agreement expressed in a study of National party politicians and other opinion leaders in the mid-1970s, namely that separate development was a good idea.[10] An opinion shift of 50 percent in a decade and a half is significant. Even more radical was the abandonment of belief in most (not all, most) aspects of petty apartheid. In van der Merwe's study in the late 1960s, 75.2 percent of the Afrikaner elite had expressed support for keeping whites and blacks apart in everything from the use of toilet facilities to buses, churches, and universities.[11] In the 1988 study, only 11.0 percent favored segregation in the workplace; 21.5 percent in transport facilities; 29.0 percent in churches; and 34.7 percent in entertainment facilities.[12]

In quantitative terms, the most marked shift in beliefs came in the economic sphere. In 1966–67, 76 percent of the Afrikaner elite sample believed in job reservation for white workers.[13] In 1988, 90.6 percent said that people who have the same job should receive the same pay, and this implied abandonment of job discrimination between blacks and whites.[14] Equally important, the Afrikaner opinion leaders in 1988 clearly had reached the conclusion that apartheid had been a bad thing economically: 66.8 percent agreed that it had hindered the development of the South African economy, and 91.2 percent believed that whatever economic development had occurred was in spite of apartheid.[15]

Did the average Afrikaner go along with the elite? Here the base line is a large-sample survey conducted in 1984 by the Human Sciences Research Council of South Africa (a body that generally has stayed politically neutral and maintained its scholarly standards through some very hard times). The 1984 survey indicated that the average Afrikaner was still in favor of maintaining each of the "seven pillars of apartheid." These pillars, and the percentage of Afrikaners in favor of keeping them were as follows: the Mixed Marriages Act (78.9 percent); the Immorality Act (81.3 percent); Group Areas Act (86.9 percent); separate education (90.2 percent); separate amenities (84.9 percent); black African homelands (89.6 percent); and separate voter rolls for "coloureds" (92.1 percent).[16] Another Human Sciences Research Council poll conducted in May 1990 found that 68.6 percent of those white South Africans who expressed an opinion favored either de Klerk's National party or the Democratic party, which was politically to the left of the National party.[17] That 31.4 percent of the white electorate, therefore, was opposed to parties committed to relaxation of apartheid prohibitions means that 47–50 percent of the Afrikaner voters disapproved of de Klerk's dismantling of the system. Nevertheless, that roughly half of the Afrikaners were now willing to abandon apartheid was quite a notable change in less than a decade. It was not as big a move as the elite had made, but significant nonetheless.

But from the viewpoint of the long-term history of the Afrikaners (and, indeed, from the viewpoint of their future), whether half or fewer have experienced the shift shown by the political elite is irrelevant. Recall that the key thing about Afrikaner ideology—ethnic, religious, and political— as it developed from 1870 onward, was that the *volk* were *one* Chosen People, that they served the *one* God, that they were bonded in a *single* covenant, that they were *singular* even within the white population, and that they were rightly the *primary* custodians of the South African society, economy, and state. Hence, the defection of even a minority from the unity of the *volk* was unremittingly fatal to the entire Afrikaner cosmology. Under the Afrikaners' covenantal belief system there was no room for pluralism. The unity of the people and their bonding together under God, gave them a mandate that was based not on majority rule, but on a belief that their covenant was absolute and right. The doubts expressed by a minority—and, particularly a minority that represented the elite of Afrikaner culture—was a direct proof that the *volk* no longer existed. Individual Afrikaners, yes; several political parties, certainly; competing economic and class interests, manifestly; but the *volk:* no more.

(3)

How did this come to be? Certainly economic pressures have been central, some in ways that conform to the neo-Marxist analysis of South African society, some in ways that conform to the Friedmanite version of classical capitalist economic liberalism. During the 1970s, the National party, which had been the voice of Afrikanerdom, and which since the late 1930s had successfully preached that there were no class divisions among white Afrikaans-speakers, perceptibly altered that position. Under P. W. Botha (1978–89) the National party quietly and systematically jettisoned its working-class elements. The National party gradually became a party overtly committed to serving the interests of the haute bourgeois: business executives, lawyers, technocrats, and upper civil servants. It reached out with some success to white English-speakers who had the same class interests. Thus, whereas the National party had drawn an estimated 85 percent of the Afrikaner vote in the 1977 election, this fell to 63 percent in the general election of 1981, with 33 percent of Afrikaners voting for far-right parties that simultaneously promoted the interests of the Afrikaans-speaking working and lower middle class and paid homage to the verities of the Afrikaner covenant as articulated in the 1949–69 era.[18]

At the same time, the haute bourgeoisie, and especially (but not solely) the business elite, came under the influence of an intellectual code that was increasingly prevalent in western societies, namely the popularized version of neoclassical economics. The success of Afrikaners in gaining a significant degree of control over the South African economy meant that the economic attitudes of small shopkeepers and bank clerks no longer fit reality. As the Afrikaners came to dominate major corporations, the upper levels of management came increasingly into contact with their overseas counterparts and with the executives of multinational firms whose corporations stationed them for a time in South Africa. Thus was spread the dominant tenets of virtually all business schools and some departments of economics in North America (and, to a lesser extent, in Great Britain), namely, that interference in the economic marketplace by the state should be limited and, if possible, reduced. A further line of thought (one that went all the way back to Adam Smith) was that unfree labor, while apparently cheap, actually was expensive, because its artificial cheapness introduced economic irrationality.[19] The degree to which these ideas captured the Afrikaner elite is shown by the fact (discussed earlier) that the elite went from a 76 percent approval of job reservation in the mid-1960s to a nine-out-of-ten affirmation of a person's pay being solely a function of economic productivity, not of race.

And the internationally fashionable doctrine of reducing state economic interference was assimilated in the late 1980s and the 1990s. In February 1988, the Botha government announced plans for the privatization of state-controlled industries, for lower subsidies to private businesses and farms, and a pay freeze for civil servants. The first targets of privatization, modeled on British and European precedents, were the state phosphorus corporation (Foskor) and the state electrical supply corporation (Eskom). South African Transport Services, which controlled South African Airways, most harbors and railways, and a good deal of road haulage, was to be privatized as well. The public iron and steel corporation (Iscor) was to be restructured to make privatization possible.[20] The diminuition of the state sector (which under high apartheid had served as an economic safety net for the bottom segment of the Afrikaner population) and the reduction of employment discrimination clearly would hurt the Afrikaner working class. Indeed, the practice and theory of modern capitalism undercuts racial apartheid while simultaneously enlarging class antagonism within the Afrikaans-speaking section of the white minority.

International sanctions against South Africa remained in effect until July 1991, when President George Bush lifted U.S. restrictions on trade and thereby effectively ended South Africa's economic penalties. (The remaining international sanctions became a cipher once the United States reestablished full trade relations.) The full degree and effect of sanctions will probably never be fully known (the amount of clandestine trade with South Africa on the part of nations who formally invoked sanctions is something that neither the South African government nor its underground trading partners wishes to publicize); nor will we ever know the actual price paid by various segments of South African society.[21] Everyone was hurt, all races and classes. The real issue is, how did each interest group judge the cost? There is no doubt that the people for whom the African National Congress speaks found the price well worth paying. For the Afrikaner elite, who already were bending away from classical apartheid because it was economically irrational, sanctions served as a confirmation of an evolving recognition that apartheid cost too much. The Conservative party and other right-wing Afrikaner groups vehemently disagreed.

(4)

In recognizing that the material concerns of Afrikaners increasingly divided them, one is pointing to a truth, but not the entire truth. There was more to the tessellation of the Afrikaner *volk* than simple material changes: "soft" changes, cultural ones, were equally significant. For instance, from the early 1970s onward, a good deal of anglicization occurred within Afrikaner society. This was part of the political *détente* between middle- and upper-class Afrikaners in the business and professional sectors. (The successful reshaping of the National party so that it appealed to many English-speakers is evidence of this process.) In part, anglicization occurred because both Afrikaans- and English-speakers were increasingly awash in a tidal wave of foreign films (most of them of U.S. origin) and television (which was introduced in South Africa only in 1975). Even though films and programs were censored or state-controlled, these media gave access to a world of international values that Afrikaner society previously had been able to keep at bay. Both Anglophones and Afrikaners were affected, but the Afrikaners much more so, because previously they had lived in a hermetically sealed cultural environment. Crucially, as this process continued, intermarriage between Afrikaans- and English-speakers, which in the days of Afrikaner cultural purity had carried a stigma, became much more frequent and less opprobrious. It is estimated that in the late 1980s, 25 percent of all white marriages were "mixed marriages" between speakers of Afrikaans and English.[22]

The linchpin in the Afrikaners' covenantal cosmology always had been their religious beliefs, and change in these can be quite precisely documented at a theological level. During the years 1969–90, the three Dutch Reformed churches, which previously had been united in their affirmation of apartheid, took three different paths. The Nederduitse Hervormde Kerk changed not a bit: apartheid to them was part of the divine plan and tampering with it therefore was morally retrograde. In contrast, the Gereformeerde Kerk (the Doppers) abandoned belief in apartheid and in the melding of the *volk,* of constitutional arrangements, and of racial segregation as being part of the divine plan. In essence, they repudiated the idea of the covenant, the bond that had made the Afrikaners a Chosen People, and the morality that the covenant implied. Thus, Dopper churches came to include a considerable number of black members. As one of the Dopper leaders explained in the mid-1980s, there should be only one prerequisite for church membership and that was faith in Jesus Christ.[23] Although small (like the NHK, the GK represents only about 5 percent of the Afrikaner population), the Doppers' defection from the ranks of those bound by the covenant was important, for it opened the path of possibility for the main Nederduitse Gereformeerde Kerk (NGK). The Doppers in many ways have resembled the extreme Independents of seventeenth-century England whose principles could push them either to extremely conservative Puritanism or to the radicalism of the Levelers. Thus, the two Doppers to have led South African political life represent these two extremes: the former slave trader Paul Kruger—who more than any single person was the evangelist of the Afrikaners' identification with the covenant, with their being a Chosen People, and with the doctrine of racial superiority—and F. W. de Klerk—who dismantled the apparatus of the state that had been framed upon those beliefs.

A study conducted in 1971 by Robert Buis, *Religious Beliefs and White Prejudice,* confirmed that attitudes toward racial matters (which in South Africa means attitudes on the proper order of society in general) vary according to the religious background of the individual concerned. Simply put, "committed" members of the Dutch Reformed faith had less favorable attitudes toward blacks than did those of committed members of the other main white faiths.[24] According to Buis, certain church-derived values permeated all of Afrikaner society:

> The teachings of the Dutch Reformed Church are evident in many other spheres of South African society. . . . A policy of Christian National Education has been made compulsory in all white schools. Here all teaching is done within a Christian and a national frame of reference.
>
> Prospective immigrants who profess to be atheists or agnostics are not usually granted residence permits despite an all-out drive to attract white immigrants to South Africa. In the legal system the Old Testament principles of justice are barely concealed.[25]

Because of the central importance of the NGK in South African society (in the 1960s it was said that the only difference between the National party and the NGK was the day of the week) the pressing question was whether the NGK would follow the path of the Doppers or of the NHK.[26] The first chance for the NGK to answer that question came in 1974 when the general synod met to discuss a policy document entitled *Ras, Volk en Nasie* ("Race, *Volk*, and Nation"). This statement of belief, which was fully endorsed by the synod, was the product of several years' work by the best theological and scriptural scholars in the NGK. The document is remarkably lucid and, if one accepts the fundamental assumptions of its authors (particularly that the Bible is a divinely inspired document), rational. It is also very subtle.

The first quarter of "Race, *Volk*, and Nation" formed a bedrock on which to erect the NGK system of racial ethics. Not surprisingly, this consisted mostly of Old Testament texts. The reading of the scriptures, though ultimately extremely traditional in its implications, did not involve an old-fashioned Hametic view of race, but rather an up-to-date hermeneutic vocabulary. The church's theologians had read their contemporary European scholarship. Thus, their report averred that the church must use as its starting point and as the standard of truth the Word of God, and yet it also warned that the scriptures were not to be used as a sociological handbook. Such literal readings, they said, had in the past resulted in mistaken views of race and ethnology, such as when the scriptures had been used to justify slavery.[27] In fact, they noted, the scriptures never mentioned race in the modern biological sense of the term.

So how could the scriptures be of any help? Through certain scriptural principles that were applicable throughout history. A welter of Old Testament references (with particular emphasis on chapters 10 and 11 of the book of Genesis) argued that the scriptures clearly taught that God had sanctioned the development of different nations, cultures, and ethnic groups. The calling of Abram by Yahweh had created an additional principle: there might be a variety of divinely ordered groups, but they were not equal. The scriptures, the NGK scholars said, included a third principle: people chosen by God had to behave differently than did other nations and cultures; they had to keep separate. It was the task of the church, the scholars said, to take these divine principles as articulated in the past and to apply them to the present.[28] What the leading scholars of the NGK were doing was obvious: they were abandoning the literal readings of the Hebrew scriptures (such as the Hametic texts) which in the past had justified the creation of apartheid structures, and in their place they introduced a set of abstract principles, drawn from the Hebrew texts, which, they believed, justified the perpetuation of the very same apartheid structures.

But the scholars had a problem. Although their reinterpretation worked for the "Old Testament," there were problems with the "New." The words of Jesus (and to a lesser extent the writings of the apostle Paul) are full of direct repudiations of the ancient Hebrew covenant and of the idea of there being a Chosen People in the physical sense; distinctions between people based on their ethnicity or social standing are specifically rejected. Indeed, the single principle most positively asserted in the teachings of Jesus is the equality of all humankind before God. The NGK theologians dealt with this "New Testament" principle by an unstated, subtle, and very effective hermeneutic shift. Whereas the general principles of the "Old Testament" were taken as having direct institutional implications in the modern world, the "New Testament" principles were interpreted as being doctrines of the heart, ones that had to reign in every righteous soul, but which had no direct institutional implications.[29] Although the NGK scholars never would have admitted the point directly, it is fair to summarize their hermeneutic as saying that the "Old Testament" ruled the visible world and the "New Testament" guided the world of the spirit. They preferred to suggest that the individual Christian had to strive for Christian spiritual virtues while living out his or her political, religious, and social life within divinely ordained ethnic and national contexts. Thus, the largest of the Dutch Reformed churches not only implicitly affirmed apartheid, but indirectly rejected their own integration with the black and "coloured" Reformed churches.[30]

That was in 1974, and whatever else the position of the NGK was at that date, it was coherent and skillfully argued. Certainly it played in Pretoria. Elsewhere, however, the church's position received little respect. In 1982, the NGK was expelled from the international body with which it most closely identified, the World Alliance of Reformed Churches.[31] European and American Reformed Church leaders declared the NGK position on social structure to be heretical. Within South Africa, the "coloured" Dutch Reformed Church—the "Sendingskerk" with about 700,000 members, a little under the number of the NGK membership—drafted in 1982 the "Belhar Confession," which called upon the NGK to confess "its guilt for providing the moral and theological foundations for apartheid."[32] The NGK's immediate response was to reject this call, but the various theological pressures were strong enough to lead the NGK to appoint a commission on doctrine to review the church's racial policy. In October 1986, everything came to a head when, at the church's general synod, a draft document, *Kerk en Samelewing* ("Church and Society") was received.

In contrast to "Race, *Volk*, and Nation" (1974), the new document was a mess, and in so being it accurately reflected conditions within the largest of the Dutch Reformed churches. Both in its preparation and in its reception, "Church and Society" was the occasion of great bitterness. The conflicted nature of serious Afrikaner Christians is indicated in this confused, staccato, and contradictory policy statement. Throughout the document one encounters what Conor Cruise O'Brien had noted in Afrikaner political life of the period, a sense of uncertainty and confusion stemming from the "unexpected force of guilt."[33] In obedience to Reformed tradition, the new document declared as its fundamental assumption, that the Bible was the sole standard of right for the church.[34] Obviously, then, if the church wished to change its position on race and ethnic relations, it had to change totally its reading of the scriptures and to repudiate not only the hermeneutics of the 1974 document, but the official interpretation of the scriptures that went all the way back to 1859, when the church founded its own seminary and and started to develop an indigenous South African Reformed theology. Now, in 1986, the synod swallowed hard and did just that. After ten pages of largely unrelated observations on the character of divine revelation—many of the statements were not even written in full sentences, so distracted was the tone of the document—the members of the doctrinal commission blurted out that, in effect, they had decided to go with the "New Testament" rather than the "Old." In the "New Testament" they pointed out, diversity of creation was always seen within the context of unity. Further, it was argued, although the "Old Testament" indeed deals with the biological factors that differentiate human groups, it is not aware of any such thing as a race problem. (The Amalekites and the Canaanites might have had a word or two to say about this assertion.) And, the NGK theologians noted, in the "New Testament" the idea of race plays no part whatsoever.[35]

Racism—defined as an attitude or theory that implies one race or ethnic group is inherently inferior to another group—was declared to be a sin. And the church authorities now argued that nothing in the scriptures implied any specific political model. Therefore the attempt of previous generations of Reformed theologians to ground the separation of peoples on biblical principles was invalid. In other words, apartheid was not biblically justified and to the extent that the NGK had spread this incorrect interpretation of the Bible, it confessed its error: apartheid was incompatible with Christian ethics.[36]

But what should be done about apartheid? In other sections of "Church and Society," the NGK distanced itself from two notions; namely, that it was in all matters as one with the *volk*, and that it was a partner with the state.[37] This degree of humility was something new for the NGK, which previously had prided itself on being the primary authentic voice of the *volk* and the moral conscience of the state. There was method in this humility: by distancing itself from both the *volk* and the state, the NGK absolved itself of the need to put forward any specific program for the elimination of apartheid. Thus was condoned, what Heribert Adam called in a similar context, "conversion without repentance."[38]

Yet, however weak was the NGK's repentance for its past errors (it did not, for example, even go so far as to prohibit individual congregations from being racially exclusive), the importance of this document is undeniable. As accepted by the synod (only minor amendments were made in passage), it completely destroyed the religious basis of everything that the Afrikaner culture had developed during the previous 125 years. No longer could the Afrikaners think of themselves as a Chosen People (because the vaunting of any group was racism and therefore a sin); no longer could the coidentity of the state, *volk,* and church be credited (the synod specifically rejected this trinity); no more could apartheid be justified by scriptural references (the church's interpretation of the scriptures had altered radically). Thus did the leading Dutch Reformed Church effectively declare that the covenant was dead.

(5)

As in Northern Ireland, "holy fragments" have been thrown off in reaction to the gradual abandonment of the old truths by church leaders, by National party politicians, and by the professional and business elite. In contrast to Ulster, these fragments of Afrikaner society are quite large and at moments have seemed to have the potential to coalesce and to form a new majority: not a new unity, but a new majority. The first such fragment was the Herstigte Nasionale party—the "Reconstructed" or "Reconstituted" National party—which arose in 1969 as the first challenge since 1948 among Afrikaans-speakers to the National party. To anyone outside of South African society, its rise is apt to appear as epiphenomenal, but it was not. In 1966, the National party under H. F. Verwoerd had been reelected with the biggest majority in South Africa's political history. After the assassination of Verwoerd in September of that year, the party had closed ranks tightly behind B. J. Vorster. He was strongly committed to continued white domination. Yet, by 1969, Vorster was being viewed by a small and vocal minority of the Afrikaner electorate as a liberal reformer and as a traitor. This was because Vorster, in order to maintain white supremacy, sided with the wing of the National party that was willing to make minor changes in apartheid. Although these changes were small within the context of the entire system, to true believers any change was heresy. Therefore, 1969 is a signal moment, for it marks the first visible fissure between the fundamentalist and the pragmatic advocates of apartheid.

The second political fragment, the Conservative party, was thrown off in 1982. Its formation was a reaction to the way the National party had responded to the pressures of the 1970s—the labor unrest of 1972 and 1973, the fall of the Portuguese colonies in Africa in 1974, the Soweto riots of 1976—by backing away from job reservation and from some of the detailed provisions of petty apartheid.[39] The Conservatives were especially incensed that in 1980 the job reservation system was scrapped, and that black unions were recognized and given limited right to strike. More changes were in train, and a sizable minority of the National party would not wear this. Thus, after two years of intense infighting, Andries Treurnicht led fifteen members of parliament out of the National party and founded the Conservative party. At the time, one prescient observer noted, "The ethnic glue of Afrikanerdom has finally dissolved."[40] The Conservative party gradually displaced the Herstigte Nasionale party as the voice of the Afrikaner political fundamentalists. Like most such bands of true believers, the Conservative party perceives the world in Manichean terms. The modifications of apartheid that occurred in the 1980s—creation in 1983 of a tricameral legislature that gave the "coloured" population a visible, but spurious, vote, the abolition of the Mixed Marriage Act and of the miscengenation clause of the Immorality Act in 1985, the abolition of the pass laws in 1986—simply confirmed the fundamentalist view. Had they not foreseen this apostasy?

If the Conservative party is the respectable face of Afrikaner fundamentalism (its parliamentary members have so far played the political game by the rules), the AWB—the Afrikaner Weerstandsbeweging—founded in 1973 by Eugene Terre Blanche, is the hard face. It is an unabashedly fascistic force (its uniforms and insignia are modeled on those of the Nazis). As is the case with most South African males, most of its members have had military training and own guns. The AWB leaders talk of resisting by force the black onslaught that they believe will come soon, and they dream of creating a *boerestaat*, an Afrikaner homeland. At their most optimistic, they claim what is now the Transvaal and the Orange Free State.

In the religious field, the increasing softening of the NGK in relation to apartheid resulted in the formation in the mid-1980s of an ultratraditional Reformed sect, the Afrikaanse Protestantse Kerk. About

60 clerics and 30,000 laymen broke away from the NGK to join this body.[41]

(6)

Despite the undeniable reality of the existence of each of these holy fragments, I think that the one that will most affect South Africa's future does not assume institutional form, and it is found in the individual human heart. The survey of attitudes of elite Afrikaners conducted in 1988 by Manzo and McGowan indicated something important: that although the Afrikaner elite now was opposed to separate development, to job discrimination, and to most forms of petty apartheid, in certain areas the majority of even this elite and "liberal" group felt that whites and blacks should be kept apart (although not necessarily by law): swimming pools (55.8 percent agreed with this proposition); hospitals (56.9 percent); residential areas (62.3 percent); and schools (67.8 percent).[42]

Undoubtedly, these beliefs are related to the pervasive white fears of black violence and particularly fear of sexual violence. And, certainly, these fears are considerably greater outside of the elite.[43] But I think that more than fear is involved. The desire to keep one's children educationally separate from nonwhites, to have one's family reside in a purely white neighborhood, and the desire to keep themselves and their families away from blacks and "coloureds" when their own bodies are in a vulnerable or semidressed state (hospitals, swimming pools) all have something in common. Each of these matters is redolent of the ancient imperative that the body, the family, the "seed" must be protected from admixture with the impure and the profane.

That fragment of belief, held deep within the heart of Afrikaners' culture, is one of the legacies of their former adherence to the covenant.

11

Israel, 1967 to the Present:
Completing the Circle

(1)

Whand, on 12 June 1967, the Israeli government announced that
it would not withdraw to the 1949 armistice line, that could
have been read as a statement of temporary intent. But when, on
28 June, the authorities proclaimed the reunification of Jerusalem, that
was permanent, a reaffirmation of a contract that the Jewish people had
made millennia in the past. Control of the Old City of Jerusalem, and
especially of the Temple Mount, gave Israel possession of the most holy
religious sites of the ancient Hebrews. The Mount itself was directly
associated with Moses and with the history of the covenant that is articulated in the Pentateuch. If any part of "the Land" was sacred, this was it.

To the Israelis, the amazing and unsettling aspect of the Six Day War
was the amount of territory that they had conquered. On the eve of the
war, Israel had control of approximately 77 percent of the old Palestine
mandate (estimates vary slightly). About 3 percent of the old mandate
(Gaza) was under Egyptian control, and 20 percent (commonly called the
West Bank) was attached to Jordan.[1] During the Six Day War, Israel
captured Gaza, the West Bank, the rest of Jerusalem, plus the Sinai and
the Golan plateau (the latter previously held by Syria). This captured
territory was three times the size of pre-1967 Israel.[2]

Thus arose the embarrassment of success. What should be done with
these territories? Jerusalem, of course, would be kept, for it was holy

311

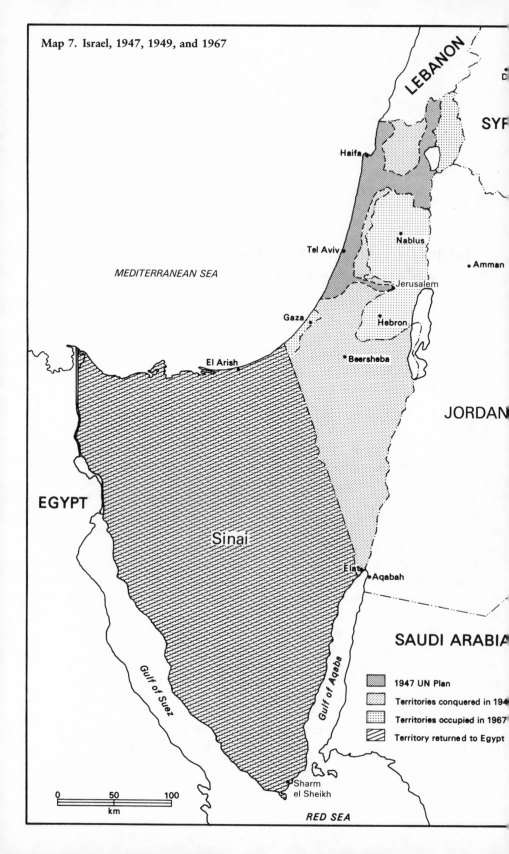

Map 7. Israel, 1947, 1949, and 1967

LEBANON

SYRIA

Haifa

Nablus

Tel Aviv

Amman

MEDITERRANEAN SEA

Jerusalem

Gaza

Hebron

El Arish

Beersheba

JORDAN

EGYPT

Sinai

Elat
Aqabah

SAUDI ARABIA

Gulf of Suez

Gulf of Aqaba

1947 UN Plan

Territories conquered in 1949

Territories occupied in 1967

Territory returned to Egypt

0   50   100
km

Sharm
el Sheikh

RED SEA

ground. Sinai, on the other hand, was mostly a vast emptiness. Although some scholars considered it part of Eretz Israel, the level of emotional attachment was low. Thus it would be used as a diplomatic chip and probably given up. But Gaza, the Golan Heights, and the West Bank were different, perhaps not automatically to be assimilated into Israel, but worth keeping. Each of them was militarily significant and, historically, each was part of Eretz Israel, in the view of most Israeli scholars. So, they were not mere matters of topography. The chief Sephardic rabbi stated that it was a religious obligation to keep the newly conquered territories.[3] The rector of Bar-Ilan University summarized the retentionist view: "There is only one nation to whom the Land belongs in trust and by covenant promise," he declared, "and that is the Jewish people. No temporary demographic changes can alter this basic fact which is the bedrock of the Jewish faith."[4]

From the end of the Six Day War until the Likud party came to power in 1977, the Israeli polity was undecided as to what to do with the various conquered (officially termed "occupied") territories. The "maximalist camp," which included the various factions that eventually became Likud, and several small extreme groups were for keeping everything save the Sinai, and a few even wanted that. The "anti-maximalists" were in the tradition of David Ben-Gurion in his latter years: they saw the West Bank, even with massive new Jewish settlement, as being more of a risk than a benefit, because of its Arab majority. This held even more true for the other "occupied territories" (always with the exception of Jerusalem, which virtually no one wished to return to non-Israeli control).[5]

Because the Labor party was the most powerful single political bloc in this era, that party's confusion about what to do with Israel's embarrassment of military spoils was crucial. The Labor party divided into three groups. One, led by Pinhas Sapir, secretary of the treasury, was dovish. This group opposed the annexation of any territory whose Arab population would change the demographic balance—that is, would seriously dilute the Jewish majority within the areas under Israeli control. A second group, led by Moshe Dayan, was hawkish. This segment held that the Palestinians had lost their right to self-determination by not accepting the United Nations' partition plan of 1947 and, therefore, the annexation of Palestinian lands was morally justified. The Dayan phalanx believed that the claims of the Palestinians were irreconcilable with Israel's right to exist, so it was best to snuff out those claims quickly. A middle ground, centering around Yigan Allon, favored selective annexation of the territories, chiefly the strategically important areas such as the Golan Heights.

Defensible boundaries were Allon's goal. For that reason, the Allon group opposed Israel's annexation of large centers of Arab population. In the actual course of events, none of these three positions became official government policy, although the middle course—articulated as the "Allon plan"—was tacitly adopted until 1977.[6]

The lack of a clear governmental policy meant that the colonization and management of the newly conquered territories progressed in a halting fashion. The result was less a piece of social architecture than a patchwork. Yet despite government ambiguity, indeed confusion, on what to do with the "occupied territories," the expansion of the portions of Eretz Israel under Jewish settlement and control went ahead, and that fact makes the process a more accurate indication of the attitudes of the people than had the government mandated matters.

Six areas were conquered in 1967, each of which opened a different set of questions and a different menu of policies. One of these, Jerusalem, was unique among the newly conquered lands, both by virtue of its sacred history and its urbanization. It is impossible to learn exactly the extent of Jewish settlement after 1967 in what previously was an Arab sector, but the mode of colonization is clear enough. Beginning in January 1968, the authorities expropriated large blocks of Arab-owned land within Jerusalem and used these to build Jews-only housing projects. These multistory apartment blocks formed a ring of concrete around the remaining Arab areas in Jerusalem.[7] The best estimates (drawn from the *Statistical Abstract of Israel, 1980*) indicate that during 1968–79 some 84,000 Jewish people moved into the newly taken areas of Jerusalem.[8]

What happened in the other five areas—Gaza, the Golan Heights, and the three distinct portions of the West Bank—the Jordan Valley, Samaria, and Judea—was similar to what happened during Israel's previous colonizations.[9] The methods used were by now well tried. Tightly guarded Jewish settlements and large-scale land expropriation were the cornerstones. The West Bank Data Project, headed by the deputy mayor of Jerusalem, Meron Benvenisti, has shown in detail how the methods developed during the 1950s were used with ever-increasing efficiency after 1967. The system of land alienation became routine, involving middle-echelon Israeli officials, rather than high-level decision makers.[10] After the 1967 war, all the time-tested ways of expropriating Arab lands were employed—military authorities closed entire areas and then seized the land as being waste, they requisitioned land for security reasons, and seized abandoned houses, lands, and stores. And now, some new methods were added. For example, "state land" previously owned by the Jordanian government was now owned by the Israeli state.

The details of the colonization machinery differed somewhat locale by locale. For instance, by 1984 Israel had acquired direct ownership of 40 percent of the land of the Gaza Strip.[11] But actually settling the area was difficult, because only about 18 percent of the Gaza population had fled or been killed during the Six Day War.[12] The Palestinian population was essentially unbroken. The Gaza Strip, then, was a new colonial situation for the Israelis, for despite the confiscation of Arab lands, there were no easy places of settlement. By 1978 only about 500 Israelis settled in Gaza, amid more than 400,000 Palestinians, and almost all of these settlers were living inside of military posts.[13] Instead of settling Gaza, the evolving Israeli practice was to use the Gaza Palestinians as a supply of cheap manual labor and to keep those Palestinians who were not needed in the Israeli economy fenced in, literally.

In contrast, on the Golan Heights, an estimated 93 percent of the pre-1967 Arab population of about 100,000 had fled or died.[14] Because of the Golan Heights' strategic importance, the actual settlement of the area by Israeli colonists was secondary to its use by the Israeli Defence Force. The Golan settlement proceeded only slowly, and by the end of 1977, there were still fewer than 4,000 permanent Israeli settlers, amid perhaps 7,000 Palestinians.[15]

In the Jordan Valley portion of the West Bank, the death and flight of Palestinian population had been very high. A pre-Six Day War population of nearly 84,000 dropped to 12 percent of that number.[16] By 1975, there were fifteen Jewish settlements in the area, but only 1,800 settlers amid an Arab majority at that time of perhaps 10,000. The Israeli settlements in this area were primarily military, rather than agricultural or civilian.[17]

When most Israelis refer to the "West Bank," they mean primarily Samaria (north of Jerusalem) and Judea (south), and that was the real cockpit of the battle to colonize the West Bank. Unlike the Jordan River Valley, Judea and Samaria had a large Arab population in absolute terms (nearly 759,000 on the eve of the 1967 war) and these areas lost through death and flight about 175,000, (that is, about 23 percent) of their Palestinian inhabitants during the war.[18] (It is impossible to know how many of these were "regular residents" of the West Bank and how many were from refugee camps; whatever the exact arithmetic, the displacement and colonization was a real phenomenon.) These areas, mostly upland and situated a distance away from strategic military points, were not colonized primarily for military reasons. Here the colonization process was one of venation. Like a growing leaf, Israeli land confiscations and, then settlements, moved slowly forward. Usually each new settlement was within hailing distance of another. Exact measurements of Israeli colonization in this period are hard to find because, in contrast to the 1950s, the government did not boast of the settlement process. The general outlines are clear, however. Considering the West Bank as a whole (the Jordan Valley, Samaria, and Judea), by 1977, considerably less than half of the land that had been in Arab hands prior to 1967 had been confiscated.[19] Probably an excess of 5,000 settlers were in place by 1977, although this number is hard to verify.[20]

Hence, we can make a rough scorecard on the colonization process (again, one must emphasize that Israeli government secrecy on the extent of the Palestinian displacement and on Jewish colonization dictates that all estimates are necessarily tentative). By 1977, about 40 percent of the previously Arab-held lands in Gaza and well below half those in the West Bank had been confiscated and placed in Israeli hands; Jerusalem was totally under Israeli control, and the Golan Heights were permanently secured; of the roughly 1.4 million Arabs who lived before 1967 in what were to become the "occupied territories," a maximum of approximately 350,000 were induced to abandon their homes and to flee.[21] Their places were taken by roughly 100,000 Israelis (including the numbers that settled in Jerusalem).[22] The number of new Jewish villages in existence, as of 1977, as estimated by two independent sources—Baruch Kimmerling[23] and Ann Mosely Lesch[24]—is shown in the table.

	Kimmerling	Lesch
Golan Heights	25	25
West Bank	28	36
Gaza and Sinai	23	22
Total	76	83

Five comments about this scorecard. The first is that although one is here dealing with territories that the Israelis well and truly conquered, and although Gaza, the West Bank, and the Golan Heights experienced large-scale land alienation, everyone had an investment in pretending that real and permanent conquest had not occurred. Thus arose the fiction of the "occupied territories." From the Israeli viewpoint that vocabulary was useful, for it gave the government flexibility in negotiating with surrounding Arab states. Talking of "occupation" rather than of annexation or conquest of the various Palestinian areas kept the disapproval of the world community a little farther away. In particular, it made U.S. moral and financial support for Israel easier in terms of American domestic politics if the territories were merely "occupied," or (in a term that became common in the 1980s) "administered." From the viewpoint of the surrounding Arab countries, "occupation" rather than conquest or annexation was preferable, because it made things appear only temporary, which is what they wanted to believe about the results of the Six Day War.

Second, the colonization of the West Bank was paralleled by a process of "internal colonization" within Galilee, the only part of pre-1967 Israel to have an Arab majority. A new type of settlement, called the *mizpe* ("the lookout"), was introduced in Galilee. A *mizpe* consisted of a small number of families settled on a strategic location, such as a high point of land that controlled a road or valley. A *mizpe* did not have the usual schools, stores, or other amenities, but depended on nearby towns for such things.[25] In February 1967, the Labor government began a campaign of land confiscation in Galilee aimed at dispossessing thousands of small farmers. This led to the first sign of Palestinian resistance, namely the protest known as "Land Day" conducted on 30 March 1976.[26]

Third, the fact that the "occupied territories" were not (save for Jerusalem) formally annexed to Israel made them easier to govern. This was no paradox; it merely reflects the fact that the Palestinians who lived in the newly conquered lands were not (unlike those living in Israel proper) citizens of the state of Israel, even in theory. Thus they were without civil rights and were controlled by military administrations that did not have to answer to the civil code. Significantly, however, Jews who lived in the "occupied territories" were full Israeli citizens and Israeli civil law governed most aspects of their lives. These are not simply theoretical matters. Everyone in Israel and the territories carried identity cards, and in the newly conquered areas, Arab drivers were issued distinctive license plates so that soldiers could immediately identify them. In the West Bank a system of territorial segregation emerged in which one part of the countryside was inhabited by Arabs, another area, next door, by Jews, creating a patchwork of hostile regions, alienated and disjointed.[27] The situation in the West Bank is strikingly similar to that of Ulster: a system of next-door hatred, with one group clearly on top, and the other with a long memory of its historical grievances, burnishing them, like votary artifacts, and waiting: not necessarily patiently, but waiting, alert and bitter.

Fourth, the Six Day War was of a piece with earlier Israeli economic policies; it built the conquered indigene into the economy as a cheap labor pool. The Gaza Strip and the West Bank provided the Israelis with a new work force, one that was much easier to regulate than was the pool of Palestinian laborers within Israel proper. The manual workers in the newly conquered areas had no affiliations with organized labor and they lived on well-defined reservations. One says "reservations," but one could also say "homelands" in the sense that that term was used in South Africa in the 1970s and early 1980s. The Gaza Strip was very similar to Transkei in that it was a captive labor pool and the "homeland" had very few colonial settlers. The West Bank, on the other hand, resembled Ciskei in that it encompassed both a large body of native inhabitants and was also penetrated in many places by enclaves of settlers. In Israel, as in South Africa in the days of high apartheid, indigenous workers were permitted to leave their homelands to take jobs in the metropoles only under strict conditions. Permits could be cancelled at any time and without explanation.

Fifth, just as in South Africa, the noncolonists benefited in some ways from the economic system (the standard of living for blacks was higher in South Africa than anyplace else in Africa and so too were health standards). In fact, it was part of Israeli government policy in the years 1967–73 (when the economic boom of the late 1960s ended) to use the provision of relatively well-paid laboring jobs as a means of making the Palestinians see the wisdom of being quiet.[28] Here a frequently used surrogate for economic well-being, the infant death rate, is revealing (see table).[29]

Year	Infant deaths per thousand	
	Jews	Arabs
1967	20.8	44.3
1974	19.2	37.0

The health of young children is one of the clearest windows we have on the economic condition of any group. What we see here is that even though the "dual economy" of Israel improved the Palestinians' economic situation, still the Palestinians were much worse off than were the Jewish citizens of Israel, despite their access to the Israeli medical system.

Finally, one must emphasize that behind all the bickering in Israel between 1967 and 1977 about how to deal with the conquered territories, there was a fundamental agreement among the great majority of politically active Israelis that Israel had a moral right to the new territories. The only question was whether it was prudent to exercise those rights.[30]

(2)

The Six Day War fundamentally transformed the nature of the Israeli polity. No longer was Israel simply a settler society. Now it had to control large numbers of indigenous Palestinians. Two other changes bear note. One of these is that the Six Day War changed geopolitics as far as Israel was concerned; the other is that the 1967 victory sparked off a series of animated and charismatic movements aimed at accelerating the "redemption" of the Promised Land. These pushed the Israeli polity more and more into the mode of classic Hebrew covenantal thinking.

Before the 1967 war, Israel was like a small coastal vessel, the sort steered by a captain who stood at the binnacle for hours, steering a compass course by old-fashioned reckoning. Now, after the Six Day War, it suddenly became a modern corsair outfitted with satellite navigational devices and all sorts of high-tech gee-gaws from foreign warlords who saw the use of such a vessel. This occurred because Israel's 1967 victory coincided with (and of course reinforced) a view that had been growing in the United States: Israel was not merely a worthy charity, it was potentially the cornerstone of the American position in the oil-rich Middle East. This relationship was bonded by the geopolitics of the Yom Kippur War: on 6 October 1973, Egypt and Syria made a surprise attack that caught the Israelis offguard. The two superpowers, the United States and the Soviet Union, supplied arms to their respective surrogates: the United States airlifted advanced weapons to Israel and the Soviets airlifted weaponry to Egypt and Syria. By 24 October, the Israelis were victorious and a ceasefire went into force. That this victory was not as great as it could have been was the result of great U.S. pressure and of Soviet threat; the United States believed that too decisive an Israeli victory would preclude a permanent peace in the Middle East.

These events brought to the fore the "special relationship" that developed between Israel and the United States in the 1970s and which continued throughout the 1980s and into the 1990s only slightly shaken. The United States backed Israel's territorial growth as long as the justification was military. For example, President Gerald Ford wrote in 1975 to assure the then-prime minister of Israel, Yitzhak Rabin, that the United States would support the position that "any peace agreement with Syria must be predicated upon Israel remaining on the Golan Heights."[31] It was an accurate indication of the view of the U.S. defense establishment when, in October 1988, 100 retired U.S. generals and admirals signed a full-page advertisement urging that Israel should not give up the West Bank. "The natural barrier and the short border provided by the Jordan River have enabled Israel to control raids and infiltration and to prevent the country from being turned into another Lebanon."[32] Israel's decision to hand over the Sinai to Egypt was at the strong urging of President Jimmy Carter. The only major bump in the road before the late 1980s was the Israeli invasion of Lebanon in 1982, which even Ronald Reagan in his fullest anticommunist phase, saw as going too far.[33]

If Israel became the cornerstone of American policy in the Middle East, the language of the relationship was money. From the foundation of the state of Israel, the United States had always been financially helpful, but in the late 1960s and especially after the Yom Kippur War of 1973, huge amounts of U.S. aid poured in. Whereas from 1948 to 1973 the United States had provided Israel with an average level of $69 million annually; between 1974 and 1981 the average rose to $2.5 billion per year. More than two-thirds of that was for military purposes, the rest for economic and social aid.[34] These monies increasingly were provided on very special terms. In theory, part of U.S. aid was in the form of loans, but these were converted into "soft loans," meaning that since 1984, they have not needed to be repaid. Moreover, to help Israel deal with its other foreign creditors, in 1984 the U.S. Senate stipulated that the U.S. level of assistance should not in any fiscal year be below the level of Israel's intentional debt repayments.[35]

To place in perspective just how large U.S. aid really is, consider the situation in the year 1990. Using round numbers, one notes that Israel has a Jewish population of about 3.5 million, and its 1990 Gross National Product was $33 billion. American aid is approximately $3 billion a year. In other words, roughly 10 percent of Israel's GNP comes from U.S. aid. This is equivalent to sending every Jewish man, woman, and child in Israel $857 annually. Of course, since most of the aid is tied to military spending, much of the money ends up back in the United States. But the arms arrive in Israel, whose demand for weaponry is prodigious.[36]

None of these things—the shifting role of Israel in geopolitics after 1967, the U.S. alliance, the vast amounts of American money, and, perforce, weaponry—changed anything at the heart of the Israeli polity. What these things did was to give Israel a license that it would not otherwise have had: a license to develop more quickly with less hesitation in the direction of classic covenantal behavior. In their own minds, the Israelis always had been situated in a fortress on a hill, and the United States's employing their land as a strategic redoubt fit that image perfectly.

(3)

Thus it was in the decade following the Six Day War that Israeli society was particularly fertile ground for new, or more intense expressions of what it meant to be a state with a mission. Here two groups were important, the Land of Israel Movement and Gush Emunim ("bloc of the Faithful"). Each group was significant in its own right as a shaper of public attitudes and of state policies, and each was an indicator of what was bubbling just beneath the surface of Israeli political culture.

To catch the full flavor of the Land of Israel Movement, one should think of it as "The Whole Land of Israel Movement." It was formed after the 1967 war and its message was simple: the entire Promised Land belonged to the Jewish people, and for the state of Israel to surrender any portion of the Land conquered in the Six Day War would be a moral transgression. The movement directed its energies primarily toward influencing political decision makers. Rael Jean Isaac, the first scholar to document the movement's character, pointed out that it had a broad basis of recruitment, unprecedented on the Israeli political scene.[37] The movement did not draw from any particular social class, from any specific ethnic segment, or from any of the cohorts that traditionally are used to explain political collectivities. The movement's supporters ranged from members of the religious parties and old Irgun terrorists to the center-left of the Labor party. Adherents were bonded by an intense form of local patriotism. Extremely nationalistic, they joined with a fervently biblical sense of the redemption of the Land of Israel in its full scriptural dimensions. In 1968, the movement backed an Israeli settlement in Hebron (a heavily Arab area), by a group of ultrareligious Jews. The government tried to stop the settlement, but was steamrollered. At elections, the movement's goal was to move the entire political spectrum to what is (somewhat misleadingly) called the right. The movement's central point was that the newly conquered lands should be kept not for military reasons, but for religious ones. As one of the movement's leaders explained, it was unthinkable to return any of the "occupied territories" because wars of conquest were mandatory in Jewish tradition in order to redeem the Holy Land.[38]

One of the movement's manifestos stated, "The whole of Eretz Israel is now in the hands of the Jewish people. . . . We are bound to be loyal to the entirety of our country—for the sake of the people's past as well as its future, and no government in Israel is entitled to give up this entirety."[39]

Another one of the leaders explained that the justification for keeping newly conquered territories was the same as the justification for setting up the state of Israel in the first place. " If someone says we have no right to Judea and Samaria because there is an Arab majority there, then there was no moral basis in the past for our settlement. . . . Why was settling Mishmar Haemek socialist implementation, and doing the same thing in the Jordan Valley today fascism?"[40]

This melding of extreme Israeli nationalism and religious traditionalism was taken to a higher level of intensity by the foundation of Gush Emunim in March 1974. Gush Emunim was a broad coalition of what is referred to as the "settler movement," groups strongly in favor of the colonization of conquered Arab lands, the West Bank and the Gaza Strip in particular. Its members were universally against returning even a square meter of land to the Palestinians. Gush Emunim founded several settlements in heavily Palestinian areas and did so against the government's wishes. Some supporters of Gush Emunim engaged in harassment and violence against Palestinians in the "occupied territories" as part of a policy of keeping tensions high and thus increasing governmental reluctance to withdraw from these areas.[41]

In a shrewd analysis of the roots of Gush Emunim, Gideon Aran of Hebrew University has shown that the merging of the demands of traditional, biblically based religion and its imperative of "redeeming" Eretz Israel with extreme Israeli nationalism resolved a major set of contradictions within Israeli society. Traditional Zionism, Aran notes, had always been potentially at odds with religious orthodoxy. In the first twenty years of the Israeli state, the Labor-dominated government had employed as much religious imagery and traditional vocabulary as possible in its evocation of the state, but this was a palliative measure. David Ben-Gurion interpreted the state of Israel as a transcendent entity, and although this sacralized state worked for some people, to orthodox leaders it came close to idolatry. What Gush Emunim did was to keep the focus, white-hot and precise, on the topographic character of Eretz Israel and upon the settlement of the entire area by Jews. By going back to the earliest scriptural texts, the parts of the Bible that defined the Promised Land and told the people to conquer it, the religious purpose of the Israeli people was declared to be the same as the purpose of the state, so long as it kept and colonized the "occupied territories." Thus, twentieth-century Israeli nationalism and some of the most ancient parts of the original Hebrew covenant were joined.[42]

The Land of Israel Movement and Gush Emunim were leading sectors

in levering the entire Israeli political spectrum away from the older generation of politicians who, though they frequently employed religious language, believed themselves to be in charge of a secular state. The old way
of talking, which was consciously to speak in metaphor, *as if* the Israeli
state were transcendent and had a prophetic mission, was replaced by a
new mode. Now, increasingly, metaphor was replaced by literal belief that
the biblical definition of "the Land" was the proper one and that God had
directly ordered Jews to take the land and to cleanse it.

If the Land of Israel Movement and Gush Emunim were emblematic of
something widespread in Israel after the Six Day War, we should not
mistake its character. This was not a religious revival in the traditional
sense. Although orthodox religion probably has gained slowly since
1967, the nation was far from being observant. An informed estimate
published in 1971 said that roughly one-fifth of Israelis were fully observant and that another one-third were partially observant. This means that
about 45–50 percent were nonobservant.[43] (The word "secular" is sometimes misleadingly used for this group; these people were definitely Jewish in their identity, so "nonobservant" is more accurate.) What actually
was happening was not a widespread revival of traditional practice, but
rather a *permeation* of all sectors of Israeli society, observant, semiobser-
vant, and nonobservant, with the ways of thinking that stemmed from
traditional Hebrew religion. The deputy prime minister said in his 1974
Independence Day speech that the Bible is what unites all Jews, "from
atheists to the most religiously devout." He was being neither ironic nor
literary. The Bible increasingly was recognized by all segments of Israeli
society as being a fundamentally religious document, not just a cultural
archive as the old-fashioned Labor-Zionists had believed it to be.[44] "Religion became an increasingly important legitimizing factor after 1967,"
Charles Liebman observed. Before the Six Day War, "it was fairly easy to
justify the demands of the state upon its citizenry in terms of Israel's
physical survival. After 1967, when survival seemed more secure, and
when Israel itself laid claim to newly acquired territory on the basis of its
'historical rights' as well as on security grounds, and when it confronted
an indigenous population which not only disputed that claim but the very
foundation of the state, Israeli legitimacy required reinforcement." "In the
case of Judaism," said Liebman, the notion of historical rights necessarily
involves "religious associations and religious claims." Liebman added, "I
do not believe that the process was anything but an unconscious one. But
that does not make it any the less significant."[45]

Independent confirmation of the permeation of all sectors by traditional religious ways of thinking (however unconscious this may be, as Liebman notes), is found in research conducted by the Israel Institute of Applied Social Research. In the early 1970s this group studied Jews' concepts of their rights to "the Land." One question was particularly revealing. It can be paraphrased as follows: "Do you accept as a basis for Jewish possession of the land of Israel, rights that go back to the Bible?" The percentages of each group espousing biblical legitimation are shown in the table.[46]

	Years of education		
Group	0–4 (%)	5–10 (%)	11–plus (%)
Weekly attend synagogue on Sabbath and festivals	84	83	86
Occasionally attend synagogue on Sabbath and festivals	74	68	56
Sometimes attend synagogues on High Holidays	70	57	45
Never attend synagogue	68	49	39

It is not surprising that the more religious the person was, the more often a biblical basis for Jewish rights to Eretz Israel was espoused. More noteworthy is that 59 percent of the entire sample accepted biblical legitimation for Israeli rights and, second, that even in the least religious sector of the population (persons with at least a high school education who never attended synagogue), almost four-tenths believed that Israel's rights stemmed in part from the scriptures.

Granted, there still existed an ever-diminishing band of old fashioned "secular" Jews, mostly of Ashkenazic background, who harked back to the socialist-humanist beliefs of many pre-1948 Zionists. In the *Jerusalem Quarterly* in 1988, Yehoshua Arieli, emeritus professor of history at Hebrew University, presented a quiet lament titled "On Being a Secular Jew in Israel." He chose his title "to suggest my growing sense that the position of the Jewish non-religious sector in the country has become more and more problematical, and to point to the growing tendency to delegitimatize its rights to shape its public and private life in accordance with its convictions." He continued, "We are reaching a state of affairs where Israel is the only country in which the legitimacy of being a secular Jew is questioned."[47] Revealingly, Arieli provided from his own secularist perspective a definition of what Jewishness meant within the context of Israeli society.

The fundamental concept of Jewishness refers to a totality of traits of a distinct collective existence which identifies a people, a land, a language, a history, a divine revelation, and a divine purpose: the sanctification of the land, of the life of the individual and the people, by fulfilling the revealed will of God and living according to his law. Jewish religion is not a framework of individual redemption, a church or institution for grace (ecclesia), but the instrument, the way and content of fulfilling the revealed will of God—to be a holy people.[48]

That definition is an unintentional, but concise, explanation of why, after 1967, many persons found that true secularity in Israel was a difficult and diminishing possibility.

(4)

The outward and visible sign of Israel's having gone over a societal watershed was in the "earthquake of 1977."[49] This was the general election that ended, perhaps permanently, the hegemony of the Labor party, which had been the dominant element in every coalition since the foundation of the state in 1948. The Likud union of parties, headed by Menachem Begin, came to the fore and since 1977 has been the leading party: not dominant, for the Israeli system of proportional representation virtually precludes any party obtaining a pure majority. But because it serves as a magnet to the small religious parties, Likud has been the most powerful party since 1977, even when, on a strictly party vote count, it has had fewer Knesset seats (as in 1984) than did Labor. The kaleidoscopically complex petty details of Israeli electoral life should not obscure what happened. Great shifts had occurred in Israeli culture after the Six Day War, but these were like tectonic plates shifting below the surface of the earth, so when they finally were made manifest on the surface of everyday political life, everyone was surprised, not least the electoral forecasters, few of whom had foreseen Likud's triumph.

Likud is frequently referred to as being part of the "political right," and that is a useful shorthand as long as one understands that the "right" in Israeli politics is not analogous to the right any place else. For example, it has nothing to do with "free enterprise" as opposed to state involvement in economics. Likud is only marginally less inclined to state action than is Labor, and, in reality, in Israel the state has a larger role in economic life than in any of the Western European social democracies. Milton Friedman, the great advocate of "free enterprise" and an informed observer of Israel, wrote a letter in the spring of 1990 to the then-finance minister, Shimon Peres, decrying the "incredibly long and complex list of government restrictions" on free enterprise. Friedman concluded, "One of the great paradoxes of history is that no people has benefited so much from free-market capitalism as the Jews, yet no people has done so much to undermine capitalism as the Jews."[50] The "right" in Israel means "religiously animated": not necessarily orthodox, not distinctive of any particular Jewish sect, but given to understanding the world in traditional Jewish religious terms and partial to the use of ancient Jewish myths and symbols not just as emblems but as literal realities.

The geneaology of Likud is nothing if not pure. It goes directly back to Vladimir Jabotinsky whose "revisionism" was the most aggressive form of Zionism in the Yishuv era. Jabotinsky's program was simplicity itself. His 1923 article "The Iron Wall" is one of the foundations of present-day Israeli colonial policy: an iron wall of bayonets, he argued, had to be placed between Palestinians and Jews. In 1925, Jabotinsky founded the League for the Revision of Zionist Policies and in the early 1930s he withdrew this league from the framework of conventional Zionism as embodied in the World Zionist Organization. In 1931, the revisionists had established their own paramilitary terrorist organization, Irgun (Irgun Zvai Le'emi, also called "Etzel"). Irgun, which in the late 1930s and early 1940s fought Christians, Arabs, and other Zionists, came under the control of Menachem Begin in 1944. When the new state of Israel came into being, Begin formed the Herut party and claimed the heirship of revisionism. Herut's platform demanded Jewish sovereignty on both sides of the Jordan River, this presumably to be achieved by force. The Herut was a minority party: it received 11.5 percent of the vote in the 1948 general election and this had risen only slightly by the early 1960s. In 1973, however, Begin was able to convince two other parties that also had biblically framed beliefs about Greater Israel (the Liberal party and La'am) to join with Herut and form the Likud bloc. Likud's platform called for the permanent retention of Judea, Samaria, and Gaza, thereby establishing Jewish sovereignty over western Eretz Israel, defined as the territory between the Jordan River and the Mediterranean Sea.[51]

That Israeli political experts were as surprised as everyone else by the Likud victory in 1977 (43 of the 120 seats in the Knesset, a massive achievement under Israeli's dotty proportional representational system) should not be held against them. The changes in cultural outlook that had been moving so quickly since 1967 were "soft" changes, the sort that do not manifest themselves in politics until late in the game. But what the political scientists of the era should have been aware of was the existence of a massive demographic lever, namely the former minority, now a majority, the "Orientals." The facts are simple. Individuals of "Oriental" background (sometimes called "African-Asian Jews" or "Arab Jews," meaning Jews whose origins were in Arab lands) became a majority in the 1970s, and because of their high birth rate, a growing one. A reasonable estimate is that in 1978, persons of Oriental background made up 52.1 percent of the Jewish population of Israel.[52] It was clear that the Orientals strongly preferred Likud to Labor: 65 percent in 1977 and 71 percent in 1984.[53] This allegiance went back a long way, right to the tap roots of Likud. Although the line of succession within Likud had been wholly Ashkenazic—Jabotinsky to Begin to Yitzhak Shamir, who was born Yizhak Yzernitzsky in Byelorussia—these leaders have had a particular sensitivity to the opinions of the non-Ashkenazim. Jabotinsky, for example, learned Ladino and supported the Sephardic pronunciation of Hebrew. Begin was an appropriate leader for the Orientals. "Like them, he felt no need to apologize for being Israeli," writes Paul Johnson. Begin "shared their hatred of Arabs. . . . Like the Oriental Jews, he regarded the notion that the Arabs had the choice of granting or withholding Israel's right to exist as an insult to the dead. . . . In strict contrast to the Labour establishment, he and the Oriental Jews had a common and precious characteristic: a complete absence of any feelings of guilt."[54]

But certainly the Oriental Jews felt resentment, toward the Ashkenazic establishment that controlled the Labor party and its institutional associations, such as the Histadrut. The actual degree of resentment cannot be quantified,[55] but the reasons for it are easily found. For example, in the late 1970s, the average income of Oriental Jewish families was 80 percent of that of the average Ashkenazic family.[56] Significantly, not only were Orientals underrepresented in the most prestigious occupations, but the gap was greater among native-born Israelis than among immigrants.[57] That meant that things were worse for sons than for their fathers, a serious cause of discontent. During the 1970s, the educational gap between persons of Oriental and of European origin declined slightly, but it still was very marked. The table shows the participation rate in academic education by people between twenty and twenty-nine years old, expressed in terms of persons per 10,000 in the relevant group.[58] Because these differences were so large and because this cohort reaches its peak earning

Foreign-born Jews	
European background	842
"Oriental" background	211
Israeli-born	
European parentage	1,405
"Oriental" parentage	299

years in the mid-1990s, it is clear that the lower occupational status and earning power of the Oriental Jews will continue until well into the twenty-first century.

As a result of the strong pressure within Israeli society to perceive the country as a spiritual unity, Israeli political scientists long resisted understanding the "Orientals" as anything other than a social class phenomenon, and thus a transient one. It is to the credit of Eliezer Ben-Rafael's pioneering work that it is now impossible to ignore ethnicity as a major phenomenon within Israel. He has documented, for example, the persistence among Yemenites in Israel of ethnic identity over three and even four generations.[59] Not only are there separate ethnic identities (Yemenite, Moroccan, etc.) among Israeli Jews, but the Orientals as a group share a constellation of characteristics, and this has been empirically demonstrated. Charles Liebman has noted that the flood of Oriental Jewish immigrants in the late 1940s and 1950s "included a disproportionately large number of religiously traditional immigrants for whom religious symbols bore their traditional resonance and for whom Zionist-Socialism had no meaning."[60] A survey conducted in 1969 revealed that Oriental Jews were half as likely to show little or no commitment to the religious aspect of Jewish identity than were Israelis of European background.[61] A number of other studies have demonstrated that the Oriental Jews were markedly more hostile toward Arabs than were those of European ancestry.[62]

In noting this second fact, I imply no moral judgment. One should merely speculate on why this anti-Arab attitude, virtually hatred, has been so commonplace among Oriental Jews. The first (and I think the most important reason) is that the anti-Arab attitude was based on the reality of a shared collective experience. Oriental Jews, with their origins in North Africa and the Middle East, had been very badly treated in several satrapies that were the heirs of the fragmented Ottoman empire. At best, the Jews in Arab countries had lived on sufferance, at worst as untouchables and pariahs. So it was hardly surprising that when, in Israel, they had the chance to walk upright, they stood and shook their fists at their former persecutors, or at the nearest substitutes, the Palestinians. Within families, the folklore of the hard life in the old Arab countries was passed down from parent to child, so that the offspring of the Orientals were raised with an abiding hatred of Arabs.

But there was something more to it than that. The experience of the Orientals *in* Israel made them more anti-Arab than ever. One straightforward reason is that the Oriental immigrants frequently were sent to development towns, most of which were in remote areas near the borders, where they were the target of Palestinian terrorist attacks. And even if they never were directly attacked, their experience as human pickets in the Israeli fence made them continually conscious of their vulnerability and of the Palestinian danger. Further, most of the Orientals were from Arab countries and sometimes they were denominated "Arab Jews." But even without that appellation, there was no disguising the fact that they had their roots in the Arab world. When the so-called Orientals wished to distance themselves from their Arab backgrounds, they did this by showing extreme anti-Palestinian attitudes and by following those political leaders who most desired to unite Israel as a holy nation in pursuit of the redemption of the whole Land of Israel.[63] What may be called the "Joe McCarthy" factor may have been operative as well. This concept comes from the fact that the keenest followers of Senator Joseph McCarthy's anticommunist crusade in the United States were Irish Roman Catholics who used the crusade as an opportunity to attack the old WASP establishment for being unpatriotic. In the same way, the Oriental Jews, by being unswervingly anti-Arab, have been able to call into question the soundness of the Ashkenazic establishment, among whom there is a notable covey of doves on the Palestinian issue. And, finally, there is the matter of displaced aggression. Although the Orientals can direct some of their bitterness for being treated badly in Israel toward the Europeans, there is a limit to how far they can go. Anger cannot be employed to question the legitimacy of the state of Israel or the corporate identity of Israelis as a special people. So the non-European Jews channel some of the animus at their second-class status toward the nearest acceptable target, the Palestinians.

All these ideas are useful in grappling with the filigree of post-1967 Israeli society, but they should not distract us from the central point: for whatever reasons, the growing Oriental majority in Israeli society pushed the polity in the direction of the classical covenantal worldview. The Orientals, being more committed than the non-Orientals to traditional religious beliefs, accelerated the adoption of the use of biblical referents, not as cultural icons, but as geomagnetic points upon which to orientate the entire life of the nation. Traditionalism reinforced the demands for maintaining control of the "whole" Land of Israel. The high degree of anti-Arab, especially anti-Palestinian, prejudice in the Oriental population reinforced the scripturally based desires to keep Eretz Israel out of the hands of the modern equivalent of the Philistines and the Canaanites. And, equally important, the traditionalism of the Oriental Jews helped to bring to the fore the sacred-profane distinction that is so central to covenantal thinking and which is especially crucial when sorting out human beings. The Jews were sacred, the Arabs profane, and this was not a point to be debated, but a divine injunction to be respected. It was the duty of the sacred to subdue the profane.

(5)

Immediately after the "earthquake of 1977," Israeli governmental policy concerning the definition and colonization of Eretz Israel shifted. In William Harris's words, "The romantic religio-nationalist drive to redeem the historic 'Land of Israel' by Jewish colonisation, a drive which had posed such a threat to the credibility of the Labour government in its last years, now dominated the apparatus of the state."[64] The government of Prime Minister Begin effected several changes immediately. One of these was ideological. The balance between "pragmatic" and "biblical" considerations was shifted further toward the biblical end of the spectrum. For example, colonization policies frequently were adopted that were of no advantage to Israel's defensive posture, or they made no economic sense; they were adopted simply because the lands being colonized were in Eretz Israel as defined in the books of Moses. In geographical terms, this meant that the focus of colonizing efforts shifted from such points as the Golan Heights into areas of the West Bank, especially the Samarian highlands, that had little strategic value.

Simultaneously, a policy of "thickening" existing settlements was adopted. This involved increasing the number of settlers and the size of the area under their control in each settlement. Surprisingly (and somewhat paradoxically, given Likud's devotion to the concept of the Land of Israel's being held conjointly by all the people), in September 1979 the private purchase of land in the West Bank was approved. This was not an indication of any belief in "free enterprise" but a way of speeding Jewish settlement in the West Bank with very little cost to the government. In the actual event, not a great deal of land was involved (about one-fifth of the land acquired by Jews in the West Bank between 1977 and 1987 was acquired privately), but Likud's willingness to abandon temporarily the honored policy of collective ownership of land gives an idea of how much it wanted to expedite colonization in Samaria and Judea. (This new policy was quietly back-burnered when, in 1985, it turned out that large-scale fraud had obtained in the private land acquisitions and that bribery of senior civil servants had occurred.)[65]

When Menachem Begin took office as prime minister in mid-1977, there were 36 West Bank settlements (counts vary slightly). By June 1981, there were more than 100.[66] The table indicates the number of Jewish colonists in the West Bank as of 31 December of each year up to 1985.[67]

1976	3,176
1977	5,023
1978	7,361
1979	10,001
1980	12,424
1981	16,119
1982	20,600
1983	27,500
1984	42,600
1985	52,000

In the same time period, the portion of land in the West Bank that was reserved exclusively for Jewish use (whether acquired through confiscation or by private purchase) reached 70 percent.[68] (This was up from well below 50 percent when Begin's Likud took power.)

This increase occurred because Likud added two new techniques to the well-tried battery of methods of alienating Palestinian lands. One of these new methods, adopted in 1980, was to make "Declarations of State Land." All uncultivated land that was not registered to a private Palestinian owner was vulnerable. This acquisition was based on the incongruous assertion that the Israeli state was the direct heir to the framers of the Ottoman Land Code of 1855, under which lands uncultivated and unregistered belonged to the state. Under the 1980 Israeli act, roughly 40 percent of the West Bank was put on a register of seizable land. In a complementary activity, the Israeli state claimed all former Arab state lands on the West Bank. The rationale in this case was that Israel was the heir of the Ottoman empire, a mordant little irony. As a result of these combined processes and of the confiscations that followed in their train, approximately 32 percent of the land of the West Bank had been declared Israel's state land by mid-1985.[69]

The other new technique was to amend the Jordanian Town and Village Planning Law of 1966 to serve as a colonization tool for Israel. Under the amended planning act, Israeli "comprehensive master plans," and "special planning zones" were decreed in areas around Jewish settlements. Areas inhabited by Palestinians were zoned for housing, public institutions, and industry, all of which were exclusively for Jewish use. The plans having been promulgated, the Palestinians were removed. Meron Benvenisti's 1986 Report on the West Bank gives specific examples of this process at work. One noteworthy point was the ubiquity of this method. By the end of 1985, there were 191 such plans in operation in the West Bank.[70] Each of these plans was a tiny and efficient piece of colonial social planning. And, crucially, each was legal. Indeed, that is one of the foremost characteristics of the entire process of the displacement of the Palestinians, from the end of the 1948–49 war onward: it was meticulously legal. That is one of the central characteristics of covenantal societies: a deep respect for the law.

This concern with law and with legalism was taken almost to the point of parody as far as the civil law in the West Bank was concerned. Israeli settlers have enjoyed all the rights of Israeli citizens even though, technically, they live outside of Israel. (Israel has not yet annexed the territories; it still "occupies" or "administers" them.) In 1984 the settlers' rights as Israeli citizens were explicitly affirmed by the Knesset. The settlers live under a separate set of laws from the Palestinians. Rather than assimilate the Palestinians in the West Bank to full legal rights, the Israeli government has insisted that the Palestinians are still governed by Jordanian law, of which the Israeli military administration merely happens to be the heir. Thus, total legal segregation reigns: one set of laws for Jews, another for the non-Jews. In 1981, the Israeli government framed a set of proposals to which it still adheres: that the Palestinians would be granted "autonomy" as far as local administration was concerned, if they would cooperate with the military administration in the West Bank. The outlines of this proposal were strangely similar to the "self-government" that was being developed in the same era in the black homelands of South Africa. The Palestinians showed little enthusiasm.[71]

In 1983 Begin was diagnosed as suffering from "endogenous depression" and he resigned as prime minister. He was succeeded by his former foreign minister, Yitzhak Shamir. Born in Byelorussia in 1915, Shamir had emigrated to Palestine in 1935. During the Arab "revolt" of 1936, he found his way into extreme politics. He became an instructor in the Revisionist Youth Movement and then a member of Irgun. He gravitated to the far extreme of the Irgun, the Stern Gang, a terrorist squad whose members rejoiced in the epithet "the maddest of the mad." The Stern Gang was responsible for a series of terrorist raids against British authorities in the pre-1948 period, including the murder of Lord Moyne, the United Kingdom minister for Middle East affairs. Irgun was responsible for the Deir Yassin massacre in the winter of 1947–48, in which more than 200 Arab villagers were rounded up and killed.[72] Uncontestably, Shamir was a hard-liner and he well understood the methods required of a colonial power. Undoubtedly, he understood the parallel between the Catholics in Northern Ireland and the Arabs in the West Bank and Gaza. How else could he tell a crowd of cheering Englishmen on Christmas Eve, 1987, that Irish rebels must be crushed "like grasshoppers," and their heads smashed against the walls of Westminster Abbey?[73]

In 1984, Likud and the Labor alignment ended a general election in a virtual dead heat. After thirty-eight days of negotiation, they formed a government of "national unity." In a bizarre system of sharing, Shamir and Shimon Peres alternated the top office and their fractious followers interlaced with one another in a cabinet that was well described as a marriage of inconvenience. This menage did not come apart permanently until the spring of 1990 when, first, the Labor alignment tried and failed to form a government and then Likud, by making concessions to the ultrareligious parties, assumed power on its own.

The salient point about the politics of the 1980s is that despite the intense bickering and despite the 1988 general election in which Likud was more hawkish on the "occupied territories" than was Labor, the actual difference between Likud and Labor was not great and was diminishing. "The Israeli electorate sensed also that the ideological rift dividing Labour and Likud had narrowed down to a mere difference of style," Meron Benevenisti noted in the mid-1980s.[74] In fact, during the 1980s the whole political spectrum was shifting toward the Likud end, which meant that increasingly politics were fought in a vocabulary formed by traditional biblically based religious concepts. As for the various "occupied territories," it no longer mattered very much which party or what sort of coalition was in office. "The seemingly opposed political cultures appeared to have enough common ground to reach a compromise formula concerning day-to-day activities in the territories, especially with regard to the settlements," Benevenisti remarked.[75] It now became a matter of bureaucratic self-interest for various parts of the Israeli state to impel the colonization process forward.[76] This worked because the general population was more and more of one mind, a hawkish one, about the conquered land. A survey conducted by the Guttman Institute of Applied Social Research in April 1990, showed that 59 percent of the populace approved of forcing the Arabs to leave the conquered territories, while offering them some form of compensation for being driven out. And 56 percent approved of full annexation of the conquered territories, while providing "autonomy" to the Arabs (that is, giving them reserves or homelands to live on).[77] When Yitzhak Shamir formed his government in June 1990, the program outlined at the beginning of the Knesset session (equivalent to the Queen's Speech in parliamentary democracies) included these declarations concerning the Land of Israel:

> —The eternal right of the Jewish people to Eretz Israel is not subject to question, and is intertwined with its right to security and peace;
> —United Jerusalem, Israel's eternal capital, is one indivisible city under Israeli sovereignty;
> —Jerusalem will not be included in the framework of autonomy [homelands, reservations] that will be granted to the Arab residents of Judea, Samaria, and the Gaza Strip, and its Arab residents will not participate, either as voters or as candidates, in elections for the establishment of representation of the residents of Judea, Samaria, and the Gaza Strip.
> —Settlement in all parts of Eretz Israel is the right of our people and an integral part of national security; the government will act to strengthen settlement, to broaden and develop it.[78]

How the indigenous peoples of the West Bank and the Gaza Strip will be treated in the future is impossible to predict, but there is a certain hard logic that cannot be avoided. Despite a myriad of options, alternatives, and "peace plans" by various groups, the fundamental fact is that the pattern of territorial mixing of settler and indigene, of Palestinian and Jew, in Judea, Samaria, and the Jordan Valley is now so intricate that the repartition of any part of the West Bank is impossible without the massive relocation of human beings. In the past, such resettlements have always meant tragedy.

(6)

The reason for paying close attention to the evolution of beliefs and actions as they affected the territories conquered in the Six Day War is twofold: (1) the ways the Israeli polity has dealt with the problems and opportunities provided by the acquisition of the West Bank, Gaza, Golan Heights, and Sinai are litmus tests that indicate fundamental values, attitudes, and ways of thinking; and (2) the "occupied territories" were in themselves a catalyst, one that stimulated Israel to develop further along the path to their reborn covenantal culture. Now, some readers may find this contradictory, for how can the same set of events be both a litmus test and a catalyst? Here, recall the Heisenberg Uncertainty Principle. It held that, for example, one could think accurately of an electron as a particle, or one could consider it, also accurately, as a wave, but one could not hold both of these true positions simultaneously. Fair enough: if one is considering the origin of the set of changes in the cultural wiring of Israeli society that occurred after 1967, then the acquisition of the "occupied territories" certainly is one major cause. And if one, at a different moment, wishes to assess how far the polity had gone along on the road to adopting a covenantal mindset, then how the government, the settlers, and the electorate acted concerning the territories is a very good gauge.

In either usage, it is clear that from 1967 onward, something very nearly congruent to the ancient Hebrew covenant was knitting together. The overarching concept of the Promised Land was continually in the forefront of political life, and the "redemption" of the land was never out of mind. Maintaining control of the West Bank (and to a lesser extent, Gaza) was justified both on military and biblical grounds, but, increasingly, biblical terms dominated: it is our land, past and future. This biblical thinking, of course, was historical thinking, and that is one of the key characteristics of covenantal thought. Significantly, even people who declared themselves complete secularists frequently had their minds formed by biblical historical modes. For example, A. B. Yehoshua, one of Israel's major novelists and a committed secularist, indicated this pervasive sense. "Here we can argue about bones and graves from over 3,000 years ago," he said. "Here at home everything belongs to you."[79] There, however inadvertently, is encapsulated a central aspect of covenantal thought: history gives us our home in the Land.

Another feature: the emphasis on law and on legalistic thinking that is so fundamental to covenantal thought characterizes all of Israeli society. Nowhere is law more important than in the myriad rules and regulations that have facilitated the consolidation of Jewish colonies in the recently conquered parts of Eretz Israel. In handling the "redemption" of the land from 1948 onward, and especially from 1967 to the present day, successive Israeli governments have acted on the presumption that actions that are legal are morally right. That the Palestinians doubtless have just the opposite view of Jewish law and its morality is hardly a drawback, for, if the modern equivalents of the Canaanites think one thing, then in the Hebrew covenantal framework, that confirms the opposite.

Blood sacrifice, on behalf of the land and for the benefit of the corporate entity of the Israeli people, has developed as a major motif in Israeli popular culture. It is not by happenstance that Israel's president, Chaim Herzog, wrote a book called *Heroes of Israel: Profiles of Jewish Courage,* which recognizes instances of bravery from Joshua in ancient times to Yigal Allon to David Ben-Gurion to the IDF commandos who effected the Entebbe rescue in 1976 in Uganda.[80] "Contractual behaviour . . . seems to be endemic to Jewish political culture," Daniel J. Elazar has written.[81] Nowhere is this more true than in present-day Israel. The overarching contract is between the people who collectively have taken possession of the sacred land and who hold it in collective ownership, rather than permit it to be fragmented into private ownership. Of course, there is another major figure in the covenant and that is the Almighty. As Elazar notes, the covenantal worldview "suggests that man and God are partners in the management of the world."[82] The supernatural nature of the senior partner in this contract sometimes makes it difficult for modern nations to deal directly with the Israelis.

Resistance to the idea that Israel is quickly finding its way to becoming a full-born covenantal polity is apt to come most strongly from the North Americans, and especially those who have a nodding acquaintance with Israeli politics and friends and perhaps relatives in Israel. "There's cousin Tami, and my old school chum Susan, now Chai Sarah, and, why, one of them is an atheist and the other was last in synagogue for her brother's bar mitzvah." Granted. But consider that for the last two generations North Americans have had ties almost exclusively with the Ashkenazic Zionists and their descendants. And, further, North Americans have dealt almost entirely with those who speak English. English-speaking Israelis tend to be much more highly educated than the general Israeli population; are more apt to be committed to North American values, such as belief in equality of civil rights; and are more likely to disapprove of religiously-rooted privilege.[83] The general Israeli population, however, now has an "Oriental" majority and is inaccessible both to speakers of English and of Yiddish, and is not in favor of liberal western values. When David Levy, an Oriental Jew who became foreign minister of Israel, cannot speak English, it should drive home the fact that most North Americans have been maintaining contact with a portion of Israeli society that is rapidly becoming atypical and secondary. And given the massive American aid to

Israel, the Israeli government has every interest in North Americans' continuing to perceive Israel through their experience with this "comfortable" group rather than dealing with the real Israeli populace.

If I am correct in believing that the covenant is locking together, piece by piece, in modern Israel, then we will find that, as in other places where we have seen the covenant in operation (ancient Israel, and among the Ulster-Scots and the Afrikaners), Israel will have very specific interactions with those outside of the covenant. When the covenantal grid is working efficiently it (1) tells those inside the society how to deal with outsiders and (2) it is strengthened and confirmed by the very act of dealing with outsiders. Here three recent test cases are illuminating: the *intifada*, the *aliyah* of Soviet Jews, and the Gulf War of 1990–91.

The *intifada* (uprising) among the Palestinians is well known the world over, because it has made good television. Unlike the Palestinians' resistance to Israeli rule in the past, this time their actions were visually dramatic and that has made all the difference to the outside world. The program of resistance began in late 1987 in the West Bank and Gaza and took everyone by surprise, not least most Palestinians. The stone throwing, rioting, and petrol bombing, aimed at the Israeli army, was notable for the participation of young people. Previously the strong Palestinian family structure had permitted parents to keep their young off the streets, but now the children defied their parents. Economic boycotts against Israeli concerns followed the rioting. Then, in late 1990, just as the IDF thought it was getting on top of the trouble, events took a new turn: individual Palestinians, in suicide missions, began knife attacks on randomly chosen Israeli settlers. Thus the *intifada* careered along, right up to the start of the Iraq-U.S. war of January 1991 (since then it has been in abeyance).

That the Palestinians would revolt is a surprise to no one, but why the uprising started when it did is a great mystery and one suspects that its specific causes will not be known with certainty for years. Up to the start of the 1980s, the efficiency of the Israelis in holding down the Palestinians was amazing. In 1988, for example, there were approximately 64,000 Israeli settlers in the West Bank and 2,500 in Gaza amid a total of perhaps 1,500,000 Arabs in those two areas (precise numbers are impossible to obtain). Even considering the presence of the IDF, this is a colonist-to-indigene ratio markedly higher than the white-to-black ratio in South Africa.[84]

That said, the ratio of colonist to native explains why heavy repression was the only possibility, given the Israelis' fundamental assumptions. One could hardly allow anything resembling democracy as a solution, because the Palestinians would not accept the notion that the "occupied territories" were properly part of a Jewish state. Besides, democracy was not applicable to the Palestinians. They were a profane people. "Democratic rules do not apply to the Palestinians because the territories are under military occupation," an Israeli political essayist commented, tautologically, "and because these rules are alien to Arab culture." He explained further that Arab thought "derives from a totally anti-democratic Arab political culture."[85] Therefore, the Arabs had to be treated undemocratically.

Faced with a very narrow range of operational choices, the Israelis must have found a certain plangency in the advice that the former U.S. secretary of state, Henry Kissinger, gave in January 1988:

> Israel should bar the media from entry into the territories involved in the present demonstrations, accept the short-term criticism of the world press for such conduct, and put down the insurrection as quickly as possible—overwhelmingly, brutally, and rapidly.[86]

Israel's leaders did not take Dr. Kissinger's advice, and this perhaps explains why, unlike Kissinger, none of them has yet won a Nobel Peace Prize. What they did instead was to fall into the same trap as did the Royal Ulster Constabulary in the 1970s in Belfast and Londonderry. "We were playing into the rioters' hands . . . making fools of ourselves in the press," commented a spokesman for the Royal Ulster Constabulary in the spring of 1988. "We watch films of Israelis attacking and we think, 'that's what we were doing ten years ago.' It looks bad and it doesn't really work."[87] That is the doleful honesty for which the Ulster-Scot is known, and it is right on both counts.

A tally kept by the Jerusalem bureau of the Associated Press indicated that in the first year and a half of the *intifada* at least 430 Palestinians were killed, 25,999 injured, 6,599 imprisoned—85 percent without trial.[88] According to the *Washington Post,* 21 Israelis were killed in the same period and 1,121 injured.[89] The world saw much of the violence on television and read of it on the front pages of newspapers. As a result, Israel managed the unprecedented triple of being condemned (late in 1989) by an Amnesty International investigative report, by the Middle East branch of the International Commission of Jurists (also late in 1989), and in the spring of 1990 by former U.S. president Jimmy Carter who undertook his own investigatory mission.[90] In an attempt to limit future violence, the U.S. secretary of state, James Baker, told the Israeli foreign minister, David Levy, in October 1990 that the United States wanted a freeze on all settlement activity in the territories conquered during the Six Day War.[91]

Far from breaking the Israelis away from their policies, this virtually worldwide condemnation of Israeli actions in the "occupied territories" served to harden them. Just as most of the Israeli settlers in the territories live in self-contained laagers, communities surrounded by barbed wire and segregated from the enemy all around, so the polity within Israel surrounded itself with intellectual barbed wire and refused to hear the words of the outsiders. Was not the *intifada* an offense against Eretz Israel? And did not the world's condemnation of Israel's defense against the *intifada* place Israel in the position of being a righteous fortress amid the profane? When, in December 1990, the United Nations Security Council passed a resolution condemning Israel's deportations of a few (actually, only four) Palestinians from the "occupied territories" and promised to protect the Palestinians in the territories by monitoring conditions there, it was an unusual vote for only one reason: for the first time the United States supported an anti-Israeli resolution in the Security Council. Israel was unmoved.

If the *intifada* confirmed the terrible, ultimate loneliness that every covenantal culture experiences, the other recent development, the *aliyah* of Soviet Jews, has confirmed another: that the land and the people are one and that by their having "redeemed" so much of the Land of Israel, the Israelis have been given the resources to save hundreds of thousands of their fellow Jews, and of drawing the members of the diaspora to their rightful historical homeland. In their turn, the new Soviet arrivals will make possible the further "redemption" of Eretz Israel, either by being settlers in the conquered territories themselves, or, more likely, by strengthening Israel's population base and thus making it easier for *sabra* to become colonists in the West Bank and Gaza. When the Likud government of Yitzhak Shamir was sworn into office in June 1990, the first items on the government's policy slate were as follows:

1. (a) In recognition of a shared fate and of the common struggle for the existence of the Jewish people in Eretz Israel and in the Diaspora, and in order to realize the central goal of the State of Israel—the ingathering of the Jewish people to its land—the government will place immigration and absorption foremost among its national objectives.
(b) The government will act to accelerate immigration from all lands and will act to save persecuted Jews.

(c) The government will act to create the social, economic, and spiritual conditions for the speedy and successful absorption of the immigrants in their homeland.[92]

The actual number of Soviet Jews who arrived in Israel in 1990 exceeded by two to five times what had been considered realistic official estimates: 200,000 arrived, including 12,000 in the last week of the year.[93] Expected numbers for 1991 were roughly another 200,000. This decline from the previously projected 300,000 to 400,000 was the result of the Gulf War and, of longer-term significance, of the poor performance of the Israeli economy.[94] The Gulf War sharply reduced incomers. Nevertheless, these numbers are harbingers of a continuing Soviet Jewish *aliyah,* which is perfectly consonant with Eretz Israel's purpose under the ancient Hebrew covenant: to be the Promised Land. Mind you, it is necessary to engage in a degree of willful blindness concerning one aspect of the Soviet migration: no serious observer has suggested that Israel is the first choice for a new homeland on the part of most Soviet Jews. Most, certainly, would prefer the United States, but a tacit agreement (and, I suspect, the next generation of historians will discover an explicit one) between Israel and the United States has channeled the great bulk of them to Israel. In fact, in September 1989, one could observe the interesting phenomenon of President George Bush preaching Zionism to American Jews. He suggested to them that it would be no tragedy if few Soviet Jews came to the United States, since the state of Israel was open to these migrants. Then, he put teeth in his remarks, by placing strict limits on the number of Soviet citizens who would be accepted as refugees by the United States. During the year 1990, this was limited to 50,000, of whom an estimated 30,000 would be Jewish. Most important, as of 1 October 1989, the U.S. administration stopped processing Soviet citizens' applications for refugee status at embassies outside of the Soviet Union. Previously, potential Soviet refugees could go to Rome or Vienna and there obtain a U.S. refugee visa. Now they could apply only in Moscow, which is to say, only with very great difficulty: it is very hard to prove persecution if the Soviet authorities permit one to go to the U.S. embassy, and if one does not go, then, of course, one cannot apply.[95] So, like a giant spillway on a large river, American policy diverted the flow of Soviet Jews to Israel.

Although it is undeniable that the level of religious observance among Soviet Jewish migrants to Israel is lower than that of Israel's general population, the Soviet influx has not upset the evolving covenantal mentalité. For one thing, the presence of Soviet migrants permits the Israelis to reduce sharply the number of Palestinians from the West Bank and Gaza that they permit to work in Israel, and perforce this allows greater segregation of Arabs from Jews. An informed estimate indicates that whereas before the Soviet Jewish influx, 120,000 Palestinians from the conquered territories had been given permits to travel to Israel proper for employment, this number had dropped to 50,000 by May 1991, as a consequence of Soviets taking the jobs.[96] Second, it is a mistake to think that the Soviet Jews, although less steeped in traditional Jewish culture than are most Israelis, are inevitably less committed to strongly "covenantal" positions. Writing in the *New York Review of Books* in mid-1991, Avishai Margalit revealed the results of a privately conducted survey of the views of new Soviet immigrants. The study, done in 1990 by a professional polling organization, revealed that the immigrants were markedly more hawkish on most geopolitical issues than was the bulk of the Israeli population. About 85 percent of the immigrants believed that the Arabs both could and should be expelled both from Israel and the territories conquered in 1967. This compares to 70 percent of Israeli Jews who held that expulsion should be carried out if this were feasibly politically, and to 15 percent who believed it not only was desirable but actually possible. Only 2 percent of the Soviet immigrants thought that the Israeli government should deal directly with the Palestine Liberation Organization (PLO), whereas one-quarter of the Israeli Jewish population favored such negotiations.[97]

In a remark that was in equal portions indiscreet and transparently honest, in March 1990 Prime Minister Shamir stated that a big immigration required "a big Israel."[98] What he meant was that if enough Soviet Jews arrived, then this would make it easier for the Israelis to overcome the extremely high birth rate of Palestinians in the West Bank and Gaza.[99] And that would make it easier for Israel to complete its colonization of the conquered territories: either by permitting an eventual Jewish majority in those areas, or, if push came to shove, by strengthening the army that would expel the Palestinians. By early 1991 it was common to talk of a million Soviet Jews migrating to Israel. Under the Law of Return (as amended) anyone with at least one Jewish grandparent has the right to settle in Israel, which makes possible wildly optimistic projections. For example, a calculation by an ultraorthodox rabbi of Soviet background ran as follows: there are at present 2 million Jews in the Soviet Union with two Jewish parents, another 1 million with only a Jewish mother, another 2 million with a Jewish father, and a total of 14 to 18 million with at least one Jewish grandparent; of that number it is "realistic" to think that some 5 million are interested in emigrating to Israel.[100] A cooler appraisal would set the number at well under 1 million, perhaps half a million.

More realistic has been the planning of Ariel Sharon, advocate of a Greater Israel, and, for a time, minister of housing. He indicated in the later months of 1990 and again in 1991, that Soviet *olim* (immigrants) would not be sent to the "occupied territories." However, he pointed out that "there is a severe influence by Arabs in Samaria, Judea and Gaza on our Israeli Arabs, who are getting more and more involved in terror and violence." Although he would not settle the new arrivals in the territories, for fear of endangering the Soviet exodus, Sharon planned on settling larger numbers of Soviet Jews along the old borders between Israel and the West Bank and Gaza. There they would serve as a buffer, cutting off Palestinians in the "occupied territories" from "our Israeli Arabs." Also, as an extension of the conquest of Jerusalem in 1967, Sharon avowed, "We are going for a massive construction plan in the heart of Jerusalem, at least 5,000 homes a year for the next eight years, most of them in East Jerusalem."[101] Thus, the "redemption of the land," the victory over the profane inhabitants of the land, and the ingathering of the Jewish people were locked integrally together.[102]

Some Israeli authorities worry that a large proportion of Soviets are not true Jews, which poses a special problem to the covenantal mindset. Rabbi Shilo Rafael, speaking at the annual conference on oral *halachah* in Jerusalem in August 1990, claimed that "for sixty rubles now you can get a birth certificate saying you're Moses's grandson." He added, "Thousands of immigrants have false documents stating that they are Jewish."[103] Various speakers at this conference, whose theme was "Immigration Absorption in the Light of *Halachah*," raised other knotty questions. Should Soviet Jews with questionable documents be required to convert formally to Judaism before being allowed to marry? And, were the divorces of Soviet female Jews valid, since most of them had not obtained a *get* (a religiously sanctioned divorce) from their husbands? Part of this concern with the Jewishness of the Soviet migrant reflected a realistic observation that the level of religious practice was low among Soviet Jews, as compared with that of Israeli Jews. But, mostly it reflected something within Israeli society, for it is doubtful that large numbers of non-Jews would wish to migrate to Israel, no matter how easy it might be to obtain false documents. That the worries were generated within Israeli society is clearly shown by a tiny wave of hysteria that began in mid-1990 when the Ministry of the Interior reported that as many as one-third of the Soviet

Jewish immigrants were not really Jews at all. This idea stemmed from the fact that only 68 percent of Soviet Jews had registered as Jews with the Interior Ministry in the first three months of 1990. Officials of the ministry then reported (inaccurately, as it turned out) that 30 percent of the Soviet and 65 percent of the Romanian *olim* were actually registering themselves as non-Jews. Interior Minister Aryeh Deri publicly warned that non-Jews "had been hitching a ride at Israel's expense and within a few years you will find them sitting on their suitcase."[104] Upping the ante, the absorption minister, Yitzhak Peretz, declared that the percentage of non-Jews was even greater than the interior minister had established and he warned that "we shall soon be getting twice as many non-Jews as Jewish immigrants.[105]

In fact, the real number of non-Jews turned out to be about 5 percent of the total. The Soviet Jews who had not registered in the first three months of 1990 (upon which all the hysteria was based) came in later in the year and an overwhelming majority of them registered as Jewish.

Yet in its very inaccuracy, and the speed with which the matter became a widespread public issue, points to the location of a sensitive nerve center in Israeli society. The interior minister had a considerable, if short-lived success, when he suggested that the Law of Return should be further amended to ensure higher levels of Jewish purity. One can react to the culture's sensitivity to the level of "Jewishness" of the new arrivals by criticizing "the seeming intent to claim Israel for a 'pure' race" as did one American letter writer to the *Jerusalem Post*,[106] but that drive for purity is a fundamental characteristic of the covenantal mindset, going all the way back to the books of Moses. Sorting out those within the body corporate from those who are outside is an absolute prerequisite for the continued existence of God's people.

Just as both the *intifada* and the *aliyah* of Soviet Jews went to the heart of what counted in Israeli life, so too the Gulf War confirmed the central directions that I have here been chronicling. The invasion of Iraq in 1990 and the subsequent United Nations's victory over the Iraqis changed nothing in the Israeli outlook, except to deepen the existing trends. The Gulf War once again placed Israel in the position of being a fortress, a citadel under siege. The Israelis understood, even if the outside world frequently forgot, that if Iraq actually possessed nuclear and biological warheads for its missiles, then they would fall primarily (and probably solely) on Israel. Thus, for a time, all of Israel became one giant Masada, a citadel on a hostile plateau.

This classic covenantal situation was reinforced by Israel's regaining the unchallenged moral ascendancy amid world Jewry. Before the Gulf War, support for Israel among diaspora Jews had been eroding, especially in the United States where the *intifada* was perceived as having parallels to the American civil rights movement of the 1960s. This changed overnight. The moment that Israel was physically besieged, it regained the moral high ground in the Jewish world. This had the important side effect of stimulating American Jews to lobby hard for U.S. government support for Israel.

What held for diaspora Jewry held even more within Israel. The Gulf War upheld the morality of the Israeli position. The nation had been attacked by evil forces situated outside Eretz Israel, and these forces had been traitorously encouraged from within Israel by the Palestinians. Therefore, the Palestinians were confirmed as evil and thus their demands for civil rights and for a cessation of Israeli colonization in the conquered Palestinian territories could be dismissed. Indeed, as the Gulf War closed, the Israeli government speeded up settlement on the West Bank. In reply to the suggestion by American authorities that this was provocative and an impediment to the "peace process," in August 1991 Housing Minister Ariel Sharon gave a classic covenantal answer: "What provocation? Is it provocation for Jewish families to want to live in their homeland?"[107]

This is not a position that outsiders, especially the U.S. government, either can or will understand fully. In particular, the United States has pushed hard for a freeze, or at least a severe limitation, on further Israeli colonization of the lands conquered in 1967. What will eventually occur is open to a wide range of guesses, but political scientists would do well to heed the words of Finance Minister Yitzhak Modai, who made it clear that Israelis should be willing to accept deep cuts in U.S. aid rather than to give up the right to control Eretz Israel fully. "We're a stiff-necked people," he said. "Whoever doesn't remember that should read the Bible."[108]

(7)

Hypotheses.

Despite the trumpery of academe, hypotheses that deal with the infinitely complex world of real human beings are really just two things: intuitive suggestions as to how things worked in the past and guesses as to how they will develop in the future. So the reader can easily test my hypotheses about the way the Israeli polity behaved from 1948 onward, and especially after 1967. Does the historical pattern make a bit more sense than it otherwise would if one perceives the Israelis as moving more and more into the classic covenantal template, as set down by the ancient Hebrews in the first five books of the Bible? And second, is my prediction—that Israel will fit that template more and more closely by the late 1990s—correct?

Part V

ENVOI

12

Conclusion: Living with God's Peoples

(1)

Beyond all of the details, the various national histories, and the complex historiographies that I have presented, I hope that I have succeeded in communicating my own sense of wonder at the structural integrity and the perdurance of the basic cultural constructs of the ancient Israelites. That the bedrock beliefs of the ancient Hebrews were laid down even before they became an iron-using people, and that these beliefs (however gentled and tidied up by later redactors) not only survive in our own time, but continue to be an independent and formative force in the history of nations, can only make one stop in awe, as one would do upon encountering some fantastic primordial natural phenomenon.

The covenant of the ancient Hebrews, with all of its legends, magical practices, obsessions, and taboos, seems to me to form the single most powerful cultural construct yet built by humankind: in fact, so strong is it that many people can deal with it only by positing its origin as divine. The ancient Hebrews' mode of thought prefigured both Christianity and Islam, and neither of those later religions has managed to escape their vassalage to ancient Israel, struggle though they may to do so. The only modern faith which in its consistency and in its demands for personal commitment to a transcendant collective identity had a chance of being a serious and independent rival to the ancient paradigm—communism— has in our own time come apart so decisively as to make one wonder if it ever will be fully revived. Three or four millennia will tell, one of the ancient patriarchs might suggest.

Only with considerable humility can we approach the ancient Hebrew covenant and its modern derivatives. In part this is because of the covenant's enduring power. It is also because the ancient covenant is something that we cannot quite step totally outside of, so fundamental is it to western thought. The if-then empiricism and, crucially, the very historical modes of thought that we employ, are based upon lessons the ancient Hebrews taught us. Of course an analogical argument such as mine is by its very nature metaphorical. My hope is that this set of analogies, based upon a wide range of historical information concerning these three peoples, will help us to deal with them as part of our world—just as their base metaphor, the covenant, helps them to understand and deal with their world. The use of analogy in this manner is one of the ways whereby we can move a fair distance away from the helplessness that we otherwise experience when we try to come to terms with the ancient Hebrew world while still being part of its solar system. Employing historical analogies is rather like dealing with the old discipline of Euclidean geometry, in which one can prove beyond dispute the congruity of certain figures, even without being informed independently of the actual absolute dimensions of any one of them. That is not full knowledge, but it is knowledge nonetheless.

In a loose way, to point to the character and influence of the ancient Hebrew covenant is to design a theory, and it shares the risks inherent in any such exercise. Unless one has been living underground for the last decade, one is aware that the single most influential development in the study of history internationally has been the infusion of the discipline with the tenets and habits of mind of what is called emcompassingly "critical theory." A veritable curry of academic herbs and spices—sprigs of everything from physical anthropology to structural linguistics to old-fashioned New Criticism to new-fashioned New Historicism are stirred in—critical theory has added a certain piquancy to historical scholarship. At its best, it has reminded observers of history of something that we always knew, namely that each society has actively constructed its own view of the world, of its own history, and of the evidence for that history. Historians and readers of history, being members of society, are not merely passive consumers of empirical evidence, but are active in shaping interpretations of evidence and in decoding and recording its meanings for the larger society. Being reminded of this situation can help all of us to be careful and to be humble and to avoid the God-like omniscience we too often assume, by virtue of our knowing how, in a limited historical period, things turn out.

My own recognition of our need for humility when dealing with the ancient Hebrew covenant and its modern derivatives comes less from reading critical theory, however, than from talking to friends who are mathematicians, statisticians, and pure physicists—and also from reading that extraordinary historian of manners (the Jane Austen of our dyspeptic century), Kingsley Amis. His Fat Englishman noted: "Most patterns are illusions based on insufficient evidence. An observer seeing red and black at roulette coming up alternately six times might conclude that he'd found a pattern, this was how it always went. Then red comes up twice running. End of pattern."[1] This does not mean that no patterns exist, merely that they often are more apparent than real, and that we must be especially humble, and work especially hard, when describing what we think is a historical pattern.

Even more so must we be humble when it comes to explanations. It is here that mathematics and pure physics come in. One of the most interesting developments in recent years has been "chaos theory," a widely divergent body of work that is to classical science what dodecaphony is to classical music: one of the things that begins where the classics end. The field of chaos study is a remarkably humbling one, for essentially it asks why scientists cannot predict anything very interesting. Chaos theory is said to have begun in the 1960s with the work of Edward Lorenz, a meteorologist who tried to use the then-state-of-the-art computer techniques to predict weather systems. After all, if scientists can predict the tides with great precision, why not the weather? But, in fact, Lorenz found that it is almost impossible to predict the weather for any given spot on earth with any degree of accuracy for more than three or four days in advance. This, it turned out, was not just a matter of having enough data or big enough computers. Ultimately, Lorenz came to the conclusion that, by their very nature, weather systems can never be predicted. Other scientists, working on other topics, were coming independently to the same conclusions during the 1970s and 1980s: a good deal of the natural world is unpredictable, no matter how much information one has. Classical science was built upon the analysis of patterns that were contingent (one event depending on a preceding event), linear (the effects were always in direct proportion to the causes), and repetitive. The trouble is, many of the most important things in the world are contingent, but nonlinear and nonrepetitive, and if the weather is among these, so too is the evolution of life forms. The inability of scholars to predict the weather over the next million years is not the result of insufficient data or a paucity of knowledge of the interrelationships in complex systems, but a result of the nonlinear aspects of these systems.[2]

This behavior would be humbling enough even if we could re-create and rerun several million times the sequence of events that potentially occurred in shaping our world, for at least then we would have an indication of the directions that chaos could have taken us. But in the real world we have only one case study out of those potential millions of cases, the way things actually did evolve, physically, and ultimately biologically and socially. In essence all life—and all human society—has evolved in a deterministic system characterized by what is (from our viewpoint within the system) a high degree of randomness. Stephen Jay Gould has described much of evolution as neither a rationally analyzable fight for survival nor a calculable process of genetic sifting, but instead, as a "grand scale lottery" in which randomness as much as anything else sets off the major series of contingent events that make our world. As Gould points out, if the film of our collective history as life forms on this planet were rewound and started again, the story would come out differently each time we let the story run forward to the present.[3]

The implications of chaos theory for the sciences are as troubling as they are obvious. Practitioners must still look for patterns and must form explanations as has been done in the classical sciences. Yet now it is with the background realization that what is being perceived may not be part of any unalterable pattern or of any set of regular long-term relationships, but merely one of the seductions that occur when chaos expresses its variant nature in apparent order.

This realization makes the historical mode of thought more important than ever, and it becomes imperative that historical thinking be done well. The really interesting things in our world—such as the development of life forms, the evolution of the human species, and the development of human society—are beyond the traditional scientific ways of thinking. Although laboratory science with its traditional tools—particularly in its reliance on repetition under controlled conditions of events—can give us some help, we need a deeper way of thinking to deal with the unique and chaos-influenced world in which we live. "Historical explanations are distinct from conventional experimental results in many ways," Gould writes. "The issue of verification by repetition does not arise because we are trying to account for uniqueness of detail that cannot, both by laws of probability and time's arrow of irreversibility, occur together again. . . .

We can explain an event after it occurs, but contingency precludes its repetition, even from an identical starting point."[4]

Hence, we must be aware that the patterns I have presented may not be patterns at all, but merely random splashes on the pond of history. That possibility I accept. What I will not accept are know-nothing reductionist arguments which claim that one cannot generalize from large populations. Of course one can: a myriad of statistical techniques describe general tendencies in large populations, without denying the existence of variations from the central trends, and one can achieve the same end with words. I have been very careful to point out in my three modern case studies not only the generalized tendencies of each population, but deviations from these generalizations. Thus, any suggestion that I have been reviving the long-discredited concept of "national character" is facile and misplaced.

At the heart of my argument, antecedent even to the concept of the covenant, is a simple assertion: ideas count. And, second, the ideas that count most are religious. Of course economic and technological developments are significant levers in effecting societal change, but to see them as the key to most major events is tantamount to confusing science with engineering. L. A. Siedentop is right when he asserts that "ideas or beliefs *are* the most important social force of all, the greatest source of social change and the primary dissolver of traditional social ties."[5]

This is not to reject the usefulness of the mirror twins of modern thought, Marxist-Leninism and neo-classical economics. Within a limited range each helps us to deal with certain historical matters, such as why a certain production technique was adopted at a certain time in a given industry, or why a given labor union went on strike when another did not. But neither tells us anything very interesting. In their unremitting emphasis on market relations, the two systems resemble a physiologist who explains the development of agriculture as occurring because the human body needs food. True enough, but the really intriguing question is why certain forms of gathering, hunting, and farming developed when they did. A coarse physiological analysis gives us no insight into that question, any more than a materialist system, focused on the market, explains very much about the myriad forms that human interactions have assumed. Yes, ideas count.

Yet I do not want to take the importance of ideas to the point of parody as has been done of late within the body of "critical theory." To say, as some critical theorists do, that all is idea and nothing else, is to walk into a world inhabited chiefly by Bishop Berkeley. Words (and therefore ideas) refer to something "real," however vaguely, and one only has to observe a serious deconstructionist giving his order in a decent restaurant to realize that in his heart he believes that words often refer to real things. Otherwise, why does he make such a fuss about the Mornay sauce not being too thick?

For most of the world's cultures, "belief remains paramount," Siedentop argues. "And they take for granted that religion provides the core of belief. Religion provides the constituents of personal identity, the crucial sources of social integration, and the key to the nature of things."[6] He does not, of course, mean religion in the narrow, institutional sense, but rather the broader belief that the material world is only a minor part of a larger transcendental order and that knowledge of this overarching order comes more by extrarational means than by simple empiricism or cold rationality. It is particularly important that we engage this religious sense when we deal with the history and the present of nonwestern cultures, and of cultures on the periphery of the west, such as the three analyzed in this book. If we focus primarily on the marketplace (whether from a Friedmanite or a Trotskyite perspective, or anything in between), we gain a false clarity, but only at the price of reducing our understanding.

(2)

Our three cultures, the Ulster-Scots, the Israelis, and the Afrikaners, are not merely historical groups. They live in today's world. So it is entirely fair to ask how the outside world should deal with those cultures that derive from the ancient Hebrew covenant. That question is the same whether uttered by an official of the United Nations, or the president of the United States: How shall a policymaker approach people who keep score on a scoreboard that is invisible and about four millennia old?

First, and most important, the policymaker must take them seriously. This is not an otiose point. It is easy for outsiders to perceive covenantal cultures as being hopelessly archaic, irrational, and morally benighted. Even if these were accurate assessments, simply denouncing a given society or treating it as if it came from the Pleistocene era is not going to work.

In addition, perceiving that culture solely from an outsider's viewpoint only obscures one's understanding of it. Covenantal cultures must be assayed from the viewpoint of the people within them, and while to do so may require an almost volitional schizophrenia on the viewer's part, it is an absolute necessity if one wishes to effect communication. If successful, the observer will understand how a given set of facts can have totally different meanings depending on cultural context, and schizophrenic or no, this is one's only hope for real understanding.

Many people automatically assume that societies dominated by the covenantal cultural outlook necessarily are to be treated as enemies. That is a third trap for any policymaker to avoid, for although covenantal cultures make hard enemies, they also make superb allies. Their emphasis on the long term, on loyalty, and on corporate identity means that they are much more trustworthy than are more conventional allies.

Beyond doubt, one of the most important elements in understanding and approaching the covenantal mindset is patience, more patience than most people believe is possible. Covenantal societies think in terms of substantial chunks of time, at least decades, and sometimes centuries. Their immediate response to any outside threat is to assume that they can outlast it, and they are usually right. Only when a covenantal society is convinced that its friend (or foe) is there to stay, can the relationship be considered in a timeframe that is part of its definition of reality.

In the short run, any pressure placed upon a covenantal society to do or think any specific thing will produce the opposite effect. Because covenantal cultures see themselves as holy peoples, surrounded by the profane, outside pressure immediately strengthens the internal solidarity of the people. Moreover, because pressure for a certain sort of change (for example, the MacBride principles, which demand Catholic employment in Northern Ireland, the abandonment of apartheid, or civil rights for Palestinians) comes from outside, then whatever goal is being sought must be seen as automatically wrong, in the short run at least. The only way that pressure on covenantal societies can work is if it is applied evenly, and over many, many years.

The language of covenantal cultures is unique, and vital to the society's understanding of itself, and anyone who wishes to begin to understand these societies must learn to speak in their language, a language of historical sequences, of law, and of if-then propositions. To guy their language, or to misunderstand its components, is to misunderstand the society as a whole, and, consequently, to be misunderstood. Anyone wishing to influence a covenantal culture must learn to speak in its codes.

And, too, geography is vital to covenantal cultures. The idea of the Land is crucial; to ignore its very precise topographical coordinates is to ignore the very core of such societies.

There are those who have tried to gull covenantal societies and those who will try to do so in the future. Doing so is virtually impossible. One aspect of these societies that makes them so difficult to deal with is their consuming empiricism. The if-then mode of thought means that they deal in terms of sequences of cause and effect; they continually test assertions of fact. To approach a Chosen People with generalities, then, is to misunderstand who they are and what they cherish. To promise what one cannot deliver, to make threats that one will not carry out, is to fail to understand who these people are.

Conversely, if one wants something specific from a covenantal culture, one must be precise in specifying just what that is. Covenantal societies have a long history of painting their rocks green when someone wants to be shown a nice pasture. For instance, in the twentieth century, South Africa, Northern Ireland, and Israel all have adopted the trappings of liberal parliamentary democracy, with public election campaigns, secret ballots, and open parliamentary debate. In each case, however, the system was skewed so as to preclude democratic rights for, respectively, blacks, Roman Catholics, and Palestinians. Only by observing closely can we see the rock face beneath its paint.

Because within covenantal cultures compromise is taken as a sign of weakness, the leaders of these nations must be given plenty of room to talk to themselves and their constituents, to become accustomed to the potential for change, and to convince themselves that the idea was theirs all along. As the cases of South Africa and of Northern Ireland show, a society can slowly redefine itself so as ultimately to accept quite radical changes, rather than go to war to resist them.

A policymaker who ignores any of these realities ignores the very core of what a covenantal culture is about. And that would be to fail to communicate, to fail to understand, and to invite failure in dealings with these, God's peoples.

(3)

The Hebrew covenantal structure has lasted from the middle Bronze Age to the present. It is one of the few things in human society that we can take for granted in the sense that it will be here longer than we will. Indeed, much longer. Modern-day Israel is only the most recent society to conform to the covenantal blueprint, but it will not be the last. Others will follow, for the covenant, as found in the books of Moses, is particularly suited to the sorts of smaller societies that are inevitably produced as great empires come apart and as small ethnic groups become independent of their former masters. Far from disappearing, I believe, the covenantal cosmology, based on the ancient Hebrew template, will be one of the most effective ways for a myriad of small nations to fortify themselves in a world that will increasingly be confusion and whirl.

Notes

1. The Oldest Code

1. Dan Jacobson, *The Story of Stories: The Chosen People and Its God* (New York: Harper and Row, 1982), p. 10.
2. Ibid., p. 13.
3. Immanuel Wallerstein, in "AHR Forum," *American Historical Review* 93 (October 1988), 881.
4. Edward Pearce, *Sunday Times,* 20 November 1988.
5. The scholar who has written most successfully about Israel, South Africa, and Ulster in my judgment is Conor Cruise O'Brien. His relevant works are cited in the chapters that follow. Although he has not directly compared the three cultures, comparison implicitly runs through his work. Two specific volumes by other scholars warrant the reader's attention. The first is *The Elusive Search for Peace: South Africa, Israel, and Northern Ireland,* ed. Hermann Giliomee and Jannie Gagiano (Cape Town: Oxford University Press and Institute for a Democratic Alternative for South Africa, 1990). Unlike most volumes based on conference proceedings, this one works. It is very present-orientated and pragmatic—no vice, given the state of the three societies. I also admire Stanley B. Greenberg's *Race and State in Capitalist Development: South Africa in Comparative Perspective* (Johannesburg: Ravan Press and Yale University Press, 1980), and this despite his comparative framework being totally different from mine. The book is fundamentally Marxist, clearly written, and honest. My respect for Greenberg's scholarship is enhanced by my learning that in his more recent work he has dropped Northern Ireland from his framework as being too complicated to handle.
6. A very useful guide to the extraordinarily rich secondary literature (albeit a slightly dated one), is Horace D. Hummel's 1966 bibliographic addition to Herbert F. Hahn's *The Old Testament in Modern Research* (1954; Philadelphia: Fortress Press, 1966), pp. 263–310.
7. Robert Stone, "The Reason for Stories: Toward a Moral Fiction," *Harper's Magazine,* June 1988, p. 72.
8. Northrop Frye, *The Great Code: The Bible and Literature* (Toronto: Academic Press Canada, 1981).
9. See William Foxwell Albright's introduction to the 1957 edition of *From the Stone*

Age to Christianity: Monotheism and the Historical Process, 2d ed. (Garden City, N.Y.: Doubleday Anchor Books, 1957). This is a reprint with a new introduction of the classic 1946 edition. Paul Johnson, in his highly serviceable *A History of the Jews* (New York: Harper and Row, 1987), provides a useful summary of the present scholarly opinion on the dating of early history of the Israelites (pp. 3–79).

10. Johnson, p. 32.

2. A Very Big Deal

1. Daniel J. Harrington, *Interpreting the Old Testament: A Practical Guide* (Wilmington, Del.: Michael Glazier, 1982), p. 56. I am of course being willfully anachronistic in my comparison of ancient and modern idioms, but the resonance of the phrases is undeniable.

2. William Foxwell Albright, *From the Stone Age to Christianity: Monotheism and the Historical Process,* 2d ed. (Garden City, N.Y.: Doubleday Anchor Books, 1957), p. 165.

3. Henry Wheeler Robinson's 1935 essay and a companion piece from 1937 have been conveniently reprinted as *Corporate Personality in Ancient Israel* (Philadelphia: Fortress Press, 1964).

4. Harold Bloom, "Introduction," in Harold Bloom, ed., *Genesis* (New York: Chelsea House, 1986), p. 5.

5. Henry Wheeler Robinson, *The Old Testament: Its Making and Meaning* (London: University of London Press, 1937), p. 2.

6. Harrington, pp. 32–38.

7. Judah Goldin, *The Song at the Sea, being a Commentary on a Commentary in Two Parts* (New Haven: Yale University Press, 1971), pp. ix–x.

8. Horace D. Hummel, "Survey of Recent Literature," in Herbert F. Hahn, *The Old Testament in Modern Research* (1954; Philadelphia: Fortress Press, 1966), p. 272.

9. Frank O'Connor, *The Backward Look: A Survey of Irish Literature* (London: Macmillan, 1967).

10. I am paraphrasing an observation made by Dan Jacobson, *The Story of Stories: The Chosen People and Its God* (New York: Harper and Row, 1982), p. 25.

11. Louis Ginzberg, "Rabbi Israel Salanter," in Judah Goldin, ed., *The Jewish Expression* (New Haven: Yale University Press, 1976), p. 44.

12. Henry Wheeler Robinson, *The Religious Ideas of the Old Testament* (New York: Charles Scribner's Sons, 1927), p. 55.

3. The Afrikaners: A Culture in Exile, 1806–1948

1. See T. Dunbar Moodie, *The Rise of Afrikanerdom: Power, Apartheid, and the Afrikaner Civil Religion* (Berkeley: University of California Press, 1975), p. 179. Moodie's analysis of the 1938 celebrations is the best available. See esp. pp. 175–96.

2. Ibid., p. 184. His source is *Die Burger* (n.d.).

3. "Every Afrikaner I interviewed, of whatever political persuasion, recalled the events and activities of the 1938 centenary with deeply personal intensity. The sacred history was constituted and actualized as a general context of meaning for all Afrikanerdom in spontaneous liturgical re-enactment during the 1938 celebrations." Moodie, p. 180.

4. Johannes Meintjes, *The Voortrekkers: The Story of the Great Trek and the Making of South Africa* (London: Cassell, 1973), p. vii.

5. Alan Paton, in Theo Sundermeier, ed., *Church and Nationalism in South Africa* (Johannesburg: Ravan Press, 1975), p. 51.

6. The development of historiography as a field of analysis among South African historians has much deeper roots in the Afrikaans-speaking community than among An-

glophones. Afrikaner historians began serious historiographic analysis roughly a quarter of a century before English-language writers did. One can take as a starting date the inaugural lecture of F. A. van Jaarsveld, *Ou en Nuwe wee in die Suid-Afrikaanse Geskiedskrywing* (Pretoria: University of South Africa, 1961). It was followed by *Die Hervertolking van ons Geskiedenes*, a joint effort of van Jaarsveld, Theo van Wijk, C. F. J. Muller, and G. D. Scholtz (Pretoria: University of South Africa, 1963). Another study was edited by G. Cronje, *Aspecte van die Suid-Afrikaanse Historiografie* (Pretoria: J. L. van Schaik, Beperk, 1967). Among van Jaarsveld's other historiographic essays are *Wie en wat is die Afrikaner?* (Johannesburg: Tafelberg, 1981) and *Omstrede Suid-Afrikaanse Verlede* (Johannesburg: Perskor, 1984). The first English-language historiographic monograph of any substance was Harrison M. Wright's *The Burden of the Present: Liberal-Radical Controversy over South African History* (Cape Town: David Philip, 1977), and not until the mid-1980s was much more of substance done. (I exclude bibliographic essays.) David Yudelman included an engaged and engaging chapter, "A Critique of the Historiography of Modern South Africa," in *The Emergence of Modern South Africa: State, Capital, and the Incorporation of Organized Labor in the South African Gold Fields, 1902–39* (Cape Town: David Philip, 1984), pp. 13–51. Christopher Saunders, *C. W. De Kiewet, Historian of South Africa* (Cape Town: Centre for African Studies, University of Cape Town, 1986), dealt chiefly with a single figure, albeit an important one. Only in the late 1980s did historiographic monographs by English-language historians appear: Christopher Saunders, *The Making of the South African Past: Major Historians on Race and Class* (Cape Town: David Philip, 1988); and Ken Smith, *The Changing Past: Trends in South African Historical Writing* (Johannesburg: Southern Books, 1988).

7. Michael Streak, *The Afrikaner as Viewed by the English, 1795–1854* (Cape Town: C. Struik, 1974).

8. Anthony Trollope, *South Africa* (London: Chapman and Hall, 1878), 2:10.

9. Ibid., 2:15.

10. Mrs. Lionel Phillips [Dorothea Sara Florence Alexandra Phillips], *Some South African Recollections* (London: Longmans, Green, 1899), p. 16.

11. Ibid.

12. Ibid., p. 15.

13. Trollope, 2:12.

14. Ibid., 2:14.

15. Phillips, pp. 13–14.

16. The most interesting exception to the trend in Victorian assessment of the Afrikaners was that of the noted historian James A. Froude, who was sent by the earl of Carnarvan in 1875 to investigate events in the Orange and Transvaal republics. His report, dated 10 January 1876, included not only contemporary impressions, but a historical background to the ongoing difficulties. Viewing the Afrikaners as people of immense courage and their Great Trek as "one of the most singular chapters in modern history," Froude noted that, though often wrong in their dealings with the natives, "if their conduct is compared with that of ourselves or any other people under similar trials, they will not be found to have deserved exceptional censure." See J. A. Froude to earl of Carnarvan, 10 January 1876, in *Correspondence respecting the Proposed Conference of Delegates on Affairs of South Africa* [C. 1399], H.C., 1876, lii, esp. p. 72. It should be noted that Froude was convinced of the necessity of force in dealing with what he believed were lesser peoples. His *English in Ireland*, published in 1872–74, held that natural rights to liberties were philosophic fantasies and that the superior force of mankind had a duty to rule the weaker. What this meant for the Irish vis-à-vis the English is obvious, and one can easily conjecture what it meant for the native inhabitants of South Africa.

17. Dan O'Meara, *Volkskapitalisme: Class, Capital and Ideology in the Development of Afrikaer Nationalism, 1934–1948* (Johannesburg: Ravan Press, 1983), p. 5.

18. Ibid., p. 5.

19. Marianne Cornevin, *Apartheid: Power and Historical Falsification* (Paris: UNESCO, 1983).

20. Leonard Thompson, *The Political Mythology of Apartheid* (New Haven: Yale University Press, 1985), pp. 12, 13, and 17.

21. For a recent treatment, even more reductionist than Thompson's, see Jay Naido, *Tracking Down Historical Myths: Eight South African Cases* (Johannesburg: Ad. Donker, 1989).

22. David Harrison, *The White Tribe of Africa: South Africa in Perspective* (Berkeley: University of California Press, 1981), p. 18; Conor Cruise O'Brien, *Passion and Cunning and Other Essays* (London: Weidenfeld and Nicolson, 1988), p. 142.

23. Hermann Giliomee and Richard Elphick, "The Structure of European Domination at the Cape, 1652–1820," in Elphick and Giliomee, eds., *The Shaping of South African Society, 1652–1820* (London: Longman, 1979), pp. 362–65. The works they criticize directly are Charles Boxer, *The Dutch Seaborne Empire* (London: Hutchinson, 1965); and Sheila Patterson, "Some Speculations on the Status and Role of the Free People of Colour in the Western Cape," in Meyer Fortes and Sheila Patterson, eds., *Studies in African Social Anthropology* (London: Academic Press, 1975), pp. 160–205. In the case of Patterson, who is a historical anthropologist, the criticism is somewhat unfair. Her article is not about Afrikaner belief systems, and the references to Calvinism in it are quite peripheral. Patterson's viewpoint is more clearly developed in *The Last Trek: A Study of the Boer People and the Afrikaner Nation* (London: Routledge and Kegan Paul, 1975).

24. Heribert Adam, "Perspective in the Literature: A Critical Evaluation," in Heribert Adam and Hermann Giliomee, *The Rise and Crisis of Afrikaner Power* (Cape Town: David Philip, 1979), pp. 16–60.

25. Elphick and Giliomee, p. 363.

26. W. A. de Klerk, *The Puritans in Africa: A Story of Afrikanerdom* (London: Rex Collings, 1975), p. xiii.

27. André du Toit, "Ideological Change, Afrikaner Nationalism, and Pragmatic Racial Domination in South Africa," in Leonard Thompson and Jeffrey Butler, eds., *Change in Contemporary South Africa* (Berkeley: University of California Press, 1975), pp. 19–50; and André du Toit, "No Chosen People: The Myth of the Calvinist Origins of Afrikaner Nationalism and Racial Ideology," *American Historical Review* 88 (October 1983), 920–52.

28. Du Toit, "No Chosen People," p. 952.

29. F. A. van Jaarsveld, *The Awakening of Afrikaner Nationalism, 1868–1881* (Cape Town: Human and Rousseau, 1961), p. 3.

30. Irving Hexham, *The Irony of Apartheid: The Struggle for National Independence of Afrikaner Calvinism against British Imperialism* (New York: Edwin Mellen Press, 1981).

31. Moodie, *The Rise of Afrikanerdom, Power, Apartheid, and the Afrikaner Civil Religion.*

32. See du Toit, "Ideological Change," p. 21.

33. Ibid., esp. pp. 29 and 50.

34. Du Toit states this latter opinion clearly: "Contrary to their own backward-looking historical self-understanding, nationalist movements are best understood as modernising enterprises in which intellectuals play a crucial role in fashioning the nation as a historical construct." Ibid., p. 50 n. 7.

35. O'Meara, p. 5.

36. André du Toit, "Captive to the Nationalist Paradigm: Prof. F. A. van Jaarsveld and the Historical Evidence for the Afrikaner's Ideas on His Calling and His Mission," *Southern African Historical Journal* 16 (1984), 77.

37. F. A. van Jaarsveld, "André du Toit: Much Ado about Nothing," *South African Historical Journal* 16 (1984), 81.

38. Because of its position on the world stage, South Africa has been served by many general histories, some of them quite distinguished. I find most admirable T. R. H. Davenport's *South Africa: A Modern History,* 3d ed. (1975; Toronto: University of Toronto Press, 1987). Of older works, Arthur Keppel-Jones, *South Africa: A Short History,* 5th ed. (1949; London: Hutchinson, 1975), is lucid and graceful. For a very reined-in older chronicle, see

C. W. de Kiewet, *A History of South Africa, Social and Economic* (1941; London: Oxford University Press, rpr. 1960).

39. J. Alton Templin, *Ideology on a Frontier: The Theological Foundation of Afrikaner Nationalism, 1652–1910* (Westport, Conn.: Greenwood Press, 1984), p. 284.

40. Du Toit, "Captive to the Nationalism Paradigm," pp. 67 and 69.

41. Templin, pp. 283 and 279–80.

42. This point is well illustrated in two historical-theological studies: B. Gemser, "Die Oudstes in Israel," *Hervormde Teologiese Studies* (August 1953), 73–82; and (perhaps unintentionally) A. Van Selms, "Die Kontinuiteit van die Kerk in der Ou en Nuwe Verbond," *Hervormde Teologiese Studies* (August 1953), 93–100.

43. The ten articles in Elphick and Giliomee, covering the years 1652–1820, are an excellent overview of the nature of black and white society before the beginning of significant immigration from the British Isles.

44. Although the Dutch element in the population became culturally hegemonic, the Afrikaner cultural genealogy included French (largely Huguenot) and German elements, and, during the nineteenth and twentieth centuries, assimilated some Anglo-Celtic peoples. With some reservations, one notes the estimates of the composition of the Afrikaner population in the mid-1980s as reported by official government sources: "The ethnic composition of the Afrikaners is difficult to quantify but a reasonable estimate would be 40 percent Dutch, 40 percent German, 7.5 percent French, 7.5 percent English and Scottish and 5 percent of other elements." *South Africa, 1987–1988* (Official Yearbook of the Republic of South Africa, 13th ed., 1987), p. 71. This had changed from the estimate for 1806, which held that the ethnicity was 50 percent Dutch, 27 percent German, 17.5 percent French, and 5.5 percent other nationalities. Theal, *Progress of South Africa* (p. 44), cited in Ernst G. Malherbe, *Education in South Africa, vol. 1, 1652–1922* (Cape Town: Juta, 1925), p. 40.

45. Malherbe, 1:41.

46. See E. Morse Jones, *Role of the British Settlers in South Africa, Part 1: Up to 1820,* 2d ed. (Cape Town: A. A. Balkema, 1971).

47. There were reported to be 43,097 white people at the Cape in 1820. A few of these were of British Isles origin, so the Afrikaner population was probably a bit under 43,000. See Malherbe, 1:41, and Patterson in Fortes and Patterson, p. 173.

48. Moodie, p. 4.

49. Eric A. Walker's *The Great Trek* (London: A. and C. Black, 1934) is still worth close attention.

50. James Anthony Froude to the earl of Carnarvon, 10 January 1876. See above, note 16. On Froude's African journey, see V. C. Malherbe, *Eminent Victorians in Africa* (Cape Town: Juta, 1972), pp. 1–58.

51. H. L. Watts, "A Social and Demographic Portrait of English-Speaking White South Africans," in André de Villiers, ed., *English-Speaking South Africa Today: Proceedings of the National Conference July 1974* (Cape Town: Oxford University Press, 1976). See tables 1 and 2, pp. 42–43.

52. Although there have been several histories of South African education since 1925, Malherbe's vol. 1 is still the fundamental work on education before 1922.

53. On the development of the Dutch Reformed polities, see M. Boucher, "The Frontier and Religion: A Comparative Study of the United States of America and South Africa in the First Half of the Nineteenth Century," *Archives Year Book for South African History* (Johannesburg: Government Printer, 1969), 2:1–114; Andres Dreyer, *Boustowe vir die Geskiedenis van die Nederduitse-Gereformeerde Kirke in Suid-Afrika, vol. 3, 1804–36* (Cape Town: N. G. Kerk, 1936); S. P. Engelbrecht, *Geschiedenis van die Nederduits-Hervormde Kerk in Suid-Afrika,* 2 vols. (Amsterdam and Pretoria: J. H. De Bussy, 1920); G. B. A. Gerdener, *Boustowe vir die Geskiednis van die Nederduits-Gereformeerde Kerk in die Transgariep* (Cape Town: Die Nasionale Pers Beperk, 1930); G. B. A. Gerdener, *Ons Kerk in die Transgariep. Geskiedenis van die Ned. Geref. Kerke in Natal, Vrystaat and Transvaal* (Cape Town: S.A. Bybelvereniging, 1934); J. P. Jooste, *Die Geskiedenis van die Gereformeerde Kerke in Suid-Afrika, 1859–1959* (privately printed, 1958); B. R. Kruger,

Die Onstaan van die Geredormeerde Kerke in Suid-Afrika (Pretoria: V. en R. Drukkery, 1957); H. D. Longland, "Die Geskiedenis van die Nederduitse Gereformeerde Gemeente Colesburg, 1825–1875," *Archives Year Book for South African History* (Johannesburg: Government Printer, 1967), 1:202–90; J. I. Marais, *Geschiedenis van der Nederduits Gereformeerde Kerk, in Zuid-Afrika, tot op de Groot Trek* (Stellenbosch: Het Administratie-Bureau, 1919); A. Moorrees, *Die Nederduitse Gereformeerde Kerk in Suid-Afrika, 1652–1873* (Cape Town: S.A. Bybelvereniging, 1937); J. A. S. Oberholster, *Die Gereformeerde Kerke onder die Kruis in Suid-Afrika: Hul Onstaan en Ontwikkeling* (Cape Town and Pretoria: H.A.U.M., 1956); G. D. Scholtz, *Die Geskiedenis van die Nederduitse Hervormde Kerke van Suid-Afrika, 1842–1885* (Cape Town and Pretoria: N. G. Kerk-Uitgewers, n.d.); B. Spoelstra, *Die "Doppers" in Suid-Afrika, 1760–1899* (Cape Town: Nasionale Boekhandel, 1963); W. A. Venter, "Die Geskiedenis van die Nederduitse Gereformeèrde Gemeente Bloemfontein gedurende die Pioniersjare, 1848–1886," *Archives Year Book for South African History* (Cape Town: Government Printer, 1963), 1:163–306.

54. F. A. van Jaarsveld's classic *The Awakening of Afrikaner Nationalism, 1868–1881*, argued that the Afrikaners became a nation in the years 1868–81. This is demonstrably true in the geopolitical sense (they took up arms and they entered into international treaty negotiations), but I think that this political consciousness was only part of the story and that other aspects of the cultural complex were not developed until early in the twentieth century. In suggesting this, I imply no lack of respect for van Jaarsveld's work. Of course it is not perfect and of course later scholars have suggested modifications: historical writing works that way. What I find puzzling is that his work has been either ignored or patronized in recent historical writing. For a useful study, much broader in its implications than its title might suggest, see T. R. H. Davenport, *The Afrikaner Bond (1880–1911)* (Cape Town: Oxford University Press, 1966). Also insightful is Hermann Giliomee, "The Growth of Afrikaner Identity," in Adam and Giliomee, pp. 83–127.

55. Peter Lambley, *The Psychology of Apartheid* (Athens: University of Georgia Press, 1980), p. 34.

56. Although several historians have dealt with the development of the celebrations that eventually became the Day of the Covenant, in my opinion the most insightful analysis is that of Wolfram Kistner, a specialist in divinity. See his "The 16th of December in the Context of Nationalistic Thinking," in Sundermeier, ed., pp. 73–90.

57. S. P. Engelbrecht "Ds. Frans Lion Cachet," *Hervromde Teologiese Studies* (August 1953), 181–231.

58. Kistner, pp. 77–78.

59. Ibid., p. 78.

60. Ibid., p. 74.

61. The quotation is from Moodie, p. 7. See also Cornevin, pp. 60–61; Kistner, pp. 79–80.

62. Templin, p. 225. Kruger's biblical text was Genesis 17:7.

63. F. A. van Jaarsveld, *The Afrikaner's Interpretation of South African History* (Cape Town: Simondium Publishers, 1964), p. 11.

64. Kistner, p. 74.

65. Van Jaarsveld, *Afrikaner's Interpretation*, pp. 36–38.

66. Stephanus J. du Toit, *Die Geskiedenis van Ons Land in die Taal van Ons Volk*, 2d ed. (1877; Paarl: B. F. du Toit, 1891).

67. Thompson, *Political Mythology*, p. 32.

68. Moodie, p. 26. Moodie believes that this distinction on Kruger's part is orthodox Calvinism. Kistner (pp. 80–81) suggests its neo-Calvinist character.

69. Kistner, p. 81. As context, see the essay by Johannes C. Coetze, issue no. 2 of *Die Ossewareeks* (1957), "Die Eerste Beginsel van die Calviniste Opvoeding."

70. Kistner, p. 82.

71. Ibid.

72. Some of this sense of unity was unconsciously directed at the political unification of the Afrikaner states. In the late 1870s and early 1880s, for example, the authorities of the

Orange Free State interlarded "practically every memorandum sent to the Volksraad or to the Transvaal [with] the idea of a single nation in a single country with a single future." Van Jaarsveld, *Awakening*, p. 187.

73. Dan Jacobson, *The Story of the Stories: The Chosen People and Its God* (New York: Harper and Row, 1982), p. 183.

74. S. du Toit, ed., *Versamelde Werke van J. D. du Toit* (Johannesburg, 1961), 7:199, quoted and translated in Hexham, p. 37.

75. Van Jaarsveld, *Afrikaner's Interpretation*, p. 11.

76. Willem Postma, *Doppers* (Bloemfontein, 1918), pp. 21–22, trans. and quoted in Hexham, p. 47.

77. An odd Afrikaner sect, the "Jerusalemgangers" bears note. In 1848 they trekked out of Natal, which had come under British (and therefore evil) rule, to the north. Their geographic knowledge came mostly from the "Old Testament" and they were convinced that the Limpopo River formed part of the Nile system. They intended to reach Jerusalem, and thus the Promised Land by this route. See J. P. Claasen, *Die Jerusalemgangers met besondere verwysing na J. A. Enslin* (Silverton, R.S.A.: Promedia-Publikasies, 1981).

78. Van Jaarsveld, *Awakening*, pp. 186–87.

79. On church discipline, see Hexham, pp. 76–83.

80. There is some interesting, but I think fundamentally misguided, work aimed at finding in some specific institutional arrangements and/or legal precedents the roots of what eventually became apartheid. As I hope is becoming clear, apartheid was the by-product of an entire cultural system, and did not have its germ in institutional arrangements. See, for example, Benjamin Kline, *Genesis of Apartheid: British African Policy in the Colony of Natal, 1845–1893* (Lanham, Md.: University Press of America, 1988); and David Welsh, *The Roots of Segregation: Native Policy in Colonial Natal, 1845–1910* (Cape Town: Oxford University Press, 1971). Infinitely more subtle is John W. Cell's *The Highest Stage of White Supremacy: The Origins of Segregation in South Africa and the American South* (Cambridge: Cambridge University Press, 1982). A useful old-fashioned compendium is J. Y. Gibson, *The Evolution of South African Native Policy* (Pietermaritzburg: P. Davis and Sons, 1919). See also the extensive discussion of pre-apartheid land segregation in Peter Walshe, *The Rise of African Nationalism in South Africa: The African National Congress, 1912–1952* (Berkeley: University of California Press, 1970).

81. Hexham, p. 53.

82. *Volksstem*, 19 December 1903, quoted and trans. Leonard M. Thompson, *The Unification of South Africa, 1902–1910* (Oxford: Clarendon Press, 1960), p. 18.

83. Moodie, p. 10.

84. No direct data exist on the Afrikaner population at the time of the Second Anglo-Boer War, although one can use as a surrogate the combined population of the three main Dutch Reformed churches, as shown by the first census of South Africa in 1911. Since only a very small proportion of the population had no religion or an unspecified faith, the surrogate is valid. The total was 694,898. See *Unie Statisiteke oor Vytig Jaar* (Pretoria: Bureau of Census and Statistics, 1960), p. A-26.

85. Van Jaarsveld, *Afrikaner's Interpretation*, p. 47.

86. G. D. Scholtz's *Die Ontwikkeling van die Politieke Denke van Die Afrikaner*, 7 vols. (Johannesburg: Perskor-Uitgewery, 1967–79) is massive and discursive, but a fundamental source. See especially vol. 6, *1910–1924* (1979) and vol. 7, *1924–1939* (1979).

87. Conor Cruise O'Brien, *God Land: Reflections on Religion and Nationalism* (Cambridge: Harvard University Press, 1988), p. 47. O'Brien's reference was to the eighteenth-century Jansenists.

88. I have found the following especially useful on mining and industrialization: Belinda Bozolli, ed., *Class, Community, and Conflict: South African Perspectives* (Johannesburg: Ravan Press, 1987); Belinda Bozolli, "Ideology and the Manufacturing Class in South Africa," in *Collected Seminar Papers on the Societies of Southern Africa in the Nineteenth and Twentieth Centuries* (London: Institute of Commonwealth Studies, 1974), 4:60–79; Jonathan Crush, *The Struggle for Swazi Labour, 1890–1920* (Montreal: McGill-Queen's

University Press, 1987); Robert Davies, "Mining Capital, the State and Unskilled White Workers in South Africa, 1910–1913," *Journal of Southern African Studies* 3 (October 1976), 41–69; Donald J. N. Denoon, "The Transvaal Labour Crisis, 1901–6," *Journal of African History* 7 (1967), 481–94; Alan H. Jeeves, *Migrant Labour in South Africa's Mining Economy. The Struggle for the Gold Mines' Labour Supply, 1890–1920* (Montreal: McGill-Queen's University Press, 1985); Shula Marks and Richard Rathbone, eds., *Industrialisation and Social Change in South Africa: African class formation, culture, and consciousness, 1870–1930* (London: Longman, 1982); Shula Marks and Stanley Trapido, eds., *The Politics of Race, Class, and Nationalism in Twentieth-Century South Africa* (London: Longman, 1987); Stanley Trapido, "The South African Republic: Class Formation and the State, 1850–1900" in *Collected Seminar Papers on the Societies of Southern Africa in the Nineteenth and Twentieth Centuries* (London: Institute of Commonwealth Studies, 1973), 3:53–65; Robert V. Turrell, *Capital and Labour on the Kimberley Diamond Fields, 1871–1890* (Cambridge: Cambridge University Press, 1987); Charles van Onselen, ed., *Studies in the Social and Economic History of the Witwatersrand 1886–1914*, vol. 1, *New Babylon*, and vol. 2, *New Nineveh* (Johannesburg: Ravan Press, 1982); William H. Worger, *South Africa's City of Diamonds: Mine Workers and Monopoly Capitalism in Kimberley, 1867–1895* (New Haven: Yale University Press, 1987).

For discussions of rural changes see William Beinart, Peter Delius, and Stanley Trapido, eds., *Putting a Plough to the Ground: Accumulation and Dispossession in Rural South Africa, 1850–1930* (Johannesburg: Ravan Press, 1986), esp. pp. 56–100; Colin Bundy, *The Rise and Fall of the South African Peasantry*, 2d ed. (1979; Cape Town: David Philip, 1988); Stanley B. Greenberg, *Race and State in Capitalist Development: South Africa in Comparative Perspective* (Johannesburg: Ravan Press, 1980), pp. 70–106; Timothy Keegan, "The Restructuring of Agrarian Class Relations in a Colonial Economy: The Orange River Colony, 1902–1910," *Journal of Southern African Studies* 5 (April 1979), 234–254; Timothy J. Keegan, *Rural Transformations in Industrializing South Africa: The Southern Highveld to 1914* (London: Macmillan, 1987); Stanley Trapido, "Landlord and Tenant in a Colonial Economy: The Transvaal, 1880–1910," *Journal of Southern African Studies* 5 (October 1978), 26–58; Charles van Onselen, "Race and Class in the South African Countryside: Cultural Osmosis and Social Relations in the Share-cropping Economy of the South-Western Transvaal, 1900–1950," *American Historical Review* 95 (February 1990), 99–123; for context, see several interesting essays in Howard Lamar and Leonard Thompson, eds., *The Frontier in History: North America and Southern Africa Compared* (New Haven: Yale University Press, 1981).

89. This viewpoint is skillfully summarized in O'Meara, pp. 12–15.

90. Van Jaarsveld, *Afrikaner's Interpretation*, p. 10.

91. Leroy Vail, "Introduction," in Leroy Vail, ed., *The Creation of Tribalism in Southern Africa* (London: James Curry, 1989), pp. 8–9.

92. Jeffrey Butler, "Afrikaner Women and the Creation of Ethnicity in a Small South African Town, 1902–1950," in Vail, p. 71.

93. Ibid.

94. Ibid., pp. 61–75. See also Isabel Hofmeyr, "Building a Nation from Words: Afrikaans' Language, Literature, and Ethnic Identity, 1902–1924," in Marks and Trapido, p. 106.

95. Female purity became a cultural icon in itself and was also instrumental to the preservation of pure Afrikaner culture. For an example, this is Hexham's summary of the views of the influential Dopper nationalist leader Reverend Willem Postma: "The woman thus became the symbol of racial purity and the institution of marriage a key to preserving the future of the Afrikaner People." Hexham, p. 53.

96. Van Jaarsveld, *Afrikaner's Interpretation*, p. 19.

97. For an outsider's evaluation of the revival process, see that of Anriaa J. Barnouw, professor at Columbia University and Carnegie Corporation Visitor to South Africa in 1932, *Language and Race Problems in South Africa* (The Hague: Martinus Nijhoff, 1934).

98. Scholtz, 7:83.

99. Malherbe, 1:315.
100. The regulations are found in ibid., 1:317. The actual cleft-stick ordinance was drafted not by Milner but by officials (see ibid., 1:317, n. 13).
101. Alfred Milner to W. A. Russell, 8 July 1903, quoted in ibid. 1:317–18, n. 13.
102. H. Goold-Adams to petitioners, 11 November 1903, quoted in ibid., 1:319.
103. See ibid. 1:335 ff. and Ernst G. Malherbe, *Education in South Africa, vol. 2* (Cape Town: Juta, 1977), pp. 4–10.
104. Vorster quoted in Harrison, p. 54.
105. Professor J. C. van Rooy, quoted in Malherbe, 2:51
106. B. F. Nel, quoted in Moodie, p. 240.
107. P. J. Meyer, quoted in Malherbe, 2:103.
108. The Reverend Willim Nicol in *Die Kerkbode*, 5 March 1941, quoted in Malherbe, 2:44.
109. As late as 1975 an informed observer was able to write: "South Africa recognises no official state church. The [Dutch Reformed Church] already lost that status in 1843 in the Cape Province—in the Boer republics it happened immediately after the war in 1902—but in spite of that many members of the church in their minds still equate Afrikanerdom = the Nationalist government = the Dutch Reformed Church. . . . The pure fact remains that to the eyes of the outside world the [Dutch Reformed Church] for all practical purposes operates as a State Church." P. G. J. Meiring, in Sundermeier, pp. 63–64.
110. For the exact numbers see *Uniestatistieke oor Vyftig Jaar*, p. A-26.
111. This is the thesis of Hexham's volume, *The Irony of Apartheid*. See also J. J. Pienaar, *Die Inspirende Opvoedings-en Opheffingsaksie van de Ned. Herv. of Gereef. Kerk in Transvaal Gedvrende 1902–1910* (Pretoria: N. G. Kerk-Boekhandel, 1970).
112. See Hexham, pp. 147–64.
113. In their emphasis upon all education as essentially sacralized and in their justification of "parental rights" as explanation of why the state should pay for this "sacred trust," the Dutch Reformed clergy used almost the same arguments employed by Roman Catholic clergy in English-speaking countries to press for state monies.
114. Moodie, p. 102.
115. Of a number of exposés of the Broederbond, the most balanced is Moodie, pp. 97–115. On Broederbond influence on economic matters, O'Meara is valuable (esp. pp. 67–148). See also Harrison, pp. 84–101.
116. O'Meara, p. 74.
117. Keegan, *Rural Transformations*, p. 27.
118. Cell, p. 73.
119. Malherbe, 2:20. For a not-unfair precis of the five-volume Carnegie report, see "Touleier," *The Poor White Problem in South Africa* (Johannesburg: S.A. Liberty Press, n.d.), pp. 3–23.
120. Harrison, p. 93.
121. Butler, in Vail, pp. 64–70.
122. Moodie, pp. 69–70.
123. Giliomee, in Vail, p. 49.
124. O'Meara, p. 78.
125. Harrison, p. 117.
126. Ibid.
127. Harrison, pp. 114–19; O'Meara, pp. 78–95.
128. O'Meara, p. 150.
129. Moodie, pp. 197–207; O'Meara, pp. 96–166.
130. The classic study of history, social science concepts, and experimental evidence is I.D. MacCrone's pioneering *Race Attitudes in South Africa: Historical, Experimental, and Psychological Studies* (London: Oxford University Press, 1937).
131. John Burger, *The Black Man's Burden* (London: Victor Gollancz, 1943), pp. 42–167; Cell, pp. 46–81; Ifor L. Evans, *Native Policy in Southern Africa: An Outline* (Cambridge: Cambridge University Press, 1934), esp. pp. 14–29; Greenberg, pp. 87–106; Paul

Maylam, "The Rise and Decline of Urban Apartheid," paper presented to the African Studies Seminar, Queen's University, Ontario, January 1989.

132. For Hametic references in Afrikaner life see van Jaarsveld, *Afrikaner's Interpretation*, pp. 6–7.

133. Those of course are general characteristics; numerous variations on the central themes are possible. It would take a great deal of space to do justice to the range and variety of Afrikaner theology in the first half of the twentieth century. See Moodie, pp. 39–72. See also Hexham, esp. pp. 158–64 and 186–99; Templin, pp. 279–314. A very perceptive discussion, from the Roman Catholic perspective, is Oswin Magrath, *An Introduction to the Theology of the Dutch Reformed Churches in South Africa for Catholic Studies* (Stellenbosch: St. Nicholas' Priory, 1956).

4. The Covenantal Culture of the Ulster-Scots to 1920

1. *The Twelfth: July 1968* (Souvenir program published by the County Grand Orange Lodge of Belfast), p. 25.

2. D. Lyle Hall, *These Seventy Years* (Belfast: Bell and Logan, 1944), p. 74. Hall's volumes consist mostly of speeches that he made at the opening of various schools. Hall was a self-made Belfast businessman, a successful draper, and one of the founders of the Belfast Chamber of Trade.

3. Steve Bruce, *God Save Ulster: The Religion and Politics of Paisleyism* (Oxford: Clarendon Press, 1986), pp. 268–69.

4. Ed Moloney and Andy Pollak, *Paisley* (Dublin: Poolbeg Press, 1986), p. 238.

5. Dixon Donaldson, *Historical, Traditional, and Descriptive Account of Islandmagee* (Whitehead: Whitehead News and Ballycarry and Islandmagee Reporter, 1927), pp. 139–40. The memoir originally appeared in the *Irish Presbyterian* in January 1910. For background information on Holmes, see Donaldson, pp. 118–19.

6. Because of the recent Troubles, much has been written about Ulster, and much of it is bad. Fortunately, the seventeenth and eighteenth centuries have not yet become flooded with "fastback" analyses, and there is a good deal of genuinely distinguished scholarship that deals in whole or in part with those two centuries. The standard commentary is the *New History of Ireland* (Clarendon Press, for the Royal Irish Academy). Vol. 3 of the series is *Early Modern Ireland, 1534–1691* (1976). Vol. 4 is *Eighteenth-Century Ireland, 1691–1800* (1986). Valuable for keeping straight the often-confusing chronology is vol. 8, *A Chronology of Irish History to 1976* (1982). Of the older works, the classic is W. E. H. Lecky's five-volume *A History of Ireland in the Eighteenth Century* (London: Longmans, Green, 1892). For a compressed, balanced discussion, J. C. Beckett's *The Making of Modern Ireland, 1603–1923* (London: Faber and Faber, 1966) is still preeminent. The historical geography of Ireland in general, and Ulster in particular, is best treated in T. W. Freeman's excellent *Pre-Famine Ireland: A Study in Historical Geography* (Manchester: Manchester University Press, 1957). Among the many useful monographs available, three stand out: T. W. Moody's pioneering work *The Londonderry Plantation, 1609–41* (Belfast: William Mullen, 1939); Michael Perceval-Maxwell's *The Scottish Migration to Ulster in the Reign of James I* (London: Routledge and Kegan Paul, 1973); and Raymond Gillespie's *Colonial Ulster: The Settlement of East Ulster, 1600–1641* (Cork: Cork University Press, 1985). Although not limited to the seventeenth and eighteenth centuries, two outstanding interpretative volumes deserve mention: David W. Miller's strikingly original *Queen's Rebels: Ulster Loyalism in Historical Perspective* (Dublin: Gill and Macmillan, 1978), and A. T. Q. Stewart's *The Narrow Ground: Aspects of Ulster, 1609–1969* (London: Faber and Faber, 1977). The latter has been criticized as too pessimistic. Wrong: it is just that Stewart has lived for a long time with the history of Ulster and knows it too well to be facilely upbeat. The historical literature in the form of scholarly articles is too rich to summarize. I have found particularly admirable and stimulating Alan Gailey, "The Scots Element in North Irish Popular Culture," *Ethnologica Europaea* 7, 1 (1975), 2–22; David C. Miller, "Pres-

byterianism and 'Modernization' in Ulster," *Past and Present* 80 (August 1978), 66–90; and Frank Wright, "Protestant Ideology and Politics in Ulster," *Archives Européennes de Sociologie* 14, 2 (1973), 213–80. Less comprehensive, but nevertheless valuable are two articles by Nicholas Canny: "Protestants, Planters and Apartheid in Early Modern Ireland," *Irish Historical Studies* 25 (November 1988), 105–15; and "Dominant Minorities: English Settlers in Ireland and Virginia, 1550–1650," in A. C. Hepburn, ed., *Minorities in History* (New York: St. Martin's Press, 1979).

    7. Aidan Clarke, "Pacification, Plantation, and the Catholic Question, 1603–1623," in *Early Modern Ireland, 1534–1691*, p. 223.

    8. Perceval-Maxwell, table 8, p. 233.

    9. Lecky, 1:58.

    10. Stewart, p. 39.

    11. Gailey, pp. 4–8.

    12. The actual numbers are as follows (note that the diocese of Meath is in the province of Leinster):

cese	Presbyterian	%	Other Prot. Dissenters	%	Anglican	%	Roman Catholic	%
nagh 36	84,837	17	3,340	1	103,012	21	309,447	62
gher 49	34,623	9	26	—	104,359	26	260,241	65
ry 41	118,339	32	1,738	—	50,350	14	196,614	54
vn 58	98,961	52	3,530	2	27,662	15	58,405	31
nor 18	193,261	53	5,924	2	66,888	18	95,545	26
more 09	69,264	37	933	—	41,737	22	76,275	41
nore 05	8,736	3	97	—	46,879	16	240,593	81
ath 59	672	—	199	—	25,626	6	377,562	93
hoe 30	28,914	14	24	—	33,507	16	145,385	70
al 505	637,607	22	15,811	1	500,020	17	1,760,067	60

ce: First Report of the Commisioners of Public Instruction, Ireland, pp. 9–45 [45], H.C. 1835, xxxiii.

    13. J. G. Simms, "Land Owned by Catholics in Ireland in 1688," *Irish Historical Studies* 7 (March 1951), 189; J. G. Simms, "The Restoration, 1660–85," in *Early Modern Ireland, 1534–1691*, map 10, p. 429; J. G. Simms, "The Establishment of Protestant Ascendancy, 1691–1714," in *Eighteenth Century Ireland, 1691–1800*, p. 13.

    14. See T. W. Moody, "The Treatment of the Native Population under the Scheme for the Plantation of Ulster," *Irish Historical Studies* 1 (March 1938), 59–63. For a mapping of one county, which shows the relationship of topography and ethnicity, see Philip Robinson, "British Settlement in County Tyrone, 1610–1666," *Irish Economic and Social History* 5 (1978), 5–26.

    15. The standard histories of Irish Presbyterianism are James Seaton Reid, *History of the Presbyterian Church in Ireland* (Belfast: William Mullan, 1867), 3 vols.; and W. D. Killen, *The Ecclesiastical History of Ireland from the earliest period to the present times* (London:

Macmillan, 1875), 2 vols. A valuable snyoptic history is John M. Barkley's *A Short History of the Presbyterian Church in Ireland* (Belfast: Publications Board of the Presbyterian Church in Ireland, 1959). J. C. Beckett's *Protestant Dissent in Ireland 1687–1780* (London: Faber and Faber, 1948) deals chiefly, but not entirely, with the Presbyterians. Several difficult matters of Presbyterian history are treated in J. L. M. Haire, ed., *Challenge and Conflict: Essays in Irish Presbyterian History and Doctrine* (Antrim: W. and G. Baird, 1961). Special attention should be drawn to Peter Brooke's *Ulster Presbyterianism: The Historical Perspective 1610–1970* (New York: St. Martin's Press, 1987).

16. Although I am here focusing on the Presbyterian Church in Ireland, it should be remembered that the largest Protestant denomination in Ireland as a whole was the Church of Ireland. This, until 1 January 1871, was the Established Church. Although church authorities did not use these terms, it can be referred to as either "Episcopal" or "Anglican" without insult. Until well into the twentieth century, "Protestant" in Irish official documents (such as the census) and in common usage outside of Ulster referred to the Church of Ireland. The Presbyterians were referred to, in the seventeenth and eighteenth centuries, as "Dissenters," or, occasionally, "Nonconformists." In most late nineteenth- and early twentieth-century government documents they are included in the category "other Protestant." Throughout this study I employ "Protestant" to encompass all non-Catholic Christians. The standard histories of the Anglican Church in Ireland are Richard Mant, *History of the Church of Ireland, from the Revolution to the Union of the Churches of England and Ireland, January 1, 1801* (London: John W. Parker, 1840), 2 vols.; Walter A. Phillips, ed., *History of the Church of Ireland from the Earliest Times to the Present Day* (London: Oxford University Press, 1933), 3 vols.; Thomas J. Johnston, John L. Robinson, and Robert Wyse Jackson, *A History of the Church of Ireland* (Dublin: A.P.C.K., 1953); Donald Harman Akenson, *The Church of Ireland: Ecclesiastical Reform and Revolution, 1800–1885* (New Haven: Yale University Press, 1971).

17. There exists a veritable library of commentary on Calvin's theology, and I have by no means mastered it. My comments are drawn from my own reading of his *Institutes*. Doubtless, I have missed nuances that technically sophisticated theologians would pick up, but I think I have clearly indicated the aspects of Calvinism that were assimilated by the clergy, and ultimately the congregations, of Presbyterian Ulster.

18. *Institutes of the Christian Religion,* ed. John T. McNeill, trans. Ford L. Battles (London: SCM Press, 1961), p. 1310.

19. Ibid., p. 1513.

20. For a useful discussion of the spread of Calvinism, see John T. McNeill, *The History and Character of Calvinism* (New York: Oxford University Press, 1954).

21. Reid, 1:96–105.

22. Quoted in A. Dakon, *Calvinism* (Philadelphia: Westminster Press, 1946), p. 145.

23. The King's Confession is found in full in J. D. Douglas, *Light in the North: The Story of the Scottish Covenanters* (Exeter: Paternoster Press, 1964), appendix 1, pp. 197–99.

24. Miller, *Queen's Rebels,* p. 13.

25. Ibid., p. 12.

26. The National Covenant of 1638 is found in its entirety in Douglas, pp. 200–205.

27. For the full text of the Solemn League and Covenant of 1643 see ibid., pp. 206–8. For the context of the covenants of 1638 and 1643, see David Stevenson, *The Scottish Revolution, 1637–1644: The Triumph of the Covenanters* (Newton Abbot: David and Charles, 1973).

28. The narrative, drawn from the diary of Reverend William Adair, by the Reverend Patrick Adair, is printed in full in Reid, 1:439–55. The manuscript that Reid employed, compiled in the later seventeenth century, was published in the mid-nineteenth as Patrick Adair, *A True Narrative of the Rise and Progress of the Presbyterian Church in Ireland, (1623–1670),* ed. W. D. Killen (Belfast: C. Aitchison, 1866).

29. The narrative says that in Antrim and Ballymena, the clerics also preached on Ezra 8:20. This manifestly is an error. Probably Ezra 6:20 was the text employed.

30. For the attenuated Scottish covenanting tradition of the post-1660 period, see Ian B. Cowan, *The Scottish Covenanters, 1660–1688* (London: Victor Gollancz, 1976).

31. Miller, *Queen's Rebels*.

32. Stewart, p. 101.

33. Bruce, p. 10.

34. R. F. G. Holmes, *Our Presbyterian Heritage* (Belfast: Publication Committee of the Presbyterian Church in Ireland, 1985), p. 9, quoted in Bruce, p. 10.

35. Denis O'D. Hanna, *The Face of Ulster* (London: B. T. Batsford, 1952), p. 34.

36. See Raymond Gillespie, "The Origins and Development of an Ulster Urban Network, 1600–41," *Irish Historical Studies* 24 (May 1984), 15–29; Stewart, p. 145.

37. Miller, *Queen's Rebels* (p. 37), makes this point about Protestants in general, but I think that it is applicable to the Ulster-Scots specifically.

38. Bruce, pp. 10–11. At present there is within the Irish historical profession a debate concerning the extent to which Protestants (in the contemporary sense: members of the Established Church) attempted to convert the native Irish and whether or not their attitudes were unusual by the international standards of their era. See Alan Ford, *The Protestant Reformation in Ireland, 1590–1641* (Frankfurt: Verlag Peter Lang, 1987); and Canny, "Protestants, Planters and Apartheid in Early Modern Ireland." For a shrewd review of Ford's thesis, see Michael P. Maxwell in *Canadian Journal of Irish Studies* 14 (January 1989), pp. 78–81.

39. Marianne Elliott, *Watchmen in Sion: The Protestant Idea of Liberty* (Derry: Field Day Pamphlets, 1985), p. 11.

40. For the historical context of Presbyterian governance, see Barkley, pp. 64–117. For a modern scheme of discipline, not much changed from that of the nineteenth century, see *The Code: The Book of the Constitution and Government of the Presbyterian Church in Ireland* (Belfast: General Assembly of the Presbyterian Church in Ireland, 1948).

41. Reid, Killen, and Brooke each discuss the various schisms in detail. Barkely (p. 118) has a convenient schematic presentation of developments from 1642 to 1956. An admirably efficient summary of eighteenth-century schism is found in three succinct paragraphs in W. H. Crawford and Brian Trainor, eds., *Aspects of Irish Social History, 1750–1800* (Belfast: HMSO, 1969), p. 100. Several of the essays in Haire discuss various tensions and schisms.

42. Stewart, p. 83.

43. The Ordnance Survey Memoir for Ballycarry (officially, the Parish of Templecorran) has been collated and published: [Whitehead Extra-Mural Study Group], *Ordnance Survey Memoir of the Parish of Templecorran* (Belfast: Queen's University of Belfast, 1972). The Islandmagee Memoir is found in the Royal Irish Academy, Dublin, Ordnance Survey, Box 11, Antrim, XI, VI. A transcript is found in the Public Record Office of Northern Ireland, Belfast. Most of James Orr's poetry is found in his two volumes titled *Poems* (Belfast: Smyth and Lyons, 1804) and *The Posthumous Works of James Orr* (Belfast: Francis D. Finlay, 1817). These two volumes were reprinted as a single edition, *Collected Poems of James Orr*, in 1935 (Belfast: Mullan and Son). For items published in fugitive sources and not included in Orr's collected poems, see Donald Harman Akenson and W. H. Crawford, *Local Poets and Social History: James Orr, Bard of Ballycarry* (Belfast: HMSO, 1977), pp. 117–19. Orr received a good deal of attention in the work of the distinguished poet John Hewitt, *Rhyming Weavers and Other Country Poets of Antrim and Down* (Belfast: Blackstaff Press, 1974). Rather more extended discussion is found in Hewitt's "Ulster Poets 1800–1870," M.A. thesis, Queen's University, Belfast, 1951. Islandmagee has a very good older history, Donaldson's *Historical, Traditional, and Descriptive Account of Islandmagee* of 1927. For Ballycarry, a useful collection of items is *Ballycarry in Olden Days*, ed. Avy Dowlin (Belfast: Graham and Heslip, 1963). The modern history of Islandmagee is Donald Harman Akenson, *Between Two Revolutions: Islandmagee, County Antrim, 1798–1920* (Hamden, Conn.: Archon Books, 1979). Useful genealogical inferences can be drawn from the material in George Rutherford, comp., *Gravestone Inscriptions: County Antrim, vol. I, Islandmagee* (Belfast: Ulster Historical Foundation, 1978).

44. *Ordnance Survey Memoir for the Parish of Templecorran*, p. 22. Later (p. 33) the surveyor says that one Catholic held land in the parish.
45. Ibid., p. 40.
46. Akenson, *Islandmagee*, p. 156.
47. *Ordnance Survey Memoir for the Parish of Templecorran*, p. 41.
48. Ibid.
49. *Ordnance Survey Memoir for the Parish of Donegore* (Belfast: Department of Extra-Mural Studies, Queen's University of Belfast, and Public Record Office of Northern Ireland, 1974), p. 18.
50. Useful introductions include W. H. Crawford, *Domestic Industry in Ireland* (Dublin: Gill and Macmillan, 1972) and W. H. Crawford, "Economy and Society in South Ulster in the Eighteenth Century," *Clogher Record* (1975), 241–58. The Ulster weaving industry is placed within the context of the early industrial revolution in L. A. Clarkson, *Proto-Industrialization: The First Phase of Industrialization?* (London: Macmillan, 1985).
51. Gailey, p. 9.
52. T. W. Moody and J. C. Beckett, *Queen's Belfast, 1845–1949: The History of a University* (London: Faber and Faber, 1959), 1:xliv–liii.
53. Gailey, pp. 10–12.
54. *Ordnance Survey Memoir for the Parish of Templecorran*, p. 28.
55. H. G. Calwell, "The Kirk Session of Broadisland (Ballycarry), Co. Antrim in the Eighteenth Century," *The Non-Subscribing Presbyterian* (June 1979–March 1980), 4.
56. Ibid.
57. On social welfare practices, see Akenson, *Islandmagee*, pp. 107–15.
58. *Ordnance Survey Memoir for the Parish of Templecorran*, p. 47.
59. An important article in nontechnical terms is G. B. Adams, "The Emergence of Ulster as a District Dialect Area," *Ulster Folklife* 4 (1958), 61–73. A more general article on Irish linguistic patterns is G. B. Adams, "Language and Man in Ireland," *Ulster Folklife* 15 and 16 (1970), 140–71. See also G. B. Adams, "Northern England as a Source of Ulster Dialects," *Ulster Folklife* 13 (1967), 69–75; and G. B. Adams, "An Introduction to the Study of Ulster Dialects," *Proceedings of the Royal Irish Academy* 52, sect. C (1)26. A valuable long article is J. Braidwood's "Ulster and Elizabethan English," *Ulster Dialects* (Cultra: Ulster Folk Museum, 1964), pp. 5–109. See also G. B. Adams, "Ulster Dialect Origins," *Ulster Folklife* 17 (1971), 99–104; Michael V. Barry, ed., *Aspects of English Dialects in Ireland* (Belfast: Institute of Irish Studies, Queen's University of Belfast, 1981), vol. 1.
60. James Orr, "Ballycarry Fair," in *Collected Poems*. For a general discussion of Orr's word patterns, see Donald H. Akenson, "Listening to Rural Language: Ballycarry, Co. Antrim, 1798–1817," *Canadian Papers in Rural History* 2 (1980), 155–72.
61. Compiled from *Census of Ireland, 1981, pt. II, General Report*, p. 59 [Cd. 1190], H.C. 1902, cxxix.
62. J. R. R. Adams, *The Printed Word and the Common Man: Popular Culture in Ulster 1700–1900* (Belfast: Institute of Irish Studies, Queen's University of Belfast, 1987), p. 48.
63. Reid, 1:242n.
64. See Adams, and Aiken McClelland, "The Ulster Press in the Eighteenth and Nineteenth Centuries," *Ulster Folklife* 20 (1974), 89–99.
65. *Ordnance Survey Memoir for the Parish of Templecorran*, pp. 31–32. Adams, *The Printed Word*, esp. p. 126. See also J. R. R. Adams, "Reading Societies in Ulster," *Ulster Folklife* 27 (1980), 55–64.
66. James Orr, "The Reading Society," in *Collected Poems*.
67. *Ordnance Survey Memoir for the Parish of Templecorran*, p. 23.
68. James Orr, "Donegore Hill," in *Collected Poems*.
69. For example, see Miller, "Presbyterianism," and, for a sharply contrasting viewpoint, see Peter Gibbon, *The Origins of Ulster Unionism: The Formation of Popular Protestant Politics and Ideology in Nineteenth-Century Ireland* (Manchester: Manchester University Press, 1975).

70. Miller, "Presbyterianism," pp. 79–80.
71. Abraham J. Heschel, *The Prophets* (New York: Harper and Row, 1962), p. 9.
William Foxwell Albright, *From the Stone Age to Christianity: Monotheism and the Historical Process*, 2d ed. (Garden City: Doubleday Anchor Books, 1957), p. 325.
72. Heschel, p. xv (footnote).
73. One recognizes, of course, that Calvinism itself did not appear ex nihilo, and that the monotheism of the later Hebrew scriptures obviously influenced Calvin in defining his doctrines. The point here, however, is that nothing in the demotic culture of Northern Ireland was inimicable to the assimilation of Hebrew prophetic modes and, indeed, some local characteristics predisposed the culture to adopt them.
74. Bruce, p. 245.
75. Stewart, p. 56.
76. Over the years literally hundreds of versions of the story of the siege of Derry have been printed, ranging from the scholarly (Macauley's being the most famous) to the luridly popular. The late J. G. Simms wrote a particularly admirable popular account, *The Siege of Derry* (Dublin: A.P.C.K., 1966).
77. Oliver MacDonagh quoted in Terence Brown, *The Whole Protestant Community: The Making of a Historical Myth* (Derry: Field Day Pamphlets, 1985), p. 8.
78. Brown, p. 8.
79. Jacques Louis de Bougrenet, Chevalier de La Tocnaye, *A Frenchman's Walk through Ireland, 1796–97*, trans. John Stevenson, 1917 (Belfast: Blackstaff Press, rpr., 1984), p. 186.
80. For a judicious and illuminating discussion of the main sources that relate to the massacres of 1641, see Michael Perceval-Maxwell, "The Ulster Rising of 1641, and the Depositions," *Irish Historical Studies* 21 (September 1978), 144–67. For a recent summary of the 1641 Rising and its consequences see Raymond Gillespie, "The End of an Era: Ulster and the Outbreak of the 1641 Rising," in Ciaran Brady and Raymond Gillespie, eds., *Natives and Newcomers: Essays on the Making of Irish Colonial Society, 1534–1641* (Dublin: Irish Academic Press, 1986), pp. 191–213, also 247–48.
81. J. L. Porter, *Life and Times and Henry Cooke, D.D., Ll.D.* (Belfast: William Mullan, 1875), p. 2.
82. Ernest W. Hamilton, *The Soul of Ulster*, 2d ed. (London: Hurst and Blackett, 1917), p. 37.
83. Ernest W. Hamilton, *The Irish Rebellion of 1641* (London: John Murray, 1920), p. vi.
84. Space precludes discussion of another strand of the Presbyterians' historical feeling of being hard done by: the inhibitions on their religious practice and social mobility during the penal era of the eighteenth century and the discrimination they experienced as compared to the state church until the disestablishment of that church in 1871. For an indication of the tone and the vigor of that aspect of the historical tradition, see the popular volume *Presbyterianism in Belfast* by James Connell (Belfast: Davidson and McCormack, 1912), esp. pp. 14–40.
85. See Akenson, *Islandmagee*, pp. 139–40, 207–8.
86. The pioneering study of industrialization in the Belfast region, still highly serviceable, in E. R. R. Green, *The Lagan Valley 1800–50: A Local History of the Industrial Revolution* (London: Faber and Faber, 1949). For a valuable compendium of more recent work, see Liam Kennedy and Philip Ollerenshaw, eds., *An Economic History of Ulster, 1820–1940* (Manchester: Manchester University Press, 1985).
87. See J. C. Beckett and R. E. Glasscock, eds., *Belfast: The Origins and Growth of an Industrial City* (London: British Broadcasting Corporation, 1967); Emrys Jones, *A Social Geography of Belfast* (London: Oxford University Press, 1960). A. C. Hepburn's quantitative study of Belfast has shown that "religion in Belfast was, indeed, a considerably more potent force for residential segregation than was social class"; or, to put it another way, in Belfast, religion made deeper splits within classes than class allegiances made within religious groups. See A. C. Hepburn, "Work, Class and Religion in Belfast, 1871–1911," *Irish Economic and Social History* 10 (1983), 37.

88. The degree of job discrimination in the private sector in the north of Ireland is not well documented before the 1960s, but it is one of the few things of whose existence "everyone knew" in the nineteenth and early twentieth centuries because it was a fact. I have never encountered a historical argument against the reality of existence in Ulster of high degrees of sectarianism in the hiring practices by members of all religious groups.

89. Of those historians who apply the concept of modernization to Ulster, much the most interesting work has been done by David W. Miller (see note 6). That I do not find Miller's argument entirely convincing should not obscure the fact that his treatment of the Ulster Presbyterians is the most original to be published in the twentieth century.

90. Brooke, pp. 154–63. On Cooke, the recent biography *Henry Cooke* by Finlay Holmes (Belfast: Christian Journals, 1981) is useful.

91. For details of disestablishment, see Akenson, *Church of Ireland*, pp. 226–74.

92. Ibid., pp. 132–42.

93. For a statement of this derivative view, applied by *force majore* to Ulster, see Gibbon, esp. p. 56.

94. Bruce, p. 11.

95. For a nearly contemporary account see William Gibson, *The Year of Grace* (Belfast: n.p., 1860).

96. Killen, 2:529–30.

97. Ibid., 2:12–13.

98. Reid, 3:511.

99. Brooke, p. 175.

100. See Donald Harman Akenson, *The Irish Education Experiment* (London: Routledge and Kegan Paul, 1970), pp. 161–87.

5. Zionism and the Land of Israel to 1948

1. Walter Laqueur, *A History of Zionism* (London: Weidenfeld and Nicolson, 1972), p. xiii.

2. In relationship to its size and the length of its existence, the state of Israel has probably the highest bibliodensity in the world. Rather than engage in portmanteau notes, in the discussion that follows I shall refer only to those works and sources that I have found most helpful. Direct quotations and facts not generally known are of course directly documented.

3. Napoleon Bonaparte's proclamation of 20 April 1799, in Jerusalem, trans. and quoted in Isaiah Friedman, ed., *From Precursors of Zionism to Herzl* (New York: Garland, 1987), p. 2, a volume in the Garland series titled *The Rise of Israel*. The series of thirty-nine volumes is an extremely valuable collection of primary material related to the creation of the state of Israel.

4. Shlomo Avineri, *The Making of Modern Zionism: The Intellectual Origins of the Jewish State* (New York: Basic Books, 1981), pp. 23–72. See also David Vital, *The Origins of Zionism* (Oxford: Clarendon Press, 1975).

5. Amos Elon, *The Israelis: Founders and Son* (London: Weidenfeld and Nicolson, 1971), p. 34.

6. Moshe Kohn, "They Also Came," *Jerusalem Post International Edition*, 28 April 1990, pp. 11 and 14.

7. Paul Johnson, *A History of the Jews* (New York: Harper and Row, 1987), p. 321.

8. Ibid., p. 356.

9. Elon, p. 43.

10. For a balanced, evocative reminiscence of *shtetl* life, see the autobiography of the Zionist leader Chaim Weizmann, *Trial and Error* (London: Hamish Hamilton, 1949), pp. 1–43.

11. Avineri, p. 5.

12. David Ben-Gurion's confidential memorandum on Zionist policy, 15 October 1941, p. 10, quoted in Michael J. Cohen, ed., *The Zionist Political Program, 1940–1947* (New York: Garland, 1987), p. 22. Another estimate suggests that the Jewish population of Palestine rose from 24,000 in 1882 to about 85,000 in 1914. Neville Mandel, *The Arabs and Zionism before World War I* (Berkeley: University of California Press, 1976), p. cxiv n. 5.

13. See Mandel, esp. pp. 223–31.

14. Baruch Kimmerling, *Zionism and Territory: The Socio-Territorial Dimensions of Zionist Politics* (Berkeley: Institute of International Studies, University of California, 1983), p. 7.

15. Friedman, pp. vi–vii; Michael J. Cohen, *The Origins and Evolution of the Arab-Zionist Conflict* (Berkeley: University of California Press, 1987), pp. 34–35.

16. See, Avineri, pp. 88–100; Alex Bein, *Theodor Herzl: A Biography* (Philadelphia: Jewish Publication Society of America, 1945); Amos Elon, *Herzl* (New York: Holt, Rinehart, and Winston, 1975); Isaiah Friedman, ed., *Herzl's Political Activity, 1897–1904* (New York: Garland, 1987); Desmond Stewart, *Theodor Herzl: Artist and Politician* (London: Hamish Hamilton, 1974).

17. On Zionist developments in the decade after Herzl's death, see David Vital, *Zionism: The Formative Years* (Oxford: Clarendon Press, 1982).

18. "The Solution of the Jewish Question" was first published in *Osterreichische Wochenscrift* 21 February 1896; it appeared in English in the *Jewish Chronicle* (London) 17 January 1896. It is included in Harry Zohn, ed., *Zionist Writings: Essays and Addresses, Theodor Herzl* (New York: Herzl Press, 1973), 1:24.

19. Maxime Rodinson, *Israel: A Colonial-Settler State?* (New York: Monad Press, 1973), pp. 39–40.

20. Chaim Weizmann, "Palestine's Role in the Solution of the Jewish Problem, *Foreign Affairs* (January 1942), p. 326, included in Cohen, ed., *The Zionist Political Program, 1940–47*, pp. 52–53.

21. Chaim Weizmann, "Memorandum on Palestine Policy Submitted by the Jewish Agency for Palestine to His Majesty's Government," 16 October 1944, in ibid., pp. 149–51.

22. Barnet Litvinoff, *Weizmann: Last of the Patriarchs* (New York: G. P. Putnam's Son, 1976), p. 51.

23. For a highly readable, if self-serving, account of the events at the sixth congress of the World Zionist Organization, see Weizmann's autobiography, *Trial and Error*, pp. 110–17.

24. Conor Cruise O'Brien, "Some Reflections on Religion and Nationalism," *Studies in Zionism* 6 (1985), 161.

25. As, for example, in Samuel J. Roberts, *Survival or Hegemony? The Foundations of Israel Foreign Policy* (Baltimore: Johns Hopkins University Press, 1973), p. 2.

26. Herzl quoted in Amos Elon, "Jerusalem: The Future of the Past," *New York Review of Books,* 17 August 1988, p. 37.

27. Freud quoted in ibid.

28. Johnson, pp. 403–4; O'Brien, p. 161; Elon, "Jerusalem," p. 37.

29. Weizmann, "Memorandum on Palestine Policy," p. 150.

30. "Statement of Mr. David Ben Gurion," in *The Jewish Case before the Anglo-American Committee of Inquiry on Palestine as Presented by the Jewish Agency for Palestine* (Jerusalem: Jewish Agency, 1947, rpr. Westport, Conn: Hyperion Press, 1976), p. 54.

31. William Chomsky, *Hebrew: The Eternal Language* (Philadelphia: Jewish Publication Society of America, 1975), pp. 233–34.

32. See Avineri, pp. 83–87.

33. Elon, *The Israelis*, p. 125.

34. Thus, when Hebrew University was founded in 1918, there was never any doubt that Hebrew would be the language of instruction. Chomsky, pp. 237–44.

35. Johnson, p. 319.

36. See, for example, Leonard Stein, *The Balfour Declaration* (London: Valentine-Mitchell, 1961). See as context, from the British viewpoint, Christopher Sykes, *Crossroads to Israel* (Bloomington: Indiana University Press, 1965).

37. Johnson, p. 440.

38. Vincent Sheean, *Personal History* (New York: Modern Library, 1934), pp. 367–69.

39. For a summary of the Palestine mandate, see *Israel Pocket Library History from 1880* (Jerusalem: Keter Books, 1973), pp. 96–98.

40. Aaran S. Klieman, *Zionist Political Activity in the 1920s and 1930s* (New York: Garland, 1987), pp. i–xii; Mark Tessler, "The Political Right in Israel: Its origins, Growth, and Prospects," *Journal of Palestine Studies* 15 (Winter 1986), 13–21.

41. Martin Buber, "The National Home and National Policy in Palestine," in Paul R. Mendes-Flohr, *A Land of Two Peoples, Martin Buber on Jews and Arabs* (New York: Oxford University Press, 1983), p. 86.

42. Resolutions passed at the sixteenth World Zionist Congress in Zurich, July–August 1929, in Kleiman, p. 14.

43. See ibid., pp. 15–68, for scores of such references.

44. Lenni Brenner, *The Iron Wall: Zionist Revisionism from Jabotinsky to Shamir* (London: Zed Books, 1984), p. 74.

45. James J. Zogby, "The Palestinian Revolt of the 1930s," in Ibrahim Abu-Lughod and Baha Abu-Laban, eds., *Settler Regimes in Africa and the Arab World: The Illusion of Endurance* (Wilmette, Ill.: Medina University Press International, 1974), pp. 94–115.

46. Kimmerling, p. 10. Kimmerling's excellent study is fundamental to any understanding of Zionist territorial acquisition.

47. Ibid., table 1.1, p. 11.

48. *Palestine Royal Commission: Memoranda Prepared by the Government of Palestine* (London: HMSO, 1937), "Memorandum no. 7," pp. 15–18, in Kleiman, ed., pp. 251–54.

49. Abraham Granott, *Agrarian Reform and Record of Israel* (London: 1956), cited in Walter Lehn, "The Jewish National Fund," in Abu-Lughod and Abu-Laban, p. 43.

50. Kimmerling, pp. 47–48.

51. Lehn, p. 50.

52. Kimmerling, pp. 21–30.

53. "Memorandum no. 1," *Palestine Royal Commission*, p. 1, in Klieman, p. 237. For information on the immigration early in the mandate period see M. Mossek, *Palestine Immigration Policy under Sir Herbert Samuel: British, Zionist and Arab Attitudes* (London: Frank Cass, 1978).

54. Sheean, p. 371.

55. Shabtai Teveth, *Ben-Gurion and the Palestinian Arabs: From Peace to War* (Oxford: Oxford University Press, 1985), p. 39.

56. Brenner, p. 74.

57. Buber, "Soul-Searching," in Mendes-Flohr, p. 77.

58. Buber, "The National Home and National Policy in Palestine," in Mendes-Flohr, p. 89.

59. Teveth, p. 38.

60. Buber, "The National Home and National Policy in Palestine," in Mendes-Flohr, p. 84.

61. *The Jewish Case*, p. 66.

62. In recent years a good deal of energy on the part of historians has been misspent on the confusion of physical dispossession (which, as we have seen, did not occur except by purchase in the interwar years) with the assertion of Zionist hegemony in Palestine, which was increasingly rapid in the interwar era. For example, Joan Peters, in *From Time Immemorial: The Origins of the Arab-Jewish Conflict over Palestine* (New York: Harper and Row, 1984), builds an entire volume on the thesis that (to her surprise) there was significant illegal Arab migration into Palestine in the interwar years: therefore, the Arabs had nothing to complain about concerning Zionist expansion. For a scholarly discussion of the matter of

Arab immigration, see Fred M. Gottheil, "Arab Immigration into Pre-State Israel: 1922–1931," in Elie Kedourie and Sylvia G. Haim, *Palestine and Israel in the Nineteenth and Twentieth Centuries* (London: Frank Cass, 1982), pp. 143–52.

63. *Financial Aspects of Jewish Reconstruction in Palestine: How the Arabs Have Benefitted through Jewish Immigration* (London: Jewish Agency for Palestine, 1930), p. 6, quoted in Klieman, p. 335.

64. Ibid., p. 8, in Klieman, p. 337.

65. Ibid., pp. 12–13, in Klieman, pp. 341–42.

66. Teveth, p. 42.

67. "Resolutions passed at the sixteenth Zionist Congress," p. 20, in Klieman, p. 18.

68. Teveth, pp. 41–42.

69. Greenberg, pp. 361–68.

70. *Israel Pocket Library, History from 1880*, pp. 96–115. See Klieman for reproductions of several of the British official documents on Palestine.

71. The discussion of boundaries that follows is based on Rael Jean Isaac, *Israel Divided: Ideological Politics in the Jewish State* (Baltimore: Johns Hopkins University Press, 1976), pp. 20–44.

72. The many-sided debate on partition that was conducted in the second half of the 1930s and the early 1940s is well summarized in Amos Perlmutter, *Israel, the Partitioned State: A Political History Since 1900* (New York: Charles Scribner's Sons, 1985), pp. 60–73.

73. Teveth, p. 181.

74. David Ben-Gurion, speech reported in *New Outlook* (Tel Aviv), April 1977, quoted in Noam Chomsky, *The Fateful Triangle: The United States, Israel and the Palestinians* (London: Pluto Press, 1983), p. 161.

75. I am grateful to my friends Gerald Tulchinsky and Michael R. Marrus for their guidance on the literature of the holocaust. Marrus's *The Holocaust in History* (Toronto: Lester and Orpen Dennys, 1987) is a scholarly tour de force.

76. Earl Berger, *The Covenant and the Sword: Arab-Israeli Relations, 1948–56* (London: Routledge and Kegan Paul, 1965), p. 9. Berger's view (p. 10) that "Nazism gave Zionism its impetus and the strength necessary to overcome the enormous obstacles in its way," misses the inherent strength in Zionism that existed before World War II, and therefore misleadingly makes the active agent in the creation of Israel the Nazi movement.

77. *The Jewish Case*, pp. 20–21.

78. Ibid., p. 66.

79. See Elmer Berger, *Memoirs of an Anti-Zionist Jew* (New York: Institute for Palestine Studies, 1978); and Thomas A. Kolsky, *Jews against Zionism: The American Council for Judaism, 1942–1948* (Philadelphia: Temple University Press, 1990).

80. Perlmutter, pp. 70–73. For the debate within Zionism during the 1940s see the documents in Cohen, ed., *The Zionist Political Program, 1940–1947*.

81. The particularly volatile aspect of this policy of shunting holocaust survivors to Eretz Israel rather than giving them the alternative of settling in America, is that Zionist leaders in the United States did very little to actually save European Jewry in its time of gravest peril. In 1980, Arthur Goldberg, former supreme court justice of the United States, headed a commission of prominent American Jews to examine this question. After fifteen months the commission split apart; its draft report was very critical of the actions of American Jewish leadership on this matter. The report stated that "what is certain is that the exclusive concentration on Palestine as a solution, coupled with its intrinsic pessimism as to other alternatives, distracted the Zionist movement as well as large segments of American Jews from giving serious attention to various rescue plans." Chomsky, *Fateful Triangle*, p. 94, quoting the *New York Times*, 4 January 1982.

82. Johnson, pp. 522–24. For background, see Ronald M. Zweig, *Britain and Palestine during the Second World War* (London: Royal Historical Society, 1986); and Roberts, *Survival or Hegemony?* pp. 56 ff.

83. Kimmerling, p. 58.

6. *Northern Ireland: A Protestant State for a Protestant People, 1920–1969*

1. A. T. Q. Stewart, *The Narrow Ground: Aspects of Ulster, 1609–1969* (London: Faber and Faber, 1977), p. 162.

2. Resolution of the convention of the Presbyterian Church in Ireland, quoted in Patrick Buckland, *Irish Unionism, 1885–1923: A Documentary History* (Belfast: HMSO, 1973), pp. 78–79.

3. The political history of the three home rule bills and of partition begins in 1885. The indispensable background is K. Theodore Hoppen's magesterial *Elections, Politics, and Society in Ireland, 1832–1885* (Oxford: Clarendon Press, 1984). A valuable study that carries the story forward is Patrick Buckland's *Ulster Unionism and the Origins of Northern Ireland, 1886–1922* (Dublin: Gill and Macmillan, 1973). See also Brian M. Walker's *Ulster Politics: The Formative Years, 1868–86* (Belfast: Ulster Historical Foundation and Institute of Irish Studies, Queen's University of Belfast, 1989). Earlier works of political history of Northern Ireland are contentious. For the southern Irish interpretation, see Denis Gwynn's *The History of Partition (1912–1925)* (Dublin: Brown and Noland, 1950). Hugh Shearman's *Anglo-Irish Relations* (London: Faber and Faber, 1948) gives the northern Protestant interpretation of Ulster's relations with Great Britain and the Irish Free State through 1948.

4. The best discussion of these events is A. T. Q. Stewart, *The Ulster Crisis* (London: Faber and Faber, 1967).

5. On David Lloyd George's negotiations with unionist and nationalist leaders on home rule, see Donald Harman Akenson, *The United States and Ireland* (Cambridge: Harvard University Press, 1973), pp. 87–90.

6. Denis P. Barritt and Charles F. Carter, *The Northern Ireland Problem: A Study in Group Relations* (London: Oxford University Press, 1962), p. 21.

7. Independent Television Authority, *Religion in Britain and Northern Ireland* (London: Independent Television Authority, 1970).

8. Frank Wright, "Protestant Ideology and Politics in Ulster," *Archives Europeenes de Sociologie* 14, 2 (1973), 247.

9. For the raw data, 1926–61, see Donald Harman Akenson, *Education and Enmity: The Control of Schooling in Northern Ireland, 1920–50* (Newton Abbot: David and Charles for Institute of Irish Studies, Queen's University of Belfast, 1973), p. 26.

10. On religiosocial stratigraphy, an excellent, but much neglected, study is Emrys Jones, *A Social Geography of Belfast* (London: Oxford University Press, 1960).

11. Barritt and Carter, p. 33. This book has a good deal of revealing material on the different social styles of the two main religious groups; see esp. pp. 143–51.

12. John M. Mogey, "The Community in Northern Ireland," *Man* 48 (1948), 87.

13. Stewart, *Narrow Ground*, p. 48.

14. Quotations from Barritt and Carter, pp. 44–46.

15. The basic documents concerning the Ulster government in 1920–69 are found in Arthur S. Quekett's, *The Constitution of Northern Ireland*, 2 vols. (Belfast: HMSO, 1933). See also Harry Calvert, *Constitutional Law in Northern Ireland: A Study in Regional Government* (London and Belfast: Northern Ireland Legal Quarterly, 1968); and Nicholas Mansergh, *The Government of Northern Ireland: A Study in Devolution* (London: George Allen and Unwin, 1936). The best modern study of the period is Patrick Buckland, *The Factory of Grievances: Devolved Government in Northern Ireland, 1921–39* (Dublin: Gill and Macmillan, 1979).

16. On financial matters see R. J. Lawrence, *The Government of Northern Ireland: Public Finance and Public Service, 1921–1964* (Oxford: Clarendon Press, 1965).

17. Until 1968, the report of the boundary commission was classified as secret. It was published in 1970, edited by Geoffrey Hand: *Report of the Irish Boundary Commission, 1925* (Shannon: Irish University Press).

18. On electoral discrimination see Barritt and Carter, pp. 39–44; Buckland, *Factory*, pp. 221–46; *Orange and Green: A Quaker Study of Community Relations in Northern Ireland* (Belfast: Northern Friends Peace Board, 1969), pp. 20–24.

19. Mansergh, p. 142.

20. Barritt and Carter, pp. 112–14; *Orange and Green*, pp. 22–23.

21. D. Donnison, "The Northern Ireland Civil Service," *New Society* 5 (July 1973), 8–10; Barritt and Carter, p. 96.

22. Frank Gallagher, *The Indivisible Island* (London: Gallancz, 1957), pp. 209–11, cited in Barritt and Carter, p. 98.

23. Richard Rose, *Governing without Consensus* (London: Faber and Faber, 1971), p. 288.

24. See Claude Mertens, "Report on Civil and Social Rights in Northern Ireland," *Revue de Droit International et Compare*, vol. 3 (1969), and *Report of a Commission of Inquiry* (1936; London: English National Council for Civil Liberties, 1972). The reader may notice that in discussing the various forms of anti-Catholic discrimination by Ulster Protestants, I do not mention the matter of primary and secondary education, despite the fact that Buckland sees educational discrimination as an integral part of the Ulster governmental policy (*Factory*, p. 6), and despite the fact that I have written the standard history of state policy and education in Ulster (*Education and Enmity*). I simply cannot be as confident of my judgments as apparently Buckland can be of his. It is clear that the Catholic schools received a somewhat lower proportion of their expenses paid by the state than did the state schools, which were de facto Protestant. (Precise figures are impossible to calculate, but if one takes salary, maintenance, and capital expenditures into account, a fair guess would be that nine-tenths of the Catholic primary schools' expenses were covered by the state, and, of course, the state school had nearly 100 percent covered.) This is much better than the Catholic schools fared in the United States or in several continental European countries, but that is not the point. The real point is that the extraordinary obstinacy of the Catholic bishops and clergy in their refusal to share control of the schools with the laity—Roman Catholic laity—prevented the Catholic schools from taking part in provisions of the various education acts which could have raised the Catholic grants to close to the level of the state schools. The situation, then, was that many Protestant leaders would have been quite pleased to discriminate sharply against Catholic schools, but in fact, provisions of the actual legislation would have let the Catholic authorities overcome their disadvantages. But they did not choose to do so. In this situation, I think it inappropriate to make a simple judgment.

25. Stewart, *Ulster Crisis*, pp. 237–43.

7. The High Noon of Apartheid, 1948–1969

1. For a comprehensive bibliography see Jacqueline A. Kalley, *South Africa under Apartheid: A Select and Annotated Bibliography* (Pietermaritzburg: Shuter and Shooter, with the Institute of Social and Economic Research, Rhodes University, 1987).

2. Dan O'Meara, *Volkskapitalisme: Class, Capital and Ideology in the Development of Afrikaner Nationalism, 1934–1948* (Johannesburg: Ravan Press, 1983), p. 167.

3. Irving Hexham, *The Irony of Apartheid: The Struggle for National Independence of Afrikaner Calvinism against British Imperialism* (New York: Edwin Mellen Press, 1981), pp. 188–89.

4. T. Dunbar Moodie, *The Rise of Afrikanerdom: Power, Apartheid, and the Afrikaner Civil Religion* (Berkeley: University of California Press, 1975), p. 235.

5. Hermann Giliomee, "The National Party and the Afrikaner Broederbond," in Robert M. Price and Carl G. Rosberg, eds., *The Apartheid Regime: Political Power and Racial Domination* (Berkeley: Institute of International Studies, 1980), p. 15. As context, see Michael Roberts and A. E. G. Trollop, *The South African Opposition, 1939–1945: An Essay in Contemporary History* (London: Longmans, Green, 1947).

6. The demographic trends among the main white cultural groups are indicated by noting the patterns of religious affiliation, 1911–51, as reported in Government of South Africa, *Uniestatistieke orr Vyftig Jaar*, (1961), p. A-16.

7. T. R. H. Davenport, *South Africa: A Modern History*, 3d ed. (Toronto: University of Toronto Press, 1987), p. 355.

8. Ibid., p. 356, citing studies by M. Legassick and Dan O'Meara.

9. Jeffrey Butler, "Afrikaner Women and the Creation of Ethnicity in a Small South African Town, 1902–1950," in Leroy Vail, ed., *The Creation of Tribalism in Southern Africa* (London: James Currey, 1989), p. 58.

10. Davenport, pp. 586–87.

11. William Hudson, Gideon F. Jacobs, and Simon Biesheuvel, *Anatomy of South Africa: A Scientific Study of Present Day Attitudes* (Cape Town: Purnell and Sons, 1966), p. 11.

12. *Die Volksblad,* 16 December 1946, quoted and trans. in F. A. van Jaarsveld, *The Afrikaner's Interpretation of South African History* (Cape Town: Simondium Publishers, 1964), p. 23.

13. *Die Transvaler,* 16 December 1942, quoted and trans. in Moodie, p. 248.

14. Moodie, p. 249.

15. B. J. Vorster, *Select Speeches,* ed. O. Geyser (Bloemfontein: INCH, UOFS, 1977), p. 75.

16. J. H. P. Serfontein, *Brotherhood of Power: An Exposé of the Secret Afrikaner Broederbond* (Bloomington: Indiana University Press, 1978), p. 243.

17. C. B. Brink, "Die Beginsels ten Grondslag van die Sendingbeleid van die Ned. Geref Kerke in Suid-Afrika," in Federal Missionary Council of the Dutch Reformed Churches, *Conference of Church Leaders (Nov. 1953),* p. 22–35.

18. *The Dutch Reformed Churches in South Africa and the Problem of Race Relations: Report of the ad hoc Commission for Race Relations Appointed by the Federal Council of Dutch Reformed Churches in South Africa* (1977), pp. 3–11.

19. Ibid., p. 13.

20. Ibid., pp. 13 and 15.

21. *Human Relations in South Africa,* quoted in Robert Buis, *Religious Beliefs and White Prejudice* (Johannesburg: Ravan Press, 1975), p. 13.

22. Conor Cruise O'Brien, *Passion and Cunning and Other Essays* (London: Weidenfeld and Nicolson, 1988), p. 147.

23. Davenport, p. 577.

24. I have found especially useful John Dugard's "Racial legislation and Civil Rights," in Ellen Hellman and Henry Lever, eds., *Race Relations in South Africa 1929–1979* (London: Macmillan, 1980), pp. 79–96. For a full register of apartheid legislation the *Annual Report of the South African Institute of Race Relations* is indispensable. It later was renamed *Race Relations Survey* and still later *Survey of Race Relations in South Africa.* A valuable overview is F. A. van Jaarsveld, "Die evolusie van apartheid 1948–1978," in his *Die evolusie van apartheid en ander geskiedkundige opstelle* (Cape Town: Tafelberg, 1979), pp. 1–23. See also Edgar H. Brookes, *Apartheid: A Documentary Study of Modern South Africa* (London: Routledge and Kegan Paul, 1968); and Muriel Horrell, comp., *Race Relations as Regulated by Law in South Africa* (Johannesburg: South African Institute of Race Relations, 1982).

25. South African Statutes, Act 30, 1950.

26. Allen Drury, *"A Very Strange Society": A Journey to the Heart of South Africa* (London: Michael Joseph, 1968), p. 31.

27. South African Statutes, Act 55, 1949.

28. Gwendolen M. Carter, in Brookes, p. 179.

29. See South African Statutes, Act 55, 1949. Notice that under the statute, marriages among the profane groups—the "coloured," Asians, and "natives"—were not prohibited.

30. A. N. Pelzer, ed., *Verwoerd Speaks: Speeches 1948–1966* (Johannesburg: AFB Publishers, 1966), p. 4.

31. South African Statutes, Act 21, 1950.

32. See the summary of changes given in the speech of B. J. Vorster during the 1962 amendment of the Immorality Act, in Geyser, ed., p. 41.

33. Carter, in Brookes, p. 186.

34. South African Statutes, Act 49, 1953.

35. For a presentation of some of the more striking aspects of petty apartheid, see E. J. Kahn, Jr., *The Separated People: A Look at Contemporary South Africa* (New York: W. W. Norton, 1968), pp. 26–35.

36. South African Statutes, Act 17, 1951; Act 48, 1953; Act 28, 1956. It should be noted that the apartheid system did not introduce anything radically new in labor discrimination (an act of 1924 had set clear precedents) but merely did it better. An ironic twist of the policy was that in certain *un*skilled occupations, whites displaced blacks and, simultaneously, the wage rates for these jobs increased sharply. The economic irrationality of such practice is obvious, but was not much commented on until the 1970s.

37. For a cogent discussion, see John D. Shingler, "Education and Political Order in South Africa, 1902–1961," Ph.D. dissertation, Yale University, 1973, pp. 278–90.

38. W. G. McConkey, *Natal Daily News*, December 1962, quoted in Brookes, p. 60.

39. South African Statutes, Act 45, 1959.

40. South African Statutes, Act 41, 1950.

41. Pelzer, p. 2.

42. Cited in Graham Leach, *The Afrikaners: Their Last Great Trek* (London: Macmillan, 1989), p. 169.

43. John Lazar, "The Role of the South African Bureau of Racial Affairs in the Formulation of Apartheid Ideology, 1948–1961," *Collected Seminar Papers no. 37* (London: Institute of Commonwealth Studies, 1988), pp. 96–109.

44. South African Statutes, Act 54, 1952.

45. South African Statutes, Act 67, 1952.

46. See Hudson et al., esp. pp. 40 ff. For a useful set of papers, see André de Villiers, ed., *English-Speaking South Africa Today: Proceedings of the National Conference July 1974* (Cape Town: Oxford University Press, 1976). For an index of the development of "liberal" Anglophone opinion from 1956 onward, see the periodical *The Black Sash*.

47. D. F. Malan, *Afrikaner-Volkseenheid en my Ervarings op die Pad daarheen* (Cape Town: Nasionale Boekhandel Beperk, 1959), pp. 46–47. For biographies of Malan, see Bun Booyens, *Die Lewe van D. F. Malan, Die Erste Veertig Jare* (Cape Town: Tafelberg-Uitgewers, 1969); H. B. Thom, *D. F. Malan* (Cape Town: Tafelberg Uitgewers, Beperk, 1986).

48. Meyer's speech is given in full, in translation, in Serfontein, pp. 230–42.

49. Ibid.

50. Harrison, pp. 154–56; S. van Wyck, *Die Afrikaner in die Beroepslewe van die Stad* (Cape Town: Academica Person, 1968), cited in Hendrik W. van der Merwe et al., *White South African Elites: A Study of Incumbents of Top Positions in the Republic of South Africa* (Cape Town: Juta, 1974), p. 80.

51. O'Meara, p. 250.

52. Ibid.

53. Dan O'Meara, "White Trade Unionism, Political Power and Afrikaner Nationalism," in Eddie Webster, ed., *Essays in South African Labour History* (Johannesburg: Ravan Press, 1978), pp. 164–80.

54. H. L. Watts, "A Social and Demographic Portrait of English-Speaking White South Africans," in de Villiers, table 10, p. 62.

55. *Beleid* (Johannesburg: Federasie van Afrikaanse Kultur Vereniginge and Instituut vir Christelike Nasionale Onderwys, 1948). Large portions are translated in Brian Rose and Raymond Tunmer, eds., *Documents in South African Education* (Johannesburg: Ad. Donker, 1975), pp. 120–29. Quotations in the text are from this source.

56. Watts, in de Villiers, table 5, p. 53.

57. Ernst G. Malherbe, *Education in South Africa, vol. 2, 1923–1975* (Cape Town: Juta, 1977), p. 95. Malherbe's views were influenced by his own earlier study of the research results concerning methods of achieving bilingualism. See his *The Bilingual School* (Johannesburg: Bilingual School Association, 1943).

58. Harrison, p. 200.
59. Malherbe, 2:95.
60. Ibid., 2:110.
61. South African Statutes, Act 39, 1967.
62. Speech of L. E. D. Winchester, *Hansard,* 22 February 1967, quoted in Rose and Tunmer, p. 130. For an apt summary of Christian National goals, see Shingler, pp. 150–54.
63. F. E. Auerbach, *The Power of Prejudice in South African Education: An enquiry into History Textbooks and Syllabuses in the Transvaal High Schools of South Africa* (Cape Town: A. A. Balkema, 1965).
64. J. M. du Preez, *Africana Afrikaner: Master Symbols in South African School Textbooks,* trans. Hope du Plessis (Alberton, R.S.A.: Librarius [1984]).
65. Auerbach, p. 1.
66. Ibid., p. x, emphasis his.
67. Du Preez, p. 11.
68. Ibid., pp. 60–71.
69. Ibid., p. 92.
70. Peter Lambley, *The Psychology of Apartheid* (Athens: University of Georgia Press, 1980), pp. 198 and 199. Lambley's observations, based on his clinical practice, are an ideal-type or analytic model, and of course do not hold for every specific case.
71. Davenport, pp. 389–94, 398–99; Harrison, pp. 160–67; James Barber and John Barratt, *South Africa's Search for Status and Security 1945–1988* (Cambridge: Cambridge University Press, 1990).
72. Sheila T. van der Horst, "The Changing Face of the Economy," in Hellman and Lever, p. 110.
73. Van der Horst notes (p. 110) that in 1960, 6 percent of domestic investment was made by public corporations, and this had accelerated to 17 percent in 1975. If jobs produced by this investment were proportional to the amount of investment, these corporations would have yielded roughly 5–15 percent of white employment.
74. Dugard, in Hellman and Lever, pp. 87–93.

8. Israel: A Singular State, 1948–1967

1. The Declaration of Independence is given in Meron Medzini, ed., *Israel's Foreign Relations: Selected Documents, 1947–1974* (Jerusalem: Minister for Foreign Affairs, 1976), pp. 1–3.
2. Zvi Gitelman, *Becoming Israelis: Political Resocialization of Soviet and American Immigrants* (New York: Praeger, 1982), p. 44.
3. James S. Diamond, *Homeland or Holy Land? The "Canaanite" Critique of Israel* (Bloomington: Indiana University Press, 1986), p. 118. The entire volume deserves study as an explanation of why secularism was impossible in Israel.
4. Charles S. Liebman and Eliezer Don-Yehiya, *Civil Religion in Israel: Traditional Judaism and Political Culture in the Jewish State* (Berkeley: University of California Press, 1983), p. 19.
5. Meir Bar-Ilan, "What Kind of Life Shall We Create in Eretz Israel?" in Aaron S. Klieman, ed., *Giving Substance to the Jewish National Home: 1920 and Beyond* (New York: Garland, 1987), pp. 36–37.
6. Liebman and Don-Yehiya, p. 19.
7. Dan Izenberg, "The Limits of Morality," *Jerusalem Post Magazine,* 30 December 1990, p. 1.
8. Shlomo Avineri, "Our Second Home," *Jerusalem Post International Edition* (hereafter *JP*), 6 January 1990.
9. Paul Johnson, *A History of the Jews* (London: Harper and Row, 1987), p. 527.
10. Ibid., p. 532.
11. Michael Brecher, *Decisions in Israel's Foreign Policy* (London: Oxford University

Press, 1974), pp. 9–55; Earl Berger, *The Covenant and the Sword: Arab-Israeli Relations, 1948–56* (London: Routledge and Kegan Paul, 1965), pp. 14–77. As background, see Yehoshafat Harkabi, *Arab Attitudes to Israel* (Jerusalem: Israel Universities Press, 1972).

12. Rael Jean Isaac, *Israel Divided: Ideological Politics in the Jewish State* (Baltimore: Johns Hopkins University Press, 1976), p. 43.

13. For an indication that this is still a hotly debated issue, see Arthur Hertzberg, "The Impasse over Israel," *New York Review of Books,* 25 October 1990, pp. 41–46. He discusses as the two poles of the controversy John Quigley's *Palestine and Israel: A Challenge to Justice* (Chapel Hill: Duke University Press, 1990), and Benny Morris, *The Making of the Palestinian Refugee Problem, 1947–1949* (Cambridge: Cambridge University Press, 1988). This is somewhat hard on Morris, who is far from being an Israeli apologist. His *1948 and After: Israel and the Palestinians* (Oxford: Clarendon Press, 1990) argues against the belief that the flight of the Palestinians was executed under the orders of Palestinian leaders and thus was not a genuine flight of refugees. For a reasonably balanced, in-depth study of the exodus in one region, see Nafez Nazzal, *The Palestinian Exodus from Galilee, 1948* (Beirut: Institute for Palestinian Studies, 1978).

14. Richard Wiemer, "Zionism and the Arabs after the Establishment of the State of Israel: A Study of Zionist Conceptions for Arabs in the Jewish State," in Alexander Scholch, ed., *Palestinians over the Green Line: Studies in the Relations between Palestinians on both sides of the 1949 Armistice Line since 1967* (London: Ithaca Press, 1983), p. 34. Just how favorable the de-Arabization was in the context of Israeli expectations is shown in the fact that the primary Zionist planning document on the Arab population, "The Memorandum of the Five," prepared in June 1936, had predicted an Arab population in 1948 of 1,240,00 and a Jewish population only two-thirds that size. David Ben-Gurion, *My Talks with Arab Leaders* (New York: Third Press, 1973), p. 103.

15. Isaac, p. 41.

16. Wiemer, p. 34.

17. Gitelman, table 1.1, p. 11.

18. Baruch Kimmerling, *Zionism and Territory: The Socio-Territorial Dimensions of Zionist Politics* (Berkeley: Institute of International Studies, University of California, 1983), table 4.1, p. 93.

19. State of Israel, *Official Paper,* no. 7, June 1948, p. 19, quoted in Kimmerling, pp. 134–35.

20. Ian Lustick, *Arabs in the Jewish State: Israel's Control of a National Minority* (Austin: University of Texas Press, 1980), p. 172.

21. Emergency Land Requisition Law, 1949, quoted ibid., p. 173.

22. Absentees Property Law, 1950, *Laws of the State of Israel,* vol. 4, 1949–50, quoted in Kimmerling, p. 135.

23. Land Acquisition (Validation of Acts and Compensation) Law, 1953, quoted in Kimmerling, p. 137. See also Lustick, pp. 174–75.

24. Michael Adams, "Israel's Treatment of the Arabs in the Occupied Territories, *Journal of Palestine Studies* 6 (Winter 1977), 28; Lustick, p. 176.

25. Kimmerling, p. 136.

26. Lustick, pp. 177–78.

27. Stanley B. Greenberg, *Race and State in Capitalist Development: South Africa in Comparative Perspective* (Johannesburg: Ravan Press, 1980), p. 363.

28. Kimmerling, pp. 122–214.

29. Israel Land Authority, *Report for 1961–62,* trans. and cited in ibid. table 5.3, p. 143.

30. Ibid., p. 143.

31. Lustick, p. 167.

32. Kimmerling, p. 143.

33. Lustick, pp. 181–82.

34. Simha Flapan, *Zionism and the Palestinians* (New York: Barnes and Noble, 1979), pp. 199–200.

35. Greenberg, p. 367.
36. Wiemer, pp. 38–39.
37. Ibid., p. 39.
38. Greenberg, pp. 374–75.
39. Flapan, p. 197.
40. Wiemer, pp. 43–44. In 1990, more than one-third of the Palestinian labor force was working in Israel, comprising 7 percent of the total workers in Israel. "Russians da, Arabs la," *JP*, 29 June 1991.
41. Wiemer, pp. 41–42.
42. Adams, pp. 26–27.
43. Lustick, p. 67.
44. Adams, p. 27.
45. Greenberg, pp. 375–76; Lustick, pp. 112–16.
46. Lustick, pp. 93–94.
47. Wiemer, p. 46.
48. P. J. O'Rourke, *Holidays in Hell* (London: Picador, 1989), p. 167. There have, of course, always been exceptions. For example, Avishai Margalit, of Peace Now, who even after the Gulf War of 1990–91 averred that "our occupation is tragically emulating South African apartheid." *New York Times Magazine,* 21 July 1991, p. 32.
49. Lustick, pp. 25–26.
50. Gitelman, p. 10. For annual immigration figures, 1948–80, see table 1.1, p. 11.
51. Eliezer Ben-Rafael, *The Emergence of Ethnicity: Cultural Groups and Social Conflict in Israel* (Westport, Conn: Greenwood Press, 1982), p. 3.
52. Ibid.
53. Arthur S. Super, *Absorption of Immigrants* (Jerusalem: "Israel Digest," 1961), p. 9. This was item no. 18 in the series *Israel Today.*
54. Ibid., p. 15.
55. For a valuable study, see Ze'ev Schiff, *A History of the Israeli Army, 1874 to the Present* (New York: Macmillan, 1985).
56. Johnson, p. 541.
57. Chaim Rabin, *The Revival of Hebrew* (Jerusalem: "Israel Digest," 1958), pp. 9–10.
58. Charles S. Liebman, "Religion and Political Integration in Israel," *Journal of Jewish Sociology* 17 (1975), 21.
59. Ben-Gurion quoted in Shlomo Avineri, *The Making of Modern Zionism: The Intellectual Origins of the Jewish State* (New York: Basic Books, 1981), p. 213.
60. Ibid., p. 215.
61. Ben-Rafael, p. 14.
62. For a strong argument that Begin's political statements, which often were logically at odds with each other and incompatible with demonstrable political facts, were nevertheless conceptually consistent—part of a single conceptual-mythological framework determined by Hebrew mythology—see Robert C. Rowland, *The Rhetoric of Menachem Begin: The Myth of Redemption through Return* (Lanham, Md.: University Press of America, 1985).
63. "A Message from the Commander-in-Chief of the Irgun to the Diaspora," *The Answer* (September 1946), 11–12, cited in Rowland, pp. 243–46.
64. Rowland's *Rhetoric of Menachem Begin* is usefully read alongside Begin's own *The Revolt* (London: W. H. Allen, 1951).
65. David Ben-Gurion, *Israel: A Personal History* (New York: W. H. Allen, 1951).
66. Ibid., p. 822.
67. Ibid., p. 803.
68. The words are those of Adin Steinsalz, quoted in S. Clement Leslie, *The Rift in Israel: Religious Authority and Secular Democracy* (London: Routledge and Kegan Paul, 1971), p. 146.
69. Liebman and Don-Yehiya, pp. 30–40.
70. Ibid., pp. 40–47.
71. Ibid., p. 86.

72. Ibid., pp. 95–122.
73. Ibid., esp. pp. 1–24.
74. The entire agreement is found in Akiva Orr, *The unJewish State: The Politics of Jewish Identity in Israel* (London: Ithaca Press, 1983), pp. 7–9.
75. Leslie, p. 37.
76. Ibid., pp. 29–37; Mordecai Roshwald, "Who Is a Jew in Israel?" *Jewish Journal of Sociology* 12 (1970), 244–51.
77. Knesset Debates, vol. 6, pp. 2035–37, 3 July 1950, quoted in Orr, pp. 27–30.
78. Roshwald, p. 242.
79. For an extended discussion of the case and the court's decision see Orr, pp. 68–98. See also Roshwald, pp. 254–55.
80. Orr, pp. 33–67; Ben-Gurion, *Israel*, pp. 545–51; Leslie, p. 40.
81. Leslie, pp. 40–41; 99–132.
82. M. Avidor, *Education for a Growing Nation* (Jerusalem: "Israel Digest," 1961), p. 8.
83. Leslie, p. 52.
84. Conor Cruise O'Brien, *The Siege: The Saga of Israel and Zionism* (London: Weidenfeld and Nicolson, 1986), p. 349.
85. Abraham Shumsky, *The Clash of Cultures in Israel: A Problem for Education* (Westport, Conn.: Greenwood Press, 1972), p. 91.
86. Ibid., p. 92.
87. Ibid., p. 95.
88. Judith Bernstein and Aaran Antonovsky, "The Integration of Ethnic Groups in Israel," *Jewish Journal of Sociology* 23 (1981), table 4, p. 13.
89. As background on the foreign relations of Israel in this period, see Shlomo Aronson, *Conflict and Bargaining in the Middle East: An Israeli Perspective* (Baltimore: Johns Hopkins University Press, 1978); Earl Berger, *The Covenant and the Sword: Arab-Israeli Relations, 1948–56* (London: Routledge and Kegan Paul, 1965); Michael Brecher, *The Foreign Policy System of Israel: Setting, Images, Process* (London: Oxford University Press, 1972); Meron Medzini, ed., *Israel's Foreign Relations: Selected Documents 1947–1974* (Jerusalem: Ministry for Foreign Affairs, 1976).
90. Michael Bar-Zohar, "No, This Time They Won't Run Away," *JP*, 26 May 1990. His book is titled *Facing a Cruel Mirror* (New York: Charles Scribners' Sons, forthcoming 1992).
91. Bar-Zohar, "No, This Time They Won't Run Away."
92. For background, see Walter Laqueur, *The Road to War, 1967: The Origins of the Arab-Israel Conflict* (London: Weidenfeld and Nicolson, 1968).

9. A Covenant Comes Apart: Ulster, 1969 to the Present

1. Since the mid-1960s, Northern Ireland has become one of the most studied of modern societies. For an index of more than 6,000 items, see B. Rolston, M. Tomlinson, L. O'Dowd, R. L. Miller, and J. Smyth, *Social Science Bibliography of Northern Ireland, 1945–1983* (Belfast: Department of Social Studies, Queen's University of Belfast, 1985). The *summa* in Ulster scholarship is the late John Whyte's *Interpreting Northern Ireland* (Oxford: Clarendon Press, 1991). In my own work I have found Linen Hall Library, Belfast, the most useful source of contemporary information, as they have a fine ephemera collection encompassing all the major, and most of the minor, political and religious sects. Much of this collection now is available on microfilm.
2. Kevin Magee, "Statistical Reminders," *Fortnight,* September 1989, p. 13. Apparently Magee obtains his massive misinterpretation by comparing a twenty-year cumulative rate to the northern Irish population at any given point in time, a procedure that produces roughly twentyfold magnification error in his interpretation.
3. David Bates's *Nature* article is summarized in *Fortnight,* 18 October 1974, pp. 8–9.

4. There are, in addition to the Troubles deaths in Northern Ireland, a few everyday homicides. The number is very low and one suspects that in many cases they are disguised as Troubles killings. If anything, the comparison between Ulster and the United States is loaded in favor of the United States, for the Troubles figures include deaths of professional military personnel from outside the province who are serving in Ulster; the U.S. figures are entirely domestic.

5. Calculated from information supplied by the "Irish Information Partnership," London, in *Fortnight*, February 1989, p. 17. It is worth nothing that there has been a good deal of intragroup killing. For instance, of the 1,570 people killed by nationalist (Roman Catholic) paramilitaries during the Troubles, 170 have been clearly identified as Roman Catholic civilians. Similarly, of the 676 people killed by loyalist (Protestant) paramilitaries, 107 were Protestant civilians.

6. Michael McKeown, "Considerations on the Statistics of Violence," *Fortnight*, July 1977, p. 5, with minor arithmetical corrections.

7. P. J. O'Rourke, "The Fighting Irish," *Rolling Stone*, 9 February 1989, p. 99.

8. Sidney Elliott, "Sharing Powerlessness," *Fortnight*, May 1989, p. 10.

9. Brendan O'Leary, "More Green, Fewer Orange," *Fortnight*, February 1990, p. 12.

10. Ibid.

11. Garret Fitzgerald, writing in the *Observer*, quoted in *Fortnight*, October 1989, p. 22.

12. *Fortnight*, November 1989, p. 20.

13. Barry White, "From Conflict to Violence: The Re-Emergence of the IRA and the Loyalist Response," in John Darby, ed., *Northern Ireland: The Background to the Conflict* (Belfast: Appletree Press, 1983), p. 191.

14. N. J. Gibson, "The Impact of the Northern Ireland Crisis on the Economy," in Alan J. Ward, ed., *Northern Ireland: Living with the Crisis* (New York: Praeger, 1987), pp. 10–11.

15. Ibid., p. 11.

16. A very useful survey of the security forces is "The Security System," in W. D. Flackes and Sidney Elliott, *Northern Ireland: A Political Directory 1968–88* (Belfast: Blackstaff Press, 1989), pp. 383–409. For an overview of the Northern Ireland policing system, in comparative perspective, see John D. Brewer, Adrian Guelke, Ian Hume, Edward Moxon-Browne, and Rick Wilford, *The Police, Public Order and the State: Policing in Great Britain, Northern Ireland, the Irish Republic, the USA, Israel, South Africa and China* (London: Macmillan, 1988).

17. Paddy Hillyard, "Law and Order," in Darby, pp. 37–53.

18. Flackes and Elliott, p. 400.

19. Gibson, in Ward, pp. 1–15.

20. Karen Trew's essay "Psychological Well-Being in Northern Ireland," in Ward, pp. 16–45, has an excellent bibliography of relevant psychological studies.

21. Trew, pp. 34–36. See especially Ed Cairns, *Caught in the Crossfore: Children and the Northern Ireland Conflict* (Belfast: Appletree Press, 1987).

22. This point about the essentially public nature of the demands of the movement is well made in Michael Moran and Rupert Taylor, "Forget the Myths: Here's the Real Story," *Fortnight*, October 1988, pp. 6–7. This issue of the magazine has a useful series of reflections on the Irish civil rights campaign of the 1960s. See also the series of articles on the history of the Northern Ireland Civil Rights Association in *Fortnight* (22 March 1974, 5 April 1974, 10 May 1974, 7 June 1974). For background, see Bob Purdie, *Politics in the Streets: The Origins of the Civil Rights Movement in Northern Ireland* (Belfast: Blackstaff Press, 1990). The following paragraphs are taken primarily from my materials collected in 1969–72 in Northern Ireland.

23. (Belfast) *Newsletter*, 20 August 1969; *Irish News*, 20 August 1969.

24. See Sarah Nelson, *Ulster's Uncertain Defenders: Protestant Political, Paramilitary and Community Groups and the Northern Ireland Conflict* (Belfast: Appletree Press, 1984), esp. pp. 49–98.

25. See comments by David W. Miller, *Queen's Rebels: Ulster Loyalism in Historical Perspective* (Dublin: Gill and Macmillan, 1978), p. 159.

26. Flackes and Elliott, p. 373; Robin Wilson, "Moving On: A New Politics," *Fortnight*, November 1987, p. 21. For a perceptive general discussion of the various impacts of the AIA, see Padraig O'Malley, *Northern Ireland: Questions of Nuance* (Belfast: Blackstaff Press, 1990). A sharply argued critique is Arthur Aughey, *Under Siege: Ulster Unionism and the Anglo-Irish Agreement* (Belfast: Blackstaff Press, 1989).

27. Frank Wright, "Protestant Ideology and Politics in Ulster," *Archives Européennes de Sociologie* 14 (1973), 237.

28. Nelson, p. 11.

29. Editorial by "Columbanus Macnee," *Fortnight*, November 1988, p. 2.

30. Miller, p. 141.

31. Calculated from Brendan O'Leary, "More Green, Fewer Orange," *Fortnight*, February 1990, table 1, p. 12.

32. David McKittrick, "The Exit of the Young Turks," *Fortnight*, October 1987, p. 6.

33. Nelson, p. 128. See also Arthur Aughey and Colin McIlheney, "Law before Violence?—The Protestant Paramilitaries in Ulster Politics," *Eire-Ireland* 19 (Summer 1984), 55–74.

34. Calculated from O'Leary, p. 12, table 1.

35. Bill Rolston, "Reformism and Sectarianism: The State of the Union after Civil Rights," in Darby, pp. 211–24; David Eversley, *Religion and Employment in Northern Ireland* (London: Save Publications, 1989) Robin Wison, "Fair Jobs: DED Acts," *Fortnight*, March 1988, pp. 6–7.

36. Gary MacEoin, "Catholics, Catholicism, and the Northern Ireland Crisis," in Ward, p. 127.

37. Ibid., p. 128.

38. Eric Gallagher, "The Faith and Its Forms in Times of Stress," in Ward, pp. 102–3.

39. Flackes and Elliott, p. 42.

40. Wright, p. 236.

41. Gallagher, p. 110.

42. These phenomena had become a major worry to the Presbyterians and in 1984 the General Assembly focused major debates on the matter (Gallagher, p. 112).

43. Ed Moloney and Andy Pollak, *Paisley* (Dublin: Poolbeg Press, 1986), p. 216.

44. Ibid., p. 215.

45. See Bernard Conlon, "Ulster as Europe's Violent Sideshow," *Fortnight*, November 1989, pp. 16–17.

10. A World Unhinged: Afrikaners and Apartheid, 1969 to the Present

1. The half-dozen English-language papers that I have examined gave no play to the celebration at all. Typical of the mainline Afrikaans-language papers was *Die Burger* (Cape Town) which gave *Geloftesdag* sixteen column inches in two stories on 15 December 1988 and in subsequent issues half of an inside page, with photographs. For coverage from the progressive viewpoint, see *Vrye Weekblad*, 16 December 1988.

2. Graham Leach, *The Afrikaners: Their Last Great Trek* (London: Macmillan, 1989), pp. 3–7. Leach's volume is an extraordinarily prescient piece of journalism. Written before the surprising political events of 1990, it indicated that the abandoning of apartheid was well in process. Another useful journalistic book (by the former editor of the *Rand Daily Mail*) is Allister Sparks, *The Mind of South Africa* (London: Jonathan Cape, 1989).

3. Heribert Adam, "The South African Power-Elite," in Heribert Adam, ed., *South Africa: Sociological Perspectives* (London: Oxford University Press, 1971), pp. 73–102; and, Heribert Adam, "The South African Power-Elite: A Survey of Ideological Commitment," *Canadian Journal of Political Science* 4 (March 1971), 76–96.

4. Hendrik W. van der Merwe, M. J. Ashley, Nancy C. J. Charton, and Bettina J.

Huber, *White South African Elites: A Study of Incumbents of Top Positions in the Republic of South Africa* (Cape Town: Juta, 1974).

5. Adam and van der Merwe et al. present their work in such a way as to permit breaking out of the Afrikaans-speakers from the rest of the data base.

6. Kate Manzo and Patrick McGowan, "Is Apartheid Dying?" (forthcoming). I am grateful to the authors for providing me with a prepublication copy of this article.

7. My interpretation of the changes differs somewhat from that of Manzo and McGowan. That is one of the virtues of their study: it provides basic data that can be widely accepted and, therefore, rationally debated.

8. Manzo and McGowan, table 4 (cf. a somewhat comparable item in Adam, "South African Power-Elite," p. 80).

9. Manzo and McGowan, table 5.

10. Theodore Hanf, Heribert Weiland, and Gerda Vierdag, *South Africa: The Prospects of Peaceful Change* (Bloomington: Indiana University Press, 1981), pp. 154–56, cited in Manzo and McGowan.

11. Van der Merwe, pp. 62–64.

12. Manzo and McGowan, table 3.

13. Calculated from Adam, *South Africa,* p. 87.

14. Manzo and McGowan, table 2.

15. Ibid., p. 41.

16. Human Sciences Research Council, *Race Relations Survey, 1984* (Johannesburg: South African Institute of Race Relations, 1985), pp. 360–61. The proportions of English-speaking white South Africans who favored keeping each of the seven pillars were as follows: Mixed Marriages Act (41.3 percent), the Immorality Act (37.8 percent), Group Areas Act (42.4 percent), separate education (55.4 percent), separate amenities (50.5 percent), black African homelands (60.3 percent), and separate voter rolls for "coloureds" (64.3 percent).

17. *Weekly Mail* (Johannesburg), 22 June 1990.

18. In the 1987 general election, 40–45 percent of the English-speakers voted for the Nationalist party (Leach, p. 259).

19. Hermann Giliomee, *The Parting of the Ways: South African Politics, 1976–82* (Cape Town: David Philip, 1982), pp. 21, 37, and 113. On the invocation of "free enter- prise" and "economic growth" as major components of elite values, see Debbie Posel, "Language, Legitimation and Control: The South African State After '78," *Collected Semi- nar Papers no. 33: The Society of Southern Africa in the Nineteenth and Twentieth Cen- turies* (London: Institute of Commonwealth Studies, 1984). On the changing orientation of the Afrikaner business establishment and on a general desire among Afrikaner intellectuals to diminish the power of the state, see Stanley B. Greenberg, "Ideological Struggles within the South African State," in Shula Marks and Stanley Trapido, eds., *The Politics of Race, Class and Nationalism in Twentieth-Century South Africa* (London: Longman, 1987), pp. 393–99.

20. *Africa Research Bulletin: Economic Series* 25 (28 February 1988), 8996.

21. For a concise summary of the major international sanctions against South Africa in effect as of the beginning of 1990, see *Africa Research Bulletin: Economic Series* 27 (28 February 1990), 9831A.

22. Leach, p. 262.

23. *Race Relations Survey, 1986* (Johannesburg: South African Institute of Race Rela- tions), part 1, p. 312.

24. Robert Buis, *Religious Beliefs and White Prejudice* (Johannesburg: Ravan Press, 1975).

25. Ibid., p. 49.

26. For a valuable survey of the history of the NGK on these matters, see Johann Kinghorn, ed., *Die NG Kerk en Apartheid* (Johannesburg: Macmillan Suid-Afrika, 1986).

27. *Ras, Volk en Nasie en Volkereverhoudinge in the die van die Skrif* (Cape Town: N. G. Kerk-Uitgewers, 1975), pp. 7–8.

28. Ibid., pp. 10–27.
29. Ibid., pp. 27–38.
30. On relations with the nonwhite Reformed churches, see ibid., pp. 83–93.
31. Leach, p. 118.
32. Ibid.
33. Conor Cruise O'Brien, "South Africa: An Ominous Lull," *New York Review of Books*, 27 September 1979, p. 28, quoted in Giliomee, *Parting*, p. x.
34. *Kerk en Samelewing. 'n Getuienis van die Ned. Geref. Kerk. Soos aanvar deur die Algemene Sinode van die Ned Geref Kerke* (October 1986), p. 6.
35. Ibid., pp. 16, 19.
36. Ibid., pp. 22, 52–53.
37. Ibid., pp. 51–57.
38. Heribert Adam, "With Spirits Unbroken," *Living*, July 1990, 40.
39. F. A. van Jaarsveld, *Die evolusie van apartheid en ander geskiedkindige opstelle* (Cape Town: Tafelberg, 1980), pp. 16–23.
40. Hermann Giliomee, *Cape Times*, 17 February 1982, rpr. in Giliomee, *Parting*, p. 11.
41. Leach, p. 129.
42. Manzo and McGowan, table 3.
43. For an empirical study and discussion on the degree of such fears among Afrikaners see Pierre Hugo, "Towards Darkness and Death: Racial Demonology in South Africa," in Pierre Hugo, ed., *South African Perspectives* (Pretoria: Die Suid-Afrikaan, 1989), pp. 18–263.

11. *Israel, 1967 to the Present: Completing the Circle*

1. William W. Harris, *Taking Root: Israeli Settlement in the West Bank, the Golan, and Gaza-Sinai, 1967–1980* (New York: Research Studies Press, 1980), p. 3.
2. Ibid.
3. Paul Johnson, *A History of the Jews* (New York: Harper and Row, 1987), p. 538.
4. Ibid.
5. Meron Benvenisti et al., *The West Bank Handbook: A Political Lexicon* (Jerusalem: Jerusalem Post, 1986), pp. 42–46. For an illustration of the attitudes in, roughly, the center of the spectrum, see Shlomo Avineri, ed., *Israel and the Palestinians* (New York: St. Martin's Press, 1971). On the extreme, see Ehud Sprinzak, "Extreme Politics in Israel," *Jerusalem Quarterly* 5 (Fall 1977), 37–40.
6. Baruch Kimmerling, *Zionism and Territory: The Socio-Territorial Dimensions of Zionist Politics* (Berkeley: Institute of International Studies, University of California, 1983), pp. 157–66.
7. Michael Adams, "Israel's Treatment of the Arabs in the Occupied Territories," *Journal of Palestine Studies* 6 (Winter 1977), 33.
8. Janet Abu-Lughod, "Israeli Settlements in Occupied Arab Lands: Conquest to Colony," *Journal of Palestine Studies* 11 (Winter 1982), 25. Natural increase could have accounted for some of this number.
9. See Harris, pp. 25 ff.
10. Meron Benvenisti, *1986 Report: Demographic, Economic, Legal, Social and Political Developments in the West Bank* (Jerusalem: Jerusalem Post, 1986), p. 25.
11. Ibid., p. 26.
12. Harris, table 1, p. 16.
13. Abu-Lughod, p. 29.
14. Harris, table 1, p. 16. I suspect that his estimate of the pre-1967 Arab population is high.
15. Compare Abu-Lughod, p. 19, and Harris, table 1, p. 16.
16. Harris, table 1, p. 17.
17. Abu-Lughod, pp. 20–21.

18. Harris, table 1, p. 16.

19. Benvenisti, *1986 Report*, p. 26.

20. Ibid., p. 46. One must stress the difficulty of obtaining accurate information in this period. Benvenisti's estimates would be considered low by other sources (Harris, for example), but my own opinion is that on this matter his data base is superior.

21. Harris, p. 17, estimates 430,000.

22. Again, the problematic nature of the numbers must be emphasized. One can derive, from respectable scholarly sources, totals that range from 95,000 to 150,000.

23. Kimmerling, table 6.2, p. 162.

24. Ann Mosely Lesch, "Israeli Settlements in the Occupied Territories, 1967–1977," *Journal of Palestine Studies* 7 (Autumn 1978), 26. Lesch lists each settlement and its basic characteristics.

25. Kimmerling, p. 166.

26. Abu-Lughod, pp. 36–37.

27. Benvenisti, *1986 Report*, p. 30. Benvenisti (p. 31) compares the situation to that in all of Ireland in the seventeenth and eighteenth centuries, but Ulster, from the seventeenth through mid-twentieth centuries, is a more apposite comparison.

28. Adams, p. 34.

29. Ian Lustick, *Arabs in the Jewish State: Israel's Control of a National Minority* (Austin: University of Texas Press, 1980), table 3, p. 159. For useful comparative data (Jewish—non-Jewish) on occupational sectors, see ibid., table 4, pp. 161–63.

30. Harris, p. 58.

31. "U.S. Backed Israel on Golan," *Jerusalem Post International Edition* (hereafter *JP*), 5 May 1990.

32. "Israel's Territorial Imperatives," *JP*, 5 May 1990.

33. On the ill-conceived Lebanon war, see Uzi Benziman, *Sharon: An Israeli Caesar* (New York: Adama Books, 1985), pp. 231–76. Israel at this point worked hard at trying to convince the United States that terrorism and the Soviet military presence were everywhere in the Middle East and that Israel was the sole safe ally. See, for example, the briefing book *National Security Issues* put out by the Israeli minister of defense in August 1982, in English, for American consumption.

34. Stuart E. Eizenstat, "Israel's Economic Crisis: What Israel Must Do," *Commentary* 79 (April 1985), 15.

35. Ibid., p. 16.

36. "The Unkindest Cut of All?" *JP*, 17 March 1990; "The Dole Phenomenon," *JP*, 15 April 1990; "How to Get Israel off the U.S. Dole," *JP*, 28 April 1990; "Banking on the Diaspora," *JP*, 7 July 1990; "Where's the Money to Come from?" by John Bainerman, *JP*, 29 December 1990.

37. See Rael Jean Isaac, *Israel Divided: Ideological Politics in the Jewish State* (Baltimore: Johns Hopkins University Press, 1976), pp. 45–72.

38. Ibid., p. 61.

39. Ibid.

40. Ibid., pp. 64–65.

41. Sprinzak, pp. 42–45; Mark Tessler, "The Political Right in Israel: Its Origins, Growth, and Prospects," *Journal of Palestine Studies* 15 (Winter 1986), 33–36.

42. Gideon Aran, "From Religious Zionism to Zionist Religion: The Roots of Gush Emunim," in Peter Y. Medding, ed., *Studies in Contemporary Jewry*, vol. 2 (Bloomington: for the Institute of Contemporary Jewry of Hebrew University of Jerusalem by Indiana University Press, 1986), pp. 116–43.

43. S. Clement Leslie, *The Rift in Israel: Religious Authority and Secular Democracy* (London: Routledge and Kegan Paul, 1971), p. 72.

44. Charles S. Liebman, "Religion and Political Integration in Israel," *Journal of Jewish Sociology* 17 (1975), 20–21.

45. Ibid., p. 23.

46. Kimmerling, table 7.2, p. 193.

47. Yehoshua Arieli, "On Being a Secular Jew in Israel," *Jerusalem Quarterly* 45 (Winter 1988), 48.

48. Ibid., p. 53.

49. Tessler, p. 12.

50. Milton Friedman to Simon Peres [Spring] 1990, in *JP,* 12 May 1990.

51. Benvenisti et al., *West Bank Handbook,* p. 142; Lenni Brenner, *The Iron Wall: Zionist Revisionism from Jabotinsky to Shamir* (London: Zed Books, 1984). Tessler, pp. 13–21.

52. This is my estimate, derived from the data in the *Statistical Abstract* for 1978, p. 57, as cited in Judith Bernstein and Aaron Antonovsky, "The Integration of Ethnic Groups in Israel," *Jewish Journal of Sociology* 23 (1981), table 1, p. 7. Foreign-born "Orientals" made up 20.4 percent of the Israeli population in 1978, and Israeli-born people with fathers born in Asian-African countries made up 25.2 percent. That covers the first and second generation of Israeli residents. However, the census authorities did not give an ethnic breakdown of the 12.5 percent of the Israeli population who were third or subsequent generations. If these had the same proportionate breakdown as the rest of the population, they were 6.5 percent of Oriental background.

53. Tessler, p. 45, citing studies conducted by the Institute of Applied Social Research and the Dahaf Research Institute.

54. Johnson, pp. 545–46.

55. For indications of the temperature and vocabulary of this resentment see Amos Oz, *In the Land of Israel* (New York: Harcourt Brace Jovanovich, 1983), esp. pp. 25–48. See also the chapter "The Second Israel," in Conor Cruise O'Brien, *The Siege: The Saga of Israel and Zionism* (London: Weidenfeld and Nicolson, 1986), pp. 333–61.

56. Percy S. Cohen, "Ethnicity, Class, and Political Alignment in Israel," *Jewish Journal of Sociology* 25 (1983), 122.

57. Bernstein and Antonovsky, p. 16.

58. Ibid., table 4, p. 13.

59. Eliezer Ben-Rafael, *The Emergence of Ethnicity: Cultural Groups and Social Conflict in Israel* (Westport, Conn.: Greenwood Press, 1982).

60. Liebman, "Religion and Political Integration in Israel," p. 19.

61. Leslie, p. 73.

62. See the studies cited in Tessler, p. 53, n. 21. "Orientals" are also more hard-line on geopolitics. A poll conducted in June 1991 revealed that whereas about half of the European Jews opposed territorial comprise with Syria on the Golan Heights, nearly two-thirds of the Orientals were opposed to any compromise. "Public against Quitting Heights," *JP,* 3 August 1991.

63. This is an expansion of the "marginal status" hypothesis put forward by Percy Cohen, pp. 127–28.

64. Harris, p. 138.

65. Abu-Lughod, pp. 17, 48–49; Benvenisti, *1986 Report,* p. 35; Harris, pp. 138–40.

66. Don Peretz, *The West Bank: History, Politics, Society and Economy* (Boulder, Colo.: Westview Press, 1986), p. 59.

67. Benevenisti, *1986 Report,* p. 46.

68. Peretz, p. 59.

69. Benvenisti, *1986 Report,* p. 27.

70. Ibid., pp. 32–34.

71. Benvenisti, *1986 Report,* pp. 37–45; Benvenisti et al., *West Bank Handbook,* pp. 37–39; Peretz, pp. 83–87.

72. Johnson, pp. 522–23, 528–29.

73. Lewis Lapham, "Notebook: The Road to Shaaraim," *Harper's Magazine,* June 1988, p. 9.

74. Benvenisti, *1986 Report,* p. 79.

75. Ibid.

76. See, for example, the full-page advertisement placed in various papers by the Minis-

try of Agriculture, arguing that giving up control over Judea and Samaria would damage Israel's viability by greatly reducing its water supply. See *JP*, 18 August 1990.

77. Yosef Goell, "Polls Show Hardening of Attitudes Towards Arabs and PLO State," *JP*, 25 August 1990.

78. "Document: The New Government's Policy Guidelines," *JP*, 23 June 1990.

79. A. B. Yehoshua, "In Praise of Normality," *JP Magazine*, Rosh Hashana edition, 1990.

80. Chaim Herzog, *Heroes of Israel: Profiles of Jewish Courage* (London: Weidenfeld and Nicholson, 1990).

81. Daniel J. Elazar, "Covenant as the Basis of the Jewish Political Tradition," *Jewish Journal of Sociology* 20 (1978), 32.

82. Ibid., p. 24.

83. Thus the civil rights movement in Israel is almost entirely a product of the English-speakers, most of them immigrants. See Daniel Gavron, "The Fight for Civil Rights," *JP*, 13 January 1990.

84. Useful background to the December 1987 uprising is Emile Sahiley, *In Search of Leadership: West Bank Politics since 1967* (Washington, D.C.: Brookings Institution, 1988). Ian Lustick's *Arabs in the Jewish State: Israel's Control of a National Minority* (Austin: University of Texas, 1980), though it focuses chiefly on "intentional" Arabs and on 1970s, is still indispensable. He makes a compelling case that military means were only a small portion of an entire system of social control of the Palestinians.

85. Yosef Goell, "Democracy and Strong Leaders," *JP*, 3 February 1990. The early 1990s saw the beginning of what I think will be one of the key debates of the future, namely whether or not democracy is compatible with the existence of Israel as a Jewish state and, indeed, whether or not democracy really is desirable. The fascinating point about this issue is that it now is being debated by "European" Jews, the sort of persons who in decades past assumed not only the desirability of democracy, but that it was perfectly compatible with Zionism. The center points of the discussion are (1) the widely accepted assertion that a Jewish state must ensure the superior status of Jews and (2) the fact that as Israel expands toward filling the ancient geographic dimensions of the Israelite kingdom, Arabs inevitably will become a majority. For each of these reasons, it is argued that democracy must give way before the demands of creating a truly Jewish state. See David Heimowitz, "Can Israel Be a Real Democracy?" *JP*, 16 March 1991; and Susan Hattis Rolfe, "A Threat to Democracy Is a Threat to Zionism," *JP*, 1 June 1991.

86. The quotation is from a confidential memorandum, summarizing Kissinger's remarks, written by Julius Berman, former chairman of the Conference of Presidents of Major American Jewish Organizations, quoted in "Readings," *Harper's Magazine* June 1988, p. 17.

87. Lindsey Cook, "Unhappy Birthday for Siege Society," *Fortnight*, 16 June 1988, p. 16.

88. Robert I. Friedman, "The Settlers," *New York Review of Books*, 15 June 1989, p. 53.

89. Quoted in ibid.

90. See *inter alia*, stories on these matters in *JP*, 23 December 1989; 10 March 1990; 31 March 1990.

91. "Down to Brass Tacks," *JP*, 13 October 1990.

92. "Document: The New Government's Policy Guidelines," *JP*, 23 June 1990.

93. "200,000 New Immigrants," *JP*, 5 January 1991.

94. "Israeli Economy Is Keeping Many Jews in USSR," *New York Times*, 5 May 1991.

95. "The Ending of Neshira," *JP*, 21 September 1989.

96. Judith Miller, "Nowhere to Go," *New York Times Magazine*, 21 July 1991, p. 32.

97. Avishai Margalit, "The Great White Hope," *New York Review of Books*, 27 June 1991, p. 22.

98. Gwynne Dyer, "Israel Pins Hopes on Soviet Exodus," syndicated story, *Toronto Star* and other newspapers, 10 July 1990.

99. Sergio Della Pergola, professor of demography at Hebrew University, has estimated that every 100,000 new immigrants will push back by one full year the long-feared day when the Arab population of Israel and the conquered territories exceeds the Jewish population. He estimates that the arrival of 1 million immigrants would delay numerical parity until the year 2025. "In 10 Years Most Jews Will Be Living in Israel," *JP*, 19 January 1991.

100. "Soviet Birth Certificates Are No Proof of Jewishness," *JP*, 18 August 1990.

101. "Soviet Jews to Reside in Buffer Zones, Sharon Says," Reuters and Associated Press Story, *Globe and Mail* (Toronto), 16 October 1990; see also "200,000 New Immigrants," *JP*, 5 January 1991.

102. On the other aspects of planning, see "Israel to Increase Immigrant Spending," Reuters story, *Globe and Mail*, 22 November 1990; "Israel Wakes up to the Big New Wave of Soviet Jews," *New York Times*, 20 May 1990. The psychological costs to be borne by the Soviet immigrants is beyond speculation. For a valuable base line, see Zvi Gitelman, *Becoming Israelis: Political Resocialization of Soviet and American Immigrants* (New York: Praeger, 1982).

103. "Soviet Birth Certificates Are No Proof of Jewishness," *JP*, 18 August 1990.

104. "Error or Canard," *JP*, 11 September 1990.

105. Ibid.

106. Lois Watts, "The Law of Return," *JP*, 8 September 1990.

107. "Sharon Says Settlement to Continue in Territories," *JP*, 17 August 1991.

108. "Israel Not Budging on Settlement Expansion," *New York Times*, 7 July 1991.

12. Conclusion: Living with God's Peoples

1. Kingsley Amis, *One Fat Englishman* (Harmondsworth: Penguin, 1966), p. 120.

2. A readable discussion is James Gleick, *Chaos: Making a New Science* (New York: Viking, 1987).

3. Stephen Jay Gould, *Wonderful Life: The Burgess Shale and the Nature of History* (New York: Norton, 1989).

4. Ibid., p. 278.

5. L. A. Siedentop, "Liberalism: The Christian Connection," *Times Literary Supplement*, 24–30 March 1989, p. 308.

6. Ibid.

Index

Aaron, 17–18, 24, 33
Abandoned Areas Ordinance (Israel), 234
Abraham, 10–11, 14, 16, 30, 31, 35–37, 39, 117, 305
Abram. *See* Abraham
Absentees' Property Law (Israel), 234
Absorption, 243–50
Acre, 232
Adam, Heribert, 56, 297, 308
Adams, J. R. R., 129–30
Africana Afrikaner, 221–23
African-Asian Jews, 327
African National Congress (ANC), 226, 296, 302
Afrikaanse Christelike Vroue Vereeniging (ACCV), 81–90 passim
Afrikaanse Protestantse Kerk, 309–10
Afrikaans language revival, 70, 81–87, 216, 218. *See also* Mother tongue
Afrikaner, as term, 45n
Afrikaner Broederbond, See Broederbond
"Afrikaner nationalism," as concept, 78, 88
Afrikaner Weerstandsbeweging, 297, 309
Agudat Israel, 165
Ahab, 18
Ahaz, 19
Alaska, 157
Albright, William Foxwell, 10–11, 20, 133
Al-Fatah, 167

Aliyah: First, 152, 154; of 1917–47, 169; Second, 152, 154; of Soviets, 339–43, 393n99
Alliance party, 283
Allon, Yigal, 240, 313–14
Amalekites, 67, 397
Amis, Kingsley, 351
Ammonites, 36, 134
Amnesty International, 338
Amorites, 23
Amos, 133–35
Analogical history, 3, 350
Anglicans, 107–11, 114, 121, 123–33 passim, 146–50, 190–202 passim, 291–94, 369n12, 370n16, 371n38
Anglo-American Commission on Israel, 177
Anglo-Boer War: first, 65, 68; second, 65, 69, 72, 76–77, 89
Anglo-Celts, 81–83, 85, 87, 204, 214–17, 222, 224, 363n47; as term, 45n
Anglo-Irish Agreement, 284–86, 292
Anglo-Irish Treaty, 196
Anglophones, 45n, 219
Anthropomorphism, 20
Anti-Catholicism. *See* Roman Catholics
Antrim (Scots settlement), 104–11. *See also* Ballycarry; Islandmagee
Apartheid: and Anglo-Celts, 214–17; details of, 208–14; and Dutch Reformed Churches, 206–8; foreign policy, 224–

Apartheid (*continued*)
26; and legalism, 205; 1948 election, 204; retreat from, 296–310; and schools, 217–24; as term, 203
Apodictic law, 27
Apprentice Boys, 279
Apprenticeship regulations, 94, 211
Arab-Israeli War (1948–49), 232–33
Arab Jews, 327
Arab revolt (1936–39), 175
Aran, Gideon, 322
Arieli, Yehoshua, 324
Ashkenazim, 153, 160, 243–50, 257–58, 327–33, 336–37, 391n52
"Asians," as term, 46n
Asquith, Herbert, 188
Auerbach, F. E., 221
Authorized Version of Bible, 8, 21, 185. *See also* James I of England
Avineri, Shlomo, 231

Baal, 18, 35
Babylonians, 11
Baker, James, 339
Balfour, Arthur J., 162
Balfour Declaration, 162–64
Ballycarry, 122–33
Ballyclare, 133
"Bantu," as term, 45n, 209–10
Bantu Education Act, 212
Bantustans. *See* Homelands
Bar-Ilan, Meir, 229–30
Barrow, John, 51–52
Basutoland, 65
Bates, David, 264–65
Bawns, 3, 120
Bedouins, 241
Begin, Menachem, 246–47, 326, 327, 331–32, 384n62
Belfast Newsletter, 192, 194
Belhar Confession, 306
Belshazzar, 289
Ben-Gurion, David, 160, 165, 230, 247, 249–50, 313, 322, 336; on Arabs, 171–72; eases travel, 239; employment of Arabs, 173; Law of Return, 253; messiah, 248; motherhood award, 242; 1956 war, 258–59; partition, 176–77; redemption of Land, 232; status quo agreement, 250
Ben-Rafael, Eliezer, 328
Benvenisti, Meron, 314–15, 333–34
Berger, Earl, 177
Berkeley, George, 354
Bessarabia, 231

Birth rate, Catholic, 290–91
"Black," as term, 45n, 209
Blood River, battle of, 46, 63, 66–72, 205, 223, 295
Blood sacrifice, 33–37, 75–77, 140–43, 202, 336. *See also* Masada; Tel Hai
Bloom, Harold, 30
Blount, Charles, eighth Baron Mountjoy, 103
"Boers," as term, 45n
"Boer War." *See* Anglo-Boer War: second
Books of Moses, 12–42 passim, 243, 311, 330, 343, 356. *See also* Pentateuch; Torah
Borders (N. Ire.), 196–97
Botha, P. W., 296, 301–2
Boundary Commission (N. Ire.), 196–97
Boxer, Charles, 56
Boyne, the, battle of, 139, 202. *See also* Twelfth of July
Brice, Edward, 108, 123
Brink, C. B., 206
British East Africa. *See* Uganda proposals
British Guiana, 157
British Isles, persons from. *See* Anglo-Celts
British policy re: Palestine, 162–64. *See also* Palestine Mandate
Broadisland. *See* Ballycarry
Broederbond, 86–92, 215, 219–22
Bronze Age, 11
Brooke, Peter, 146, 148
Brown, Terence, 139
Bruce, Steve, 138
B-Specials, 201, 270, 280
Buber, Martin, 166, 171
Buckna, 100–101
Buis, Robert, 304
Burntollet Bridge, 277–78
Bush, George, 302, 340
Butler, Jeffrey, 81, 205

Cachet, Frans Lion, 66–67
Caledon, 276
Callaghan, James, 280
Calvin, Jean, 56, 111–19. *See also* Calvinism
Calvinism, 56–59, 71–72, 111–19, 262n23, 373n73
"Calvinist paradigm," 57–59
Campaign for Social Justice (N. Ire.), 275
Canaan and Canaanites, 13–42 passim, 67, 69, 74, 94–95, 98, 119–20, 143, 184, 243, 307
"Canaanism," 229–30, 246

Carter, James, 320, 338
Chaos theory, 351–53
Chichester, Sir Arthur, 273
Chichester-Clark, James, 278–82
Chinese, 209, 212
Chosen People, 17–42 passim, 60, 74–75, 83, 119–22, 134–43 passim, 247, 300, 308, 356. *See also Volk*
Christian National Education. *See* Education
Churchill, Winston, 162, 164
Church of Ireland. *See* Anglicans
Cilliers, Sarel, 68
Circassians, 241
Circumcision, 14, 16, 23
Ciskei, 214, 318
City of London Company, 105
Civil rights: in Northern Ireland, 272–82; of Palestinian Arabs, 240–41, 317, 332–33
Civil War (Irish), 1641, 140–42
Class, 80–83, 89–92, 144–46, 287–90, 301–3
Code, Bible as, 9–10
Colonization (Israel), 166–79, 311–25, 332–34, 341–42
Colour Bar Act, 94
"Coloured," as term, 45n
"Coloured" church. *See* Belhar Confession; *Sendingskerk*
Compulsory Education Act (Israel), 1949, 256
Concentration camps, British, 72, 76–77
Confiscation of Arab lands. *See* Land acquisition
Conservative Party (S.A.), 296, 309
Constitution Act, 1973 (N. Ire.), 282–83
Contractarian thought, 118
Cooke, Henry, 141, 146
Cooper, Ivan, 277
Cornevin, Marianne, 54
Corporate personality, 21–22, 73, 120, 234
Council of Ireland, 189
Covenant in Afrikaner historical thinking, 63–64; and Afrikaner oath, 47; ancient Hebrew concept of, 13–42; and apartheid, 203–4, 206–8; and blood sacrifice, 33–37; Chosen People, 21–42 passim; corporate personality in South Africa, 73; earliest forms of, 14–16; the Exodus, 32–33, 42; historical thinking, 28–31; if-then thinking, 13–42 passim; in Ireland, 119–22, 142–43; and the Land, 31–33, 73–74; legalism, 28–39,

42, 73; in modern Israel, 246–50, 335–36, 343–45; in modern world, 249–57; prophecy, 133–43; sacred-profane, 26–27; in Scotland, 114–16; and seed, 22–26, 41–42; topographic, 31–32. *See also* Chosen People; Corporate personality; Day of the Covenant; Exodus; Great Trek; Land; Seed; Ulster Covenant
Craig, James, 186, 189, 196
Craig, William, 276, 277
Critical theory, 350–51, 353–54
Cultivation of Waste Ordinance (Israel), 235
Curragh mutiny, 188
Currie, Austin, 276
Custodian for Enemy Property (Israel), 234

Daniel, 113, 134, 135–36, 177
Daughter of Jephthah. *See* Jepthah
Davenport, T. R. H., 208, 362n38, 364n54
David, 16, 176
Dayan, Moshe, 313
Day of the Covenant, 4, 45–49, 66–72, 91–92, 222–23, 295–96, 364n56
Day of the Vow. *See* Day of the Covenant
Decalogue. *See* Ten Commandments
Declaration of Independence (Israel), 227, 232, 239
Defence Regulations, 1945 (Israel), 235, 240
De Gaulle, Charles, 247
De Klerk, F. W., 296–97, 304
De Klerk, W. A., 56
De La Tocnaye, Chevalier, 140
Democracy, 241; and Israel, 227–28, 337–38, 392n85; and Ulster-Scots, 121–22
Democratic party (S.A.), 300
Democratic Unionist party (N. Ire.), 283–88, 293–94
Depopulation (Palestinian), 232–37, 311–18, 383n13
Deri, Aryeh, 343
Derry Citizens Action Committee, 277–78
Development Authority (Israel), 234, 236
De Wet Nel, M. C., 213
Diamond, James, 229
Diamonds, 65
Dietary laws, 251–52
Dingaan's Day. *See* Day of the Covenant
Dingane, 63
Diplock courts, 269

Direct rule, 282–94
Discrimination: against Oriental Jews, 327–30; against Palestinians, 231–43; against Roman Catholics, 197–202, 274–82, 374n88
Disestablishment, 146
Divorce. *See* Family law
"Domestic imperialism," as concept, 231–32
Donegore Hill, 132
Don-Yehiya, Eliezer, 248–49
"Doppers." *See* Gereformeerde Kerk
Down, Scots in, 104–11
Dowth, 11
Dror, Yehezkel, 231
Druze, 238, 241
Dual economy (Israel), 232, 236–39, 242, 318, 340–41
Dual social system (N. Ire.), 192–95
Duncan, William, 100–101
Du Plessis, L. J., 92
Du Preez, J. M., 221–23
Dutch Reformed Churches, 64–66, 68, 71–72, 84, 86, 206–8, 365n84. *See also* Gereformeerde Kerk; Nederduitse Hervormde Kerk; Nederduitse Gereformeerde Kerk
Du Toit, André, 56–59, 61
Du Toit, J. D., 74, 76
Du Toit, S. J., 82

Easter Rising, 188, 274
Ebenezer, 99
Edom, 134
Education: in Israel, 255–58, 327–28; in South Africa, 83–88, 90, 211–12, 216–24, 300, 367n109; in Ulster, 125–26, 129–30, 290–91, 379n24
Eglon, 25
Egypt, 12, 258–59, 319
Ehud, 25
Eilat, 240
Einstein, Albert, 159
Elazar, Daniel J., 336
Elliot, Marianne, 121
Elon, Amos, 152
Elphick, Richard, 56, 363n43
Emergency Land Requisition Law (Israel), 234
"English" persons in South Africa. *See* Anglo-Celts
Enniskillen, 140
Entebbe, 336
Ephraimites, 83
Episcopalians. *See* Anglicans

Eskom, 302
Established Church. *See* Anglicans
Ethical monotheism, 135–36
Etzel. *See* Irgun
Euphrates, 175
"European," as term, 45n
European Jews. *See* Ashkenazim
Evangelicalism, 147–48
Exodus, 31–34, 92, 113, 133. *See also* Great Trek; Voortrekkers
Extension of University Education Act (S.A.), 212

Fair Employment Agency (N. Ire.), 290
False-apodictic law, 27
Family laws (Israel), 251–55
Faulkner, Brian, 278, 281–83
First *Aliyah*. *See* Aliyah
First Anglo-Boer War. *See* Anglo-Boer War
First War of Independence. *See* Anglo-Boer War
Fisher, Joseph R., 106
Fishman, I. L., 250
Fitzgerald, Garret, 266, 284
Flight of the earls, 103–4
Ford, Gerald, 319
Foskor, 302
Free Presbyterian Church, 292–94. *See also* Paisley, Ian R. K.
Freud, Sigmund, 159
Friedman, Milton, 325–26, 354
Froude, James A., 64, 361n16
Frye, Northrup, 9

Gailey, Alan, 108–9, 125
Galilee, 176, 317
Garment Workers Union (S.A.), 217
Gaza, 259, 311–18, 334–44
Geddes, Sir Patrick, 255
General Mining and Finance Corporation, 217
General Zionists, 165, 250
Gereformeerde Kerk ("GK"), 71, 74–75, 87, 88, 226, 303–4
German, 161
Gibson, N. J., 269–70
Giliomee, Hermann, 56, 90, 204, 363n43
Ginzberg, Louis, 42
Girgashites, 23
Gladstone, William Ewart, 146
Golan, 259, 311–25 passim
Gold (S.A.), 65
Goldin, Judah, 7, 33
Gould, Stephen Jay, 352–53

Government of Ireland Act, 1920, 188–89, 195, 196
Graetz, Heinrich, 152
Grand apartheid, 208–9, 297–300
The Great Code, 9
Great Trek, 47, 49, 63, 74, 92, 297, 361n16. *See also* Voortrekkers
Greenberg, Stanley B., 235–36, 359n5
Group Areas Act (S.A.), 212, 300
Gruenbaum, Isaac, 250
Gulf War, 343–44
Gush Emunim, 321–33
Guttman Institute, 334

Habakkuk, 133
Haganah, 178, 232, 249
Haggai, 134
Haifa, 161, 232
halachah, 73. *See also* Covenant; Legalism
Hall, D. Lyle, 98
Hametic myth, 75–76, 94–95, 305
Hamilton, Ernest W., 141–42
Hamilton, James, 106
Harris, William, 330
Hashomer Hatzair, 165
Hazael, 134
Heath, Edward, 281–82, 284
Hebrew language, 160–61, 245–46
Hebron, 321
Hecataeus, 30
Helpmekaar, 89
Herenigde nasionale party, 88. *See also* National party
Herodotus, 30
Herstigte nasionale party. *See* Reconstituted National party
Hertzog, Albert, 91
Hertzog, J. B. M., 91
Herut, 326
Herzl, Theodor, 156–58, 159, 249
Heschel, Abraham, 133
Hess, Moses, 152
Hexham, Irving, 57, 203
Hibbat Zion, 156
Hillsborough agreement. *See* Anglo-Irish Agreement
Hirsch, Baron Maurice de, 157
Histadrut, 173, 238, 327
Historical thinking: in ancient covenant, 28–31, 335, 350; in South Africa, 66–72; and Ulster-Scots, 137–43
Historiography, of South Africa, 49–59, 77–78
Hittites, 23

Hivites, 23
Holmes, William, 100
Holocaust, 177–79, 249, 377n81
Holy fragments, 292–94, 308–10
Homelands, 213–13, 300, 332
Home rule (Ireland), 183–89
Homicide rates. *See* Murder rates
Hosea, 133
"Hottentot," as term, 45n
Huet, Rev. Mr., 66
Human Relations in South Africa, 207
Human Sciences Research Council (S.A.), 299–300
Hume, David, 15
Hume, John, 277
Hummel, Horace D., 33–34

If-then thinking, 13–42 passim, 350
Immorality Act, 1950 (S.A.), 210, 300, 309
Independent Television Authority (N. Ire.), 190
"Indian," 212; as term, 46n
Industrial capitalism and covenant, 78–80, 89–94; and apartheid, 216–17, 225–26, 287, 301–2; and Ulster-Scots, 144–46. *See also* Class
Intermarriage, 193–95, 209–10. *See also* Seed
Internal colonization, 317
Intifada, 337–39
Iraq, 175, 343–44
Irish language revival, 185
Irish News (Belfast), 192
Iron Age, 11
Irqun, 178, 246, 249, 321, 326, 333
Isaac, 15, 36–37
Isaiah, 133, 136, 143
Islandmagee, 108–9, 122–33 passim; "massacre," 142–43
Israeli Defence Force, 241–42, 245, 249, 336–37. *See also* Land acquisition

Jabotinsky, Vladimir, 165, 171, 326–27
Jacob, 15
Jacobson, Dan, 4, 5, 73
Jaffa, 232
Jahweh, 13–42 passim
James I of England (=James VI of Scotland), 106, 115, 185
James II, 98, 138–39
Japanese, 209
Jebusites, 23
Jehovah. *See* Jahweh

Jehu, 18
Jepthah, 35–37, 94–95
Jeremiah, 133
Jerusalem, 19–42 passim, 176, 240, 247, 259, 311, 313, 317
Jerusalemgangers, 365n77
Jesus, 41, 136–37, 305–6
Jewish Agency for Palestine, 172–73, 228–29
Jewish Colonization Association, 157
Jewish emancipation, 153–55, 229
Jewish National Fund, 168–73, 234–36
Johnson, Paul, 327
Jordan River valley, 175, 176, 314–15, 321. *See also* West Bank
Joshua, 67, 143
Judah, 134
Judea, 314, 322, 334–44 passim. *See also* West Bank
Judenstaat, Der, 156

Ker, R. G., 131
Kerk en Samelewing, 306–8
Khoikhoi, 45n
Khoisan, 83
Kilroot, 124
Kimmerling, Baruch, 167, 316
King's Confession, 115
Kissinger, Henry, 338
Knowth, 11
Knox, John, 114–16
Korah, 17
Kruger, Paul, 69, 71, 304
Krugersdorp, 68
Kuwait, 175
Kuyper, Abraham, 71–72

Labor party (Israel), 243, 246–47, 249–50, 313–45 passim. *See also* Ben-Gurion, David
Lallans, 128
Lambley, Peter, 223–24
Land: under covenant, 31–33, 76, 155, 159–62, 218, 233, 231–40, 311, 319–25, 334, 335, 340; in South Africa, 79–80; in Ulster, 138
Land acquisition (Israel), 155, 167–72, 231–40, 311–25, 330–35, 376n62
Land Act, 1931 (S.A.), 94
Land Day, 317
Land of Israel Movement, 321–32
Laqueur, Walter, 151
Laud, William, 114
Lauwerys, Joseph, 221
Law. *See* Covenant; Legalism; Mosaic law

Law of Return, 253–55, 343
League of Nations, 164
Left Poalei Zion, 165
Legalism, 28–39, 330–36
Lemass, Sean, 274
Lesch, Ann Mosely, 316
Levy, David, 336, 339
Liebman, Charles S., 246, 248–49, 323–24
Likud, 246, 313–45 passim
Lilienblum, Moshe Leib, 152
Lithuania, 231
Lloyd George, David, 162, 188–91
Locke, John, 118
Londonderry, 145; commission, 280; siege of, 139–40. *See also* City of London Company; Discrimination
Lorenz, Edward, 351
"Lundy," 194
Luther, Martin, 112

McAteer, Edward, 277
MacBride principles, 355
McConkey, W. G., 212
MacCrone, I. D., 367n130
MacDonagh, Oliver, 139
MacDonald, Ramsay, 196
McGowan, Patrick, 297–300, 310
Macmillan, Harold, 225
MacNeill, Eoin, 196–97
Madagascar, 157
Malachi, 134
Malan, D. F., 92, 203, 205–6, 208, 212, 215
Malayo-Portuguese, 83
Malherbe, Ernest G., 220, 363n52, 381n57
Majuba Hill, 69
Manasseh, 19
Manzo, Kate, 297–300, 310
Mapai, 165, 243, 246. *See also* Labor party
Margalit, Avishai, 341, 384n48
Marriage. *See* Family laws; Mixed Marriages Act; Seed
Masada, 248, 250, 343
Master symbols, 222–23
"Maximalists," 313
Mediterranean Sea, 175
Meier, Golda, 230
Meighen, Arthur, 162–64
Meintjes, Johannes, 47–48
Merkaz Ruhani. See Mizrachi
Methodists, 147–49, 291–92
Meyer, Piet, 215–16

Micah, 133, 136–37, 143
Midianites, 42
Military governors (Israel), 239–40
Miller, David, 118, 287, 374n89
Milner, Alfred, Viscount, 72, 84
Miriam, 18, 33
Mishmar Haemek, 322
Mixed Marriages Act, 201–10, 300, 309
Mizpe, 317
Mizrachi, 165
Moab (also Moabites), 24, 25, 134
Modai, Yitzhak, 344
Modernization, 145, 150
Molech, 35
Montgomery, Hugh, 106
Moodie, T. Dunbar, 57–58, 90, 204, 360n1
Moore, Francis, 100–101
Morning Post (London), 197
Moroccan Jews, 152, 328
Mosaic law, 11, 13–42 passim
Moses, 15, 17, 18, 23, 33, 67
Mother tongue, 85–87, 218, 220
Murder rates: N. Ire., 264–65, 386nn4, 5; USA, 264–65

Napoleon, 152
Nasser, Gamal Abdul, 258–59
"national character," as concept, 59, 353
National Covenant, Scots, 115
National Education Advisory Council (S.A.), 220
National Education Policy Act (S.A.), 220
National party (S.A.), 88, 204, 296, 299–310 passim
"Native," as term, 45–46n, 209
Native Irish. *See* Roman catholics
Natives (Urban Areas) Act, 94
Nature, 264
Nazareth, 233, 238
Nebuchadnezzar, 113
Nederduitsch Hervormde Kerk ("NHK"), 87, 206, 303–4
Nederduitse Gereformeerde Kerk ("NGK"), 86–87, 90, 304–10, 367n109
Negev desert, 236, 240
Nelson, Sarah, 287–89
New Criticism, 350
New Grange, 11
New Historicism, 350
New Jewish Version, Bible, 8
Newsweek, 271
"New Testament," 230, 306–8
Nile, 175

Noah, 94–95
"Nonwhite," as term, 45n
Nordau, Max, 166

O'Brien, Conor Cruise, 77, 159, 208, 307, 359n5, 365n87
"Occupation," as concept, 317
O'Connell, Daniel, 137
O'Connor, Frank, 39
Odessa, 231
O'Donnell, Rory, earl of Tyrconnell, 105–6
Official Unionist party, 282–89, 293
"Old Testament," 7; and Afrikaners, 61, 63–64, 67–83, 94–95, 206–8, 210, 304–8, 365n77; and Israel, 247, 323–25, 344; and Ulster, 98–100, 102–3, 111–22, 129–30, 133–43, 263
O'Meara, Dan, 53, 56, 58–59, 88, 90, 203
Onan, 22–23
O'Neill, Con, 106
O'Neill, Hugh, earl of Tyrone, 103
O'Neill, Terence, 273–79
Orange order, 98–99, 285. *See also* Twelfth of July
Ordnance Survey, 123–33 passim
"Oriental" Jews, 243–50, 257–58, 327–30, 337–38, 391n52
O'Rourke, P. J., 242, 265–66
Orr, James, 123–33 passim
Ottoman empire, 154–55, 161–62, 164, 235, 331–32

Paardekraal, 68
Paisley, Ian R. K., 99–100, 137–38, 283–88
Palestine Liberation Organization, 341
Palestine Mandate, 164, 169–79 passim
Palestinians, 164, 166, 227–59 passim, 319–25, 356; and civil rights, 337–38; Zionist view of, 170–73. *See also* Arab revolt; Depopulation
Parallelism in Bible, 15–16
Parliamentary election (N. Ire.), 288–90
Parnell, Charles Stewart, 156
Partition: of Ireland, 188–89, 195–97; of Israel, 173–77, 232
Pass laws: Israel, 242, 318; South Africa, 214
Paton, Alan, 49
Patriarchial era, 10–12
Patriot, Die, 70
Pearce, Edward, 6
Peel Commission, 173, 175–76

Pekah, 19
Penal code, Irish, 109–10, 208
Pentateuch, 12–42 passim, 136, 222. *See also* Books of Moses
People's Democracy (N. Ire.), 276
Peres, Shimon, 326, 333
Peretz, Yitzhak, 343
Perizzites, 23
Perlmann, Eliezer Yitzhak, 161
Petty apartheid, 208–9, 297–300, 310
Philistines, 42, 242
Phillips, Dorothea, 52–53
Philo Judaeus, 30
Phinehas, 24
Phoenicia, 12
Picts, 11
Planning Law (Israel), 332
Plantation of Ulster, 105–11
"Pluralism" (Israel), 227–31
Poor Law (Irish), 127
Poor whites (S.A.), 89–90, 215
Population Registration Act (S.A.), 209
Porter, J. L., 141
Postma, Willem, 74, 76
Prague, 231
Predestination. *See* Calvinism; Presbyterian doctrine
Presbyterian doctrine, 111–19
Presbyterians, 146–50, 185–86, 190–202 passim, 291–94, 369n12
Prescopacy, 114
Prescription Law (Israel), 235
Pretoria Minute, 296
Promised Land: Argentina, 157; Palestine, 158–59. *See also* Land; Uganda proposals
Prophets, 133–43, 373n73
Protestant ethic, 16
Protestants (Ireland). *See* Anglicans; Methodists; Presbyterians
Protestants and Zionism, 152, 153, 162
Provisional IRA, 264–72 passim
Purified National party (S.A.), 88, 92

Queen's University, Belfast, 276

Rabbah, 134
Rabin, Yitzhak, 319
Race, Volk, and Nation, 304–6
Racism, 24, 75–78, 92–95, 121, 299, 304–8
Rafael, Shilo, 342
Raloo, 98
Reading societies, 130

Reagan, Ronald, 320
Reconstituted National party (S.A.), 308–9
"Redeeming" the Land (Israel), 319–25, 335. *See also* Land; Land acquisition
Registration of Population Act (Israel), 254–55
Religious adhesion (N. Ire.), 190–91, 323–25
Remaliah, 19
Republican referendum (S.A.), 225
Reservation of Separate Amenities Act (S.A.), 210–11
Revisionists, 165, 246, 326–27, 333. *See also* Jabotinsky, Vladimir
Revival of 1859 (N. Ire.), 147–48
Rhodesia, 6
Robinson, Henry Wheeler, 21, 30, 42
Rolling devolution, 283–84
Roman Catholics, 106–12, 115, 119–20, 123, 138–44, 146–50, 184–201 passim, 126–72 passim, 356, 369n12
Rosenzweig, Franz, 30
Rothschild, Lionel, 162
Royal Belfast Academical Institution, 125
Royal Ulster Constabulary, 268, 279, 338
Rufeisen, Oswald, 253–54
Russian Jews (pre-1917), 154–55

Sabbath, 250–52
Sabras, 248–49
Sacred-profane, 26–27, 102, 119, 144, 330, 355
Safed, 232
Salvation deed, 92
Samaria, 311–18, 322, 334–44 passim
"San," as term, 45n
San Domingo (Jewish colony), 157
Sanlam, 217
San Remo agreement, 164
Sapir, Pinhas, 313
Sarai, 14
Saudi Arabia, 175, 258
Saunders, Christopher, 361n6
Schalit case, 254–55
Schools. *See* Education
Scottish covenants, 114–16
Scottish migration to Ulster, 106–11
Seaton, James Reid, 116
Seceders, 100–101, 121
Second *Aliyah. See* Aliyah
Second Language Movement (S.A.), 82–83
Secular Jews, 324–25
"Secular," the, re Israel, 227–31, 324–25

Seed, 14, 22–24, 75–77, 94–95, 126–27, 193–95, 209–10, 222, 252–53, 299, 310, 343, 366n96
Sendingskerk, 306
Separate development (S.A.), 214
Sephardim, 153
"Settlers," in Israel, 166–79, 311–25, 330–34
1798 Rising, 131–33
Shakespeare, William, 185
Shamir, Yitzhak, 327–45 passim
Sharon, Ariel, 342, 344
Shem, 94–95
Siedentrop, L. A., 353–54
Sinai, 175, 259, 311
Sinn Fein, 266
Six Day War, 259, 311; and land acquisition, 311–18; and social structure, 319–25
Six Mile Water revivial, 148
Slagters Nek, 76
Smith, Ken, 361n6
Smolenskin, Peretz, 152
Social class. *See* Class
Social Democratic and Labor party (N. Ire.), 281, 283–85
Social discipline (Ulster Scots), 126–28
Society of Right-Minded Afrikaners, 70, 83
Solemn League and Covenant, 116
Somme, 202
Song at the Sea, 33
South African Airways, 302
South African Bureau of Racial Affairs, 213
Soviet Jews. *See Aliyah*
"Special relationship" (U.S.-Israel), 319
"State land" (Israel), 315, 331
Status quo agreement (Israel), 250–55
Stern Gang, 333
Stewart, A. T. Q., 108, 118–19, 138, 184, 368n6
Stone, Robert, 8
Stone Age, 10
Stonehenge, 11
Stormont, 195, 275–82
Strange fire, 18
Streak, Michael, 51–52
Strijdom, J. G., 208, 212–13
Suez Canal, 175, 258–59
Sumerians, 11
Sunningdale agreement (N. Ire.), 283
Suppression of Communism Act (S.A.), 217, 226

Swift, Jonathan, 124
Syria, 175, 319

Tel Hai, 248, 250
Teman, 134
Temple Mount, 311
Templin, J. Alton, 60–61
Ten Commandments, 11, 16, 27
Terre Blanche, Eugene, 309
Terrorism (N. Ire.), 264–72
Terrorism Act (S.A.), 226
Thatcher, Margaret, 99, 284, 286
Thingamatrope, 24
Thomists, 114
Thompson, E. P., 51
Thompson, John, 292
Thompson, Leonard, 54–55
Thucydides, 30
Tomlinson Commission, 213
Torah, 12–42 passim. *See also* Books of Moses
"Totius." *See* Du Toit, J. D.
Trade unions (S.A.), 90–92, 127
Transjordan, 176
Transkei, 214, 318
Transvaal Indigency Commission, 89
"Trends," in Israeli education, 256
Trollope, Anthony, 52–53
Troubles (N. Ire.), 264–93
Truman, Harry, 178
Trumpeldor, Yosef, 248
Trusteeship, 206, 210
Twelfth of July, 98–99, 202
Tyrus, 134

Uganda proposals, 157–59
Ulster Covenant, 4, 150, 186–89, 201
Ulster Defence Association, 289
Ulster's Solemn League and Covenant. *See* Ulster Covenant
Ulster Volunteer Force (pre-1920), 188, 202
Ulster Workers' Council, 286
"Undertakers," 105
Unemployment (N. Ire.), 267–68, 270–71
UNESCO, 224
United Nations, 179, 339
United party (S.A.), 204–5
United States, and Israel, 178–79, 319–20, 336–37, 340–41
Ussher, James, 29

Vail, Leroy, 80
Van der Merwe, Hendrik W., 297, 299

Van Jaarsveld, F. A., 55–59, 75, 77, 79–80, 361n6, 364n54
Van Rieback, Jan, 62
Venda, 214
Vereeniging, treaty of, 84
Verwoerd, H. F., 208, 210, 215, 225, 308
Volk, 73, 90–91, 204, 217, 220, 224, 295, 300, 303–5, 364n72. See also Chosen People
Volkskapitalisme, 92
Volkskas Bank, 216
Voortrekker monument, 3, 295
Voortrekkers, 46–47, 52, 54, 61, 63, 66, 80. See also Great Trek
Vorster, B. J. 206, 308–9
Vorster, J. D., 85

Warsaw, 231
Washington Post, 338
Weaver poets, 127–28
Weber, Max, 16
Weizmann, Chaim, 158–62, 177–78, 255
West Bank, 3, 311–25, 330–44 passim. See also Judea; Samaria
West Bank Data Project, 314–15. See also Benvenisti, Meron
"White," as term, 45n
"Who is a Jew?" 228, 253–55, 341–43
Whyte, John, 385n1

William III of Orange, 98, 138–40
Wilson, Harold, 279
Women and Afrikaner culture, 81–83. See also Afrikaanse Christelike Vroue Vereeniging
Woodhead Commission, 173, 175
World Alliance of Reformed Churches, 306
World Council of Churches, 224, 292
World Jewish Congress, 228
World Zionist Organization, 156–79 passim, 326
Wright, Frank, 190, 292
Wright, Harrison, 361n6

Yahweh, 13–42 passim, 67–68, 72, 74, 77, 92, 98, 134–43 passim, 305
Yehoshua, A. B., 335
Yeminite Jews, 152, 328
Yiddish, 160
Yishuv, 161, 166, 169, 234, 244
Yom Kippur War, 320
Yudelman, David, 361n6

Zephaniah, 134
Zionism (pre 1948): inter-war, 164–77; orthodox opposition, 159; to World War I, 151–64. See also Aliyah; Herzl, Theodor; Land, Revisionists; World Zionist Organization

God's Peoples: Covenant
and Land in South Africa,
Israel and Ulster.

Donald Harman Akenson

BL617
.A44
1992

DATE DUE
